1993

THE ROMANS

THE
ROMANS

EDITED BY
ANDREA GIARDINA

TRANSLATED BY
LYDIA G. COCHRANE

THE UNIVERSITY OF CHICAGO PRESS
Chicago & London

ANDREA GIARDINA is professor of Roman history at the University of Rome and editor of several multivolume works on ancient Rome.

The University of Chicago Press, Chicago 60637
The University of Chicago Press, Ltd., London
© 1993 by The University of Chicago
All rights reserved. Published 1993
Printed in the United States of America
02 01 00 99 98 97 96 95 94 93   5 4 3 2 1

ISBN (cloth): 0-226-29049-2
ISBN (paper): 0-226-29050-6

Originally published as *L'uomo romano,* Rome and Bari: Editori Laterza, 1989.
© 1989, Guis. Laterza & Figli, Spa, Roma-Bari.

Library of Congress Cataloging-in-Publication Data

[Uomo romano. English]
The Romans / edited by Andrea Giardina ; translated by Lydia G.
Cochrane.
    p.   cm.
Translated from the Italian.
Includes bibliographical references.
    1. Rome—Social life and customs.   2. National characteristics,
Roman.   3. Social classes—Rome.   4. Occupations—Rome.
I. Giardina, Andrea.
DG78.R58313   1993
937—dc20   92-24582
                                                        CIP

CONTENTS

TRANSLATOR'S NOTE

CHAPTERS 10 AND 11, originally written in English, have been given in their English versions with some editing; the chapters originally written in French have been checked against the French texts; chapter 7 has been translated from the translation into Italian of Celeste Zawadzka.

In chapters 10 and 11 quotations from the works of classical writers have been given in the translations of the authors of the chapters. In other chapters some modern translations into English have been used and are credited. Because the series is readily available, the Loeb Classical Library translations have been used, with editing, for many other quotations.

ABBREVIATIONS

AE *L'Année épigraphique*

BGU *Aegyptische Urkunden aus den Staatlichen Museen zu Berlin, Griechische Urkunden*

CIL *Corpus Inscriptionum Latinarum*

CJ *Corpus Juris Civilis*

CSEL *Corpus scriptorum ecclesiasticorum Latinorum*

CTh *Codex Theodosianus*

FGH *Fragmenta Historicorum Graecorum* (Karl Müller)

FIRA *Fontes Iuris Romani Antejustiniani*

IGRR *Inscriptiones Graecae ad res Romanas pertinentes*

IlAlg *Inscriptions latines d'Algérie*

ILLRP *Inscriptiones Latinae Liberae Rei Publicae*

ILS *Inscriptiones Latinae Selectae*

IRT *The Inscriptions of Roman Tripolitania*

P.Bad. *Veröffentlichungen aus den badischen Papyrus-sammlungen*

P.Dura *The Parchments and Papyri: The Excavations at Dura-Europos. Final Report*, Wells, Fink, and Gilliam. New Haven: 1959

PG *Patrologia Graeca*

P.Hamb. *Griechische Papyrusurkunden der Hamburger Staats- und Universitätsbibliothek*

PIR *Prosopographia Imperii Romani*

PL *Patrologia Latina*

P.Mich. *Papyri in the University of Michigan Collection. Miscellaneous Papyri*

P.Oxy. *The Oxyrhynchus Papyri*

P.Princ. *Papyri in the Princeton University Collections*

P.Wisconsin *The Wisconsin Papyri*

P.Yale *Yale Papyri in the Beinecke Rare Book and Manuscript Library*

RMR *Roman Military Records on Papyrus.* Princeton: 1971

SHA *Scriptores Historiae Augustae* (Loeb Classical Library)

Sel.Pap. *Selected Papyri*, Hunt and Edgar. 2d ed. London: 1956

Syll. *Sylloge Inscriptionum Graecarum* (Wilhelm Dittenberger)
3d ed.

INTRODUCTION

Roman Man

Andrea Giardina

ROUGHLY A CENTURY BEFORE the fall of the Western Empire, the military writer Vegetius offered an anthropological synthesis of the "Roman" built on a set of simple oppositions. The Romans were less prolific than the Gauls, shorter than the Germans, weaker than the Spanish, not as rich or astute as the Africans, inferior to the Greeks in technology and in reason applied to human affairs. This human type defined by negations had one decisive superior quality, however: a vocation for dominion assured by the exercise of arms (*armorum exercitio*), camp discipline (*disciplina castrorum*), and skill in use of an army (*usus militiae*). This refined science of war suffused with ethics had become the foundation of the audacity, the sure success, and the special character of the Roman type.[1]

Cicero found this explanation insufficient. The military factor alone could not account for Roman domination of the world: "We have excelled neither Spain in population, nor Gaul in vigor, nor Carthage in versatility, nor Greece in the arts." Rather, Rome ruled by scrupulous observance of *pietas, religio,* and the distinctively Roman theological wisdom that perceived all things as being ruled and governed by the power of the gods (*sed pietate ac religione atque hac una sapientia, quod deorum numine omnia regi gubernarique perspeximus*).[2]

Vegetius was not a particularly cultivated or intelligent person. The military tract he wrote at the turn of the fourth century A.D. proposed

---

1. Vegetius *Epitoma rei militaris* 1.1, Lang ed.

2. Cicero *Haruspicum responsis* 9.19. (It is evident from a comparison of Cicero and Vegetius that the latter's statements were directly or indirectly based on Cicero.) On Cicero as interpreter of Roman history, see Santo Mazzarino, *Il pensiero storico classico*, 2 vols. in 3 books (Rome and Bari: Laterza, 1966), vol. 2, pt. 1, pp. 175ff., 184ff.

as a model the Roman legion composed of citizens, which was an archival relic—a fossil. His reflections were nearly always commonplace, which suggests that his summary anthropology also reflected an image widespread in middle to lower cultural circles (I am tempted to say, in popular circles). Thus it is hardly surprising that the same image—independent of Vegetius—is still a prominent part of the common representation of the "Roman man." The Roman was not particularly brilliant, he was less cultivated than the Greeks and was shorter than the Germans, but because he was a disciplined warrior, he had no equal for efficiency and valor. We might add that he was gifted with an admirable sense of organization.

Even after Vegetius and even after the fall of the Western Empire, this association between a warlike character and Romanness was to have a flourishing career rooted not only in purely historical perspectives but also in an awareness of all who considered themselves the true heirs of that ancient virtue. When Bishop Liutprand of Cremona arrived in Constantinople in 968 to request of Nicephorus Phocas, the Byzantine emperor, the hand in marriage of a princess "born to the purple" for the son of the emperor Otto I, he extolled the merits and the power of his lord, like any good ambassador. His interlocutor interrupted him, however: "You lie. Your lords are ignorant of the art of horsemanship, and they do not even know what an infantry battle is. The size of their shields, the burden of their cuirasses, the length of their swords, the weight of their helmets totally prevent them from fighting." The emperor continued scornfully, "They are also unable to fight because of their *gastrimargia*—the voracity of their stomachs. The stomach is their god; their audacity, lechery; their force, drunkenness. For them fasting is dissolution and sobriety, fear." He summed up tersely: "You are Lombards, not Romans!"[3] The Eastern Roman emperor was clearly not using a rhetorical argument but rather expressing his moral stance (if moral it was also racist) in so cruelly comparing the cowardice of the Westerners to the courage and experience in warfare of the Byzantines, the only true

3. Liutprand of Cremona *Relatione della sua ambasceria a Costantinopoli,* in Joachim Becker, *Die Werke Liudprands von Cremona,* 3d ed. (Hanover-Leipzig, 1915; reprint 1977), "Scriptores rerum Germanicarum in usum scholarum ex Monumentis Germaniae Historicis separatim editi," 182. Benedetto Croce saw in Nicephorus Phocas' harsh response to Liutprand a "solemn moment" in the "prehistory" of contemporary racism: see Benedetto Croce, "La Germania che abbiamo amata" (1936), in his *Pagine sparse,* 2d rev. ed. 2 vols. (Bari: Laterza, 1960), 2:511ff.

heirs of the Roman Empire. The people he ruled was proud still to be called *Rhomaioi*.[4]

This is hardly the occasion for a review of all the familiar (and laudatory) interpretations of the Roman character formulated in antiquity by writers from Polybius to Livy, Virgil, and a host of others. No single one of them could be adopted today as a key to the "Roman type" throughout all, or even almost all, Roman history. It would be more novel to survey the representations of Romanness rooted in popular opinion in our own day, now that the propagandistic use of "Romanità" on the part of reactionary mass regimes is safely in the past.[5] A fascinating book could be written on the topic.[6] Such an image would certainly include the arena full of dust and blood, with slaughtered gladiators, Christians being thrown to the lions, the specter of the cross, and so forth. In other words, it would be the image of a cruel Roman. Where cruelty is concerned (as Paul Veyne observes in chapter 12 of the present volume), it is difficult to ascribe primacy to any one great civilization in world history: some will be moved by conjuring up palpitating images of Roman amphitheaters; others will find more hair-raising the memory of the great Michael Servetus being slowly burned by John Calvin. It is a question of inclination. There is no doubt, however, that the Roman, as a type, has been castigated for his cruelty in better than a millennium and a half of Christian apologetics. Not even Edward Gibbon could minimize the human cost of pagan persecutions by comparing them with the horrors of modern wars of religion. He writes at the end of his analysis of Christian persecution in the ancient world:

> We shall conclude this chapter by a melancholy truth which obtrudes itself on the reluctant mind; that even admitting, without hesitation, or inquiry, all that history has recorded, or devotion has feigned, on the subject of martyrdoms, it must still be acknowledged that the Christians, in the course of their intestine dissensions, have inflicted far greater severi-

4. The Byzantines' attitude regarding their distant past was not always so clear: see Alexander Kazdhan, "L'eredità antica a Bisanzio," *Studi classici e orientali* 38 (1988): 139–53.

5. See Mariella Cagnetta, *Antichisti e impero fascista* (Bari: Dedalo, 1979). This debate was launched by *Quaderni di Storia*, director Luciano Canfora.

6. Its author might, for example, take inspiration from Roland Barthes, "The Romans in Films," in his *Mythologies*, trans. Annette Lavers (New York: Hill & Wang, 1972), 26–28. See also below, page 117.

ties on each other than they have experienced from the zeal
of infidels.

Gibbon concludes with a reference to the Low Countries at the time of
Charles V: "If we are obliged to submit our belief to the authority of
Grotius, it must be allowed that the number of Protestants who were
executed in a single province and a single reign far exceeded that of
the primitive martyrs in the space of three centuries and of the Roman
Empire."[7]

Anthropology has accustomed us not to judge and not to be scandalized, particularly where no striking individual action is involved but only
the reiterated constraints of invasive collective behavior patterns. As Jean-
Louis Voisin has recently demonstrated, the Romans were particularly
fond of cutting off people's heads.[8] Obviously there was no particular
concentration of severed heads in any one period, as in historical times
closer to our own, but rather a constant and recurrent presence of this
practice distributed throughout Roman history. Heads severed with great
finesse or lopped off clumsily, from the bodies of the living and the
dead, wrapped in bandages and carefully protected with layers of honey,
cedarwood oil, wax, or other substances, stuck up on pikes or poles in
military camps, exposed at the focal point of civic life, or catapulted at
the feet of the enemy; heads of common folk or of the great actors in
history (this was the fate of Pompey, Cicero, Nero, and Maxentius);
heads of political rivals or enemies in war; heads of criminals or bandits.
The definition of Celtic society as the "civilization of the cut-off head"
would apply equally well to the Romans. For the Romans the act of
cutting someone's head off was by no means to be defined as *crudelitas:*
it was not only an obvious means of intimidation but also a sign of power
and a manifestation of efficiency and prowess. The Romans were a people
of refinement, and they saw *crudelitas* in activities that were, on occasion,
associated with decapitation. Such, for example, were showing unseemly
enjoyment in contemplating the severed head of a long-feared adversary
or making too many tasteless comments about one part or another of the
victim's physiognomy. These were acts that transformed the decapitation

7. Edward Gibbon, *The History of the Decline and Fall of the Roman Empire,* ed. J. B.
Bury., 7 vols. (London: Methuen, 1909), 2:145, 148.

8. Jean-Louis Voisin, "Les Romains, chasseurs de têtes," in *Du châtiment dans la cité:
Supplices corporels et peine de mort dans le monde antique.* Table Ronde (Rome 9–11 novembre
1982) organisée par l'Ecole française de Rome avec le concours du Centre national de la
recherche scientifique (Rome: Ecole française de Rome, 1984), 241–92.

of an enemy from an admirable and manifest externalization of power into *crudelitas*.

The Romans themselves did not always agree on what was typical of Rome. A rite of human sacrifice attested on three occasions (in 228, 216, and 114 B.C.) but undoubtedly practiced much more often required the burial alive in the Forum Boarium of a couple (male and female) of Greeks and a similar couple of Gauls (*Gallus et Galla, Graecus et Graeca in foro bovario sub terram vivi demissi*). This sacrifice of live burial evidently was originally connected with the ritual *exterminatio* of two peoples who lived beyond the limits of Italy of the time, but it long remained rooted in Roman civic religion in its dual perception (not always clear, however) of "ritual death" and "human sacrifice."[9] In commenting on this rite Livy reacted with spontaneous horror, calling it "a sacrifice wholly alien to the Roman spirit" (*minime Romano sacro*). Pliny the Elder was of a quite different opinion: in order for the act of burial to deploy its full potential for the city, it must be accompanied by a *praecatio* (prayer formula), the efficacy of which had stood the test of time for 830 years. He also stated that the rite could be applied to other peoples as well, as was still the case in his day (*etiam nostra aetas vidit*).[10] What for Livy was a strange and aberrant rite in comparison with the typical forms of Roman religious expression was instead for Pliny (and he was correct) a practice rooted in civic life. It is not often that we can turn directly to the Romans to discern an aspect of Roman quiddity, however.

Whatever noun we place with the adjective "Roman" (the Roman world, Roman man, etc.), the result is the same: what we are constructing is an abstract and totalizing, thus a partial, category. The more such a construction seems an obvious empirical datum so taken for granted that it requires neither verification nor clarification, the stronger is the likelihood of its being an ideal type. The same is of course true in all complex civilizations, but it is even more valid concerning the great civilizations that, like Roman civilization, stretched the dimensions of time and space to extreme limits. To take time first: throughout the thirteen hundred years that represented the minimum duration of Roman history (other, longer, periodizations could also be proposed), how can one speak of a

9. The basic study on these rites is Augusto Fraschetti, "Le sepolture rituali del Foro Boario," in *Le délit religieux dans la cité antique*. Table Ronde (Rome 6–7 avril 1978) (Rome: Ecole française de Rome, 1981), 51–115.

10. Livy 22.57.6; Pliny the Elder *Naturalis historia* 28.12. On the complexity of priestly functions in Rome, see below, chapter 2.

Roman man substantially identical in the Rome of the Tarquins and in that of Augustus or Theodosius the Great? As for space: the geographical distribution of an empire that soon became "supernational" embraced a broad range of cultures and human types, and the unifying Greco-Roman culture and the shifting values of the *humanitas* of the ruling classes were imprinted on the territory like the leopard's spots, following the path of the implantation of cities and the establishment of areas under the direct control of the city of Rome.

When Vegetius offered his image of the Roman type, he compared it with other ethnic types that all were a part, in greater or lesser measure, of the Roman Empire. Thus he did not immediately equate Romans and citizens of the Empire. Many other authors had done the same. Cicero, for instance: at a time when all the Italic cities had for some decades enjoyed Roman citizenship, he found no unifying image. The nature of places created and fixed ethnic types. Besides the Carthaginians—always seen as *fraudulenti et mendaces* (liars and cheats), thanks to their harbors frequented by too many merchants—Cicero recalls the Campanians, made proud by the fertility and the beauty of their land, and the Ligurians, *duri atque agrestes* (rough country folk) like all peoples who have to struggle to wrest a living from their mountain terrain.[11]

When in A.D. 212 the emperor Caracalla decreed that Roman citizenship be granted to all free inhabitants of the empire, he was obliged to acknowledge the existence, within Rome's confines, of peasant masses untouched by Romanization—the freedmen known as *dediticii*—who were excluded from the edict. What is more, in the age of St. Jerome, around 400, Celtic was spoken in the outskirts of Augusta Treverorum (Treves), a totally Roman city.[12] The same was of course true in a number of other regions of the Empire. After Caracalla's decree, however, by strict juridical criteria, everyone who enjoyed Roman citizenship could be called a Roman. This strict interpretation would not have canceled distinctions that operated in people's minds concerning behavior patterns, physical aspect, and social position. Even after Caracalla, there were Roman citizens whom a Roman of average culture would have found difficult to recognize as Romans. There were some, for example, to whom terms such as *rusticus* or *agrestis* were applied: nonurbanized peasants, shepherds, and, more generally, all who lived in the great outdoors. City

11. Cicero *De lege agraria* 2.95.

12. Santo Mazzarino, "La democratizzazione della cultura nel 'Basso impero'," in *Antico, tardoantico ed èra costantiniana* (Bari: Dedalo, 1974), 74–98.

dwellers resisted recognizing as their peers any individuals (they made up the majority, however) who, living in the fields, pasture lands, or woods, were too far removed from urban standards of civil behavior. The physical connotations attached to terms such as *agrestis, rusticus,* or *montanus* recalled a hairy individual with black teeth who smelled of goats, garlic, and soup. This particular human type could be recognized at first sight by his clothing, by his long hair (long hair was never considered "a sign of virtue" and made such people resemble the barbarians). At the other extreme, he stood out by virtue of too short a haircut, razed nearly to the scalp; by his speech, which prompted laughter; by his loud voice; and, above all, by the way he carried himself. His gestures would be too brusque; he would be incapable of the composed, slow gait that typified the good citizen; he would not sit down gracefully; his untutored hands would gesticulate without harmony.[13]

This congeries of psychological exclusions and of distinctions make one thing clear: in order to define the Roman as a type, we need to turn to the city. But the question is not that simple. If distance from *urbanitas* was a clear indication of a state of barbarity,[14] there were forms of an exaggerated *urbanitas*—genuine degenerations of civilized life—expressed in behavior so vulgar as to create something like a new barbarism. In a famous description, the historian Ammianus Marcellinus (a Greek from Antioch counted among the major historians of the Roman age) expressed his utter disgust for the *otiosa et desides* (at-leisure, indolent) plebs of Rome. His account teems with names that in themselves are eloquent testimony to a world of sordid activities and culinary fixations: Messores, Statarii, Semicupae and Serapini, Cicymbricus, Gluturinus, Trulla, Lucanicus, Porclaca, Salsula. For people of this sort, the Circus Maximus was all—a temple, a house, a civic assembly. They spent their time talking about the latest feats of the chariot drivers, then, on spectacle days, they rushed en masse to the Circus at dawn, faster than the chariots being readied for the race. Ammianus Marcellinus' description ends with the plebs' obsession with food, symbolized in the image of people fixedly watching a nauseating piece of meat as it cooks. It is almost like Democritus foreseeing the well-being of later generations in his anatomical stud-

13. See Andrea Giardina, "Uomini e spazi aperti," in Arnaldo Momigliano and Aldo Schiavone, gen. eds., *Storia di Roma,* 4 vols. (Turin: Einaudi, 1988–), vol. 4, *Caratteri e morfologie* (1989), 71–99. See also below, chapters 7 and 11.

14. One citation will have to suffice: Quintilian states that even the *rustici* and the *barbari* have some appreciation of a quality as primordial as justice: *Institutiones oratoriae* 1.11.6.

ies! This historian from Antioch assuredly felt himself more "Roman" than the Romans of Rome.[15]

Leaving aside such exaggerated visions, however, one would be mistaken to equate *urbanitas* with *Romanitas* unequivocally. The question with which Jean-Paul Morel begins chapter 8 of this volume, "Could one be a craftsman and be truly Roman?" could apply to many other social figures in the Roman world.

The Romans' own portraits of the Roman "type," as they have been handed down to us by ancient literary culture, are thus extremely varied. They reach a reasonable level of coherence and homogeneity only on the very narrow plane of *humanitas*, which by definition restricts the pure Roman "type" to only a few thousand individuals.

In A.D. 449 a Roman diplomat was waiting to be received by Attila at the latter's headquarters somewhere between the Tibiscus (now Timis) and the Danube rivers. Evening fell, and our man decided to take a walk around the fortifications. He was approached by a man who, from his aspect, seemed a barbarian, but to the Roman's surprise this barbarian greeted him in Greek with *"khaire!"* (*salve*).

Thus begins one of the most famous (but least studied) accounts left us by ancient historiography. The narrator was one Priscus, a functionary of the imperial administration, who was on a diplomatic mission to the leader of the Huns. Born some thirty or forty years earlier in Paniun in Thrace, Priscus had taken part in various legations for the Eastern Roman emperor, to Rome, to Egypt, and to the Huns. His historical writings, which have reached us through excerpts in Byzantine authors, had a notable success precisely because of the importance of relations between the Romans and the barbarians. This historian of classical tastes, who recalls Herodotus and Thucydides, was also a rhetorician, and the lexicon known as the *Suda* tells us that he published orations. Thus it is not surprising to find in his historical works a number of carefully written, credible "discourses" like those found in many other ancient historians.

Priscus asks the man who has greeted him how he happens to speak Greek. The "barbarian" then recounts his adventurous life. He was a Greek, and for reasons of trade had traveled as far as Viminacium, a city in Moesia on the banks of the Danube. He had lived there many years, created a position for himself, and married a wealthy woman. But fron-

15. Ammianus Marcellinus 28.4.28–34.

8

tier life had its risks: when the city was occupied by barbarians in 441–42 he ended up as the slave of a prominent Hunnish commander. As was the custom among the Huns, he went to war with his owner, and he fought valiantly, even against the Romans, to the point of accumulating enough booty to win his freedom. He later remarried, with a barbarian woman, and now lives a much happier life than before.

Among the barbarians, Priscus' Greek continues, one could live better than among the Romans, first of all for reasons of safety: the Romans themselves did not fight but preferred to entrust their cause to mercenaries; furthermore their generals were cowards. This made them easy prey for their enemies. But the man had other reasons of a civic sort: "For the laws are not applied to all. If the wrongdoer is rich, the result is that he does not pay the penalty for his crime, whereas if he is poor and does not know how to handle the matter, he suffers the prescribed punishment—if he does not die before judgment is given (since lawsuits are much protracted and much money is spent on them."[16]

In late antiquity this choice of life-style on the part of a Greek ex-merchant must not have been unique. The cases we know must be only the tip of an iceberg. Indeed, Salvianus, a priest in Marseilles and a contemporary of Priscus, speaks of Romans who emigrated among the rebel Celts, among the Goths, or to other barbarians because they "would rather live as free men, though in seeming captivity, than as captives in seeming liberty." According to Salvianus, they sought *humanitas Romana* among the barbarians because "they have . . . been driven so far by the cruelty of Roman injustice that they no longer wish to be Romans." Salvianus complains that the tax collectors, who used fiscal obligations as a way to personal enrichment, even subverted the basic rules of life in society: in the *urbes,* the *municipia,* and the *vici*—that is, the fundamental structures of the *civilitas* whose very reasons for being lay in balanced norms—the curials (who were responsible for collecting taxes) were transforming those norms into tyrannical rules.[17] As if to give a historical example of Augustine's maxim ("And so if justice is left out, what are

16. R. C. Blockley, *The Fragmentary Classicising Historians of the Later Roman Empire,* 2 vols. (Liverpool: Francis Cairns, 1981–83), 266–73; quotation, 269.

17. Salvianus *De gubernatione Dei* 5, quoted from *On the Government of God,* trans. Eva Sanford. (New York: Columbia University Press, 1930), 142. On this *translatio humanitatis* from the Romans to the Germans, see Claudio Leonardi, "Alle origini della cristianità medievale: Giovanni Cassiano e Salviano di Marsiglia," *Studi Medievali,* 3d ser., 18 (1977): 491–608.

kingdoms except great robber bands? For what are robber bands except little kingdoms?"),[18] Salvianus even draws a parallel between the representatives of power and bandits.

There was no easy answer to the accusations of the Roman citizen who had chosen to live among the barbarians, particularly when such accusations were common in Roman society in the mid-fifth century A.D. "There is an endless sadness in this exchange," Santo Mazzarino has written. "Men prefer a happy savagery to the weight of a superior civilization."[19]

Priscus' response is a tissue of stereotypes, conventions, and evasions. It is an assertion more than a demonstration. He touches (somewhat laboriously, particularly in his analysis of the division of civic functions) on the Platonic ideal of the *polis* but without grappling with the criticisms of the refugee among the Huns. His arguments are weak and trite. All, that is, except one.

Priscus says: "For your freedom you should give thanks to fortune rather than your master. He led you out to war, where, through inexperience, you might have been killed by the enemy or, fleeing the battle, have been punished by your owner. The Romans are wont to treat even their household slaves better. . . . Amongst the Romans there are many ways of giving freedom. Not only the living but also the dead bestow it lavishly, arranging their estates as they wish; and whatever a man has willed for his possessions at his death is legally binding."[20]

This was an old argument, but it still had some life in it. In his famous oration before the Senate in A.D. 48 the emperor Claudius, a highly cultivated man (he had written, among other things, a work on Etruscan antiquities, the *Tyrrenika*), attempted to persuade the Roman senators to admit members of the Gallic aristocracy, representatives of populations by then long and solidly linked to Rome and imbued with Roman culture, to their assembly.[21] It was not an easy task: pride of

18. St. Augustine *The City of God* 4.4. The topos already existed, for example, in Seneca *Naturales quaestiones* 3.5, pref.

19. Santo Mazzarino, *La fine del mondo antico,* 2d ed. (Milan: Garzanti, 1988), 68, quoted from *The End of the Ancient World,* trans. George Holmes (London: Faber; New York: Knopf, 1966), 66.

20. Blockley, *The Fragmentary Classicising Historians,* 273. See also Gilbert Dagron, " 'Ceux d'en face.' Les peuples étrangers dans les traités militaires byzantins," *Travaux et Mémoires* 10 (1987): 229–32.

21. *ILS* 212; see also Tacitus *Annales* 11.24.

group, fear of losing their exclusive privileges, and jealousy of rising fortunes led the senators to a rigid veto.

The emperor gave a broad-ranging speech centered on a definition of a "style" in Roman history. From its origins in the remote past, Roman history had been characterized by an open attitude toward foreigners. There were even many kings who had come from outside Rome: Numa was a Sabine; Tarquinius Priscus was born of a Corinthian father and a mother from Tarquinii. This openness toward the surrounding communities was accompanied by the rise of individuals of servile origin to the highest posts: chief among these was Servius Tullius, a positive example and a legendary king of early Rome. "Born, according to Roman tradition," Claudius stated, "of a prisoner named Ocresia, he reigned to the greatest advantage of the common good."

But slavery was recorded even in connection with the founding of Rome. Plutarch recounts that according to an obscure author named Promathion, who probably lived around 500 B.C., the twin founders of Rome, Romulus and Remus, were not of royal birth (as in popular tradition) but were born of a slave mother:

> Tarchetius, king of the Albans, who was most lawless and cruel, was visited with a strange phantom in his house, namely, a phallus rising out of the hearth and remaining there many days. Now there was an oracle of Tethys in Tuscany, from which there was brought to Tarchetius a response that a virgin must have intercourse with this phantom, and she should bear a son most illustrious for his valour, and of surpassing good fortune and strength. Tarchetius, accordingly, told the prophecy to one of his daughters, and bade her consort with the phantom; but she disdained to do so, and sent a handmaid in to it. When Tarchetius learned of this, he was wroth, and seized both the maidens, purposing to put them to death. But the goddess Hestia appeared to him in his sleep and forbade him the murder. . . . And when the handmaid became the mother of twin children by the phantom, Tarchetius gave them to a certain Teratius with orders to destroy them. This man, however, carried them to the river-side and laid them down there. Then a she-wolf visited the babes and gave them suck, while all sorts of birds brought morsels of food and put them into their mouths, until a cow-herd spied them, conquered his amazement, ventured to come to them,

and took the children home with him. Thus they were saved, and when they were grown up, they set upon Tarchetius and overcame him.[22]

A strange city, Rome, which, at least until a certain age, told of mythical founders not of divine origin, as would be normal and predictable, but born of a slave woman.

The Romans' special relationship with slavery seemed odd to foreigners as well. The Greeks were impressed by it. In another famous document, the letter written in 214 B.C. by King Philip V of Macedonia to the inhabitants of Larissa,[23] the Romans' attitude toward slavery prompted his evident admiration, and he even suggested it as a model for Greece.

Obsessed (with good reason) by the problems of *oliganthrōpia* (scarcity of men) that afflicted the Greek cities, Philip was attempting to persuade the citizens of Larissa to extend citizenship to metics—foreigners resident in their city. Think about the Romans, Philip wrote, who had even granted citizenship to slaves: "Once they had liberated them, they welcomed them into citizenship and they made them participants in magistracies; in this way, not only did they enlarge their homeland but they also founded some seventy colonies." Philip's inaccuracies aside (it was in fact the sons of freedmen who could become magistrates and not the freedmen themselves, and in 214 there were nowhere near seventy colonies), what counts is, first, Philip's recognition of a Roman specificity, seen as contributing to their vitality and force, and, second, the connection between this specificity and the flexible, open assimilation of foreigners and slaves.

Modern historians have often followed Philip's example to insist on a contrast between Roman "generosity" and Greek "avarice" in the extension of citizenship. The Roman *polis* was much more open than the Greek, and it was the secret of the success of the one and the failure of the other. Furthermore, in Greece, only the citizens' assembly could cre-

---

22. Plutarch *Life of Romulus* 2.4–8. Plutarch's account has been validated by Santo Mazzarino as Etruscan-Italic koine, and Mazzarino is the source of the quite credible dating of Promathion to ca. 500 B.C.: Mazzarino, "Antiche leggende sulle origini di Roma," *Studi Romani* 8 (1960): 383–92, esp. 389ff.; Mazzarino, *Il pensiero storico classico* vol. 1, 197ff. For a recent critical view of the problem, see Carmine Ampolo in Plutarch, *Le vite di Teseo e di Romolo,* ed. Carmine Ampolo and Mario Manfredini (Milan: Fondazione Lorenzo Valla, Arnaldo Mondadori, 1988), 272–76, where he defends the archaic character of at least the nucleus of this tradition against hypotheses that favor a later date.

23. *Syll.* 543.

ate new citizens. It was a complex and difficult procedure that involved a city's "sovereign right" and in which neither magistrates nor—for even greater reason—private citizens could vote by proxy. The scenario was completely different in Rome, where the magistracy operated beyond the institutional control of the people. Even more striking is the personal initiative of the individual *dominus* in Rome: his will, accompanied by a simple ritual and by the formal approval of a magistrate, was all it took to liberate a slave and make him a citizen. In other words, the citizen created the citizen.

Can we generalize about the history of Rome or, like the emperor Claudius, discern a "style" in Roman history on the basis of this contrast between rigidity and flexibility, closure and osmosis?

Some historians have disagreed strongly with the way this question is put. Philippe Gauthier has asserted the need to take such considerations of general profiles and return them to the political context. He notes that the Roman city was indeed "permeable" when it came to conceding individual citizenship but was less so when it was a question of absorbing entire communities, when a vote of the *comitia* (electoral assembly) was necessary and favorable decisions were relatively rare. There is a reason for this apparent contradiction: whereas the single individual was one isolated person lost in the whole of the electoral body, communities assimilated in toto would need to be constituted into new tribes for electoral purposes, which risked disturbing the political equilibrium.[24] Whereas Greek *politeia* meant integration into a sovereign political community in whose decisions the new member took a part, Roman citizenship meant, above all, civil rights, since the normal single citizen, outside clientage networks, counted for nothing. Gauthier states:

> Subject to the laws of the city and protected by them, with
> access to the courts as prosecution or as defense, the Greek

24. Philippe Gauthier, " 'Générosité' romaine et 'avarice' grecque: sur l'octroi du droit de cité," in *Mélanges Seston* (Paris, 1974), 212ff. For another point of view, see Augusto Fraschetti, "A proposito di ex schiavi e della loro integrazione in ambito cittadino a Roma," *Opus* 1 (1982): 97–103, where he points to texts that show the clear presence in Rome of a "jealousy of citizenship." One such text is a fragment of the oration *De sociis et nomine Latino* of Gaius Fannius, the consul in 122 B.C. Fannius insisted that the function of the citizen consisted in participation in the *contio*, in the *ludi*, and in the *dies festi* (public assembly, games, and holidays), places and moments that he accused the Latins of usurping and from which, obviously, slaves were rigidly excluded. On Rome as an "open city" as early as the archaic period and on the "structural nature" of this theme in Roman history, see Carmine Ampolo, "La nascita della città," in Momigliano and Schiavone, eds., *Storia di Roma*, vol. 1, *Roma in Italia*, 172–77 in particular.

freedman was, as a subject under the law, slightly less than the citizen. And from that point of view he was in a situation comparable to that of the Roman freedman. Politically he counted for nothing, but if one day he became a citizen, he would be one fully. The Roman freedman was immediately numbered among the *cives*, but that promotion would have political significance only if it was followed by social success.[25]

In Rome, only the members of the senatorial aristocracy, supported by their wealth, their prestige, and their clients, were full citizens in the Greek sense of the term.

Calls to return to context are always valuable, especially when they are formulated, as in this case, with constant attention to the relevant categories. Yet Gauthier's observations are useful, paradoxically, more for their insistence on "formalization" than for their invitation to keep in mind specific historical situations. Furthermore, although it is true that many modern historians have erred by following King Philip V in his reproach to the Greek *poleis* for not being what they neither wanted to be nor could be—that is, Roman—it is also true that the contrast between Greek "avarice" and Roman "generosity" is simply a noble historical meditation (by analogy or by difference) on two different political destinies. As such, this opposition must take into account the exceptional duration of the Roman *polis*, its ability to survive not only external trials but, above all, internal ones, and its self-renewal (in some cases, its transfiguration) as it weathered the storms of civil war and political crises. In this light, we absolutely cannot ignore the value of the ideological (better, the psychological) repercussions of the opportunity, in theory offered to all, to accede, through the rights of citizenship, to full political rights and to the social advantages and the public responsibilities deriving from those rights.[26]

Politics was not merely the full exercise of political rights theoretically possessed in equal measure by all citizens (a model that did not exist in the pure state even in the most democratic of the Greek *poleis*); it was also consensus and stability in consensus, emotive participation, and hope. There is no doubt that the success of Rome owed much to this psychological component: it does not take much effort to imagine the desperation of Spartacus and his followers or to understand the cruel

25. Gauthier, " 'Générosité' romaine," p. 214.

26. On the freedmen's limitations as citizens and more generally on the problems of their integration into Roman society, see below, chapter 6.

efficacy of repressive measures in Roman law (the *senatusconsultum Silania-num* is a striking example),[27] but neither is it difficult to imagine the eager cooperation of a slave who knows that by the simple decision of his owner he can obtain liberty, and with it the glittering title of Roman citizen.

What is more, the fact that the opportunity was not simply theoretical is confirmed thousands of times over. How can we not believe Tacitus when he says that freedmen formed a category so widespread and so well assimilated into society (*late fusum corpus*) that many senators and knights were descended from freedmen?[28] Roman history is imbued with this mixture of flexibility and a violent urge to dominate; of a profound and unbending sense of *imperium* and a talent for thinking up elastic solutions. One telling example of this is the terrible power of the *pater familias,* one of the pillars of Roman society. In the abstract, this power can be seen as a source of rigidity and sclerosis, but the *pater familias* who autonomously liberates a slave and creates a citizen is at the same time a source of social osmosis and flexibility. There are an infinite number of further examples of this contrast on the strictly historical plane, but one more will have to suffice. It is the most dramatic of all—the terrible and strange "Social War" at the end of which the defeated obtained all they had fought for.[29]

The only way to reach a definition of the "Roman man" is to discern a "style" in Roman history. This will always imply choice, however, and the existence of other competing choices.

27. On this and other repressive measures having to do with slavery and on their relationship with forms of "assimilation" of the slaves, see below, chapter 5.

28. Tacitus *Annales* 13.27, cited by C. R. Whittaker, chapter 10 below.

29. See below, chapter 1.

1

The Citizen; The Political Man

Claude Nicolet

"THE WORLD IS EMPTY after the Romans": Saint-Just's discouraged cry echoes a nostalgia that Rousseau had already expressed. Sparta, but even more, republican Rome, represented the last and perhaps the only example of civic organization in history. It was by turning his back on modern society that Rousseau, in *The Social Contract,* sought to identify the underlying conditions of all "civil society." But he could only conceive of that society as leading to and being completed by a *political* contract that transformed all men into citizens or, more accurately, that defined humanity by citizenship: only the citizen could truly be a man; only a free and sovereign people was a true people. These principles, which in one sense provided a foundation for the future, were for Rousseau deeply rooted in a nearly inaccessible and bygone past in the Golden Age of the city, which lay in the past, on the banks of the Eurotas and the Tiber.

In a certain sense modern ages have only perpetuated this nostalgia. The Roman Republic has continued to fascinate historians and haunt the collective unconscious. First of all we are fascinated by success: Rome's legionaries, its generals, its administrators, and its colonists conquered, pacified, and unified a gigantic space—one-third of the ancient "known world"—and the mark they put on that world was, by and large, the matrix of modern Europe. Rome's image of grandeur as an "imperial republic" reflected on all its "citizens." The grandeur of the Roman Republic that Rousseau admired was not uniquely in Rome's conquests, however. The modern age has also admired the internal history of the Roman people because it is exemplary and unique in covering all the underlying principles of politics, including the birth of a community, the organization of the powers necessary to a city, the conquest of equality of rights by the people against "the great," demands for liberty against oppression, and the great social questions (though no one called them that at the time) of poverty, debt, agrarian legislation, and public aid. At the end of the eighteenth century, when the dawn of liberty seemed to reintroduce ancient procedures into the modern world, deviation from the Roman model was still what was feared: revolutions resembled civil wars, and both Robespierre and Catherine the Great predicted that "Caesar will come." In its grandeur and its depravity, Rome was a model to be admired or dreaded; it offered humanity a complete range of patterns for the citizen.

This obsession is hardly surprising. Our ancestors were the willing victims of a moralizing academic tradition going back to antiquity itself. It was by reading Cicero, Livy, Plutarch, and perhaps Tacitus that they formed an idea of ancient Greece and Rome. These authors (represented, what is more, by their most famous passages alone) were all didactic writers. Directly or indirectly, they wrote to exalt an exemplary and perhaps embellished image of Rome's moments of glory. Theirs was a world in which civic and military virtue prevailed, a world shown in action in the Golden Age of the conquering Republic or else, tinged with searing regret, under dehumanized rulers. There is dedication to civic virtues, if only in negative terms, in Tacitus or Suetonius.

Both under the Republic and under the Empire, then, Romans were citizens. Humble or powerful, governed by assemblies, by annually selected magistrates and a senate, or by a ruler for life (at whose side the magistrates and the Senate continued to exist), all Romans, it seems clear, were citizens, and any man who possessed or acquired the "rights to the city" that were equivalent to Roman "citizenship" was, by that token, Roman. The "Roman people" was never anything but the sum total of Roman citizens. No distinctions were drawn within the Roman people between some who enjoyed rights to the city and others who did not. In principle the Roman city was one.

Does this mean that Rome provides a striking anticipation of the theoretical situation of the modern states that emerged from the "principles" of 1789, where nationality and citizenship coincided almost perfectly and, in principle, the entire population (though with restrictions of age and sex) enjoyed the same civil rights, was regulated by the same criminal law, and participated equally in political rights? Some historians have taken this position, and all the more legitimately because the founders of modern liberties (among others, the French Jacobins) were seeking a lost antiquity. This is a problematic assertion, however, which requires qualification in a number of ways.

First, there is the problem of the number of citizens in relation to the total population. A fundamental juridical inequality aside (on which more later), one might indeed state that in the earliest days of the Republic, when Rome did not even control Latium, its territory contained slaves, who had no rights, and free men, who were all citizens. One basic and characteristic trait of Rome should be noted immediately: freed slaves had full citizenship, in principle, enjoying all civil rights and even certain political rights. Nevertheless, by the end of the fourth century—that is, as soon as Rome set out to conquer Italy—the "people" and the "population" (the citizen body and all who might be called Romans) were no longer one and the same. When the conquest of Italy was complete in 272 B.C., populations of varying size and status were united under the sovereign rule of Rome. On the one hand there were "Romans" and full citizens (*optimo iure*), not all of whom by any means were descendants of the ancient inhabitants of the city; on the other there were Italians who, as (often unwilling) members of the Roman "alliance" (*symmachia*), were in some ways (concerning military and fiscal obligations) like Romans but in other ways not. On the one hand, they had no sovereignty rights, and decisions affecting everyone were imposed on them unilaterally; on the other hand, they enjoyed a large amount of local autonomy, had their own codes of private law, and had institutions different from those of Rome.

If, then, we consider "alliance" as a homogeneous whole—after all, in spite of defections, it resisted secession attempts during the war with Hannibal—and as an entity that then turned to the profitable conquest of the entire world, we need to note that full citizens soon became a minority within the total population. Thus, it is that minority that is reflected in the texts transmitted to us of the Roman census. Incomplete and at times dubious as they are, they provide us with our only solid basis for knowledge of ancient demography. The figures vary from 165,000 around 340 B.C. to 270,000 at the beginning of the Second Punic War, 325,000 around 150 B.C., and about 395,000 around 115 B.C. Furthermore, in this period such figures are far from reflecting the entire group of *cives Romani,* since they represent only adult males eligible for military service; thus they certainly exclude women and children, perhaps older men as well (this is less sure, since men over military age were never excluded from political functions), and, at times, perhaps the poorest citizens as well.

The entire citizen body (old men, women, and children included) was thus perhaps in reality three or four times greater. Aside from the full citizens, however, there were the many Italian "Latins and allies" who lived in cities or territories that did not grant formal citizenship or who had emigrated to Rome or to one of the Roman municipalities or colonies. I should also note that within the "autonomous" communities of Latins and allies there was a growing minority of the population who received full Roman citizenship, either as a privilege granted on an individual basis or even (for the Latins) automatically by magisterial decree. This meant that for those populations Roman citizenship did not represent the egalitarian condition of everyone but rather defined a privileged juridical status involving fiscal and political privileges in particular. Hence it defined a specific social group. The only information on which we can base an estimate of this non-Roman (thus noncitizen) population is indirect and comes—when figures are available—from the numbers of the contingents of auxiliary troops furnished at the request of Rome. Such units accounted for something between one-half and two-thirds of the Roman armies. Therefore the Italian representation reflected a global population at least equal to that of the Romans. This estimate undoubtedly falls short of the truth, for it is not certain that the Romans were as stringent with their allies as they were with their own citizens concerning military obligations.

Still, it is obvious that citizens, in the midrepublican period, were a minority within the total population of Roman Italy. They were to remain so until the Social War of 90–89 B.C., an immense war of secession paradoxically won by the vanquished, who obtained from the victors in defeat what they had been unable to wrest from them by armed insurrection. From that moment on (though it took several decades to register and integrate the entire population), all the free population of Italy (with the natural exception of transient foreigners) was considered citizens. Adult males numbered perhaps more than one million around 70 B.C., and the total free population was perhaps three or four times that figure.

With the Empire (and for reasons I have attempted to show elsewhere), the procedures and the purposes of census taking changed. In 28 B.C. and again in A.D. 47 and 73 all the citizen population—old men, women, and children included—was counted in Rome, in Italy, and in the provinces (members of colonies and municipalities of citizens, plus those who had received citizenship rights elsewhere). Between 28 B.C. and A.D. 47, the citizen population rose from something over four million to nearly six million. If these impressive figures (which are enormous in comparison with ancient cities) are to be evaluated accurately, however, they need to be seen in relation to figures for all inhabitants of the Empire subject to the authority of Rome and its emperor, including the populations of the "provinces of the Roman People," the "free cities" (which formed theoretically independent enclaves in those provinces), and the client kingdoms. In spite of the unreliability of our sources, we can estimate that population at between fifty and sixty million people.

As in Italy three centuries earlier, then, the citizen population formed only a minority among all the subjects of Rome. It was a privileged minority (as we shall see) that, despite its diverse origins and variations in social status, could be considered as a distinct and relatively homogeneous social group. During the second century A.D., however, more and more *peregrini* (that is, from the Roman point of view, foreigners) were naturalized. The spectacular culmination of this process was the famous Antonine Constitution of A.D. 212 granting Roman citizenship to all free inhabitants of the empire (except for a very limited minority called *dediticii*).

Once again, every "Roman" was, in appearance, a "citizen." It is obvious, however, that neither the word nor the status had the same meaning throughout such a long time span. To be a *civis Romanus* at the time of Hannibal's War, during the civil wars, under Tiberius, or under Caracalla meant totally different things. It was in civic life that these differences appeared most clearly: in war and military obligations, in fiscal policy (and in the public dole, a positive and prominent aspect of ancient fiscal policy), in the citizen's participation—direct or indirect—in decision-making and power. In the last analysis this highly structured set of complex relations determined the concrete conditions of the exercise of citizenship and the common destiny uniting (at times dividing) the citizen body.

Before being a way of life and, at some epochs, something like a profession, however, citizenship was and would always remain a juridical status: in Latin, a *ius*. It was even the *ius* par excellence, and when applied to everyone was called the *ius civile,* the "right of citizens." We should not forget, though, that in Latin *civile* ended up simply referring to private law and criminal law rather than to political obligations and advantages. In the last analysis, Roman citizenship rights signified that their possessors would have their personal, familial, patrimonial, and commercial relations—and their quarrels or their crimes—judged by a common law. That was the ideal of the ancient city that Plato and Aristotle had expressed in philosophical terms and that Cicero had taken up and applied, without difficulty, to Rome. Equality before the law was thus—apparently—the basis and even the goal of the city, the form of association that was one among many but was the greatest of all.

Of course, equality before the law did not mean that everyone had exactly the same condition or the same rights. Differences due to nature or to fortune were inevitable, and the city, a community under law, adapted to them very well. But those inequalities, in principle, did not touch the sphere of private relations: marriage, the family, relations with one's children, inheritance. Moreover, inequalities were ignored when crimes were committed (except, of course, political crimes). This meant that a *ius civile* could be developed gradually, by a successive accumulation that preserved individual *iura* but tended toward the universal. This was the majestic history of "classical" Roman law described in the broad sweep of tradition from Cicero to Pomponius through Livy, Tacitus, and the emperor Tiberius: Rome was a "state of law."

This advance toward an increasingly rational juridical equality was in part illusory, however. In private affairs the juridical equality of all citizens (which never really existed, either in politics or in civic life) lasted only a short time. Until the early third century B.C., plebeians and patricians were still separated by constraining prohibitions, and the procedural terms of midrepublican law still contained striking inequalities according to whether the accused was *assiduus* (a taxpayer, i.e., upper-class) or *proletarius*. Generally speaking the most egalitarian period was the last century of the Republic, when, for instance, the obligations of freedmen were greatly lightened. But with the establishment of the Empire there was a strong reaction that continued to gather force; in fact, inequality once more became an organizing principle in politics and in a society structured around a hierarchy of *ordines* (ranks). Inequality also extended to private and criminal law. The senators and the knights (whose status became hereditary officially) had a special matrimonial and testamentary law. Moreover, they enjoyed juridical privileges (judgment by the Senate, for example), procedural privileges (exemption from torture, introduced for commoners under Augustus), and, eventually, a criminal law distinct from that of the *humiliores*. After the second century A.D., immunities and lesser penalties for the *honestiores* and heavier sentences for the *humiliores* make the unity of citizenship explode before our eyes, defining at least two classes whose rights were all the less equal for being largely hereditary. The *ius civile* was no longer an *aequum ius*.

Community of rights was well and good, but the ancients rarely conceived of the "city" as a transcendent abstraction. It was also, and above all, a community of interests. *Res publica* was for Cicero *res populi,* and *res* in this case had both an abstract and a concrete sense, as common property and as the global interest common to all the citizens. Philosophers such as Plato had (without paradox) assigned to the constitution of cities the superior purpose of making each of the "associates" not only "happier" (better protected or richer) but "better" because of their association. This was, of course, another way of saying that a "moral" nature of man arose out of association and out of the initial social and political "contract," since all had to agree, at least implicitly, on a hierarchy of ends and means. It also meant that the constraint the city (that is, society) necessarily exercised over its members could not be pure force, and that the same constraint supposed an internalization of violence and an effort on the part of each individual to achieve self-control.

These things were, of course, profoundly true. But most of the citizens, as they lived their daily lives, experienced their collective life quite differently. What struck them most vividly were the obvious advantages that association brought them: the day-by-day protection of a community that, through its institutions and through the law, guaranteed one and all security for themselves and their property (Cicero *De officiis* 2.21.73), and an accumulation of wealth and commodities that permitted commercial relations and organized markets, festivals and fairs, and seaports. The modest organism of the city sought to realize a practical ideal: "common properties" belonging to all—a bridge, a river, a shore, pasturelands, mines—whose reasonable exploitation would, in principle, support the normal organizational needs of the community, for instance carrying out the worship of the gods (who also had their own wealth), constructing buildings and public places, and the usual tasks of fiscal and other sorts of public administration that depend upon employees and paid wages. The ancient "will to live together" was above all a "will to live better" in a stable equilibrium.

Such were the advantages of the constitution of cities that each citizen could see before him and that he had a right to expect. Seen from this utilitarian perspective, civic life was a natural association resembling both the family, because it grouped men of a more or less common origin, and a commercial association (one of the meanings of the word *societas*) ruled by the calculation of each person's contributions and earnings. All cities were in fact torn between these two conceptions, which were not easy to reconcile. On the one hand there was the instinctive (and often false) solidarity of a "common origin" (this was strong among the Greeks, who often claimed a mythic autochthony that set one group apart from the "others"). On the other hand, there was the supersensitive egotism of each "associate," who considered it his right constantly to weigh the advantages and disadvantages of his participation in common affairs and who, in extreme cases, imagined breaking the contract, when he felt too put upon, by emigration, secession, revolution (*stasis*), or a civil war that reestablished a threatened equilibrium by the use of violence. This was the rational view, the juridical view, or the accountant's view of the basic pact.

This view took it for granted that the great advantages of life in common supposed some sacrifices in the form of responsibilities or duties. It can be found not only in the philosophers who established the theory of the city (a priori, like Plato, or a posteriori, like Aristotle and Cicero) but in speeches or official texts and in daily life in such frequently used terms as *utilitas, commoda, munus, honores,* and *officia,* all denoting usefulness, service, or duty. In exchange for all that he received, every citizen was expected to respond when necessary to the common call for the maintenance and upkeep of "common things." As a citizen, then, the individual was constantly and a priori in the debt of the community: he owed it services (as the sources often say) relating to his person and his goods, but also relating to something more immaterial but equally important: his "good advice" or his "enlightened counsel." Obviously, these involved military service, the payment of taxes, political deliberation, and the exercise of certain responsibilities. In short, the citizen was, by his very nature, a soldier awaiting mobilization, a taxpayer, and a voter and, eventually, a candidate for certain offices.

These three aspects of his nature were, in fact, intimately connected, and if the collectivity appealed to them only periodically, they nonetheless could be invoked at any time. There was no need to take any decision based on principle to justify or create these duties: they preexisted all law and were contemporary to the foundation of the city itself. These duties concerned and obliged all citizens the minute they entered into the "city," either when they came of age or, if they were born elsewhere, by virtue of the act that made them citizens. The principle was not negotiable; it was inherent. A city was like a living organism: when it faced external threats it had to be defended; when it needed resources they had to be supplied; when it needed to manifest its will that will had to be expressed collectively; when it needed to act it needed men to speak, command, count, administer, provide for worship, and obey. Every citizen had to respond immediately to such appeals, coming to the aid of the collectivity according to his abilities and his concerns. He could not shirk without taking the supreme risk of departure or secession (questions to which I shall return).

In principle, however, in most cities (in republican times, in any event) these various roles affected all citizens equally. There was no such thing as some who gave their blood and others who gave their money; some who commanded and some who obeyed. Everyone, according to circumstances and need, could be soldier, taxpayer, voter, or magistrate; everyone (as Cicero and Livy said) had to know how to obey and to command. Everyone must take part in decisions, since they involved the "people," that is, everyone. Thus there was no such thing, in principle, either in Rome or most of the other cities, as specialization by function or a structural (and hereditary) inequality between soldiers and producers, priests and governors, taxpayers and the tax-exempt, "active" and "passive" citizens. Rather there was a unified and demanding (it has been called totalitarian) conception of civic life that obliged everyone to take his turn at each of these various roles. Even in the rhetorical "selections" of the schoolbooks (which nonetheless reveal a shared ideology), Roman political and historical literature—the two are often confused from Cato to Tacitus, Cicero and Livy included—insists constantly on the city's importance for *all* its citizens. Cincinnatus in his fields being called to the dictatorship, the sacrifice of Decius Mus that assured a Roman victory, or Spurius Ligustinus (Livy 42.32–35) giving an example of blind obedience to military recruitment and of abandonment of acquired rights; senators and knights competing to fill the empty treasury during Hannibal's War; Cicero preaching modesty and resignation to unsuccessful candidates for election—all these were illustrations of love of homeland and devotion to the public cause without which, we are told, no state can exist. In Rome this structure was particularly strong (Polybius 6.54).

This "totalitarian" city that seemed to demand everything from everyone, drawing no distinctions, was neither a monastery nor a democracy. The ancients—the Romans, quite evidently—were persuaded that physical and moral constraint could not accomplish everything. No matter how demanding it might be, a city could not hope to command contributions up to the supreme sacrifice from all citizens or at all times if it failed to win a reasonable commitment from them, and commitment arose primarily out of each citizen's interests. There were immense advantages to life in common, but there were also disadvantages, dangers, and responsibilities. Just as in private law Greek and Roman jurists criticized contracts that awarded the lion's share of advantages to one side and all the disadvantages to the other, so the city must expel such contracts. The citizenry could be imbued from earliest childhood, beginning in the family, with a collective morality that encouraged civic spirit, loyalty, and resignation, but if the burdens were too heavy (and especially if they were too unjustly distributed) the bond would eventually break. The fundamental problem of the city was thus that of the distribution of responsibilities and advantages. In principle, the advantages should outnumber the obligations; they should be distributed over time and should alternate (responsibilities in particular should not be definitive or permanent). They should also be fairly distributed among the citizens, not falling always on the same people, nor should some always have the duties and others the advantages.

These highly empirical principles (they are also realistic, if not cynical) were those of all cities. Plato, Aristotle, Theophrastus, and Dicaearchus had discussed them and theorized about them, and they inspired a "common opinion" discernible in the language of decrees and inscriptions. Nowhere did this theory appear more clearly than in Rome, however, because the Romans, who had retained archaic institutions longer than most of the Greek cities, were acutely conscious of possessing a highly coherent and structured system of civic organization aimed at introducing as perfect an equilibrium as possible in this distribution of the advantages and disadvantages of responsibilities and honors. The entire system was founded on an operation of counting and categorizing the citizens (*discriptio*) that the city performed periodically and that was called the *census*. Once again, all the ancient cities, even the most democratic ones, had a *census* (*timēma*) and were to some extent census based and timocratic. No city remained so as long and as fully as Rome.

Romans attributed the invention of the census to one of their last kings, Servius Tullius, thus placing its introduction at the origin of their republic. Its original purpose was to provide an exact count of all citizens—that is, all who could be conscripted during wartime, who paid taxes, and who participated in decisions and common action. This meant adult males only. The rest of the population appeared as an adjunct to these "useful heads" as a help to their identification. Aside from his name, which carried a good deal of meaning, speaking of his origins and clearly indicating his status, every citizen was identified by a set of other facts relating to his age, geographical and familial origin, merit, and, above all, his "patrimony"—that is, his wealth. It was by taking into account these various criteria (which reflected the common opinion) that the magistrates charged with carrying out the *census* distributed the citizens according to a system (*ratio*) that assigned each one a precise place in a rigorous hierarchical order. This place was essential: every citizen had to know it or demand its definition. It alone would determine the exact role that he was to play on the stage of civic life: his rank and his duties in the army, the amount of his eventual tax payments, but also (and this was unique to Rome) his right to participate in political deliberations and to accede to the city's higher ranks and "honors."

In short, it is clear that each individual's social status and his concrete existence depended largely on his being assigned a precise place in a vast system of orders, classes, tribes, and centuries. If participation in the city on the most general level turned natural man into a man subject to the law, involved reciprocity (*civis* also means "fellow citizen"), and called him to a sort of abstract juridical life, it was only after the periodic taking of the *census* that he received his true life and received it officially by a proclamation that engaged the entire city. For some, this classification could involve a measure of blame or praise: a magistrate who wanted to reward or punish someone could change the relevant data, advancing him or putting him down a notch. The roles were fixed in advance, but in the last analysis it was the task of opinion—that is, of the state—to proclaim them and see that they were played.

The citizens played these roles grouped into intermediary categories—subunits of the city—in which the true solidarities of collective life were clearly manifest. Empirically set up, one after the other during the course of history, these subunits had an essential place in both political and social organization. The civic drama was played out at their level and filtered through them; conversely they defined and provided a model for everyone's "status"—called in Latin *condicio* or *dignitas*. This structure, which lasted to the late Empire and operated in a variety of economic and social systems, was founded on the state and made for the state, and it prevailed over all other forms of differentiation. Roman society was and remained political.

It is not enough to speak of hierarchy, which supposes that some will be first and some last, some governors and some the governed. We need also to understand what that hierarchy was founded on. When they described the "censorial system" credited to Servius Tullius—even anachronistically and idealizing it—Cicero, Dionysius of Halicarnassus, and Livy thought of it as still operative in their own times, and they cited it as the best illustration of the philosophical principle of geometric equality. As in an ideal commercial exchange, the best possible balance needed to be struck between the individual's responsibilities and his burdens, taking into account such factors as his status as a free citizen and the "purity" of his "race" (his family), his age, his physical and moral bent, his property, his wealth, and, where appropriate, his descendants. Thus there were, within the city, "tribes" defined both territorially (a property was "in such and such a tribe") and in human terms, since individuals and families were also grouped according to origin or at the pleasure of the legislator or the magistrate. There were censorial classes of all whose wealth amounted to more than one certain figure and less than another.

Within these classes (which were extremely unequal in size, since the poor were much more numerous than the rich), men were divided into a set number of "centuries" according to age (in other words, according to a military criterion). Until the Second Punic War, the censorial classes (there were eventually five of them) in turn determined the sort of arms each man was entitled to bear, hence his place and role on the battlefield. Among the wealthy, for example, the richest (and the "best") served on horseback; thus there were 18 equestrian centuries to 175 infantry (and "worker") centuries. At one time there was a visible relationship between the number of men in these 193 centuries and the overall size of the army (the *legio*) that had actually been raised, but this relationship soon disappeared. In any event, it is obvious that the system led to the existence of units that may have borne the same names but that varied enormously in size. Cicero tells us that there were more men in the last "classless" century, made up of *proletarii*, than in all the others combined. Thus more than half the citizen population served in $1/193$ of the centuries!

This seems incomprehensible until we realize that the century served not only as a recruitment category but also as a category for taxation purposes and voting privileges, which explains the imbalance. Equality of duties was calculated at the point of arrival, not the point of departure. Each century was to furnish the same number of men and the same fraction of total tax income and to express an opinion that counted as one "vote." Since the wealthy were numerically fewer in their centuries than the poor were in theirs, the wealthy automatically contributed both blood and money more massively and oftener. On the other hand, because the century system was (and long remained) also a system of political *comitia* (assemblies), the centuries of the wealthy were proportionally more numerous than those of the poor: the first class and the equestrian class accounted for a majority (98 centuries out of 193; 88 out of 193 as the system was modified in the second century).

Everything was arranged (admirably, the Romans thought) so that military and fiscal responsibilities fell disproportionately to the rich, the powerful, and the well-born, which also meant that in the city the best soldiers and the most loyal taxpayers were those who had something to defend. Conversely and in compensation (otherwise the tension would have been unbearable) the same wealthier people had a preponderant influence in assemblies in which voting took place for elections, laws were passed, and cases of law were judged. In principle, no one was excluded from any duty or any advantage: although the rich were mobilized more often and called upon for greater contributions, the last classes, the proletarians, could be called on when needed, and, during the Second Punic War, slave volunteers bought up by the state and to be freed later and even convicts were conscripted. Similarly, if the poor at times enjoyed de facto exemption from taxes, exemption was never de jure (as can be seen during the Punic Wars). As for the vote, the presence of a century of proletarians saved appearances and principles: "No one was deprived of the suffrage," Cicero declared (*De re publica* 2.40). That would be tyrannical. Still, the "multitude" had no real influence, since that would be dangerous.

So much for principles. Practice, as it evolved over several centuries of history, was of course quite different. All hasty generalizations (and any existential portrait of a "typical Roman citizen") are doubly dangerous, first, because of profound changes that took place over time and from place to place and because the theoretical system in the second and first centuries B.C. gradually disintegrated, leading eventually to the shift from the Republic to the Empire; and second, because the system itself, as we have seen, in reality involved differences and inequalities, since it ended up providing a minimum of honors and advantages for some and an accumulation of both for others (at least before "popular" institutions made a necessary correction in this imbalance).

We need next to examine these questions, first as they pertained to the military, the first of the three essential domains of civic life.

This is hardly the occasion for a full outline of the military role of Roman citizens. Nonetheless, it was an essential role. Also the needs and consequences of conquest (particularly where recruitment was concerned) were what forced the Republic into a crisis that, in the long run, resulted in a new army and a military monarchy. Even without full consideration, we need to recall the salient points of this evolution and emphasize one or two of its underlying conditions.

From its origins to the early second century A.D. the Roman army was a citizen militia recruited annually for a predetermined campaign and, when possible, demobilized afterward. The soldier was paid not a wage but an indemnity funded by a special *tributum,* a direct tax on wealth paid by all men of military age (though, obviously, predominantly by the wealthiest). This tax was also levied for the circumstance, and it was so far from being permanent that if booty permitted it was reimbursable. The system was a simple one, well structured, and economical. I should also note that, in principle, the rich were the first to be called to serve in the army.

The first blow to this system came with the war with Hannibal. The disasters that marked the war's beginning and the difficult campaigns in far-off places that followed had drastic demographic consequences: 13 percent of the total population was mobilized, and 20 percent of adult males died in the war. It was a cataclysm that recalls World War I. One obvious result was a shortage of men and chronic recruitment difficulties during the succeeding century. The war probably also contributed to the authorities' need to lower the wealth requirements (listed in the census) for conscription. From that date on, moreover, wars were fought overseas, which made for a more permanent army and a longer term of service (in Spain, then in Africa) and led to a reliance on volunteers when possible (though this was not always possible). A volunteer army had little hope of reaching sufficient numbers unless it appealed to the poorest in the population and offered financial compensation. War had to "pay." This led to the familiar spiral of an increasingly permanent army that was also increasingly professional and proletarian and, in its politics, increasingly imperialist. It was, of course, not an army of mercenaries. Rome employed non-Romans, but they served under the banner of its allies. Rome did not "buy" its soldiers. The Roman army continued to be a citizen army up to the Empire.

The army was also not a true professional army; that would make its formal appearance only with the Empire. Even under Augustus there continued to be massive civil mobilizations in times of crisis or civil war: 25 percent of the *juniores* were under arms in 44 B.C. In ordinary times, though, military obligations did not weigh equally on all citizens, and entire sectors of society could avoid them. Ideology did not keep pace, however, and it is curious to see, toward the end of the Republic and under the Empire, the persistence of military models in milieus that were less and less military (a phenomenon that has not received the attention it deserves). The "political class" was just as subject to these models as ever, since military service as an officer was obligatory for anyone who sought the honor of holding office.

These changes also brought on considerable financial stress. For one thing, after 167 B.C., successes abroad permitted the suspension of direct taxation (though in principle it was not eliminated). Thus all Roman citizens enjoyed a fiscal privilege that gave them an incentive to pursue conquest. In the short term it was the wealthy (the only ones who were truly taxable) who benefited the most: they served less and paid less. The poor, however, were encouraged or constrained to answer the call to arms, and the suppression of the *tributum* did them little good. Army pay during this period remained strangely stable and by itself was hardly an inducement, since a slave worker might earn more. It is hardly surprising, then, that various forms of compensation (the notion was inherent to the logic of a censorial system) began to appear.

The "agrarian law" revived by Tiberius Gracchus in 133 B.C. was the first of a series of measures relating to the problem of compensation for the military. Leaving aside the difficult question of exactly whom these provisions were intended to benefit (veterans? future soldiers?), their connection with military questions is undeniable. The "grain laws" introduced (cautiously) by Gaius Gracchus in 123 were the next of such measures. They attempted to guarantee to the *cives* the simple possibility of buying a generous amount of wheat at a fairly low fixed price, subsidized by the public treasury. Here, too, we have questions, for instance: Was this privilege originally restricted, by law or in fact, to the inhabitants of the *Urbs*? Three-quarters of a century later, with the *lex Clodia* of 58 B.C., this was certainly the case, and freedmen were admitted to the distributions, which had become completely free. We have some figures: 320,000 people benefited from the distributions, or from one-fourth to one-third of the male adult population of Rome—perhaps one-half of the total population. According to Cicero, if we interpret him correctly, the dole absorbed one-fifth of the fiscal revenues of the state. An accurate figure is less important than the order of magnitude, which is impressive enough. Here too, however, the precise connection with the proletarianization of the army is not clear, for at this point it was probably civilians, men exempt from service and little anxious to serve, who, as Florus put it "profit from their treasure."

Soldiers who were currently serving in the army benefited from other mechanisms that were more or less spontaneously put into operation at that time, one of which was the distribution of booty, both during campaigns and on the day of the triumph. The distribution of lands to veterans was another. The latter institution was a sort of cancer for the state for nearly a century (from 103 to 13 B.C.) and one of the reasons for its fall. For one thing, the stock of available public lands was diminishing; for another, the Senate often voted down the claims generals had made for their soldiers or made the veterans wait an inordinately long time. This explains one of the effects (if not the goals) of the civil wars: to appropriate land (lands of the vanquished who had been killed, exiled, or dispossessed) in order to distribute it to the soldiers (and the friends) of the victors. The transfers of property effected on this enormously large scale undeniably contributed to a "revolution" in Rome: tens of thousands of veterans were settled as a result of Sulla's proscriptions or by the triumvirs after 43 B.C. The memory of these expropriations (and the threat of their like) still haunted Romans fifteen years after the foundation of the principate. Thus when Augustus decreed (in 13 B.C.) that, as a matter of principle, the system of distributing land to demobilized soldiers would be replaced by money distributions, one cannot say that a world was ending. Rather, the imperial system was born.

The second of the three essential domains of civic life was politics. As a soldier and a taxpayer (both were theoretically obligatory until the Empire), the Roman citizen was not a passively obedient subject with no recourse against those who governed him; he was also a member of a community—the *populus Romanus*—endowed with a high degree of autonomy and activity. The "liberty" of the Roman people is often evoked, along with its "sovereign grandeur" (*maiestas*) and even its "authority." In more technical terms, however, the Roman people is said to have had a will, to have willed and demanded things, and in order to manifest that will, to have given orders (*voluntas, iussus populi*). As we have seen, however, the people was simply the sum total of the citizens. Thus it was up to the citizens to express what the people wanted in a formal, verifiable, and concrete manner. In other words, the Roman citizen—the possible conscript and the taxpayer—also had a will and an opinion on matters of common interest that he was expected to express. In modern parliamentary democracies, this aspect of citizenship can be summed up in the term "voter." Things were both less direct and more complex in Rome.

The ancient city was a simple and practical organism. In order to know what its constituents wanted, never (or very seldom) was any means imagined other than consulting them directly and listening to their response. Representation was unknown. This meant that the citizens had to be united in an assembly. Unlike the ephemeral abstraction of election days in our own day, this was an extremely concrete and very prosaic reality: all who had the right to do so met together at a given place. Everyone, in principle, came, listened, and spoke. This is, roughly speaking, the model for deliberation and decision making that the smaller Greek cities—and even the big cities such as Athens—offered to the "democratic" constitution. It was a simple model, but it was also a fragile one. Since open-air direct democracy demanded the repeated and assiduous presence of all citizens, it ran into difficulties when the city reached a certain size or degree of complexity in its economic and social relations. It also involved considerable practical and psychological difficulties.

Like all cities, then, Rome had its assembly. Or rather—and this is a characteristic that was both archaic and original—it had several of them, composed in principle and in fact of the same citizens, but convened and, above all, distributed differently according to the nature and the purpose of the assembly. What characterized Roman assemblies most fundamentally was precisely that, rather than grouping an indefinite number of individuals, the assemblies provided a limited and set number of units within which each individual gave his opinion, but whose collective opinion was what was counted. This is why the notion of "assembly" is expressed in Latin by *comitia,* in the plural. These units were of course those we have already encountered and that operated for military recruitment or tax collecting: the classes, centuries, and tribes of the census system, which also provided the framework of the comitial system. Thus it was the thirty-five tribes and the 193 centuries that were consulted and not (or at least not formally) the individuals who composed them. Obviously this system functioned as a sort of negative image of fiscal and military obligations: the poor, who were infinitely more numerous than the wealthy and, in practice, were less affected by military mobilization and direct taxation, were practically without any political influence, since it was the tribes and centuries that were counted in a majority vote, not individuals.

This statement requires some reservations according to the type of assembly called and its agenda. The timocratic principle operated fully only in the assembly of the centuries: the knights (who had the highest census listing, four hundred thousand sesterces) and the first class together held a near majority; thus when they agreed, they could sway any decision. In the assembly of the tribes, however, citizens were (at least in principle) grouped according to their place of origin or residence. The vote in this assembly was no more egalitarian, however, since the number of rural tribes (thirty-one) was far greater than urban tribes (four), whereas the population of the city of Rome certainly exceeded the rural population until 89 B.C. Furthermore, since the censors and the Senate determined assignment to a tribe, the tribes were extremely unequal in size. Thus there were tribes of fewer members in which one elector's voice could be determinant and others with a great many members in which one man's opinion counted for little.

Why did Rome choose this complex organization? And why did it have two sorts of assemblies? Cicero offers a clear explanation:

> Our forefathers . . . were wise and scrupulous men, and they gave no power to the mass meeting, such was their will. The commons passed their bill, the people passed their law; but first the mass meeting was dismissed, areas were assigned, orders, classes, ages were apportioned separately in their own tribes and centuries, the supporters of the act were heard, the text was published and studied for weeks—then whatever those two bodies passed as law was commanded or forbidden—such was their will. But all the states of the Greeks are managed by irresponsible seated assemblies. And so, not to discuss this later Greece, which has long been troubled and vexed by its own devices, that older Greece, which once was so notable for its resources, its power, its glory, fell because of this defect alone—the undue freedom and irresponsibility of its assemblies. Untried men, without experience in any affairs and ignorant, took their places in the assembly and then they undertook useless wars, then they put factious men in charge of the state, then they drove most deserving citizens out of the country. (*Pro Flacco* 7.15–16.)

Thus it was a simple question of molding the expression of opinion and the taking of decisions to fit into a hierarchy. Roman assemblies had a general competence covering all aspects of collective life, but that competence was exercised essentially in two domains—"rewards and punishments," as Polybius put it. The first of these domains included the granting of public responsibilities, the election of most magistrates, and jurisdiction in certain criminal cases. The second included the elaboration of rules and decrees (in practice, voting on laws and plebiscites) concerning nearly all questions of private and public law, diplomacy, war and peace, and more. In principle, nothing (unless it was custom, which was revocable) limited the competence and the sovereignty of the people. There was no domain reserved to the magistrates or the Senate. It was in order to set practical limits to this apparently unlimited power that the rulers of Rome jealously preserved the ancient, complex, and hierarchized comitial organization.

The assembly organized by centuries was more timocratic than that of the tribes and had the privileges of electing the higher magistrates who held military power, of legislation concerning war, peace, and treaties, and of judgments involving capital punishment. The tribal assembly chose the other magistrates (including the tribunes, of course) and handled the remaining legislation and trials. At least this was how the system operated in principle and at its beginnings, since this schematic description leaves out a remarkable historical evolution that profoundly altered electoral practices toward the end of the republican era.

Such, then, was the framework within which the Roman citizen exercised the power of opinion and will that was part of his very nature and that offered each individual a place (and only one place) in a complex and inegalitarian structure. There were, however, other essential characteristics of the comitial system in Rome that will help us to understand the individual's roles.

First, although their competence was universal, the Roman *comitia* never met by right, for example at a fixed date, but were always convened to discuss a precise order of the day at a meeting called by a magistrate who held juridical competence for that specific agenda. The people could not call its own meetings; others had to call the *comitia* into existence. It might happen (but seldom did) that no assembly would be convened at all. Conversely, however, the various magistrates could not submit to an assembly whatever they wanted, when they wanted, or as they wanted: a "comitial law" of sacred origin and accumulated through the ages regulated recourse to the people. This law determined a calendar and, in part, the meeting place for the *comitia,* two elements that greatly influenced both the procedures and the vote itself and that limited use or abuse of them on the part of some magistrates. In short, the people could not meet on its own initiative; assembly was dependent on the gods, on tradition, and on custom.

Neither could the people express itself freely and without aid. The simple citizen in Rome did not choose the questions put to him. Moreover, he did not deliberate. Whatever the assembly—electoral, legislative, or judicial—the people in its *comitia* and the citizens individually could do no more than answer yes or no to a question (*rogatio*) put to them. This was even true of elections. Thus, as a matter of principle, the individual citizen not only had no right to initiate legislation, he also had no right to participate in a debate, to interrogate, or to object to or amend a proposition. He was given a voice, yes, but—like a judge or a silent witness—only at the very end of a long process and in terms that apparently strongly limited his liberty.

This liberty was also restricted and, in a certain sense, supervised by the technical procedures of the vote—at least in the early period—since until the late second century B.C. this yes or no vote was also a voice vote carried out according to a long and meticulous procedure. When a vote was to be taken, the citizens were called together by units (the tribe, the century) and were asked to pass in single file, in an order that was more likely to be hierarchical than alphabetical, before an impressive array of city magistrates and employees and officers of their unit (the curators of the tribes, centurions of the centuries, "rogators," and so forth). Each man, in full sight of the assembly, responded orally. By its procedures, the Roman oral vote was thus a solemn occasion for complete manifestation of the control exercised by the hierarchy and of the full weight of the superior orders and the established authorities. These authorities might even contest a vote that had already been taken, as in 167 B.C., on the occasion of the vote for the triumph of Lucius Aemilius Paulus.

This unwieldy, solemn, and timocratic system responded to the needs of the rural, oligarchical, and virtuous city of Rome's origins. Did it ever function in this ideal manner, even in the golden age of republican civism? I could not swear to it: Dionysius, Cicero, and Livy describe it more as a principle than as a reality.

The more telling questions concern instead the real effect of this system and its consequences for the life of the citizen. By the same token, we need to investigate the profound differences that it implied, particularly in the social sphere. Inegalitarian in principle, the system neither affected all citizens equally nor asked equal participation from them, but rather it encouraged and promoted considerable differences of behavior between the rich and the poor, the freeborn and the freed, inhabitants of the city of Rome and of the *ager,* city dwellers and rustics—above all, as we shall see, between the "full-time" members of the "political class" (the candidates for office and honors) and the rest. By its distribution of roles, the system of the census, which piously asserted the unity of the body civic, in reality tore the city apart. This means that it evolved, and the changes that it underwent between the second and the first century B.C., which nearly led to its disappearance, also introduced a certain number of substitute procedures and a true redistribution of both influence and the issues at stake.

A first indication of these changes is in the calendar. We can estimate the number and the frequency of the times that, on the average, the presence of the citizens was required in Rome. Every five years they needed to take part in the census. Until the Social War, for most of the citizens who lived in the *ager Romanus* (the municipalities and the Roman colonies), this operation took place in Rome itself. A long and painstaking procedure carried out tribe by tribe, it took eighteen months to complete (at the rate of something like a thousand declarations per working day). The citizen's presence was obligatory, and failure to appear involved serious punishment. At that time some well-organized collectivities of the *ager Romanus* may have conducted such operations locally, transmitting partial results to Rome in documentary form. In any event, this was the procedure followed for all Latins in Italy who were not Roman citizens. It offered the advantage of saving people a trip, but it could be seen as a disadvantage (even a liability) if *formulae* sent from Rome had to be applied. In any event, until 89 B.C. the majority of the citizens had to go to Rome if they wanted the full benefits of the *census*. I might also note that, at least until Polybius' days, in the mid-second century, citizens were also obliged to gather in Rome for the *dilectus* (selection) of those eligible for military service. By definition, however, this affected only young men of military age, hence a minority.

The chief strictly political activity of the *comitia* involved elections. Every year some forty regular magistrates had to be elected, plus twenty-four military tribunes. These operations—some carried out by the *comitia* of the centuries and others by tribal assemblies—were often long and complex, lasting more than an entire day for each electoral college (consuls, praetors, tribunes). The citizens could not vote when they wanted to, but had to vote in strict order within their units and when called. The roll call—by name—was long and subject to specific controls. In short, even if all the three hundred thousand to four hundred thousand citizens in second-century B.C. Rome (or the million citizens of the first century

B.C.) did not vote, elections involved repeated and interminable operations that occupied at least ten days out of the year.

There were also occasions when laws and trials brought before the
comitia required a vote. Here the only fixed rule regarded regulations
concerning procedures and the interval between a proposition and the
vote. The number of such occasions depended wholly on the political
situation at the moment, on whether anyone wanted to have recourse to
popular vote, on the legislative activity of the magistrates, on conflicts
between "parties," and so forth. The available documentation is not complete enough to enable us to made a reliable estimate of the frequency of
such operations, but we can discern trends. Beginning with the age of
the Gracchi, votes on tribunician laws became an essential instrument
of policy and no longer required the approval of the Senate. There was
of course a sharp increase in the number of laws, and, as we shall see,
legislation was of growing political, social, and economic importance.
For certain years we can identify tens of assemblies. The presentation of
a proposed law (this was also true of elections, but on a lesser scale) was
a long and complex procedure that could require at least twenty-four
days (the *trinundinum*). During this time it was customary to convene
several semiofficial preparatory assemblies of the people (*contiones*) where
the author of the proposal and others defended it, where his adversaries
had the right to speak against it, and where the citizens were strongly
encouraged to be present in great numbers and to show their enthusiasm.
Thus it is easy to see that all this could occupy a considerable number of
hours and days—twenty, thirty, and often many more. In short, certain
sources were justified in calling the Roman citizen a *forensis, comitialis,
contionalis* (or *contionarius*). Citizenship was indeed a full-time job.

Under such conditions a question of central importance naturally
becomes, Who really participated in these electoral and political activities?
We have absolutely no reliable figures. Furthermore, it is not sure (given
the system of voting by units) that any permanent account was kept. It
is certain, however, that, by definition, participation varied enormously
according to circumstances but also over time, as long-term institutional
and political changes took place. Can the topography of Rome furnish
any answers? We know that the tribes were convened within the *pome-
rium,* the sacred space of the city, usually in the Forum either in front of
the Curia or elsewhere, at times on the Capitoline. The Forum did not
provide a very large space, but we also know that in the late second
century, when votes were taken, the people at times filled it entirely, and

even that on one occasion (in 124 B.C.) those who were crowded out of the Forum itself occupied the surrounding rooftops and terraces. This tells us nothing about normal attendance, though, for, according to the circumstances, the tribes might be called to vote one after the other, which meant that a smaller electoral arena, used thirty-five times, would suffice. In principle, all male adult citizens could come to the *comitia* of the tribes, which would represent several hundred thousand potential voters in the second century B.C. and nearly a million in the first century. It seems highly improbable—even supposing that voting operations took place successively—that such figures were ever realized, and a few tens of thousands of voters, on the most important occasions, seems a maximum.

This is not the important point, however. The system of thirty-five tribes (a fixed number, although the size of the single tribes varied greatly) gave an advantage to the thirty-one "rustic" tribes. In reality, it offered them a second advantage: only very few members of the rural tribes needed to make the trip to Rome to represent their tribe and cast the one global vote that was counted. As long as the population of the city of Rome was composed of longtime citizens enrolled (normally) in the four urban tribes, and as long as the *ager Romanus* was not too far from the center, these country people's vote had considerable weight. During the second and first centuries, however, an evolving economic and political situation introduced notable changes: the urban population grew, in part because of a veritable rural exodus from the regions of Italy in which great landed properties were forming and when landless peasants, Latins, and people from among Rome's allies flocked to Rome seeking citizenship. Furthermore freedmen (most of whom lived in the city of Rome) made up an increasingly large part of the urban population and could not always be fitted into the four urban tribes. In short, toward the end of the second century B.C. more and more of the inhabitants of Rome were enrolled in the rustic tribes. As long as their rural origin remained noticeable and they retained an interest in rural affairs, this shift compensated for the geographical distances involved in the territories of Rome. We know from reliable sources, however, that the great political reforms of the late second century (the agrarian laws of Tiberius and Gaius Gracchus and of Saturninus) prompted agitation and disturbances in the rural districts themselves and brought on sizable electoral migrations to Rome both for the *contiones* and the vote.

Things changed during the first century B.C. After the Social War, the enrollment of new citizens in the tribes (the rustic tribes for the most part) had swelled their ranks, so an individual vote carried less weight. Moreover, the number of inhabitants of Rome (uprooted countryfolk, freedmen, new citizens) inscribed in those same tribes increased constantly, to the point that in the tribal assembly (in which the "rural" tribes were still in the majority) Rome's "urban plebs" now outnumbered the others. Active and ambitious politicians seeking success for its own sake henceforth had less need to recruit partisans from afar. It is not certain that the urban populace was willing to support any and all candidates. What is certain is that the plebs' automatic majority (so to speak) in the tribal assembly—the privileged instrument of the tribunes— profoundly modified the unwritten rules of the political game.

The centuriate assemblies operated as a powerful counterbalance to this system, however. There, as Cicero and the enlightened conservatives said, the "true people" was "distributed" and "ordered" in hierarchical fashion; there, votes were weighed, not simply checked off. The spectacle of the centuriate assemblies, in which "orders," fortunes, and ages were organized under the sign of *gravitas,* was often contrasted to that of the democratic assemblies of the Greek cities, which met in the theater, where, comfortably seated, everyone mingled and the multitude dominated. The centuriate assemblies pondered serious matters: the election of the consuls, praetors, and censors; death sentences; laws affecting the status or the life of a citizen; votes concerning war, peace, and diplomacy (until the second century). Such matters required age, the experience acquired by the exercise of public office, and wealth (which encouraged prudence). The assembly of the 193 centuries was, in fact, extremely oligarchical. The wealthy and the senators were distributed among the seventy units of the first class (one unit of *juniores* and one of *seniores* for each of the thirty-five tribes). The knights (both young and old before 123 B.C.; the young only after that date) had eighteen centuries.

We have only one indication of the number of persons within these groups: more than half of all citizens (at that date some 175,000 persons) were packed into the last century, that of the *proletarii* and *capite censi* (those taxed per capita), which was hardly ever convened. Thus the various migrations and changes in the urban population had little real effect on the oligarchical nature of the centuriate *comitia,* since the members of the rural tribes who lived in Rome were for the most part proletarians or people of modest means. In the early centuries, if by chance a notable (Cicero's father, for example) came to the city to live, his voice would carry some weight. This explains the vast migratory movements to participate in the centuriate assembly before and especially after the Social

War, when candidates campaigned in the most remote districts, in particular in the rich and fertile areas of Cisalpine Italy. Veritable "marches on
Rome" were organized, such as the one that turned out the vote for
Cicero's recall from banishment in 57 B.C., when, duly propagandized
by Pompey and his friends, notables from the colonies and the municipalities, after voting through a certain number of decrees, came in force to
Rome to assure the triumph of their cause. We can call them "notables"
with confidence, as only the notables' voices mattered. They may on
some occasions have been accompanied by more modest citizens who
swelled the delegation or offered their strong right arms in the event of
a brawl. For the vote, however, only the notables counted.

The *comitia* of the centuries were held in the Campus Martius, which
is also where the tribal assembly was held (in the late Republic) to elect
low-level magistrates, the aediles, and perhaps the tribunes (Varro *De re
rustica* 3.2). Curiously space was at less of a premium there than in the
Forum. Enclosures (*saepta*) were erected near the *Villa Publica* to delimit
thirty-five areas (one per tribe) in which the citizens would gather to be
called, in order by class. The crowds were apparently smaller at the
centuriate *comitia*. It was in that place and for that purpose, however, that
the most impressive permanent construction in antiquity designed for
electoral purposes was built (under Caesar and Augustus). This was the
Saepta Julia, a vast rectangle 310 × 120 meters surrounded by a portico,
with special rooms at both ends for checking off the electors and counting
the votes. It has been calculated that seventy thousand citizens could
exercise their right to vote in that space, simultaneously or during the
course of one day. (At the time, Italy had perhaps slightly over one
million eligible voters). It is an irony of Caesar's and Augustus' munifi-
cence that these sumptuous arrangements were provided just as the Roman assemblies were about to become simple relics of the past and as the
Republic was about to be replaced by the monarchy.

In spite of the difficulties and the weaknesses of the comitial organization, it would be a mistake to think that before that point, "electoral life"
in Rome was completely oligarchical, mere ritual, or pure form. If this
were so, we could not account for the importance, for political history,
of the reforms that were either introduced into it or proposed for it.
Certain of these reforms restricted the Senate's and the magistrates'
power to manipulate or control the assemblies (often through religion).
Others were aimed at the timocratic nature of the system itself. They
were unsuccessful, but the fact that a man such as Gaius Gracchus even
thought of trying is significant. Many reforms aimed at a different, per-

haps a more just, distribution of new citizens (freedmen and Italians) among the tribes. The most important of the reforms was the introduction, between 137 and 107 B.C., of a written vote (hence a secret vote), put into effect by a series of "tabellary laws" that applied to the various tasks of the assemblies: passing laws, judiciary judgments, and elections. Henceforth, the voter chose a *tabella* marked "yes" or "no" or, in the case of an election, wrote the name or the initials of his candidate on his voting board.

This change in voting techniques affected voting procedures, the way assemblies were conducted, and the arrangement of the voting precincts. It was of course intended to assure the secrecy and the freedom of the vote, and it deliberately opened a breach in the system of clientage influence dominated by an oligarchy. In antiquity, voting in elections was not necessarily a democratic process, but to assure at least some degree of genuine choice and liberty in that process was considered an eminently "popular" measure in Rome. The tabellary laws included extremely ingenious and meticulous procedures for assuring an honest vote— "gangplanks" led up to the voting urns, voters were checked off by means of individual tokens, taking the final count of the votes was supervised, and so on. They also facilitated, if not explained, the enormous rise in electoral legislation that was characteristic of the Roman political scene between 133 and 40 B.C. It is in this area rather than in the recruitment of political figures that we should seek the effect of those laws. At times, the conservative oligarchy contested them; unscrupulous leaders sought to pervert them; military dictators attempted to impose their will in spite of them. Nonetheless, voting procedures in Rome emerged with improved morality and efficiency and, in ordinary times, protected elections and legislation from the worst sorts of pressure.

Another and more insidious threat remained: corruption. To judge by a visible increase in the number of laws attempting to combat corruption (*leges de ambitu*) during the second and first centuries, the voting process was clearly not free of it. In a system in which one could learn in advance where everyone voted and what group had the better chance of determining the result, the temptation to buy votes was unavoidable. Conservative moralists even considered it a form of corruption to propose to the people or the plebs measures to their advantage.

There was also a more brutal and more reprehensible form of corruption, however, which consisted in simply buying (at a predetermined price and for cash) the vote of an entire group. The practice spread in the first century B.C.; we can see it operating (unsuccessfully) against

Cicero in 71 B.C. and against Cato in 52, though it was more likely to be used in consular and praetorian elections, the centuries of the first classes being the prime targets. The strong corporate structure of the plebs and the people—the tribes, the centuries, the neighborhood associations, and the guilds—facilitated contacts, negotiations, and distribution of the proceeds. Some sort of high point was reached when Augustus offered an ongoing "electoral pay" of one thousand sesterces apiece to all members of his two tribes, the *Scaptia* and the *Fabia,* to eliminate outside interference (Suetonius *Lives of the Caesars, Augustus* 40.2).

At times, the high sums that corrupt and corrupting candidates openly paid for election caused a steep rise in interest rates in the financial markets. Cicero, a consular lawyer, provides striking and deplorable examples in the "secrets" of his correspondence. Like the bacchanalia under the Directory, they seem to reveal the precipitous decline of a corrupt oligarchy and to call for the "clean sweep" of a regenerating dictatorship. Caesar, for his part, was content to "recommend" to a tribe the candidates of his choice with *imperatoria brevitas.* How serious and how widespread were such abuses? A detailed and objective study remains to be made.

The emergence of organized violence between 101 and 19 B.C. was perhaps even a more serious threat than corruption. The Roman comitial system was too rigid, too partitioned, and too carefully controlled to permit the diversified and demanding population of a gigantic city such as Rome to express its thoughts on all possible matters. Alongside the formal assemblies, in which decisions were reached, the system tolerated a broader system of meetings (*contiones*) in which simple citizens, although they did not have the right to speak, could at least become informed by listening to magistrates and senators debate, in principle, discussing both sides of every question.

Aside from these *contiones,* which were always called by a magistrate in office, all meetings of the people or even of a handful of citizens were considered an invitation to sedition, though they were neither forbidden nor repressed. Examples of *coetus*—crowd movements, agitation, even riots—were not lacking, even in the third and second centuries B.C. They have not yet been sufficiently studied. What roles did the "notables" of the "corporate" structures of the *Urbs* (tribes, neighborhoods, guilds) play in them? Or the various social and economic categories: shopkeepers and butchers, but also the money changers of the Forum? Such questions merit closer analysis. Certain traditional events in civic life—triumphs, the funerals of great persons, religious festivals and the theatrical representations that accompanied them—also offered an occasion for legal assembly; and, as time went by and with the encouragement, for their own purposes, of leaders or factions, opinions came to be expressed at them, on occasion raucously. Toward the end of the Republic, political leaders made use of such occasions (by the choice of plays or simply by their ostentatious presence) to sound out public opinion or enlist public support. Major criminal or political trials, with their public and dramatic procedure, offered a similar range of possibilities.

It was thus marginal circumstances such as these, much more than the rigid comitial ritual, that established an intermittent communication between the "masses" and the political class, that permitted the circulation of political messages, and, in the long run, that created a sort of substitute democracy alongside the oligarchical structures of the city. Once again, the possible advantages of such contacts were rapidly obliterated in the late Republic by abuses engendered by violence. The first formal evidence of intimidation and the use of force (a thrashing) in the assemblies came in 103 B.C., when Marius' veterans were somewhat heavy-handed in seeing through the vote for the *lex Appuleia*.

The age of the civil wars, which began in 88 B.C. and continued for more than half a century, pitted against one another citizen armies raised in the traditional manner, fighting in Rome, in Italy, and later throughout the Empire to settle quarrels between their generals and decide who was to hold supreme power. I cannot go further into the question here, except to note that the civil wars considerably raised the level of mobilization in 49, 43, and 32 B.C.; took an incredible toll in violent deaths, proscriptions, and brutal transfers of property; and led, in the long run, to nearly revolutionary social upheavals. The disciplined and conscientious citizens of the time of Hannibal's War had become—even for contemporaries— wolves preying on one another. It was enough to disgust an entire generation, and liberty suffered the same reprobation as civil strife. It was time for a master.

This sort of military armed conflict over half a century had a remarkable influence on the conduct of political life in Rome, notably in the appearance and the development of *partes* (poorly translated as "parties") organized along paramilitary lines. The armed conspiracies and the coups d'état (successful and unsuccessful) of Lepidus (78), Catiline (66), and Caelius and Milo (47) show that for some contemporaries political action was simply a foretaste of civil war. For some of these factions—those of Catiline between 66 and 63 B.C. and of Clodius between 58 and 52—we have detailed information on membership and organization. Catiline, for example, attempted to appeal to fairly well defined social groups—shopkeepers and impoverished veterans with land grants. Clodius, ten years later, seemed to count more on the urban plebs, in whose interest he proposed and put through the free distribution of "public grain," a measure of extreme importance that persisted for more than five centuries. The support of the "masses" no longer sufficed, however, and strong arms were needed; so the factions used organized troops (*copiae, operae*) made up of a nucleus of gladiators who could be counted on to fight to the death and supplemented by slaves or freedmen (*decuriati*) enlisted from Rome, but often from the wilder corners of Italy as well. With the aid of such armed bands, the factions fought one another by day and by night for control of the streets, and armed brawls could spring up in the *contiones* or even on voting days. At this point "the people" had become a caricature.

This was the final stage in the breakdown of the system—which does not mean that it had not functioned correctly for a fairly long time. Now that we have seen the forms that this system took we need to look briefly at its actual content—that is, at the real questions that it permitted Rome to decide. The most obvious of these—rightly or wrongly—was the settling of individual or group rivalries within the political class by the recruitment of rulers and elections to the magistracy. This was essential for both social and political reasons, and the maintenance of family status and the continued success of clientage relations depended upon it. It is an exaggeration to state, as some have done—Tacitus, for example—that such rivalries only involved prestige or power for their own sake; that they simply established who would be first on each level; in short, that they were a zero-sum game. Throughout the history of the Republic, a political choice can often (though not always) be discerned behind the choice of a man, especially in a military or imperial context. Since the ancient city—even an oligarchical city such as Rome—was a place for public debate, men's ambitions did not long remain hidden. The citizens, even of rank, could not have been unaware of the consequences of their choices.

This was the case, for example, concerning the strategy and the tactics adopted against Hannibal between 218 and 216 B.C., as shown in several famous episodes. It was also the case concerning the declaration of the second and third Macedonian wars. It seems to me also to have been the case during the first triumvirate, in the troubled years around 60–55 B.C. The division of power among Pompey, Crassus, and Caesar (which tends to blind us to other questions) was accompanied by an extremely systematic series of conquests in both the East and the West, which involved considerable and diversified interests that were perhaps their true stakes. It is our challenge to decipher—when we can—a Roman political life that has been oversimplified by the historians.

There was one domain, however, in which the citizen was directly and vitally concerned by the decisions submitted to him, and which might make us suspect that he solicited such legislation or suggested it more spontaneously than has been supposed. This was the area designated as *commoda,* the "material advantages" that conservatives often contrasted with *utilitas publica.* Cicero tells us that these were (in modern terms) the program of the popular classes. The Latin word *popularis* refers both to "one who loves the people" and "one who is loved by the people"; thus it designates an attitude more than a program or a policy. Nonetheless, the people was (quite naturally) particularly sensitive and attentive the minute certain questions were raised. Three of four of these became the great leitmotifs of Roman politics, in particular between 133 and 44 B.C.: first, of course, came the agrarian laws; then the grain laws (the distribution, at first at a reduced price and then free, of a minimal ration of forty liters of wheat per month); then the suppression or suspension of taxes (as in 167 and in 60 B.C.); finally the laws concerning debts and interest rates. We might also count as advantageous to the people such guarantees of liberty as the tabellary laws.

These are familiar matters, and this is not the place to recall them in detail. I would like to insist instead on a quasi-necessary and often misunderstood aspect of such measures: their demographic and financial importance. The well-being of the citizens (impoverished peasants, proletarians, former soldiers to whom the various agrarian laws attempted to distribute land parcels) was not an aim totally within itself. The ultimate justification of such legislation, under both the Republic and the Empire, was always to "provide citizens for the City"—that is, to nourish future soldiers and reestablish in the city an ideal equilibrium, expressed by the census, that had been compromised by Rome's excessive development and proletarianization. The grain laws (which were extremely costly: in 58 B.C. one-fifth of the state revenues went into the free distribution of wheat to 250,000 to 300,000 recipients of the dole) were simply the extreme logical result of the principles underlying this system.

As we have seen, this system initially tended, as much as possible, to exempt the poorest citizens from both military and fiscal obligations, which were neither fixed nor obligatory but resulted wholly from imme-

45

diate need. If the city's external successes brought in sufficient revenues from other sources (first in war booty, then from exploitation of the provinces), why should its citizens—rich or poor—continue to pay taxes? And if such revenues increased, why should they not be used to benefit the city's citizens? No one, conservative or not, rejected this idea; everyone approved of filling the treasury, and opinions differed only on how to do so. The poorer citizens and their "popular" leaders proposed to use part of these sums to bring tangible individual benefits to the dispossessed: lands, wheat, and soon, under Caesar and the Empire, distributions of money, which was basically simply an adaptation of the *misthos* of the democratic Greek cities. Everyone grasped the logical connection between the suspension of the *tributum* in 167 and the wheat law of 123: As Florus said, "It is just that a victorious people live on the product of its treasury."

Army recruitment displayed a similar reaction structured on need. A constraining and inexorable *dilectus* had placed a heavy burden on the first classes in the census until about 120 B.C., as was normal under the system. They had paid a heavy blood tax against Hannibal and against the Spanish. It was probably during the second century that the standards for census criteria for conscription had to be lowered appreciably. In the late second century and the first century (with Marius in 106), recruitment began to include "proletarians"—that is, when possible, poor peasants, which meant that once again the number of volunteers was generally sufficient to assure the *supplementum* needed to fill the ranks each year. Thus for the first time proletarians were subject to the blood tax. In precisely the same period we see their influence increase in the tribal *comitia* (thanks to the tabellary laws), and the grain laws and the agrarian laws assured their existence and improved their civic status.

Things were of course not quite this simple, for it was not exactly the same categories that won or lost in this game (one of the reasons for its eventual overthrow). Still, this vast game of losses and gains (and this is what interests me most) was neither secret nor spontaneous. The mechanisms that have just been described resulted from a series of extremely precise, clearly defined decrees (laws, or *senatusconsulta*) to which we can put a date, a name, and a content. We know that they were conceived, debated, proposed, and combated publicly. Their aims and their consequences were clear, and, when all was said and done, they depended on a vote and on majority support. Once again, Roman public life was not a shadow play. The Roman citizen, even in the first century B.C., the century of the civil wars, was not simply a wild beast, a grasping puppet ready to sell a vote that interested him only for its price, or a corrupt spectator of the quarrels of the great. He thought in terms of his own interests—and why not?—but those interests were broader than the wages of corruption. It was only after twenty years of atrocious civil war, toward the end of the triumvirate, that public spirit seem to disappear forever and the *cives* could quote Horace: "Money you must first seek; virtue after coin" (*Epistles* 1.1.53). So many massacres gave them some reason for doing so.

Thus far I have spoken of the citizen or of citizens, attempting, as much as possible, to detach them from their idealized image. I have left aside the third domain of civic life, what I have called the "political class." The portrait of the Roman "political man" as he changed through time and according to the hierarchies of power and success would be both a possible and a necessary addition to our portrait gallery. Not only are both space and time lacking here, but the task might seem useless, since the ancient texts that have come down to us seem fascinated by successive types of the political man and information on him seems plentiful and dependable.

The first types to appear (in Livy and Plutarch) are the somewhat legendary heroes of the pure, "lean and mean" Republic—Fabricius with his *"grande âme"* (Rousseau, *Discours sur les sciences et les arts*, Pléiade edition, 3:14), Cincinnatus at his plow, Manlius and his pitiless *imperia.* Later, there were unflinching generals like Fabius Cunctator; new men of brilliant talent and tottering finances like Cicero; other generals fighting for top place. Still later there was Nepos' extraordinary *Life of Atticus,* something like a negative image of the ambitious senator; Tacitus' galleries of courtiers that included a few heroes and a few sages; and, the most extreme case, Suetonius' monsters perverted by supreme power.

All this is of course too close to the schoolbooks to be truly useful. Perhaps more to the point are the few moralistic or didactic philosophical works that sketch the ideal qualifications, the morals, and (more interesting) the intellectual baggage and the sort of culture judged appropriate or desirable in those who governed or ruled the Republic or the Empire. Such texts include Cicero's *De officiis* and *De oratore* (and some fine passages in the *Pro Murena,* the *Pro Sestio,* and the *Pro Rabirio,* but also in the *De re publica*); a few pages of Sallust, Velleius, Valerius Maximus, and Seneca; and, once again, Tacitus. Have these texts, which at times mask their true intent, really been sufficiently interrogated? The part that social conformity, education, ambition, and interest played at the various levels of power and in various periods deserves further investigation in all the available texts, including the ostentatious and, of course, extremely biased image furnished by epigraphy. This is hardly possible here.

What I would like to do instead is to recall a few things one tends to forget, limiting my remarks to the republican era. First, about words. There is no word in Latin for the "political man" except for the bare term *civis,* which also designates the citizen. The ideal "political man" was the *bonus* or the *optimus civis.* This might lead one to think Rome an ideal democracy, but Rome was a city ruled by the census in which not all were eligible for public office, just as not all citizens were admitted into Rome's legions or into the centuries that dominated the *comitia.* It was true that after the decline of the patriciate in the fourth and third centuries B.C. plebeians were no longer barred from office by their birth (as was still true in the case of freedmen). But (as is often forgotten) there were qualifications based on the census. Indeed, anyone who aspired to honors, the first echelon of which was the grade of military tribune, had to be able to serve in the cavalry, which meant that he had to be listed in the census as equestrian and *ingenuus* (freeborn). Furthermore, at least until the early first century, such a man had to have actually done his years of military service, though this condition seems to have slackened around 75 B.C. Some service in the camps, albeit brief, remained an indispensable precondition to the exercise of municipal office. Under the Republic, although no law or regulation stated that eligibility for office was hereditary (that is, for one to qualify, one's father must have been a senator or magistrate), this was nonetheless the practice. The "new men" (sons of notables) and simple knights had the recognized right to aspire to honors and even, following the steps of Marius or Cicero, to aspire to high office, but the way was far from smooth. Under Augustus, access to honors was closed and, in principle, reserved to senators' sons. This did not represent a radical change, however, as the opportunity for political and social promotion (the two amounted to roughly the same thing) continued to be available to the equestrian order and, exceptionally, to others. But now this promotion did not depend exclusively (as it had under the Republic) on the vote in the *comitia.* From now on, it was under the control and the will of the emperor, who could bestow the rank which would qualify one to seek office. He could do this either by conferring the right to wear the purple stripe (*laticlavus*) of senatorial rank, or by directly installing (*adlectio*) a person in the Senate, and thus he kept a tight grip on what had formerly been one of the people's "benefits."

A second term that requires definition is "politics." For the moment, politics can be defined by access to the magistracy, which is the precise meaning of Latin expressions such as *rem publicam capessere* or *ad rem publicam adire*. Politics was not only a career; it was also a source of status—that is, it determined not only influence and power but "dignity" (*dignitas*), official rank in the social hierarchy, and the juridical framework of social levels. In short, politics to a large extent molded and organized social life. The status of senator (under Augustus all males in senatorial families were officially included in the *ordo senatorius*) brought not only a monopoly on political deliberation and political posts but also a variety of external signs of privilege and precedence, as well as particular advantages and obligations (matrimonial and testamentary) in the domains of private and criminal law.

One can, of course, discern other divisions in Roman society and other structural principles than this rigid organization of juridical status and "orders": economics, wealth, race, and residence played a role as well. However, nothing was as constant, as constraining, and, above all, as official as this political hierarchization of society that, in all official documents, placed the consul above the praetor and set up a careful calculation of degrees of "nobility" or commonality for the families of the "establishment" based on the number of their ancestors who had been granted a triumph or had served as censors. This was, in any event, the model imposed by the law and by upbringing (soon by the emperors), but also by the rhetorical tradition and by literature. Because it brought status and thus dignity, the political realm tended to dominate the social. Sociological reality may have been different, even within the senatorial families. Some may well have revolted against these constraints (as has recently been claimed) and escaped to the spheres of money-making, finance, and industry. But it is extremely significant that such flights were covered over and that those who attempted them were excluded from collective memory.

Given these three fundamental and nearly permanent characteristics—the qualification requirements of the census, the obligation to do military service, and the determination of social status by political honors—we now need to go further and attempt a definition, in several of its aspects, of the existential condition of the Roman political man and of the characteristics that condition imposed upon him. The narrow range of military recruitment quite naturally made the Roman political man the very model of the oligarchical man. It should be noted that quite early in Roman society, which was totally patriarchal and in which age had a positive value in a man or a custom, the fact of having ancestors ("political" ancestors) was regarded favorably. De facto heredity (de jure as well where the patriciate was concerned) was thus determinant. Unlike modern systems of nobility, however, heredity was not always sufficient to guarantee maintenance of status: in each generation status had to be earned by the sanction (or the anointment) of popular vote. No one could forget that *honores* were granted neither for life nor automatically. There were instances and epochs in which the people bowed before icons, but it was always free to express its refusal and exhibit its inconstancy. Fact did not create a right. Even if history did not always bear it out, such *honores*—titles, dignities, offices—were not free gifts but functions necessitated by the *res publica*. After the late second century, some went so far as to say that they were gifts granted by the people, and that those who received them were in the "service" (the word was used, and not only by the "democrats") not of some abstract collective interest but rather of the concrete wishes of the citizens. In extreme cases, a vote could revoke the charge of an elected magistrate, and in fact did so (on rare occasions) after 133 B.C.

The fact that in the long run nearly everything depended on the vote of the people had one notable consequence, both in Rome and in most other cities: even though a decision was at times obtained by purely ritual procedures, it often involved real debate, even concerning candidates for election. This implied a common language, methods of argumentation, and techniques of persuasion. Thus eloquence played an important role, not as a constraining incantation but, at least in principle, as the art of persuasion. This in turn required knowledge, and recognition, of one's opponent. Cicero, following Greek models and writing in the first century, gave these principles ideal and theoretical expression, treating both the people's and the politician's points of view. In the end, these principles made the art of oratory the crucible and the synthesis of all public virtues. At all times, of course, there were other forms of dialogue with the citizenry that coexisted with oratory—brutal recourse to authority, ruse, intimidation, calumny, pamphleteering, invective, and so forth. In an increasingly rapid whirlwind that swept Rome toward the disaster of the civil wars, Roman politics embraced the best and the worst, the eloquence of Tiberius Gracchus (or of Cicero or Cato), Verres' money, Vettius' ignoble accusations and Clodius' invective, the obscene calumnies of pseudo-Brutus, the anonymous pamphlets, false witness, and haughty pride of Pompey. Still, as if on a vast stage, everything (or nearly everything) was played out in public. Secrecy and silence would come only with the Empire.

These were just words, perhaps, but words counted for something. The Republic, at once conformist and turbulent, inspired loyalty and even sacrifice. How the political system assured a minimum of competence in the men who filled the necessary posts—military, financial, diplomatic, and juridical—is another question. Ancient education and culture showed little interest in such matters. The organization of the *cursus honorum* (path of perferment) wisely provided for a graded apprenticeship by the imposition of age requirements and the establishment of a fixed order among magistracies, which meant that experience took the place of a nearly nonexistent training in theory. This potential gerontocracy carried its own antidote: the tribunate of the plebs, which was often open to younger men, noble and nonnoble, was an outlet for action and a sort of "magistracy of sedition." It held a near monopoly on legislative initiative, which was a headier but also a more dangerous way to attract the gaze and the favor of the people than, for example, surfeiting them with games and spectacles during a free-spending aedilate.

The oligarchy had a firm hold on only two areas of competence: military science (which in Rome, according to Polybius, was all discipline and application) and the law, civil law in particular, the great school of action and of thought. Theirs was not a lawyer's profession of pleading cases—that was to come later, in the first century B.C. and under the Empire—but the science of the jurisconsult interested in the point of law, not in the facts, who dispenses his *responsa* to clients, friends, or others obliged to him with an authority conferred as much by his function as by knowledge or logic. That authority gradually became juridical practice, and it contributed to the construction of the law.

A good soldier (he first had to have learned to obey), a good officer, and a good general, the Roman "political man" was also this man of wise counsel surrounded by consultants, clients, and students, who, by virtue of his wisdom, his good sense, and his morality (he was a *vir bonus*), defined the law, enlightened the praetor, and thus contributed to the well-being of the homeland by giving everyone his due (when possible). Later, of course, judicial rhetoric entered into the picture, as did the art of moving a jury (and the spectators), manipulating witnesses, persuading at any price—in short, of staging the great spectacle that was a Roman criminal trial. These were played out in the Forum, in the same space and involving the same actors as politics: the game was very similar to the political game, and, for better or for worse, it quite naturally led to politics.

Curiously enough, we are struck by the apparent absence of anything specifically related to administration and finance in these channels for the formation and selection of the governing class. The ignorance of some who were charged with fiscal responsibilities is legendary. There is a relatively simple explanation for this. To begin with, there was a fairly clear break between the responsible magistrate and the administration itself (for example, in the treasury), which was abandoned to professional scribes, often recruited by dubious means and organized in a "corporative order," who managed the actual operations. There was no fiscal administration, since the collection of taxes was farmed out by contract to private companies of publicans from which senators and magistrates were strictly excluded. This meant that such contracts were concentrated in the hands of knights, rich men perhaps, but, by definition, not senators. It is certain that there were clandestine contacts (and dealings) between the two groups, but the law was opposed to them and, on occasion, was applied.

This may explain why financial competence was not used as a qualification for high office. The inconvenience was slight, however. In Roman society, every "great" man was, in practice, surrounded by a large private force of slaves, freedmen, and clients specially trained to serve their patron's needs: "the wit of others served to supplement what little wit the good man had." The retinue devoted to the exclusive service of the princeps already existed, in embryo, in a number of instances during the latter days of the Republic.

Furthermore, no matter how great a magistrate's responsibilities might be, the collective control of the Senate had the final say. Collective group memory and the vigilance of the elders or of adversaries forcibly created or supplemented competence. Social pressure, group cohesion, and respect for tradition served as the cement that bound together the rustic and military republic whose irresistible rise earned Polybius' admiration.

Roman political life was not a life of repose, however. From the earliest days, the political man ran constant risks. First, he risked his life: magistrates and former senators were, above all, officers and generals, and war in the ancient world did not spare its leaders: 170 senators (out of 300) had died by 216, after three years of the war against Hannibal. A time came, however, when it was in internal struggles and even in civil war that Roman men risked their lives. After 149 B.C., and, in particular, after 123, the major criminal trials became an essential part of the conflicts. They marked the stages of a normal career, but often they broke a career as well, and men paid the price of political activities with civil death or actual death. The causes of this spiral of risk lie beyond the scope of this study, but I might note that it culminated, with the civil wars, in death on the battlefield, in massacres and murder for revenge, and in proscriptions, a banishment without trial or appeal. Even if our sources exaggerate the number of victims (40 senators in 81 B.C.; 300 in 43 B.C.), they represent a considerable proportion of what we might call the political class. Well before these bloody episodes, reliable witnesses tell us, some Romans clearly perceived increased dangers, which led some senators' sons and a good many knights to put aside their personal ambitions in favor of retirement in a life of *otium*. Literature and business may perhaps have gained from this renunciation, but the Republic died of it.

Bibliography

Brunt, P. A. *Italian Manpower, 225 B.C.–A.D. 14.* 2d ed. Oxford: Clarendon Press, 1987.

———. *The Fall of the Roman Republic and Related Essays.* Oxford: Clarendon Press; New York: Oxford University Press, 1988.

Cohen, Benjamin. "La notion d''ordo' dans la Rome antique." *Bulletin Association G. Budé,* 1975:259–82.

Ferrary, Jean-Louis. "Le idee politiche a Roma nell'epoca repubblicana." In Luigi Firpo, gen. ed. *Storia delle idee politiche, economiche e sociali.* 6 vols. Turin: UTET, 1972–87. Vol. 1:723–804.

Gabba, Emilio. *Esercito e società nella tarda Repubblica romana.* Florence: La Nuova Italia, 1973.

Gruen, Erich S. *Roman Politics and the Criminal Courts.* Cambridge, Mass.: Harvard University Press, 1968.

Harmand, Jacques. *L'armée et le soldat à Rome de 107 à 50 avant notre ère.* Paris: A. & J. Picard, 1967.

Hinard, François. *Les proscriptions de la Rome républicaine.* Rome: Ecole française de Rome, 1985.

Hinard, François, et al. *Dictatures.* Actes de la table ronde réunie à Paris les 27 et 28 février 1984. Paris: De Boccard, 1988.

Nicolet, Claude. *Tributum: Recherches sur la fiscalité directe sous la république romaine.* Bonn: Habelt, 1976.

———. "Les classes dirigeantes romaines sous la République," *Annales E.S.C.,* 1977:726–54.

———. *Le métier de citoyen dans la Rome républicaine.* Paris: Gallimard, 1976; 2d ed. 1979. Available in English as *The World of the Citizen in Republican Rome*. Trans. P. S. Falla. Berkeley: University of California Press, 1980.

―――. *Les structures de l'Italie romaine*. 2d ed. Collection Nouvelle Clio. Paris: Presses Universitaires de France, 1979.

―――, ed. *Des ordres à Rome*. Paris: Publications de la Sorbonne, 1984.

Nicolet, Claude, et al. *Demokratia et Aristokratia: A propos de Caïus Gracchus: mots grecs et réalités romaines*. Paris: Université de Paris I, 1983.

Sherwin-White, A. N. *The Roman Citizenship*. 2d ed. Oxford: Clarendon Press, 1973.

Syme, Ronald. *The Roman Revolution*. Oxford: Clarendon Press, 1939.

Taylor, L. Ross, *Party Politics in the Age of Caesar*. Berkeley: University of California Press, 1949.

Veyne, Paul. *Le Pain et le cirque: Sociologie historique d'un pluralisme politique*. Paris: Editions du Seuil, 1976. Available in English as *Bread and Circuses: Historical Sociology and Political Pluralism*. Abr. and trans. Brian Pearce. London: A. Lane, Penguin Press, 1990.

Virlouvet, Catherine. *Famines et émeutes à Rome, des origines de la République à la mort de Néron*. Rome: Ecole française de Rome, 1985.

Yavetz, Zvi. *Plebs and Princeps*. London: Oxford University Press; Oxford: Clarendon Press, 1969.

2

The Priest

John Scheid

THERE WAS NO ONE PRIESTHOOD in Rome and no one priestly power. Religious functions must be seen as plural and tied to a precise social context. Since religious situations came in many forms, so did priestly tasks. This means that there is a wealth of Roman priestly figures that far exceeds the distinction between those who were called priests (*sacerdotes*) and others who did not bear that title, or between *sacerdotes* with public and with private functions. No matter what category we look at, it will contain persons active in cultic activities, some of whom were called priests and some of whom were not. Furthermore, besides the priestly powers of Rome itself, there was a throng of priestly figures who functioned in the various other cities of Italy.

In other words, we will always need to make a good many distinctions and explanations if we want to speak of priests in Rome. For one thing, we need to decide whether we are speaking of Romans as citizens or as inhabitants of the city of Rome, keeping in mind that an increasing majority of Roman citizens no longer lived in Rome but in the various cities of the empire, which had their own sacred institutions. For reasons of both space and accessibility, I intend to treat the priesthood in the traditional Roman context, concentrating on the city of Rome, which will permit me to speak of both republican and imperial Rome and to offer a description of priestly matters complex enough to serve as a model for most of the other cities of Roman culture and law. Furthermore, if I adopt the viewpoint of a contemporary of Cicero or Marcus Aurelius the reader will need to remember that priestly figures and religious functions different from the strictly Roman ones were present in Rome. A Roman might meet and have daily intercourse with religious figures who served the foreign communities established on the banks of the Tiber—Egyptians, Jews, Greeks from Syria and Asia Minor—communities that often exerted a spiritual influence in the city at large and whose cults, as events dictated, often became part of the religious heritage of the Roman people. Thus, before the definitive victory of Christianity, the number of Roman priests constantly grew and their nature constantly diversified. We need also to keep in mind that all catalogs of Roman priestly figures will be provisional and partial.

I shall speak most about public cults, not because they were superior to other expressions of religious ritual in Rome, but because they had a longer and more marked effect on the Roman people as a whole; also, quite simply, because they are the best known. In any event, public religious life in Rome offers a model that can be applied, without too much risk, to private forms of religious ritual in the *collegium* or in the family, and even to cultic practices in the cities of the empire for as long as the traditional forms of religion operated.

Whom, then, can we call a priest in Rome? Even within the framework of traditional religion, the term cannot be applied automatically to someone who was called "priest" (*sacerdos*), as, for example, in Christianity. Experience invites us to consider all persons who performed cultic acts for a given community in Rome to have been Roman priests. But that definition would still be incomplete. Notably, it would lead to a paradox: those who best corresponded to this definition would be not the people who were called priests (*sacerdotes*) but the magistrates and heads of families. The priests, properly speaking, had a further qualification: they were also the depositaries of sacred law, which they alone administered and developed, an activity in which they were necessarily assisted by the Senate; but that body had no cultic activity in its own right. Thus it would be preferable to define the priestly function as the exercise of a religious authority, whether that power of initiative concerned activities connected with the cult or control of the religious system. Any notion of the originality and the richness of this priestly power requires first a description of the various priestly roles in Rome, then an examination of the nature of priestly functions.

Who was a priest in Rome? As in most ancient religions the first response seems simple: he was a man. The cult and the priestly powers were, above all, men's business, on both the public and the private levels. The priestly act, celebrated in the name of a community, could not be entrusted to a woman, considered incapable of representing anyone but herself.

This does not mean that women were excluded from religious ritual, however. It is common knowledge that women served in such female priestly functions as the service of Vesta; they also served as flaminicas (the wives of flamens), and Roman matrons played a role in religious observance both in public and in private. Whenever a woman took on a priestly role, however, she either was subordinate to a man or was no longer truly considered to be a woman. The flaminicas, and indeed mothers of families, were in fact adjuncts to their husbands, and their tasks were usually marginal or complementary to those of the flamen or the *pater familias*. The ritual act par excellence, sacrifice, was forbidden them. One exception was the Vestal Virgins, who officiated at the Damia. The Vestals, however, were under the authority of the *pontifex maximus;* furthermore, they were neither maidens nor married women but fell between gender categories. On occasion, matrons officiated and probably sacrificed, as on the day of Fortuna Virilis, but the sources add that this was an exceptional privilege accorded to women for having saved the city when men had failed to do so.

In time, other cults with a female priesthood entered Rome, such as those of the Aventine Ceres, of Bacchus, and of Isis. These priestesses were sacerdotal figures introduced into Roman public or private religion, however, who accompanied the foreign divinities whose cult they celebrated. Inseparable from the cultic practices to which they were attached, they enriched the Roman religious system rather than bringing it any significant variation. As with the gods naturalized into Rome, it was not so much that these priestesses reflected an evolution in Roman religious convictions; rather, they were a sign that the very concept of what was Roman had broadened to include both the old Roman and Italic nucleus and the gods, the lands, and soon the elites of the entire world. In public religion these naturalized cults and priesthoods were, in any event, under the authority of the priestly college of the decemvirs, later the quindecemvirs, which was exclusively male.

The Sibylline Books provide a telling example of this process. These books, the only Roman oracle that predicted the future, came from Campania, thus from outside Rome, and had been dictated by a woman, the Cumaean Sibyl. An indispensable motive force in Roman institutions and venerated as one of the city's talismans, these pronouncements seem, on first view, to show the intrusion of a prophetess, a priestess, and a foreigner into the heart of Roman public life. Nonetheless, this distant prophetess and the books that, according to tradition, she had sold to King Tarquin were under the total control of the college of the quindecemvirs, who were the only persons permitted to consult them and interpret them for the magistrates and the Senate.

These facts and others suggest that we not misconstrue the role of women in the exercise of sacerdotal power. Excluded from the primary role, women nonetheless (and necessarily) occupied a secondary one as indispensable coadjutors to men: the flamen of Jupiter could not fulfill his responsibilities separate from the flaminica; without Vestals, Rome itself could not continue to play its historical role. In other words, the priestly function was often presented in Roman traditions as a necessary collaboration of women and men.

This definition is still imprecise, however. If men's gender qualified them (with the aid of women) to represent the interests of a community, they must also be an integral part of that community. Thus only citizens were eligible to play a cultic role in the religious aspects of the *res publica,* and only male members of a family directed the domestic cult. Although foreigners were not absorbed into the Roman religious system, they could celebrate their cults in Roman temples on the condition that the Senate or some other competent authority had authorized them to do so. Within their families and within the foreign communities, they celebrated their own cults in total freedom. As for slaves, their status resembled in part that of women and in part that of foreigners: they aided their masters in the exercise of religious functions, but they could also be empowered to represent them.

Reserved to male citizens, priestly authority was nonetheless exercised neither by all citizens nor in all contexts. In a community of any size—all the people or one segment of the people—the power to act in the community's name was given to only a few, and in Rome not everyone who might have wanted to be a priest could be one. Priesthood was a question not of vocation (at least not in traditional cults) but of social status. Because religious acts were celebrated in the name of the community and not in that of individuals, only those who, by their birth and their status, represented the community could take on priestly functions.

Within the *familia,* it was the *pater familias* who assumed responsibility for all the cultic activities of the domestic community—sacrifices, nuptial rites, funerals, and so on—acting in person or delegating his authority to a member of his household (his son, his freedman, or his slave). Outside the domestic context, however, a male could act for himself if he had the means and eventually for the small community directly dependent on him (his nuclear family), but his actions did not engage his entire *familia.*

Sacred roles were distributed within the family by birthright, but in the community life of the Roman people they were determined by the traditional rules of public life. Thus sacred acts were entrusted to all who were or who had been legally elected as magistrates or priests of the people of Rome.

All magistrates had to perform priestly tasks. The consuls had to offer a great many of the numerous sacrifices that punctuated the political calendar. The first of these occurred at the festivities of 1 January and were celebrated to dissolve the vows their predecessors had pronounced a year earlier for the continued prosperity of the *res publica* and, under the empire, for the health of the reigning emperor. Following this sacrifice, the consuls formulated new vows of their own. Soon after taking office, the consuls presided over the ancient federal sacrifice on the Albanus Mons on the occasion of the *Feriae Latinae* and then sacrificed at Lavinium. They also presided at games, for example at the *Ludi Romani* on 15 September (before these games were directed by the curule aediles), and later, under the Empire, at festivities celebrating the victory of Actium, Augustus' birthday, and other occasions. The praetor of Rome supervised the sacrifices to Hercules at the Ara Maxima and presided over other games (the Apollonian Games and the *Ludi piscatorii*). The praetors could also replace the consuls if need be. All other magistrates, according to their rank and their functions, spent a part of their time in public sacrificial rites. Along with such regular acts (*sollemnes*), there were exceptional sacrifices and vows performed on the initiative of the consuls.

Such sacrifices were no hasty rituals that required no more of the magistrates than their presence; they were long and complex liturgies that demanded a significant amount of time and means, to the point that the consuls, whose responsibilities grew with Rome's conquests, increasingly delegated their performance to other magistrates. Sacrifice entailed arranging for sacrificial victims, obtaining the help of a colleague (perhaps a priest), and then spending the greater part of the civic day (from daybreak to early afternoon) at the place of sacrifice. All the various acts of this liturgy required authoritative attitudes, actions, and words from the magistrate, beginning with the immolation of the victim up to the offering of the *exta* to the gods and the appropriation of the parts reserved for the participants. The magistrate quite probably also arranged for the sacrificial banquet or the distribution that took its place. On the occasion of the great feast days, several sacrifices took place, as well as games organized and presided over by the officiating magistrate.

Sacrifice and the dedication of sanctuaries to public gods were not the only priestly duties of the magistrates. Their second major religious function was taking auguries. By law all important acts in public life were preceded and determined by the consultation of auspices and, should such arise, by consideration of spontaneous auspices. Taking auspices meant interrogating the gods (Jupiter in particular) as to whether a public act was appropriate, the god in question limiting his or her response to a negative or a positive. Techniques of interrogation were multiple and complex and included the observation of flights of birds and often, at the end of the Republic, the examination of the behavior of sacred fowl. As with sacrifice, the magistrate officiated with assistants and, on occasion, with the aid of priests who specialized in augury. In all cases, it was the magistrate who was the "master" in the consultation.

Finally, the consuls had the authority to initiate action in the religious sphere—a not inconsiderable power. It was they who informed the priestly colleges and consulted the Senate about religious problems or innovations. When new public gods were installed in the Roman pantheon, it was at the request of the consuls. When innovations or crises arose, the Senate, a body of former magistrates, exercised sacerdotal prerogatives by counseling, supervising, and aiding the magistrates in the administration of their decisions and religious tasks.

Another collective body—the patricians—had priestly functions. In case of a power vacuum or an interregnum, the patricians had the right to take auguries in the absence of a magistrate capable of doing so.

Before turning to the place of the priestly colleges in the system of Roman religion, we need to look briefly at the principal sorts of public priests in Rome.

With the exception of a few priests attached to a particular cult or temple (the public priestesses of Ceres, for example), Roman priests were grouped in colleges or sodalities of fixed membership. In the late Republic and under the first dynasties of the Empire, four great colleges grouped most of the priests. The first of these, the pontifical college, presided over by the *pontifex maximus,* included the pontiffs, the flamens, the *rex sacrorum,* and the Vestal Virgins. Next in importance came the college of the *augures,* followed by that of the *decemviri* (which became *quindecemviri* around the year 80), who were charged with the consultation of the Sibylline Books, and the *septemviri,* who had charge of ritual feasts for the gods. There were also smaller priestly sodalities more exclusively dedicated (under the Republic) to cultic tasks: the *Salii* of the Palatine and the Quirinal; the *Luperci,* the *Fratres Arvales,* and the *sodales*

Titii. Under the Empire, a number of dynastic sodalities were created, as required, when rulers became divinities, such as the *sodales Augustales Claudiales,* the *sodales Flaviales Titiales,* and the *sodales Antoniniani.*

I shall examine the ritual function of these priests later; for the moment it is enough to note that, by and large, they celebrated in the same sorts of ceremonies as the magistrates, but they also had prerogatives of their own. How, then, did they differ from the magistrates, whose function in ritual acts they often seemed to duplicate?

Roman tradition recounts that the first priests aided the original king —the mythical magistrate—in the exercise of his sacred prerogatives. At the rise of the Republic the priests became partially separate from the magistrates, since they continued to exercise the portion of the royal powers that could not be transferred to magistrates of the Republic once the king himself had disappeared or become a simple priest (the *rex sacrorum*). Indeed, except for the great liturgical acts of the *res publica* (for example, vows, sacrifices, or the taking of auguries directly connected with the government), the pontiffs, flamens, and augurs celebrated the rites of the archaic calendar much as if they were perpetuating a ceremonial that did not concern the magistrates in office under the Republic. With time their priestly functions broadened, and the priests of the four major colleges also became the only legal depositaries of sacred law. Their decisions had no executive force (unless their *ius* had already given them this right), but they controlled and communicated sacred law to the magistrates and to the magisterial assembly, the Senate.

Priests thus differed from magistrates by a division of ritual tasks and by their ultimate juridical competence. Finally, by their ritual attitudes, certain priests represented the powers, qualities, and function of their divine patron—which was true of the magistrates only exceptionally, notably when they embodied the archaic plenitude of public and sacred power during the triumph that followed a great military victory.

Priests also had their own particular mode of recruitment. The sacerdotal powers of the magistrates were accorded, along with *imperium* and *potestas* (military and civil powers), by popular election, which was followed, after taking appropriate auguries, by investiture. The power of the priests had a different origin, and their personal status appeared to differ from that of other representatives of the Roman people. At first sight, public priests generally came from the same senatorial circles as the magistrates, and for the most part they followed the same sorts of political careers. At closer inspection, however, differences appear. Because Romans usually expressed in the form of rules or formal customs everything that seemed to them indispensable for both maintenance of a certain equality within the senatorial elite and control of the exercise of power, the rules governing the choice of the priests (and changes in those rules after the rise of the Republic in 504 B.C.) provide an invaluable indication of the position of priests within Roman "constitutional order."

Whereas the choice of the magistrates and the procedures by which they exercised their powers were rapidly subjected to strict control after the expulsion of the kings, the priests perpetuated a system of recruitment that one might be tempted to call prerepublican. The priestly colleges co-opted their members without external control and independent of the criteria based on census categories or age that regulated access to the magistracy. As we have seen, the priests exercised powers in the religious field equivalent to those of a consul without having been elected and even without being senators. They might be chosen at a very young age, and their election was for life. They did not dispose of *imperium* and could not convene the people or the Senate, but the augurs had the right to dismiss an electoral assembly immediately if they remarked unfavorable signs; and, in more general terms, the advice and opinions of the pontiffs, augurs, and quindecemvirs, not to speak of the *pontifex maximus,* exerted an enormous influence on public life. In other words, we have every indication that the Romans gave their priests a position at the center of the *res publica* that in some ways counterbalanced that of the magistrates.

Not only the influence of the priests but also their relations with the magistrates are clearly revealed by the evolution of the procedures of co-optation into the priestly colleges after the founding of the Republic.

In a first phase, when the rules concerning the magistracy were evolving rapidly, the institution of the priesthood perpetuated other forms of recruitment and remained an extremely conservative force that, following tradition, steadfastly resisted the co-optation of nonpatricians until 300 B.C. After that date the modes of recruitment to the priesthood seem to have been a symbol of oligarchical privilege and were the object of a number of conflicts. Until the late second century B.C. the priesthood was replenished by simple co-optation—that is, without popular or senatorial involvement. Still, at least from the mid-third century, the most important priest, the *pontifex maximus,* was no longer elected by the pontiffs alone, as in earlier times, but by a special assembly of seventeen tribes, probably chosen by lot from among the thirty-five tribes for the purposes of the election. Thus for the first time the people acquired some control over the choice of a priest, even though this control remained limited, since the high priest had to be chosen from among three pontiffs selected by the pontifical college, whose members were chosen in the traditional way. A century and a half later, in 104–103 B.C., the *lex Domitia* applied that electoral procedure to all priests by giving the partial assembly charged with the election of the *pontifex maximus* responsibility for choosing the members of the pontifical, augural, decemviral, and septemviral colleges as well.

Several steps were involved in this procedure. First, the members of each college offered "nominations" by issuing a proclamation, under oath, naming candidates they judged worthy of priesthood. Each individual priest could "name" only one candidate, and no candidate could have more than two "nominations" at any one time. Thus Cicero was proud of being "named" by the augurs Pompey and Hortensius. On the day of the priestly election (in an assembly called when vacancies had occurred in a college), the seventeen tribes drawn by lot chose the persons they wished to elect (*creare*) from among the *nominati*, a list that was public knowledge. In a third phase each college co-opted candidates, and certain priests (the augurs for example) were also "inaugurated" by consultation with the heavens.

The new system was applied only in the four major colleges. The sodalities continued to elect and co-opt behind closed doors until the end of the Empire. Certain specific priests and priestesses under the pontifical college (the flamens, the *rex sacrorum,* and the Vestals) were neither elected nor co-opted but "taken" by the *pontifex maximus,* perhaps from among several candidates selected by the other pontiffs or by the Senate.

The *lex Domitia* was intended to put an end to the control of the priesthood on the part of an extremely limited number of families who had used this means to appropriate a public power in the Republic that they did not share with their peers. Without being truly democratic (and one might well wonder whether this term had any meaning in the oligarchical regime of Rome), the new procedures for the selection of priests undeniably opened up recruitment to the priesthood and gave the people some control over co-optations. In this the *lex Domitia* was "republican." In short, priests became quasi magistrates. They also acquired an extremely brilliant position: it is probably from this date that the four colleges mentioned in this law were called *amplissimi* (very brilliant). Nonetheless, it is clear that the difference between the status of a magistrate and that of a priest remained great; in spite of the reforms of 104–103 there was still a noticeable gap between the two.

The new law was first abolished in 80 B.C. by Sulla, who intended to restore the prerogatives of the nobility over the people, but it was reestablished in 63 by the *lex Atia*. Sulla, like Caesar a half-century later, had raised the number of priests to match an increase in the number of magistrates (which shows that in the mind of Romans there was still a connection between the priests and the magistrates). The priests still retained their specificity, however. Even when Augustus reorganized priestly recruitment between 29 and 18/13 B.C. he did not change the way they were chosen. Rather, he consecrated traditional procedures by distributing public priesthoods between the senatorial and the equestrian orders, thus emphasizing the quasi-magisterial rank of priests of the senatorial class. Some details aside, recruitment procedures remained nearly the same.

In the year 29 Augustus received the privilege of "naming" as many candidates as he wished, even beyond the number stipulated in the *lex Atia*. Later, when he was a member of all the priestly colleges and functioned as *pontifex maximus* as well, he exercised his privilege within each college, as did his successors. After Tiberius, nominations for members of the four colleges took place annually, not in a special meeting but in the Senate, and henceforth that body chose the candidates that the priestly elections simply confirmed. We do not know how long elections were held to confirm the Senate's choices, but it is possible that the procedure lasted until the early third century. As before, the sodalities were not included in this procedure, even though some of its mechanisms (notably, the three phases of *nominatio, creatio,* and *cooptatio*) were adopted internally. In any event, this is the way the Arval Brethren seems to have proceeded.

Thus, in spite of a similarity in status with the magistrates and although they performed rites like those of the magistrates, the priests were public personages quite different from the magistrates, even if there was no radical opposition between the two groups and nothing prevented anyone from holding both offices. The difference seems rather to lie in a division of tasks and in a necessary collaboration of priests and magistrates both for reasons inherent in the "constitutional" rules of the Republic, which systematically divided powers, and (as we shall see) for purely religious reasons. Basically, however, it is impossible to separate magistrates and priests on the basis of the religious nature of the ritual acts the two groups performed or on that of debates concerning religion and sacred law. They celebrated the same sort of rites, and although their competence was different they both worked with the Senate to administer the religious life of the *res publica*. We can conclude that in the public religion of the Roman people, the priestly role was conferred on all those who were the elected representatives of the people. Their role changed according to their function and their rank, but they all had basically the same religious competence.

The same was true of the communities of Roman citizens outside the city of Rome. It goes without saying that the promagistrates who governed the provinces of the empire from Sulla on operated in the same manner as the magistrates. During their mandate they assumed all the priestly tasks that the public life of their province might require: taking auguries and making vows, sacrifices, and dedications. The powers of the promagistrates diminished, however, and under the Empire their religious initiatives were subordinated to those of the princeps, whose auguries were superior to those of the legates or proconsuls. More accurately, the princeps alone had the right to auspicate, at least in the provinces he governed directly. The most obvious consequence of this was the rapid disappearance, under the principate of Augustus, of the triumphs of promagistrates, since the first condition for having a triumph was to possess the right of augury. Still, in the place that was theirs, the governors exercised the ordinary religious responsibilities of the people's representative, even without the presence of priests.

Within an army camp the chief priest was the legion commander, who was charged with the celebration of regular rites (as listed in an extract from a calendar from an auxiliary wing dating from A.D. 223/227 found in Dura-Europos) and all exceptional celebrations. In the same manner, in the districts of the city of Rome, local cults were celebrated at street crossings by the *magistri* of the *pagus* (district), who under Augustus became the *magistri* of the *vici* (wards). On a more general level, in the colleges of artisans, shopkeepers, and officeholders elected *magistri* had charge of liturgy, which they performed and supervised in cooperation with the association's popular assembly.

Other cities in the empire had a similar religious organization, which makes it useless to enter into detail about them. Let me only note that the magistrates and the priests exercising sacerdotal functions were fewer and less varied than in Rome, which eventually led to a greater concentration of priestly functions. In such cities, moreover, priesthood proper was not a lifetime appointment but simply one stage in a career of "honors"; hence priestly responsibilities were merely one aspect of public responsibilities. Thus it was not a special competence, title, or ritual behavior that distinguished priests from magistrates. Before we go on, however, we need to look briefly at how many priests there were.

After two millennia of Christianity, we are accustomed not only to a religious life largely organized under the supervision of the clergy but also to a verifiable structure of religious power and a systematic representation of this hierarchical power in all communities of the faithful. Simple observation of the structure of Jewish communities is enough to show that, even within the Western world, the Christian model was not universal. Be that as it may, this model did not apply to Rome before the Christian era, with the exception of an ephemeral attempt at structure in the mid-third century. In Rome, in fact, priestly acts were very broadly distributed, ranging from sacrifices offered by the consuls to the domestic rites celebrated by every *pater familias*. There was no "clergy" who celebrated all religious acts: each magistrate or priest performed only a portion of the various priestly functions and served a specific community. The magistrates and priests of Rome, who represented the people as a whole, were too few in number to serve all the citizens. Nor did the religious rule call on them to do so.

It never occurred to any Roman to call on a priest to celebrate the cult in his home. Public priests, the pontiffs for example, only celebrated rites that concerned all the Roman people, or else, on the request of a magistrate, they considered such questions as harm done to public sacred places or general problems that might arise. As public priests they were not competent to officiate for a restricted community of citizens. The one attested exception to this concerns patrician marriage, the *confarreatio,* which was celebrated by the *pontifex maximus* in the presence of the flamen of Jupiter. However, patricians had a unique status, notably on the religious level, and their example cannot be extended to other citizens.

Moreover, the priests in the various colleges would never have consulted together or supported one another in view of a common religious policy. In order to create a sacerdotal lobby, Roman custom would have required bringing together not only the priests but also the magistrates, at least the ones currently in office. On occasion, conflicts opposed priests and magistrates (more accurately, one priest or priestly college and a magistrate), but these quarrels concerned specific rules pertaining to ritual, not any pressure that the priests might have wanted to exert on "lay" power (so to speak) or vice versa. Indeed, just as there was no priestly milieu in Rome distinct from the magistracy and from public life, so there was no discernable lay power.

There were never any great number of public priests in Rome. At the beginning of our era, the Roman people amounted to something like four million adult male citizens. The number of magistrates in office at any one time, with slight variations from one epoch to another, was around 50, with some 60 promagistrates. Added to these 110 officials of senatorial rank there were another 40 or so specific offices filled by men of senatorial rank and about 70 by knights. These 220 persons, with the emperor, represented the essence of public power, and they were joined by about 83 members of the major priestly colleges and perhaps 100 members of the sodalities, making some 190 priests in all or, if we include the 60 or so persons in the specialized sodalities (very young people, *Salii,* and *Luperci* for the most part), 250 priests. If this is true and if we take into account the very limited scope of most of the sodalities, the religious destiny of the Roman people was thus in the hands of from 400 to 500 people.

This very number makes it absurd to imagine any priestly control—even if "priest" is taken in the very largest sense—over the religious life of all Roman citizens. Not only would this have been materially impossible, but control was not the task of the priests or the magistrates. Their competence concerned one body of the faithful—the *res publica,* the Roman people as a whole—not the individuals who made it up; their role involved acts of sovereignty and government, not the aid or the control of the citizens. Citizens assumed their own sacerdotal responsibilities in their own homes or in the narrower communities to which they belonged. Even when some scandal involving religious practices emerged there, it fell to the magistrates to settle the affair, as the ones responsible for public order, not to any sort of religious power nor even to magistrates acting as "priests." These were affairs for the police: the religious aspects of criminal behavior were used as evidence of disturbing or subverting public order and were not the province of any religious authority. Thus in 213 B.C., in the darkest months of the Second Punic War, when the people, gripped by religious panic, turned to all the superstitions currently being marketed, it was a magistrate, the praetor, who repressed such excesses from the middle of the Forum, the seat of public cults (Livy 25.1.6–12). Clearly, the Christian experience in the West is not always a sufficient basis for even a superficial appreciation of the true situation of the Roman priesthood.

Up to this point this description of Roman priestly figures has been external, defining the social and political status of the persons charged with religious responsibilities in the name of the Roman community. We now need to take up priests from another point of view. We have seen that, by criteria for their selection and by their place in community life, those responsible for the religious aspects of Roman life were far from what a Christian, for example, would call a priest. In spite of the heritage of language and gesture that Roman priests left to Christianity, their ritual behavior was also unlike that of Christian priests. Ritual behavior can be divided into two major attitudes: in the first, the priests celebrated and supervised rites establishing relations with the gods; in the second they were the physical signs of a divine function. Before describing these two areas of priestly behavior, it may be useful to pause briefly over one of the fundamental principles of Roman religion that will help us to understand the various roles of the Roman priest.

Both in texts that speak of religion and in philosophical reflection, the Romans conceived of the city (or any civilized community) as the place in which gods and men cohabit, *hic et nunc*. The gods participated with men in community life and, somewhat like magistrates, they worked for the realization of the common good. According to Roman tradition, this cohabitation went back to the origins of the city, and religion was the entire set of relations that the city (or any given community) maintained and should maintain with its gods. The material form of these relations was called the cult of the gods (*cultus deorum*). Romans understood that term to mean the homage due these most powerful fellow citizens in recognition of their supremacy and in exchange for their benefits. It also entailed regular dialogue with them.

All aspects of cultic acts—execution, supervision, and the definition of rules—fell under the competence of the magistrates and the priests. The various sacerdotal activities thus had a mission to realize, maintain, enlarge, and supervise the relations between a community and its gods. This generalization holds true even though priestly activities varied enormously in a polytheistic religion like that of the Romans. Because the public cults of Rome are infinitely better known than the private cults (domestic or collegiate), my examples will be drawn mainly from Roman public religion.

One essential general question needs to be examined first: If the city was the place where men met the gods, and if religion was the means for realizing and maintaining these relations, what difference was there between purely public acts (of the magistrates) and the priestly acts performed by both magistrates and priests? In other words, when you come right down to it, What was the relationship between a priest and a magistrate, or between a magistrate when he governed and a magistrate when he sacrificed or took auspices?

These questions have no simple answer, particularly since the Romans had neither a political constitution nor a religious code that was systematic and complete. Thus any answer to them will depend on indications alone. The first indication lies in the distinction that Romans made in public law (*ius publicum*) between the two complementary provinces of public law, the domain of the magistrates, and sacred law, the domain of the priests. Does this division answer our needs? We can note that events attest to a close collaboration between priests and magistrates in most public acts. The magistrate often needed the aid and advice of priests for his authoritative acts, and any consul whom the pontiffs or the augurs refused to assist would find himself blocked, or at least hampered, in his action. Furthermore, when the republican "constitution" came under increasing pressure as Rome grew, and when the elite governed more and more by exploring the lacunae in the sets of rules and customs that took the place of a constitution rather than by following these rules themselves, priestly counsel might be indispensable for giving somewhat audacious institutional and governmental innovations a semblance of legitimacy, given that such counsel attested to—or contested—the conformity of such innovations with sacred law. The opinion of the priests was thus an important element in the political game. Furthermore those who held civic power at any given moment had little control over the priests, thanks to the priests' lifetime tenure and the particular ways in which they were selected. This meant that all political forces attempted to gain greater control over the priests through the laws governing their recruitment.

This ongoing process came to an end during the last decades before the Common Era, when Augustus was co-opted into all the priestly colleges, one by one, a privilege transmitted to his successors. From that time on, the emperor participated in the decisions of the priestly colleges as a member of those bodies, and he held in his own hands the full powers that earlier Romans had granted their kings.

The fact that the magistrates could perform sacerdotal acts and had the right to initiate religious legislation did not mean that they could do without priests: the magistrates served only a part of the liturgical calendar and, above all, they could not act alone to pass judgment on the validity of their religious acts. The priests and the Senate had to be consulted in any crisis and about any innovation; and even if tradition gave magistrates the right to initiate such a consultation and granted them final decision, it was also customary for them to follow the advice of the priests and the Senate.

Recruited in quite a different way from the magistrates (as if to mark a necessary distinction between their functions), the priests had a broad range of competence, from the celebration of rites to responsibility for sacred law. Nonetheless, the priests had an absolute need of the magistrates' collaboration. Like the Senate, priests had to be consulted before they could intervene in public life. One exception to this was if they held their own *ius,* rights inherent to their charge, that gave them a permanent mandate for certain acts. Thus they needed no invitation save that of the president of their college to fix the dates of the archaic feast days of the calendar and to take complete charge of them. There were other rituals on the calendar that they did not control, notably the ones celebrated by the magistrates. Thus it was the consuls, not the pontiffs, who fixed the dates of the *Feriae Latinae.* Similarly, no magistrate needed to consult the augurs in order to take auspices. Even the *pontifex maximus* kept silent unless expressly interrogated by the consul. Still, the magistrates were nearly always surrounded by pontiffs, augurs, or quindecemvirs; and, more generally, the sacerdotal colleges and the Senate always had to be consulted concerning religious questions.

Even if it is difficult to interpret the complex relations between priests and magistrates, we can presume that they were not totally senseless. It would be a mistake to suppose that the magistrate represented men and the priest the gods, for in the exercise of their ritual responsibilities magistrates also represented the gods. Actually, it was more often the magistrates who represented the interests of the gods, and when the gods were "represented" (in a ritual sense), that role could be taken equally well by magistrates or priests.

Thus the more pertinent distinction lies on the plane of public acts, since that was what Roman religion was all about. The magistrate disposed of broader powers on the religious level than did the priest (or the Senate), because he could act with both the people and the gods, whereas the priests, who (like the senators) held neither *imperium* nor *potestas,* could only act with the gods. Even the augurs, who held formidable power in the late Republic and were one of the kingpins of the political game, had no real way to oppose a magistrate. They could adjourn an electoral assembly, but they could not stop it from taking place. Although the augurs, like the pontiffs and the quindecemvirs, interpreted the sacred law that was their charge with total liberty, they could only do so with the magistrate and on his request, and the final decision belonged to the consulting magistrate.

The preeminence of the magistrate over the priests and the Senate, but also the ultimate superiority of the sacred, is perfectly described by an anecdote reported by Cicero. During a consular election, the consul Tiberius Sempronius Gracchus, the father of the Gracchi, refused to heed a negative augury (an *omen*). When his decision aroused murmurs among the people, Sempronius informed the Senate, which consulted the haruspices. They agreed that the *omen* was indeed a bad sign and concluded that the electoral assembly was therefore not legal. Sempronius refused to heed this advice and returned to the Campus Martius to conclude the electoral procedures. Some time later, however, he informed the college of augurs that he had done so, because after consultation of the augural books he realized that he had indeed committed an infraction to the sacred laws when he left the Senate to complete the election. The advice of the augurs was presented to the Senate (probably on the initiative of a consul), and the consuls who had been elected in the incriminated assembly resigned.

In short, to be a priest in Rome meant acting with the gods and knowing how to act with them. The sacerdotal activities of the magistrates, on the other hand, consisted in being able to act with the gods in a certain number of circumstances and in becoming informed about and deliberating on the sacred value of such actions.

We cannot conclude, however, that the priest was anchored in the atemporal and the metaphysical. Despite the magistrate's undeniable preeminence in temporal matters, the priest had a unique dignity that gave him higher rank than the magistrate, and he intervened in the life of the city in discreet but efficacious ways. He alone could pronounce on and interpret sacred law and offer a solution when grave conflicts arose between the gods and the city (more accurately, he chose the norms that fitted the events), even though he could do so only with the aid of a magistrate, usually assisted by the Senate.

There is no better description of the relations between a priest and a high magistrate than the famous dialogue between King Numa and Jupiter in Rome's earliest days (Ovid *Fasti* 3.277–377). Fearlessly confronting the terrible supreme god who behaved in just as brutal and uncivilized a manner as the inhabitants of Romulus' city, Numa used verbal skills and inflexibility to win the sympathy of the celestial ruler, who ultimately let the terrestrial ruler tell him what to do and who came, summoned by

Numa, to the *comitium* (assembly) to give Rome's first citizens tokens of his "entry into the city." Jupiter, without for a moment abandoning his superiority, thus bowed to the will of the magistrate. Similarly, the priests, by their permanent and lifelong proximity with the sacred, were more venerable than a consul, but within the government of the city, they were subject to the consul's authority.

Some scholars have supposed, on the basis of this sort of relationship, that republican priests—the pontiffs in particular—had originally been aides to the archaic king, who alone was empowered to act with both the gods and the citizens, and that after the fall of the monarchy they had "emancipated" themselves eventually to become the fixed number of colleges that we know in the historical era. This is possible, although the ancient documents cited in support of this notion may well be historicizing explanations of the institutional relations that existed between priests and magistrates in the late Republic.

For the Romans, however, relations between priests and magistrates probably had even deeper implications, because relations existed not only between priests and magistrates but also within the priestly colleges. Thus when the *magistri* of the priestly colleges (whose titles were eponyms of their college) acted they frequently had a flamen standing passively at their side as though outside of time and indissolubly linked with the *magister*. The same division of religious roles is attested in the domestic cult, where the wife was a necessary adjunct to the husband. The case of the Arval Brethren, a sodality in which this sort of collaboration between a *magister* and a flamen appears with exceptional clarity, shows that these two sacerdotal roles were a dual version of the same power, particularly since the *magistri* had been flamens the year before their presidency. It is as if the Arvals had to bring together the two ritual functions to celebrate the rites with which they were charged, but were unable to fuse them. A similarly bipartite division of all sovereign acts was profoundly anchored in the Roman mind, as in the legendary traditions concerning the two first kings of Rome: Romulus, the young, vigorous, active, and violent king who founded the city, and Numa, the peace-loving older man, averse to action, and the pious creator of religion and the law.

Imitating the intellectual Romans of the first century A.D. we might interpret these ritual events to say that relations between the magistrate and the priest seem to represent something like the notion of an action and a sovereign power that, in order to be perfect, had to have the approval of men and the gods. The republican "constitution" to which the institutional examples cited above belong and, more generally, Roman custom seem to avoid giving any one man control of all the relations with the gods and with the people. Traditionally the magistrates were deprived of a part of their powers (and to some extent the most prestigious part) when those powers concerned close relations with the gods. Under the Empire, the emperor—the supreme magistrate—gained control over all the various relations that intermingled in the city, not by any swift strike but by traditional co-optation into all the colleges and sodalities. Basically, the disappearance of the priests' formal autonomy from the supreme magistrate was only another aspect of a new balance of powers, all the more so since even in the golden age of the Republic the leaders of the senatorial aristocracy were nearly always members of a sacerdotal college.

Thus when Caesar and, above all, Augustus accumulated religious roles, these were not, strictly speaking, revolutionary acts but rather the sacerdotal counterpart of privileges conceded to the ruler on the plane of the powers of government. A power given into the hands of the magistrates and the priests was replaced by a power given into the hands of a princeps invested with both powers of government and sacred powers. This does not mean, however, that the two sorts of power were mingled. In fact and in law, they remained just as separate, on the formal level, as they had been under the Republic; only the manner in which they were exercised changed. Probably one reason for the scandal caused by the emperor Elagabalus was that he attempted to reign as a priest instead of governing as princeps and controlling religious life as a priest.

To return to the questions posed earlier, the complex relations between priests and magistrates that can be found at all levels of Roman public and private life also express (for anyone inclined to exegetical meditation) one of the major principles of the ancient conception of religion: the city resulted from an alliance between men and the gods under the guidance of the magistrates.

The ritual activities of those who held sacerdotal powers in Rome can be grouped under two major headings: celebration of the cult, and representation of divine functions.

The celebration of the cult by both magistrates and priests took two basic forms: the offering of sacrifices (with numerous variations and secondary rituals), and the taking of auspices. As he sacrificed, the officiant expressed solemn homage by act and word by means of a meal consumed in the company of the divinity who was being invoked and in accordance with strict hierarchic rules. This "act of faith" recognized the superiority and immortality of the god by according him (or her) the vital parts of the victim (the *exta,* which included the liver, the gallbladder, the lungs, the peritoneum, and the heart) and the place of honor, and by the different modes of consumption of god and participants. During such banquets, a dialogue was set up in which the community, speaking through the mouth of the officiant, thanked the divinity for favors received and solicited further favors. A sacrifice included a number of secondary rites and took some time to accomplish. The great feast days often had one or more series of sacrifices, on occasion also including theatrical spectacles, games, or races at which the officiant also presided.

During the second of the two basic Roman rites, the taking or receiving of auspices, the magistrate and, on occasion, the augurs consulted or heeded a divinity (Jupiter, for the most part) concerning acts of government. The divinatory ritual of augury was a clear expression of the civic nature of Jupiter, in which the supreme god showed his direct participation in public life by signs that he sent to those who guided the destiny of the Roman people. The consultant observed celestial signs (the flight of birds, for example, or the behavior of sacred fowl) within the framework of rigid procedures that left him little liberty. The Romans' cultic acts were always the expression of an objective will—that of the Roman people—and the priest was expected to disappear behind that common will. The rigid formalism of the cult expressed this common will, and it guaranteed that public piety would be free from subjectivity (for example, in the personal sentiments of the celebrant). Thus, as Cicero testifies, the taking of auguries consisted in a dialogue between the magistrate and an assistant (in the case in question, a *pullarius* charged with observing the sacred fowl) rather than the magistrate's attentive and respectful observation. The pace and the tone of such exchanges show that the responses were codified and seldom surprising. They varied only in the face of spectacular and truly disquieting phenomena, and even then we can presume that, as with the inspection of the *exta,* the desired responses could be arrived at if the dialogue and the observation were pursued.

There is nothing unusual in the purely formal nature of the taking of auspices or the recourse to an assistant for the act of consultation. The participation of assistants in sacred acts—here the *pullarius,* the haruspices for the consultation of the *exta,* or, more generally, the throng of apparitors, senators' offspring, and slaves that surrounded the sacrificers—was a constant of the cult and of the sacerdotal act. The chief function of the person who assumed a sacerdotal responsibility was to exert his authority—rather, to express the authority of the Roman people. He fixed the dates and the modalities of the liturgy, presided at the rites, and made all authoritative statements. Specific acts required by the cult but not expressing the will and the authority of the celebrant were usually entrusted to assistants of inferior age or social rank. This meant that all the categories of Roman society had a role in the cult, each according to rank and function, thus defining those differences under the very gaze of the divinity. When a rite was split up among several officiants, the most humble of whom did the acts that might seem to later Western eyes the most essential, it was not a sign of a desiccated or dead religion but, quite to the contrary, a prime condition for its success. It was not the sacred act itself that defined the sacerdotal role but the *authoritative* sacred act: as the very term indicates, the *sacerdos* (from the hypothetical root sakro-dhōt-s, "he who *does* the sacred act," in the sense that *facere* [to do, to effect] had in public law) acted for the people. By his permanent *ius* or on the demand of a magistrate, he had power and authority in the sacred sphere just like the magistrate's in the purely human sphere. In historical times, the term *sacerdos* was applied only to "priests," but nothing prevented it from being applied to anyone invested with that sacred authority—priest or magistrate—in a given context.

The apparent rigidity of the dialogue connected with taking auspices might seem systematic manipulation, but this is misleading. Jupiter, as we have seen, was reported to have acquiesced in the decisions of the magistrate, who acted in the religious interests of the community. Thus while the formulas for the consultation of auspices attest the transparency of the public rite, they also imply Jupiter's approval. The supreme god, according to his function and to the legendary pact, was to work for the public welfare and approve all just and legitimate measures. Thus, on the condition that such measures bore no incongruity or offense, he more properly expressed his assent than the officiant sought to obtain it. The taking of auspices, like the offering of sacrifices, normally expressed Jupiter's presence among the citizenry, and Jupiter cared more about the correct execution of the gestures by which he was addressed or that pronounced his assent than he did about the consultant's intentions or personal whims. Such rites did not express Jupiter's disagreement. Disapproval was usually signified by spectacular and menacing phenomena unconnected with the consultation proper that obliged the celebrant to abandon his routine psalmodizing to analyze the celestial master's discontent and act accordingly.

In short, during the consultation of auspices, the initiative was on

Jupiter's side, not on the magistrates'. Their function was to associate Jupiter with all acts of sovereignty and to establish publicly, by means of stereotyped rituals, that the god approved. As long as Jupiter did not object, the consultant had no reason to stray from his cold and solemn observance.

When the god showed his discontent by sending unexpected signs, the celebrant had to consult specialized priests, as in any situation that could not be resolved by current tradition. This consultation was usually carried out before the Senate. Thus, whenever good relations with the gods were seriously and lastingly interrupted, the magistrates summoned the Senate and consulted the quindecemvirs, who were directed to seek in the Sibylline Books for the oracle that corresponded to the crisis. This oracle was then announced and interpreted to the Senate, and its prescriptions were transformed into decrees published by the magistrate. It is significant that in this consulting process the augurs, pontiffs, and quindecemvirs were not (or were no longer) in direct contact with the divinity. The crisis was resolved by turning to an immutable tradition (immutable in principle at least) and to a fixed corpus of prophecies—rules taken from sacred law or Sibylline oracles that took for granted reconciliation with the gods. The gods, in fact, had no apparent role in the search for a solution to the problem. It was as if the priestly colleges always had available ways to assure the assent of the gods and to bring back peace with the heavens. Their knowledge was sufficient for restoring logic to events or for revealing that events contained both a hidden rationality and guarantees of success.

Both the sacerdotal wisdom and the sacred law that were divided among the various colleges and cults occupied a central place in Roman culture, not only because they were directly connected with the birth of Roman law or because they typified "priestly" functions but also because they contained a global representation of the nature of things.

Roman priests—the pontiffs in particular—were men of law and men of the written word. Their writings contained no metaphysical revelation; instead they registered all the important facts relative to the public acts of men and of gods and compiled all the decrees and the *responsa* given by the priests. In short, they formed an entire sacred jurisprudence. Even the Sibylline Books did not contain any revelation in the modern sense of the term, but rather held secret recipes for resolving serious crises that the Sibyl had apparently foreseen. Nonetheless, these priestly books, the rules they contained, and, even more, the exegetical and casuistic traditions attached to them, constituted a uniquely Roman world system that was capable of explaining and justifying everything. Along with the ritual pronouncements made at sacrifices or in the great liturgical moments, these innumerable traditions and the know-how of those who guarded them formed something like a Book of Revelation for the Romans, a revelation inscribed in the history of Rome. They transmitted an assurance that the gods were the patrons and the unfailing allies of the Roman people.

Priests and magistrates served as officiants and as jurists, but they exercised still another ritual function. Some as part of their permanent role, others in certain circumstances, represented the functions of a particular divinity—"their" divinity.

The flamens were first among the priests specially dedicated to such tasks. A full record remains of the cultic regulations pertaining to the most venerable of the fifteen flamens, the flamen of Jupiter. In particular these regulations are expressed in permanent prescriptions and prohibitions that reveal a complex symbolism. Not that the flamen of Jupiter was a being apart; he was a citizen like any other, and he underwent no special preparation for his function, which began the day of his "taking" by the *pontifex maximus*. From that moment on, his life was totally different, but it was not a life of renunciation. The life of the flamen, and of the flaminical couple, appears to have been normal, and it even seems to have provided a model for conjugal life in Rome. The flamen and the flaminica were married according to the most fully elaborated rite, that of the *confarreatio;* they had to be married to be appointed, and (accidents aside) they remained in office only as long as their marriage lasted. Aulus Gellius describes the flamen's role in book 10, section 15 of *Attic Nights.* "If the Dialis has lost his wife he abdicates his office," he states. "The marriage of the priest cannot be dissolved except by death." Indeed the *flammeum,* a bright red veil, was worn by brides to bring good luck because the flaminica, who did not have the right to divorce, wore it permanently.

The flamen of Jupiter was actively present in the life of the city. Not only did he participate in sacrifices to "his" god, where he had the place of honor (thus taking a prominent part in the city's most important ceremonies); he was the only priest who had the right to sit in the Senate. His eminent presence was signaled by the curule seat and the *praetexta* (a purple-bordered toga), signs of the high magistrates and even of the ancient king, and he enjoyed the privilege of using a chariot to go from place to place within the city. Furthermore, the flamen of Jupiter was literally rooted in Rome. He could not spend a single night outside the city without committing an impiety, and he could not sleep for three consecutive nights out of his own bed, whose feet, plastered with a thin coat of clay, expressed permanent and physical communication with the soil of Rome. This bed was placed in the vestibule of his house in order to give his fellow citizens access to him. The most Roman of the Romans, the flamen of Jupiter was also the most human of humans. He was forbidden to touch fermented flour or raw meat, substances not (or not yet) proper for human consumption.

That the flamen of Jupiter was ever-present also made his life totally "other." He lived permanently within the sacred context and bore it with him as he went: all work had to stop as he moved through the city, so that he lived surrounded by the solemn silence of a major feast day. The only fire that could be taken out of his house was fire for sacred uses, and a box of sacrificial cakes had to be kept by his bedside. The flamen's headgear, a hat called an *apex* or *albogalerus,* was made out of the skin of a sacrificial victim, and at its peak there was a stick wound around with a strand of wool, also from a victim, that expressed the sacred context as well. Sacrality invested his very body: when the flamen went to perform a sacrifice he was accompanied by a *lictor,* who kept people at a distance, and when he shaved he had to use a bronze razor, "a material appropriate to the religious context."

It would be an exaggeration, however, to claim that at his investiture the body of the flamen was transformed into a sacred object. Sacrality was not attached to his person but rather to the function that he incarnated. This sacrality ended immediately if the flamen committed a serious error in ritual or if he divorced. The fact that he could not separate from his wife shows that, strictly speaking, it was the couple that was a sacred object, not either partner.

Furthermore, sacrality did not derive from the priest's being but from his unusual activities: it was an "acted" sacrality. The flamen had to wear insignia of his charge at all times. He was not allowed to go about without his *apex,* and it was only fairly late that he could remove it inside his house. Finally, it is noteworthy that by custom it was not other citizens who were enjoined not to touch him but rather he who had to defend himself from contact, as if to show the sacred nature of his person when it was most appropriate.

Another rule defined this quality even more clearly. The flamen was forbidden to eat beans because of their unfortunate connotations. More generally he was not allowed to see or touch a dead body, from entering the area surrounding a funeral pyre, or from even hearing funeral music. This last proscription emphasizes the sacred context that surrounded the flamen: it was forbidden to bury bodies in a sacred place, and the regulations of the sacred wood of Luceria, in Apulia, forbade "depositing a cadaver or celebrating a funeral rite in this sacred wood."

Thus by his costume, by his life-style, and by certain acts he must or must not perform the flamen gave constant notice to his fellow citizens that he was "elsewhere" and represented something "other." The operative symbolism gave notice of this absence by referring to the sacred context of the celestial gods. By his unusual behavior, which contrasted strongly with ordinary life, the flamen introduced into the world of the city signs of a beyond in total contrast to both the world of men and the world of the dead. At first sight, the flamen's behavior permitted everyone to understand that he put the city in communication with the world of the gods. Several rules permitted a more precise definition of the god he served.

Although his name—the flamen of Jupiter (Flamen Dialis)—and the sacrifices in which he participated or officiated made his function perfectly clear, there were a certain number of traditions and prohibitions that manifested other elements of the divine power that he embodied. We have already seen the royal or consular insignia that set this priest apart; those same signs of supreme power implied that it was the god who enjoyed plenitude of power. This same sovereign competence prohibited the flamen from viewing the army in battle array and even from seeing a horse, a fact that, as Georges Dumézil has pointed out, clearly separated him from the areas of human activity that involved warfare— that is, from the province of Mars.

By being excluded from swearing oaths, the flamen of Jupiter showed that his god was the master of the oath and the master of the law and that Jupiter, as master of the law, was master *tout court*. An oath meant binding oneself: the Flamen Dialis could not possibly accept such a tie, either for himself or for his divine patron. Aulus Gellius tells us that he wore no knot on his *apex* or his belt, and he could wear no ring unless it was perforated and had no gem. He could not touch or even mention ivy because ivy binds everything it clasps (*vincit ad quodcumque se applicat*); he avoided passing under a grape arbor.

Customs concerning contact between the flamen and a prisoner were even more spectacular: "If anyone is being taken to be flogged and falls at his feet as a supplicant, it is unlawful for the man to be flogged on that day." Furthermore, although any man in fetters should be prevented from penetrating into the house of the flamen, if a prisoner did manage to do so, "he must be loosened, the bonds must be drawn up through the *impluvium* [an opening in the roof of the atrium] up to the roof and from there let down into the street." Plutarch gives a reason for one such regulation regarding flamens, the tabu on naming or touching a she-goat or a dog. The goat, more subject to epilepsy (literally, "tied" by epilepsy: *epilēpsiai katalambanesthai*) than any other animal, was thought to contaminate anyone who touched him, which meant that the flamen who had contact with the animal might in turn be bound. To explain why flamens could not touch dogs, Plutarch recalls that dogs were chased away from sanctuaries for fear that their aggressive nature might keep supplicants from taking refuge there. Thus the dog was seen as a sort of impenetrable wall or a tie thrown around the sanctuary or around the priest. Finally, the *flammeum,* the veil worn by the flaminica, was a vivid orange-red, "the color of the fire of Jovian ire," Paul the Deacon commented.

Thus the actions of the flaminical couple referred directly and unambiguously to Jupiter. There were undoubtedly other rules we are unaware of, and we do not always understand the ones that have come down to us. Still, the sources indicate that reference to Jupiter was not always systematic or immediate. The actions that evoke Jupiter refer to the Jovian attribute of lightning, the messenger of his will; to his sovereign power, free and absolute; to his dominion over law and good will. They also limit his sphere of influence in relation to Mars. Such actions gave a content and a limit to sovereignty that fitted with the tolerant cohabitation of polytheistic pantheons: Jupiter was sovereign, but that was all he was. This choice of elements—few but perhaps essential—that served to inscribe the figure of Jupiter into daily reality was not intrinsic to the priest's physical person. That is, these signs did not derive from a consecration that transformed the flamen and his wife into divine bodies. These theological constructs were exterior to their person; they had to be put into action to be perceived, and they came into existence only when the other citizens reacted to this incessant ritual and perceived them.

Was the flamen a statue of Jupiter—that is, a figure of the god but not the body of the god? Plutarch leads us to understand this was the case. At the end of his digression on the right of asylum (which clarifies the relations between the flamen of Jupiter and dogs) he concludes: "It is thus natural that the priest of Jupiter, who is like an animated and sacred statue [*hosper empsychon kai hieron agalma*], can also be approached like a refuge by implorers and suppliants, without having anything drive them away or frighten them." Aside from the right of asylum, other regulations—the use of bronze and the prohibition of contact with the world of death—made the flamen resemble a divine image.

Still, Plutarch does not say the flamen was a statue; he notes that this priest was *like* an idol: *hosper agalma*. And rightly so, given that the flamen—even more the flaminical couple—obviously could not be reduced to a copy of Jupiter or one of his statues. The flamens were more than a statue of the god, and more than an image. Like the Greek *kolossos* studied by Jean-Paul Vernant, they were more like a double. Without being a natural object or the imitation of a real object, nor a pure product of the mind, this double is a reality external to the subject that, by its very appearance and when it appears, contrasts, because of its unusual nature, with the ordinary course of life. It reveals itself as something that is not present. The *kolossos* introduces the power of death into the universe of the living, expressing it in visible form. By means of unusual behavior and a chosen set of signifying elements the flaminical couple brought a visible form of the power of Jupiter into the universe of the city of Rome.

Augustine gives a good description of an ephemeral rite to keep a woman after childbirth from being bothered by the god Silvanus, and his description confirms my interpretation of the behavior of the flaminical couple. Three custodian gods (*dei custodes*) protected the woman, and "to represent the three guardian gods [*eorumque custodum significandorum causa*], three men go about the thresholds of the house at night and strike the threshold first with an axe, next with a pestle, and in the third place sweep it with a broom." The very names of these guardian gods reflect the ritual acts performed by these three men: Intercidona (*a securis intercisione:* "from cutting down with an axe"), Pilumnus (*a pilo:* "from the pestle"), and Deverra (*ab scopis:* "from the broom").

The term the bishop of Hippo uses to designate the activity of the three men (*custodum significandorum causa*) is interesting as well. Unlike the verb *imitor*, linked with *imago* (appearance, as opposed to reality; like *eikōn* and *phantasma*), *significare* expresses the substitution of a sign or a real act for an activity, a message, or an event to be reproduced. In my view, this term (which was to have a quite understandable success in linguistics) perfectly designates the production of the double in the course of a figuration. In the ritual surrounding childbirth, these three men *signifying* the three gods "show" the divine powers by perfectly tangible "signs." The three banal acts they perform are enough to make the *signum* of these three divinities appear at the threshold of the threatened house.

This picturesque ritual attests that in private religion customs that involved priestly functions in all ways resembled those of public worship. The three major flamens were involved in similar rituals. Every year as they made their way to the sanctuary of Fides (Good Faith), where they were to sacrifice, the flamens of Jupiter, Mars, and Quirinus went through the city in a chariot with a veil over their right hands. The right hand was the seat of good faith—its sanctuary, so to speak. It was the veil, which according to ancient commentators signaled the sacrality of the object it covered, that transformed the right hand of the flamen into a *signum*, a "statue" of Fides. This "veiled Faith" has baffled some modern commentators who supposed that the expression referred to a cultic statue of the goddess, but on coins Fides is never represented as veiled. "Faith veiled" was simply the veiled hand of the flamen that represented—like the *dextrarum iunctio* (clasped hands)—a living image of the qualities of Fides.

The eminently sacerdotal role of "signifying" was very frequently played by the priests (in the stricter sense of the term). It might be seen as an invitation to interpret the collaboration of the magistrate and the priest from another point of view. This role was not reserved to the priests, however. A magistrate—or, more generally, anyone sacrificing—took it on during a sacrifice when he described the divinity invited to the sacrifice and rendered it present by his actions. The hero of a triumph, who was not only the ultimate and perfect magistrate but also something like a living "image" of Jupiter, is a classic example of this.

The triumphant general moved in procession from the Campus Martius to the temple of Jupiter Capitoline in a chariot drawn on some occasions by white horses. He wore the *tunica palmata* decorated with embroidered palm fronds and the purple *toga picta*. In his right hand he carried a scepter topped by the Jovian eagle. Over his head, which was wreathed with laurel, a public slave held a heavy gold crown. From time to time the slave cried out to him: "Look behind you and remember that you are a man!" Indeed, this purple garb might be misleading. Not only was Jupiter represented at the peak of his temple in a quadriga but the use of white horses by the legendary Camillus was an even more direct evocation of the god. "That isn't something for a citizen, or even for a man," the Romans murmured, according to Livy, "for they regarded a chariot of the sort as sacred and reserved for the king and for the father of the gods." Moreover, the clothing worn by the triumphant general, the golden crown, and the scepter reflected the portrayal of Jupiter in his temple. Better still, the face of the triumphator was reddened with minium, as was the statue of Jupiter.

Historians of Rome are clear on this point: for the majority of them the triumphator was the living image of Jupiter. Sir James George Frazer, in one of the logical shortcuts that have assured his celebrity, concluded that the first triumphators, the early Roman and Italic kings, were considered gods by their subjects. Other historians, considering that the kings were dressed in that fashion, have rejected this Jovian epiphany and credited primitive royal costume with both the attributes of the sovereign god and those of the human triumphator. Recently a more balanced attitude has become commonly accepted: during a triumph it was the ancient triumphant king who was resurrected for the day in the guise of the victorious general. The basic reference for this *rex* for a day was nonetheless Jupiter and his statue.

The ambiguity inherent in the triumphator that prompts the historians' reflections—was he a king of bygone days or a god?—is a perfect expression of his relationship with the god he met at the end of the procession. The Romans' murmured comments as Camillus passed by with his team of four horses and the famous phrase pronounced by the public slave accompanying the general prove, if need be, that the Romans perfectly comprehended the figure that passed before them. Throughout the parade the soldiers accompanying their triumphant *imperator* shouted *io triumpe,* which seems to have been an invitation to a god to manifest himself. These shouts alternated with pleasantries and songs mocking the general, however, and a slave, the humblest of humans, indefatigably reminded him of his human condition. Finally, the triumphator played this role only for the duration of the procession; he became a simple citizen once more as soon as he reached the Capitoline and had celebrated the fulfillment of the vows he had made at the outset of his campaign. The regular magistrates who presided over games also traditionally wore the triumphal costume only for the duration of the games.

All the limits put to the deployment of the Jovian image reflect the status of this figuration. As with the flamen, that image fell more in the category of the double than in that of the "resembling" image or the actual incarnation of the god. During the triumph—a splendid manifestation of the power of Rome—the general served as a support for a certain number of characteristics that unambiguously evoked the presence and sovereignty of Jupiter. However, these traits were countered by other acts signifying the uniqueness of the triumphator and the absence and otherness of Jupiter. Present but superhuman, the god was somehow manifest as a result of the ritual that the triumphator celebrated as he moved from the Campus Martius to the Capitoline.

Undeniably, then, this ritual behavior cannot serve to define the figure of the Roman priest any more clearly than the others. But why should we seek a precise definition at all costs? Obviously the Romans did not do so. In the last analysis, everything seems to suggest that we respect the ambiguity of the Roman "priest"—an ambiguity that perfectly expresses the great variety of priestly figures in Rome. One even has the impression that each one of these complementary sacerdotal roles forms something like a partial sketch of the priesthood, scattered among the citizenry as a whole, in conformity with the very Roman habit of controlling the universe by representing it in separate parts.

Bibliography

Beard, Mary, and John North, eds. *Pagan Priests: Religion and Power in the Ancient World*. Ithaca, N.Y.: Cornell University Press, 1990.

Porte, Danielle. *Les donneurs du sacré: Le prêtre à Rome*. Paris: Belles Lettres, 1989.

Scheid, John. "Le flamine de Jupiter, les Vestales et le général triomphant." In *Corps des dieux*. Ed. Charles Malamoud and Jean-Pierre Vernant. Le temps de la Réflexion 7. Paris: Gallimard, 1986. Pp. 213–30.

Wissowa, Georg. *Religion und Kultus der Römer*. 2d ed. Munich: C. H. Beck, 1912; reprint of 2d ed. 1971. Pp. 479–566.

3

The Jurist

Aldo Schiavone

ELABORATION OF THE LAW and knowledge of the law (the *ius*)—a distinct, identifiable intellectual exercise that demanded and developed particular talents and attitudes—persisted throughout the history of Rome. We today still find it a relatively easy task to follow almost ten centuries of their uninterrupted practice of the law from the heart of archaic Rome, the epoch of the Twelve Tables in the mid-fifth century B.C., down to the publication of Justinian's *Corpus iuris civilis* in the heyday of the Byzantine Empire.

This continuity is all the more remarkable if we consider that what we perceive is not merely the forced and perhaps misleading product of our own retrospective gaze, nor is it the result of a historiographic operation combining a variety of elements and itineraries and recognizing common characteristics in them that historical actors themselves never consciously identified. On the contrary, throughout this long history the protagonists of this story were acutely aware of being immersed in an ongoing current of thoughts and mental (and even social) habits steadily flowing down from a remote past. This sensation was even the polestar of their labors and the focus of their identity.

Roman jurists were not only "sages," "experts," or "scholars" of the law. For a considerable part of their history they were also its most important and prestigious "constructors" and "producers." Even more, the golden age of juridical science (from the late second century B.C. to the first decades of the third century A.D.) almost completely coincided with the period of the total affirmation of a model of "jurisprudential law" within the institutional fabric of Roman society—that is, the normative power was to a large extent concentrated in the class prerogatives of the jurists, who, independent of the public charges they took on, were permitted to create the law (*permissum est iura condere*), to cite the somewhat bureaucratic formula of one second-century A.D. author (Gaius *Institutiones* 1.7).

Nonetheless, we need to guard against becoming hypnotized by consistency in such a long time span. There were also signs of great changes during this long evolution that are just as important to note as continuity is. One of these regarded the sociological position of legal experts as a class and included their relations with the community as a whole and with the institutions of the city and later of the empire; another concerned the formal characteristics of jurisprudence—the structure and the quality of the knowledge produced, accumulated, and transmitted. And since jurists were also in great measure the creators of the law that they elaborated (more accurately that they formed in the very act of elaborating it), cultural changes that they set in motion were immediately reflected in the normative organization of society. Roman law was unique among ancient systems of law not only because it was elaborated "scientifically" but also because it was the only system in large part produced by a class of experts "professionally" engaged in this task over the centuries.

For the purposes of the present volume, I shall concentrate on the first of the two levels of the history of Roman jurisprudence, privileging the sociological experience of jurists as a class over the development of the cognitive paradigms of juridical knowledge. We need to keep in mind, however, that the distinction is precarious and that every change in knowledge brought modifications of status, and vice versa.

I shall present a four-part polyptych, each panel of which contains a well-known sort of person who also represented a type: respectively, the archaic priest, the republican aristocrat, a counselor and "friend" of the princeps in the years between Augustus and the Antonines, and a high functionary in the imperial administration under the Severi and in late antiquity.

The most archaic Roman mind-set (as it is revealed to us when we decipher later tradition) left a genetic imprint of two distinct elements—in part contiguous and superimposed, in part precociously separated and "specialized"—that we could call veritable preestablished, integrated fields, or valences. With inevitable approximation and accepting the risks inherent in all definitions at the point of intersection between history and anthropology, I propose to call these two areas "magico-sacral-religious knowledge" and "knowledge of the *ius*." Religion and law: it is not surprising that the few surviving fragments of written Latin that predate the fourth century B.C. clearly refer to these two realms alone. Thus, from the outset, religious experience, which probably played a determinant role in the fashioning of the city's most ancient organizational structure, combined with a somewhat different mental and cultural patrimony that tended not toward the production of cults or magical experiences but rather to a slow and multistrata construction of a network of rules destined to cover all the most important aspects of the "social" behavior of the *patres,* rules that were the oldest nucleus of the *ius* of Rome.

The effects of the practice of the law were inevitably reflected in the many relationships of the collectivity, and the mental connection between magic, religion, and *ius* contributed notably to creating the first "public" space—both ideal and physical—in the history of Rome.

From the outset, pronouncement of the *ius* was rigorously reserved to a circle of priests, the college of the *pontifices*—literally, "road makers"; more figuratively, "those who open the way." Along with the three major flamens (of Mars, Jupiter, and Quirinus) and with the augurs and the Vestal Virgins, they were an essential component in the institutional organization of archaic Roman religion. Historiography has debated at great length the origins of the exclusive privileges that distinguished the pontiffs from the other priestly groups. There is nothing surprising about such privileges, however. The city's oldest forms of religion already operated according to a separation of tasks, and the hypothesis that there was a genetic differentiation between the sacrificial and symbolic ritual reserved to the flamens and a concentration of wisdom among the pontiffs is by no means absurd. However the division of functions may have come about, the pontiffs ended up as the custodians and the interpreters of all the most important reserves of the "civil" wisdom of the community. They controlled the calendar and kept count of the full moons, the new moons, and the *dies fasti* (court days), thus holding an important social control over time; they set the formulaic sequence of prayers and ritual invocations of the gods; they probably even controlled writing after its introduction in Rome around 600 B.C. Moreover, they registered the most significant events in the life of the city, from famines to eclipses, and they took part in the *comitia calata* (assemblies) that made decisions fundamental to the life of the community. They were, in short, the "sages" of the city.

The most suggestive and profound mental and cultural focus of their talents but also of the definition of their role in society—which was almost an anthropological device—was still discernible in the historical period. It was a constant impulse in the direction of a rich and invasive "regulative imagination." This impulse might be defined as a continuous "ritualistic overdetermination" of the social relationships and the relations between men and nature, for both individual and collective stability and reassurance. It was a perception of ritual that closely approached a genuine "prescriptive syndrome": the social space of the relations between the *patres* and the supersensitive and transfigured space of the divine and the magical seemed closed within an armature of rules and detailed, minute, and implacable—one might even say obsessive—precepts. Once formulated through the revealing word of the priests, those commands acquired a separate and irrevocable objectivity according to a phenomenon of projection known in many primitive cultures and ancient societies. Scrupulous respect of such rules brought ample remuneration, however, and their observance lent certitude and strength to the community. They also gave power to the pontiffs, whose words and interpretive skills appeared to contain the secret of the city's connection with the sacred and the magical world, a world imagined to be concerned with protecting and making invincible those who knew how to understand its language and how to heed the will of the gods that inhabited it.

The pontiffs' store of knowledge was thus more and more markedly "social," and their prescriptive pronouncements were always aimed at assuring an immediate advantage for those who knew how to benefit from such wisdom. The presence of the pontiffs eventually guaranteed a genuinely "urban" recasting of the earlier religiosity of the *gentes* (patrilineal clans) and contributed to reining in its early tendency to be aristocratic (the structure of the *gentes* was primarily founded on and ruled by aristocratic selection). The preexisting patrimony of Latin myths (which were already somewhat contaminated by Greek and Etruscan influences) was reinterpreted in a "historical" and "urban" key. In modern historiography this hypothetical "mythic disintegration" in the long run also favored the transposition out of the sphere of the sacred of models and mental schemata originally formed as purely magical and religious fantasy.

Not only did the pontiffs reelaborate the most remote strata of the religiosity of the *gentes* but, by the pronouncement of the *ius*, they used the same store of knowledge—and followed the same prescriptive mentality—to regulate relations between the various family groups within the community, combining the staying power of the preurban "systems of power" of the king and the flamens. The creation of the *ius* was founded above all on recall of the *mores,* the ancient traditions of behavior conserved within the system of kinship within the *gens* and laid down in the earliest days of the collectivity. The manipulation of these memories was accomplished by combining social experience and religious imagination. It was manifested under the form of the pontiffs' responses, given in a typically oracular manner, to questions put by the *patres* when they asked for a definition of the *ius* in a particular set of circumstances. That is to say that they asked for a definition of the conduct, in action and in words, to follow so that each individual's acts would be appropriate, both in respect to other heads of family and in respect to the gods, to reaching specific objectives in group relations.

This was how the model of the *responsum* was formed as a type of authoritarian communication of great importance in the life of the archaic city. Through an infinite number of adaptations (but nonetheless always keeping traces of its original nature), it became one of the most solid paradigms of Roman juridical wisdom.

Responding to the questions of the *patres* who interrogated them became an increasingly peremptory task for the pontiffs and their principle function in the city. The questions that required the protection of pontifical pronouncements were, above all, the mechanisms of patrilinearity, landownership, reciprocity, and exchange (both matrimonial and exchange of goods), all of which were essential bonds in a society based on *gentes.* The pontiffs gave guidance in such matters as drawing up a will, alienating or acquiring a *res in mancipio* (a category of property including land, slaves, beasts of burden, and farm implements), disciplining relations between the owners of neighboring landholdings concerning exploitation of the land, enforcing an obligation, and ruling on adjustments in kinship relations and their consequences for patrimony and power at a death or a marriage.

In this way, filtering through a homogeneous and narrowly restricted group, a particular wisdom was constituted. This store of knowledge was also potentially new in respect to the usual resources of the archaic mind-set: intrinsically casuistic, "local," and operating point by point, it offered a different *responsum* for every demand. Cognition of the *ius* did not emerge elsewhere, nor had the *ius* any meaning except to resolve immediate and concrete problems corresponding to the needs of the community. Knowledge of the law permitted the formation of a particular talent for the interpretation of social questions (even in a society of little complexity)—a talent indissolubly connected with the particular occasions on which it was called upon.

The original superposition of magico-religious experience and law, which had led to reciprocal reinforcement of the two functions in the unstable context of the early city, assured the pontiffs an importance that persisted well beyond the first centuries of community life, throughout Rome's Etruscan period, to a much later date well into the republican period. Although in the course of the history of the Republic an increasing dissymmetry came to be established between the two camps and juridical knowledge gradually emerged as Rome's one great intellectual vocation, the unique nature of that relationship continued for centuries to come. As late as A.D. 90 we can see Quintus Mucius Scaevola, *pontifex* and jurist, intent on untangling some of its more complex knots.

The connection between pronouncing on the *ius* and religious experience, though it had not dissolved, had nonetheless slowly begun to weaken, parallel to the consolidation (first with the Etruscan monarchy, then with protorepublican institutions) of a genuinely "political" dimension in the functioning of society. The legislation of the Twelve Tables—an unexpected, mysterious, and traumatic episode that probably contained elements of an explicitly antipontifical tenor—made an undeniable contribution to the first breaks in this bond.

A fairly precise sequence of events became discernible involving politics, religion, and law, although the pace of the various stages is less than clear and synchronic combinations prevailed everywhere over the linearity of temporal succession. The more the political sphere was reinforced in Rome, even as early as the sixth and the fifth centuries B.C., the less weight was borne by religion and the old structures of kinship within the *gens*. Moreover the relative shrinkage of the magico-religious world in turn signaled the irresistible expansion of the *ius*, which emerged as a distinct entity and the product of a "civil" knowledge organized according to criteria of its own. Already toward the end of the fourth century B.C. it figured as the true *logos* of Rome. The ancient interweaving of the sacred and the law was slowly joined by and then slowly replaced by a different alliance, fully recognizable in the early third century B.C., between juridical knowledge and the political power of the new patrician and plebeian aristocracy. Religion, for its part, was also subjected to notable pressure from the new dominant bloc.

Between the fourth and the third centuries B.C., the image of the priest-sage faded and nearly vanished, its place being taken by that of the noble/sage. Giving *responsa* came to be seen as an aristocratic privilege tied to a hegemony of the patrician and plebeian *nobilitas* that had emerged from the social struggles of the fifth and the fourth centuries. This attitude was part and parcel of the political predominance of an oligarchy. Juridical knowledge came to be yoked to the primacy of the great families, a combination that was to last at least through the Republic. One thing did not change, however: knowledge of the law remained a function of the exercise of power in the city.

We cannot say how much "rational" thought (even of a "low" level of rationality, without concepts or abstractions) had been concentrated in the pontiffs' earlier powers, as distinct from the nuclei (certainly more prevalent originally) of magico-religious thought and ritual. We can legitimately suppose, however, that the new context not only continued the casuistic approach but also favored the development of models of empirical realism and distributive calculation.

The *responsa* provided an better and better embodiment of the living *ius* of Rome (now a city in full expansion); they constituted a discontinuous but solid framework for the relationships that were crystallizing in the city. Nonetheless, unlike the *lex publica* they did not establish general rules. They were valid only for the questions that had been posed. In a certain sense they were consumed in their pronouncement; their duration was the time it took to put them into effect. They were not forgotten, however, and their memory was entrusted first to the oral tradition of the college of pontiffs, then to that of the aristocratic families. Each new question was first of all measured against existing precedents—opinions already given that had accumulated layer upon layer. The survival of each individual *responsum* was tied to a subtle interplay between the magnetism of the event, memorized in its unrepeatable individuality, and a search for a possible and prescriptive typicality. This analogical tension established the persistence of the *responsum* in real life. Still, the decision to innovate, to stray from the past, was traumatic.

For a long time *responsa* were not even accompanied by any explanation: they appeared as the manifestation of a secret skill and competence that was to some extent still oracular and prophetic even though it was less and less tied to pontifical practice. When he examined the question put to him the sage concentrated on the details, on the minute signs that only for a trained mind became revelatory and indicative of a response. At the same time, every new situation had to be brought into alignment with the ancient *mores*. Social reality was registered through a network of verbal tesserae, only one of which might prove decisive for a solution. These were tiny segments of words, of time, of behavior: a precedent, a repetition, a ritualistic formula, an act. This search was in some sense diagnostic or semiotic in type, in that it developed the special relationship with the particular and the mental aptitude for the concatenation of signs that can be found in a roughly contemporary age in the logic of Greek medical texts of the "clinical" tradition. Between Roman sages of the central centuries of the Republic and the Greek physicians who preceded or were untouched by the "anatomical turning point" there is more than a vague comparison. They shared a bias toward a "semiprofessional rationality," empirical and easily available, and a habit of day-by-day investigation centered on man and on the individual. Rather than becoming inert fossils, these were elements that were to continue to play an active part in more mature Roman juridical thought; they gave the great Roman jurists their inimitable tone of concreteness and realism (despite their penchant for gelid abstract thought) and provided them with the fundamental trait of their unique "humanism."

The force of the *responsum* and the guarantee of its "truth" as law no longer resulted from its basis in religion and sacrality. These were now founded on a body of almost totally "civil" notions and interpretive doctrines. This body of knowledge was no less admirable and austere, however, in the consciousness of the citizens, and mastering it was still the exclusive patrimony of a restricted group of powerful men, even if such men no longer had to have any connection with sacerdotal tasks. We cannot yet call them "jurists" in the modern sense of the word, however. Knowledge of the law continued to be only one intrinsic and not completely specialized aspect of a still-global aristocratic education that included other and equally important bodies of knowledge and that prepared for other tasks. Still, they were "experts" for whom juridical knowledge and the activities connected with it could become true "service in the city," as Cicero was to write, and the nucleus of an intense and prestigious public presence.

When the field of attraction including the law and its language shifted from religion to politics (a process that has wrongly been defined as "secularization"), it did not bring about any internal change in the components of juridical knowledge. The mental style of the new aristocratic expert presented no radical break with his pontiff predecessor. He brought hermeneutic refinements and a quantitative accumulation in experience, not changes of a qualitative sort. As late as the mid-third century B.C., the tradition was still almost exclusively oral, deeply rooted in the particular cultural and social patterns of the most ancient civic history. It was a wisdom of words and of signs that persisted within formulaic models and that conserved substantially archaic schemata as it interpreted *mores* and *leges* and drew from them rulings on individual cases that the citizens put to their experts.

On the rare occasions in which it appeared in juridical culture before the mid-second century B.C. (and in which it did not simply operate as a marginal expedient for documentation and mnemonics), writing was exclusively connected with problems involving political strife. There is in fact a single thread uniting writing and politics in the first texts of Roman jurisprudence of which we have any reliable word—the *De usurpationibus* of Appius Claudius Caecus (and the work of his freedman Gnaeus Flavius) at the end of the fourth century and, roughly a hundred years later, the *Tripartita* of Sextus Aelius Paetus Catus. It is probably risky to apply the adjective "democratic" to the genesis of these works; and in any event, Sextus Aelius operated in a context—perhaps in Scipio's circles—that cannot be directly compared with the milieu of Appius Claudius and his possibly demagogic and "tyrannical" propositions. Nonetheless the presence of writing always betrays an intent to "popularize" juridical knowledge, or at least an interest in moving it toward awareness of it among a more general audience. The written word mitigated an exaggerated dependency on the aristocratic oral tradition. The closed and verifiable space of the text, of the *liber,* of the tables, opposed the arbitrariness of secret memory: this was what had already taken place with the Twelve Tables.

An entirely oral body of knowledge, though, like a uniquely casuistic body of knowledge, was inadequate to the investigation or regulation of complex structures. When, during the course of the third century B.C., Roman society totally abandoned its archaic traits, the old juridical thought, crystallized in the anonymous and collective tradition of the *ius civile,* proved insufficient by itself. For a moment the very "jurisprudential" nature of the Roman juridical experience seemed shaken as never before since the institution of the Twelve Tables. At this point, the center of juridical innovation tipped toward the activity of a magistrate of the Republic—the praetor—whose annual edict proved a prescriptive process that made him a less hampered and swifter interpreter of the needs of the new imperial city.

Aristocratic jurisprudence soon recuperated its threatened primacy, however. It did so, first, by basing its own operations on a more sophisticated ethics of the *responsum* that reflected a well-articulated and mature morality of persuasion and truth vis-à-vis the strata rising to prominence

in the city's life. Second, it threw the old pontifical primacy into permanent crisis. Cicero recounts that Quintus Mucius Scaevola stated, "How
often have I heard my father say that no one could be a good pontiff
without a knowledge of the civil law" (Cicero *De legibus* 2.19.47). The
admonition contains in full the sign of the times. The old model of
knowledge was turned upside down: no longer did pontifical practice
serve as the basis for knowledge of the *ius civile;* the doctrine of civil law
justified the pontifical role. Thus there arose a "specialists'" and, in its
way, a "modern" image of the tasks of the priests and of competence in
the law, even if those tasks and that competence were still anchored to a
univocal and totalizing *paideia.*

Finally, in little more than a century—the tormented and crucial
years between the Gracchi and Augustus—the aristocratic tradition effected an unprecedented revolution in the content and the methods of its
own body of knowledge. The intellectual transformation that signaled
the rise of the new thought and of a genuine juridical literature (writing
by this time was a vehicle for the various authors' diverse personalities)
to a large extent coincided with the biographies of some of the major
figures in late-republican jurisprudence. Such figures spanned four generations: Publius Mucius Scaevola, his son Quintus Mucius, Servius Sulpicius Rufus, and Marcus Antistius Labeo, all of whom were also magistrates and leaders amid the senatorial *nobilitas.* These men were not
conscious creators of a unified discipline; rather they worked in different
directions, urged on by differing pressures and demands. Still, their
methods enabled each successive generation to profit from the experience
of the previous one and recast it within a more complex model.

Their history tells us of the laborious emergence of new conceptual
parameters, of a "rational" and "formal" law for the first time conceived
abstractly and in terms of a true juridical ontology. They provided schemata adequate to a less elementary society but that nonetheless succeeded
in finding a grounding in a reelaboration of the ancient, archaic, and
protorepublican tradition of wisdom, mingling the two in a way that
remained one of the most typical traits of Roman juridical thought. It
was also a history that witnessed the progressive fragmentation, under
the burden of the political crisis that struck the *nobilitas,* of the link between political primacy and juridical knowledge, the symbol of all aristocratic jurisprudence. Consequently, that same history witnessed the constitution of a group of "jurists" (we can use the word) as a completely
autonomous professional elite embodying interests and values distinct
from the reasons of politics. This group was of course still an expression

of the dominant strata, but it was no longer totally and unmediatedly identical with the groups that successively held power.

The "scientific revolution" of Roman jurisprudence can be said to have concluded under Augustus with the death of Labeo. For nearly two centuries after this date, jurists were to deepen the autonomy of their doctrine and the vocation of its practitioners as technicians and specialists, enhancing them by the choice of and the control over ever more complex forms of logic. By this time, the system of operative concepts constituted a new and great science that was watched over by a particularly compact group of men who made themselves its jealous interpreters and with whom rulers in power found it indispensable to enter into alliances and compromises whenever power relations were determined by the current situation.

Henceforth, an intense and uninterrupted dialogue, constantly punctuated by changes of tone and emphasis, characterized the relations between jurists and the imperial power. The history of these events has not yet been written, and I must be content here simply to sketch only a few points referring to situations that have caught the eye of recent historiography.

We can suppose that the beginnings of the new jurisprudence could not have been tranquil. The greatest jurist of Augustus' time, the same Labeo whom we have already encountered, was also a subtle and severe opponent of the new regime in the name of loyalty to an aristocratic primacy thrown into crisis by the institutions of the principate. It is probable that one of the major objectives of his work, which aimed at establishing the parameters of a dialectic between the interpreter and the normative text (be it a praetorian edict, the *leges,* or the *senatusconsulta*) capable of placing the traditional hegemony of jurisprudence on a more advanced basis, was the implicit but evident intention in opposition to the monopoly of juridical innovation with the new political power.

Labeo's "ideological" hostility was not destined to be kept up by successive generations of jurists, however, and Augustus' flexibility and caution (and perhaps the prudent restraint of Labeo himself) had helped to limit and sterilize its most immediately political effects from the outset of the new regime. Nonetheless, even though Labeo's work and his example had little effect on the future of the principate, they traced the confines of the great "power compromise" that later jurisprudence practiced and successfully maintained for more than a century.

The point to which Labeo clung most tenaciously was a defense of

95

the "jurisprudentiality" of Roman law against any tendency on the part of the regime to shift the ancient balance in a "legislative" direction (an idea that may have entered the mind of the last of the Caesars). In the tacit pact that successive jurists made with the new power, that ancient equilibrium assured loyalty to institutions and collaboration with them; in exchange the jurists received the substantial guarantee of a full respect of the primacy of jurisprudence in the hierarchy of the sources of the production of the law. The prerogatives of the men of the highest levels of jurists were untouched; in fact their prestige grew and broadened, sheltered and protected by politics.

All that initially was a difficulty could thus be transmuted into a solid alliance, and the most important jurists became quasi-institutionalized as consultants and counselors of the princeps. The age of Hadrian was the high point of this integration, which coincided with a season in politics and culture unequaled in the history of imperial Rome. The career and the intellectual biography of Salvius Julianus—the greatest jurist of the age, among the greatest in the entire history of jurisprudence, and the man who inspired many of Hadrian's decrees, if not also his model of governance—summarized and brought to their highest level all the most significant traits of this age, both in the eyes of his own contemporaries and for those who followed in his tradition.

Dialogue with the imperial power was not the only characteristic of jurisprudence in the century after Augustus' death. Besides testing their strength against that of the princeps, the jurists also argued among themselves—at times peacefully, at times even bitterly; in the process they established the rules, the cadences, and the areas of an intense and persistent colloquium between the generations and the ages, weaving their thought into a single set of problems that was enlarged by a continual process of proposing hypotheses, solutions, and new figures and disciplines. The jurists disagreed, at times passionately, but they never lost their fundamental solidarity as a "corps." The underlying options, laid down during the century of the "scientific revolution," were no longer questioned. Onto that shared base of methods, principles, and concepts, however, they grafted a variety of offshoots, some technical and leading to specialization, some leading to a "politics of the law."

In the years between Labeo and Julianus it seems that even within jurisprudence at least two orientations—two "schools," as the jurists themselves called them—came to be defined. Each of these in turn split into distinct branches that drew sustenance and suggestions (always with original reelaborations) from the major philosophical currents of the times. The first current, the "Sabinian" (from the name of a jurist of the age of Tiberius), might be characterized as a generically empiricist tendency, although on occasion it embraced skeptical overtones and arguments in its assessment of reality and its evaluation of juridical events. The second current, the "Proculan" (from the name of another jurist of the first century A.D.), seems to have been more open to a nondogmatic rationalism and cautiously trusting of a primacy of concepts and categories over data and the materials of social experience.

Following a reconstruction already in circulation in the late second century A.D, the work and the doctrine of the great Julianus put an end to the debate of the "schools" by reaching beyond the reasons for the old antagonisms. There is probably something excessive in this judgment, but there is also an element of truth in it if we recall the lines along which Julianus' "politics of law" developed. Jurists intent on creating a science of jurisprudence and emperors working to put order into their decrees collaborated, the jurist class and the principate still to some extent operating on equal terms as one power with another, to consolidate a system of law within the parameters of "utility" and "certitude."

In the final years of the second century A.D. the role of jurisprudence and the place of its long history changed once more. This transformation took place in the background, behind a process that was exceptional in a number of ways—the birth, on the ruins of the Hadrianic model of imperial government, of a true "state" machinery, immediately bureaucratic and centralizing and with ever-increasing responsibilities for social and economic direction and control. Before then only with a dubious use of analogy could one call the political and administrative institutions of Rome a "state."

The new configuration of power and government completely absorbed the autonomy of the jurists. Just as the great experts in republican law had all been magistrates of the Roman people, so now the most prominent persons in Severan jurisprudence were the high functionaries in the imperial administration. These men were intellectual bureaucrats of an almost Hegelian sort, called to manage a worldwide power mined by contradictions, threats, and dangers. But whereas the jurist-magistrates of the Republic had behind them an administrative organization (and in a certain sense a political organization) that was relatively simple and "light," the minister-jurists of the Severi gave form and direction to an apparatus of a complexity hitherto unheard of in the ancient West.

This created a totally new situation: the traditional "Labeonian" autonomy of jurisprudence, the model for which had remained valid up to Julianus (though it was revised and updated), was not eclipsed or dismantled by any external force. Rather it was the jurists themselves (probably in full awareness) who changed the nature of "their" law and their own role. When they accepted high administrative posts, they reserved to themselves the role of godfather to the "state" form of politics and government and put their own stamp on it. Furthermore, if by conceding to the imperial chancellery a consequent and inevitable primacy in the production of the law (through the *constitutiones*) they put an end to the "jurisprudentiality" of Roman law, their change of guise also assured them a voice in a form of juridical production that was now openly "legislative."

But in the act of fitting the old jurisprudential law into the new fact-oriented constitutional reality, the jurists gave it a "definitive" systemization, gathering it together with endless commentaries designed to help it resist the ravages of time. At the same time, they used new literary genres to create a new organization in which, to be sure, the old normative autonomy of jurisprudence no longer had a place, but in which the now unlimited power of the princeps and sovereign could be tempered and to some extent mitigated within an ecumenical natural law that was benevolent but rigorous.

If Julianus was the most luminous example of the "jurist-counselor," Domitius Ulpianus (even more than his colleague and perhaps rival, Julius Paulus) was the prototype of the "jurist-high functionary." Ulpian's vast writings, broadly utilized by Justinian's compilers and hence relatively well known to us, still await full investigation using truly modern criteria. In some of his works, and particularly in long passages of the comments *ad edictum* and *ad Sabinum,* the dense web of citations that punctuates the discourse seems to become its true guiding thread: in the existent extracts of the *ad edictum,* we can count more than a thousand references to earlier jurists. His references are often subtly manipulated, however, in accordance with a plan in which the systemizing of doctrine clearly prevails over accuracy.

In reality, although Ulpian made broad use of the debate of the golden years of jurisprudence, he nonetheless operated totally outside the bounds of that debate. It was no longer the collective voice of the jurist class, persisting through time, that spoke through him; it was now the Severan legislator, who approached juridical texts as Julianus had the praetorian edicts, subjecting them to a crystallization that sanctioned·the end of a tradition.

For some time, perhaps two decades, the work of these last great jurists seemed to maintain a miraculous equilibrium between new forms and the tenacious memory of the old ways. A moment of extraordinary intellectual intensity began just as the century of crisis loomed. Precisely while its own decisions helped to create the conditions of its own disappearance, Roman jurisprudential law had the time to raise up its own monument in a full profile of a "formal" law (formal in Hegel's sense, but also in Weber's). Its actual application in the imperial society of the time was limited, but it prepared the way for all successive updatings of ancient juridical thought from Justinian to more modern times. Roman law was to last an extraordinarily long time; under many flags it came to be nearly identical with the destiny of all "rational" law.

Bibliography

The present essay presupposes and reworks parts of my preceding publications: Aldo Schiavone, *Giuristi e nobili nella Roma repubblicana: Il secolo della "rivoluzione scientifica" nel pensiero giuridico antico* (Roma and Bari: Laterza, 1987); Schiavone, "I saperi della città," in *Storia di Roma*, gen. eds. Arnaldo Momigliano and Aldo Schiavone (Turin: Einaudi, 1988), vol. 1, *Roma in Italia*, 545–74.

I am also indebted to, among other works, Mario Bretone, *Tecniche e ideologie dei giuristi romani*, 2d ed. (Naples: Edizioni Scientifiche Italiane, 1982); Federico d'Ippolito, *Giuristi e sapienti in Roma arcaica* (Rome and Bari: Laterza, 1986); d'Ippolito, *I giuristi e la città: Ricerche sulla giurisprudenza romana della repubblica* (Naples: Edizioni Scientifiche Italiane, 1978); Vincenzo Scarano Ussani, *Valori e storia nella cultura giuridica fra Nerva e Adriano: Studi su Nerazio e Celso* (Naples: Jovene, 1979); Scarano Ussani, *L'utilità e la certezza: Compiti e modelli del sapere giuridico in Salvio Giuliano* (Milan: Giuffrè, 1987); Scarano Ussani, *Empiria e dogmi: La scuola proculiana tra Nerva e Adriano* (Turin: G. Giappichelli, 1989); Valerio Marotta, *Multa de iure sanxit: Aspetti della politica del diritto di Antonino Pio* (Milan: Giuffrè, 1988); Tony Honoré, *Ulpian* (Oxford: Clarendon Press; New York: Oxford University Press, 1982); Francesco Casavola, *Giuristi adrianei* (Naples: Jovene, 1980), bibliog. Giacomo de Cristofaro.

4

The Soldier

Jean-Michel Carrié, C.N.R.S.

TO ANYONE SEEKING EXOTIC times and figures, the Roman soldier may
not, at first glance, seem picturesque. As early as the reign of Augustus
(my chronological point of departure here), Rome had already invented—long before in certain cases—many elements of what was to become
the universal and obligatory framework of military life and military institutions that still pertains in Western societies today. Among these (and
in no particular order) are barracks life, promotion rolls, bugle calls, the
camp infirmary, the personnel office, tours of duty, morning report,
permissions and leaves, "the army offers you a career," discharge review
boards, and even theatrical performances for the troops. Encouraged to
anachronism by so much modernity, some historians have projected their
own memories of military service onto the Roman soldier to declare that
"the legionaries probably suffered more from isolation and boredom than
from the enemy." This arbitrary generalization was rightly contested by
one of the best-informed scholars of the Roman army, the late R. W.
Davies. Still, the legions continue to guarantee the success of professional
"anachronists," naive filmmakers, and clever comic strip writers.

Romans themselves must have agreed that the soldier lacked picturesque qualities, as he is strikingly absent as a character in Latin fiction.
Although the genre was subject to constraints inherited from Greek literature and relied on a conventional repertory of situations and heroes,
some Latin novelists, picaresque before the letter, nonetheless introduced
social types drawn from current society into their works. Still, in one of
the two examples we do have the soldier who appears in the *Satyricon*
remains atypical and without personality; it is not because he is a soldier
but because he is guarding the site of her sacrifice that he becomes an

actor in spite of himself in the episode of the lady from Ephesus. The same is true in Apuleius' *Metamorphoses* (which is, incidentally, in closer conformity with the Greek ideal). The narrator, transformed into an ass, is for a while in the service of a legionary, about whom we know all we need to know by his introduction: "We met with a tall soldier (for so his habit and countenance declared) who was a legionary." Succinct as it is, this portrait is not totally without interest: it illustrates recruitment criteria of height and general aspect, and it reflects the instinctive respect (perhaps dictated by simple prudence) that the soldier, selected to embody and defend imperial authority, inspired in civilians. What is surprising is that once Apuleius introduces the military milieu into his story he furnishes no local color, no traces of military jargon, not even any clichés about military life.

This absence of a fictional mirror to transpose reality to the plane of the imaginary is of little help to our attempt to construct our own representation of the Roman soldier. We are left with two sources difficult to use for comparison and confirmation: a civil and basically ideological discourse that offers only immutable *topoi* that attempt a configuration of an evanescent referent; and iconographic representations of soldiers, on rare occasions accompanied by statements that are lapidary in all senses of the term.

Today there are a number of works, both scholarly and popularizing, on the Roman army, but no general study of the Roman soldier. Not that some studies have not borne that title, but they turn out to be descriptions of the conditions of service in the Roman army or of the "daily life of the soldier"—works useful and interesting for what they are, but that see the soldier only from the angle of his professional life. The soldier as a social actor; as he creates, reproduces, or diffuses patterns of behavior and ways of thinking; the image that soldiers had of themselves and that other groups had of them; what they and others had to say on the subject—all that has up to now been taken up only topic by topic and essential points in that story continue to elicit controversy among historians. We shall soon seen how delicate an operation it is to use civil sources; yet they have been the basis for the opinions of the earliest modern commentators, even for works that claimed to be technical, such as treatises on the "art of war," on strategy, on poliorcetics (the art of the siege), or on military history—works written, for the most part, by civilians with little experience of military life.

A proper sociological and anthropological study of the Roman soldier would, by definition, have to be comparative and contrastive. Unfortunately, if our grasp of the "soldier" is insufficient, so is our grasp of the "civilian," with the exception of a few privileged groups favored by the existence of contrastive sources. In a sense, then, the present study is premature in anticipation of the many systematic inquiries that would be needed to trace a definitive portrait of the Roman soldier. I shall at least attempt to summarize preliminary studies that are now available and that point the way for future research. The necessary limits on bibliography prevent me from acknowledging more than a small part of my debts.

The Roman army, the instrument of an exceptional historical destiny, long drew its strength from the perfect congruity between the political and the military structure of the city-state. The individual's resources determined both his political responsibilities and his military participation, which, more than a duty, was a right and even a privilege. The city's only army was its citizens, mobilized in their turn according to its needs and solely for the duration of the war. As the conquering city grew, longer wars and the need to maintain a military presence in the conquered provinces threw these traditional arrangements into crisis, and by becoming a de facto permanent army the army had to open its ranks to the poorest citizens, the proletarians; to provide payment for the troops; and to accept an increasing dissociation between the profession of arms and the "profession of the citizen." When the Roman soldier became the ends and the means of rival ambitions, his behavior tended to resemble that of the mercenaries who served the Hellenistic monarchs. Then, when Augustus put an end to the crisis of the city-state by establishing an authoritarian regime founded on absolute control of the army, he created a new and durable version of the Roman soldier. The modern historian often skips over this change or grants it an indifferent glance, but it launched a lasting debate in Roman political opinion and was the target of widespread criticism. When he became a professional, the imperial soldier was perceived as a mercenary; when his service became permanent, people saw him as an idler and a useless mouth to be fed when he was not fighting. Often a recent citizen (perhaps only from the date he enrolled), he was also considered a barbarian.

The new military institution retained the fundamental principles of tradition, however: the citizen-soldier, albeit reinterpreted as a soldier-citizen, and the monopoly of command for the upper classes, a survival from the old timocratic system. At the same time, however, the concept of "citizen" was being emptied of all real content in a regime that drew all its power from the soldier, the faithful servant of the princeps and soon a maker of emperors.

I might also note that in Rome it was the professional soldier who created the "civilian," a figure up to then unknown because all citizens were potential soldiers. The new concept had a name taken from military jargon: *paganus* (literally, a country person, from which, later, "pagan"), probably because the civilians who had the most contact with garrisons were country people. I will not be referring to them when I speak of "civil discourse" concerning the soldier, however, but rather the small fraction of Roman society that was or thought itself associated with political power and that, for all practical purposes, acquired a monopoly on the ideological messages that have come down to us, often muffling the voice of the soldier himself.

By professionalizing the army, then, Augustus replaced revolving enlistment for all citizens with continuous service by some. During the last two centures of the Republic the population under arms (where Italians were in the majority) often reached 10 percent and at times as much as 20 percent of citizens. How could Italy conceivably have continued to contribute soldiers for a permanent army at that rate? This simple question is enough, in my opinion, to disqualify the various hypotheses (a fall in military vocations, depopulation, economic crisis, etc.) that have been advanced to explain the dwindling number of Italians in the legions after the beginning of the Empire. At least during the first two centuries of the Common Era, Italy maintained its military prerogatives by furnishing the initial personnel for newly created legions or legions raised to replace others that had been wiped out. In particular, Italy kept its hold, at least until the Severi, on direct access to the praetorian guard, a prestigious and economically privileged corps and a seedbed for officers for the legions. Furthermore, as J. C. Mann has established, at least in the first century A.D. it was the policy of the central government to distribute Italian soldiers throughout the provinces.

The growth of the Roman army and its components to the dimensions of the civilized world and the extension of Roman citizenship to most of Rome's defenders (which opened the way to Caracalla's even more radical edict in A.D. 212) could not but satisfy the idealistic philosophies predominant at the time. The Hellenistic sovereigns had shown the way by according a status of "juridical entities" (*politeumata*) to their mercenary regiments, thus making them politically comparable to the Hellenic communities and recognizing their cultural identity. In the satisfied judgment of the Roman Empire of men such as Plutarch and Aelius Aristides the Augustan reforms were seen as the application of a Platonic program (not that of the *Laws* but that of the *Republic)*: a permanent army created for a specialized function thus guaranteeing technical excellence; soldier-citizens chosen for aptitudes that were further developed by training, thus permitting the other citizens to pursue their own professions unhindered; soldiers who were not driven into military service by necessity, such as the poor or the mercenaries. In a purely Platonic view their remuneration would be no more and no less than what covered their needs. Plato would also have soldiers fed at public meals; Aelius Aristides preferred to have them strictly separated from civilians, according to a precept that he traced to Egyptian wisdom (Aelius Aristides *Roman Oration* 72–87). More useful even than the farmer, because he assured the liberty of all (Maximus Tyrius *Dissertationes* 23), the soldier was at the service of the princeps, who was himself trained in war, like the philosopher of the *Republic,* and who was the soul of the world and would infuse the body of the world with reason and permit it to accede to happiness. Obviously, in this vision the soldier was to realize a particularly lofty model of moral rectitude; metaphorically speaking he must be Plato's "purebred dog"—an image repeated by Plutarch and (without reference to his breeding) by Dio Chrysostom (*Orationes* 1.28). Good breeding— this time without the dog—entered into the official nomenclature of the soldiers of the early empire: *gennaiotatoi,* a more expressive term than its Latin equivalent, *fortissimi.*

Closer perhaps to Roman political realism was Dio Cassius' reasoning, which he attributes to Maecenas, justifying the Augustan institution of the professional soldier (Dio Cassius 52.27.1–5): Given that the principle of utility prevails even over that of honesty, it is good policy to turn to the advantage of the collectivity the strongest and the poorest of the population, who are potential delinquents. Money now counts for more than glory, and one must learn to live with one's times. In Horace as well, the soldier appears with the laborer, the innkeeper, and the sailor as an example of those who must toil (*labor*) for money in order to ensure an old age without need, of those who must give up personal liberty to submit to others (in the case of the soldier, quite a submission!) and struggle for subsistence—in short, of those who are refused *otium,* which was both leisure and peace of soul (Horace *Odes* 2.16). It is very likely that a good many citizens quietly rejoiced that a professional army freed them from military service and left them free to pursue their trades or enjoy their *otium.* This did not prevent them from publicly deploring the disappearance of the ancient Roman mind, founded in abnegation, courage, and endurance, or from demanding that the volunteer soldier practice those same virtues.

In a more Roman, more traditionalist analysis that describes the evolution of Roman society and institutions in terms of corruption, the soldier occupies a place abandoned by the citizen, in moral decline. This intransigent ideology could not even consider the soldier a citizen, even though in fact the overwhelming majority of soldiers of the princeps were Roman citizens or foreigners doing their best to become citizens.

Tacitus' pessimistic view presents the military reality of the empire as a perversion or inversion of the Platonic models. The *thymos,* or noble anger, that had characterized the "guardians of the city" had become degraded into *ira, furor,* or even *ferocia* (the terms that return constantly when Tacitus speaks of soldiers)—that is, into a savage and impassioned anger with little resemblance to the state of sacred trance and superhuman personality dissociation of the archaic *furor.* That *furor* was itself a ritualized vestige of a functional ideology, also tripartite, buried deep in the night of Indo-European origins and unsuspected by the Romans. The fact that the soldier was prey to tyrannical desires (for pleasure, for fortune, for power, eventually for glory) (Juvenal *Satires* 10.140–41) made him a dangerous being who threatened the public welfare with the very arms with which he was supposed to defend it. He was apt to be described as a subhuman being whose faults were multiplied by group psychology (for which he provided an ideal occasion for observation). His numbers inspired fear. Tacitus often designates the rank and file, the *gregarii milites,* by the term *volgus,* a term that gave pejorative connotations to any "mass" (Tacitus *Historiae* 2.29.5, 37.2, 44.5, 45.6, 93.2, 3.31.2). Varro traced the etymology of *miles,* the soldier, from the number *mille.* The word lent itself particularly well to Tacitus' habit of using a singular noun in a collective sense: *miles* for "the soldiers" as a whole.

This ideology, which exerted a strong influence on the upper classes of imperial society and was more alive than ever in the fourth century, called for an ideal soldier of peasant extraction—a *topos* indefatigably repeated from Cato to Vegetius (Cato *De agri cultura,* pref. 4; Maximus Tyrius *Dissertationes* 24; Vegetius *Epitoma rei militaris* 1.3). He also had to be as "Roman" as possible (whatever that might mean); he must be even more cut off from civil society (here they agreed with the neoplatonics); he should be paid little (social jealousy blinded the civilians); he should be better disciplined and kept in line by the application of merciless punishments. Because Plato's dog had turned into a wolf (Suetonius *Lives of the Caesars, Tiberius* 25.1) it was up to his leaders and his generals to protect the soldier from the assaults of desire (*libidines, cupido*) by rebuilding within him the ramparts of reason (*sapientia, prudentia*) and morality (*devotio* in its broadest sense), and by instilling in him a respect for human values that the *miles impius* had forgotten.

Such "theories of the soldier," sometimes convergent, sometimes contradictory, have had an equally powerful attraction for modern historians, who for many years used them as a point of departure for their own attempts to reconstitute the Roman soldier. Even recently opinions have diverged on such essential points as the origin of military recruitment and the soldiers' relative wealth, cultural level, and "Romanness." Some of these topics are still debated today. As documentary sources have gradually prevailed over the ideological sources, however, and the latter have been recognized as such, significant advances in knowledge have been made possible. By the same token, long-accepted ideas have required reconsideration.

In particular, Theodor Mommsen's theory that obligatory conscription was still the principal means of recruitment under the Empire has been largely abandoned, despite the efforts of P. A. Brunt to revalidate it. Volunteers outnumbered conscripts well before local recruitment became the general practice in the second century A.D., even before the Severi improved conditions of service. Brian Dobson has shown how Augustus instituted permanent legions, replenishing their ranks annually with only a few hundred men rather than forming new, completely manned legions by the time-honored practice of the *dilectus* (draft), which reconstituted old units that had been dissolved or wiped out. In light of this, it seems evident to me that from its inception the permanent army was conceived as a means for avoiding forced conscription and, in particular and in the special circumstance of the end of the civil wars, as a means of not imposing the *dilectus* on Italian citizens, even if this risked overly prolonging the tour of duty of the soldiers who remained under arms. (The last troubles in that transition period between the old and the new political systems continued until the revolts of A.D. 14 under Tiberius.) Thus voluntary service is to be seen as the inevitable corollary of a permanent army rather than as a gradual and spontaneous evolution.

At the same time, many *peregrini* (free subjects of nations allied to Rome) had to be enrolled not only in the auxiliary units but also in the legions. At first sight, the study of the names of legionaries gave credit to the idea that citizen recruitment continued. But the example of Egypt, which we know thanks to correspondence on papyrus from recruits informing their families and their friends of their new civil identity (for example, *P.Bad.* 72; *BGU* 2.423; see also *P.Yale* 1545) as nonchalantly as we today would inform people of a change of address, leads us to think twice. There is one M. Longinius Valens, for example, who up to then was named Psenamounis, son of Asemos, or one Lucius Pompeius, son of Pompeius, Niger, of the Pollia tribe, in reality son of Syrus and grandson of Apion. Are we to conclude that any Egyptian "fellah" could become a soldier, hence a citizen, of Rome? Certainly not. But a Hellenized Egyptian city dweller was no longer considered an "Egyptian" by the recruitment bureaus, even if a "Roman" from Italy would not have recognized him as a fellow citizen. It is clear that from the time of Augustus the line of demarcation between those who could and could not be enrolled in the Roman army no longer fell between Roman citizens and the *peregrini* of the provinces, but rather, within each province, between small and middling property owners assimilated into an urban structure (Aelius Aristides *Roman Oration* 78: *phylokrinesantes,* chosen according to civic criteria), or at least into a village, and propertyless common folk, urban or rural. Furthermore, this economic line of demarcation coincided with a cultural frontier that ran not between "Roman culture" and "non-Roman cultures" but between a culture of the classes that were dominant or associated with domination, a sort of supernational koine molded or influenced by Hellenism, and classes that were dominated and later identified with a number of nonprestigious "local cultures."

Recruitment in the first century A.D., by reaction against the "proletarian" recruitment of the last two centuries of the Republic, was drawn from provincials enrolled in the cities rather than in the *pagi,* or rural districts. The social level of recruits probably rose in Italy as well, to judge from the concentrated recruitment in the most prosperous regions, Campania and the Po Valley. Extending the levying of troops to the whole of the Mediterranean world permitted the Empire to reconcile voluntary enrollment with the selection of soldiers who were physically fit and did not come from the lowest economic and cultural levels—not famished creatures who had no roots or even modest interests to defend and consequently were ready for any sort of adventure, including revolt or desertion, but men capable of equating the defense of the Empire and sworn service to the princeps with the survival of a society from which they were not excluded. Such men were not about to sell their services for a simple promise that they would not die of hunger: they expected from military service either a decent economic condition (in the legions), a better one (by promotion), or a gain in prestige and personal status (in the auxiliary corps). When recruitment eventually encountered difficulties (which incidentally proves that conscription had been abandoned), these came more from a shortage of acceptable candidates than from any growing civilian disaffection (as has often been claimed) regarding the risks, toil, and constraints of military life. Aelius Aristides confirms that Rome had no trouble finding volunteers throughout the provinces in his days (ibid., 85–86). The specialized corps were one sector that always fell outside "civic" recruitment in its new guise. Here Rome had no compunctions about calling on populations outside its provinces that offered a high potential in fighting skills and "military cultures" that complemented its own (Moors, Thracians, Caucasians, Persians, etc.).

Augustus and his immediate successors by no means intended to create or even encourage the constitution of a military class that would reproduce itself socially as a sort of hereditary army. Moreover, the fact that soldiers were forbidden to contract (legal) marriage during their tour of duty or to acquire real estate in the province in which they were garrisoned was intended to keep them from founding a family and to encourage them to return to their places of origin after discharge. Stationing soldiers in the provinces brought unexpected results, however. The four hundred thousand to five hundred thousand veterans of the civil wars whom Augustus settled as colonists in Italy failed to produce anything like a proportional number of soldier offspring, but it was soon apparent that in the provinces there was a direct relation between the size of a garrison and the province's contribution to recruitment. Thus during the first half of the first century A.D., when the Iberian peninsula was the seat of three legions, Spanish soldiers could be found nearly everywhere on the frontiers of the empire, and a gradual reduction of troops to one legion brought on a reduction in the Iberian contingent in the other provinces. From Augustus to Trajan, and even more after the conquest of Britain (ancient Britannia), the military center of gravity of the empire was situated on the Rhine. In the second century it shifted to the Danube, where it long remained, leading in the third century to the preeminence of the Illyrians, first as soldiers, then, from soldiers, as emperors. Provincial recruitment spontaneously and rapidly became first regional, then local. The soldiers themselves were the most persuasive recruiting agents. The prestige of the uniform, of the soldiers' military bearing, of military ceremonial, but also a secure future and direct experience of the spectacle of a life that (until Marcus Aurelius) was tranquil more often than it was exposed to danger made a favorable impression on young minds that, if they had been far from any camp and had been influenced by the clichés, commonplaces, and traditional jokes about military life, would have recoiled from the idea of joining up. Even in the provinces on the periphery of the empire, the outer fringe (the zone of the camps) created a specific and cohesive milieu, fashioned its collective identity, and eventually furnished the better part of the troops and instituted a de facto hereditary military class well before the legislative power felt obligated to establish one by law when the barbarian invasions upset the equilibrium and shook the structures of those same frontier zones—soldiers' lands.

Whereas in the East the soldier tended to return to his native city when he was discharged, eventually taking his place among the magistrates and public benefactors of his municipality (see, for example, *AE* [1981]:775 for Sebaste in Asia Minor), in the West, which was originally more rural, the camps often propagated urban civilization, thanks to discharged soldiers who settled near them, independent of the official veterans' colonies. The statistics gathered by Eric Birley for four western provinces show that an overwhelming majority (from 65 to 97 percent) of veterans remained where they had been stationed after their discharge. Historiography has amply developed the theme of the contribution of the Roman soldier to the diffusion of sedentary agriculture and urbanization, consolidating Rome's efforts for military defense by enhancing the value of the land in the conquered territories. The more simplistic formulations of such views have rightly been criticized for misconstruing both the agrarian and the urban situations before the installation of Roman rule. To take the most studied and debated case, that of North Africa, the military "frontier" was far from being a great wall sheltering a settled Roman or Romanized population and protecting it against nomadic natives chased out of their territories. Moreover, from the second century on, Roman soldiers were no longer ethnically different from the local population; thus they could hardly have embodied the confrontation of two irreducibly opposed civilizations, impermeable to one another's influence. Must we, then, totally reverse the old theories to state that soldiers played no role at all in urbanization and the extension of lands under cultivation? That would be paradoxical indeed.

The soldiers no longer came from agrarian backgrounds, nor could they spontaneously turn themselves into farmers the minute their discharge benefits were delivered (more often in land than in coin). Still, they did not necessarily rush to sell their land grants. As property owners they were on an equal footing with the middle class of the provincial cities, whose wealth was also in land. We know from soldiers' wills that soldiers and veterans owned slaves. Their names often appear in agricultural lease contracts when they rented out cultivatable land. They were not peasants but rentiers, men who lived off land, and there is ample documentation of their rights of "possession" of imperial lands. This was already the system of the citizens' colonies in the Hellenistic cleruchy: tenants of the king, the soldiers exploited their land allotment by waged laborers or tenant farmers.

Regionalization thus led to a local attachment that made the soldier less likely to want to leave his area. Does that mean, though, that the Roman army had become, as René Cagnat once said, "a provincial militia paid by the state"? Was it able to maintain the moral unity it needed in the face of an implantation that threatened to dilute it culturally in the surrounding milieu? In his consideration of a limited but significant example, the diffusion of epigraphy in Britannia, J. C. Mann has remarked that the local population's lack of response to the Italian soldiers' introduction of lapidary inscriptions eventually slowed the military's enthusiasm for epigraphy as the soldiers became increasingly provincial.

The Syrian soldiers of Intercisa, in Pannonia (now Hungary), studied by Jenö Fitz offer a different picture. For nearly a century, from Antoninus to the 260s, the Syrians of Emesa (Homs), who jealously guarded their cultural traditions and were a people of an ethnic homogeneity, used strict endogamy and successive troop levies to make Intercisa a focal point for the oriental identity of the entire province even though they were far from their native province and in a profoundly different environment. The cultural pull was so strong that when their sons served in the Pannonian legions they returned to Intercisa to retire and be buried. In this case, Roman authority conferred an officialized status on a regional particularism that was the image of Rome on their soil for the civilian population. This example, better known than others, illustrates the variety of the situations in which a relationship could be established between civil and military society—a variety that shows just how insufficient and inappropriate the problematics of what was "Roman" and what was "indigenous" were in some historians' interpretation of acculturation in the Roman Empire.

These variations from one region to another and the strength of the ethnic entities accepted by the emperors would seem to support the criticisms that return in Tacitus like a leitmotif: "armies whose habits and speech were so different" (*Historiae* 2.37); "an army of many languages and customs, in which citizens, allies, and foreigners mingled"

(3.35.5). The soldiers' growing attachment to their camp, which had become "their very hearths and homes" (*in modum Penatium*) (2.80.5), appears in the account of the revolt against Vitellius, curiously picked up by the *Scriptores Historiae Augustae* as one of the reasons for the murder of Severus Alexander. Severus Alexander had ordered troops from the Rhine and the Danube regions to the East for an inconclusive expedition against the Persians, thus leaving undefended the provinces in which these men had left their families and their goods and to which he then had to return them to hold back the barbarian attacks that the soldiers had predicted and feared. What the soldiers took to be a strategic error set them against the emperor. The author (*SHA, The Two Maximini* 7.5) suggests, however, that the episode was a clear expression of the men's emotional identification of the defense of the empire with defense of "their frontier" and their "piece of empire."

Nonetheless, how can we fail to recognize, with J. F. Gilliam, that "it was the loyalty to Rome of these incomplete Romans in the army that sustained the Empire even during the long crisis of the third century" (Gilliam, *Roman Army Papers*, 287)? Even though that army had become permanent, professional, provincial, and local, and even though citizenship had been emptied of its political content, this mixture of men never behaved like mercenaries. Even the accounts of military uprisings show us that they continued to identify with the collective ends of the Empire. They could be moved by resentment, manipulated by ambitious or scheming men, or demoralized by certain specific conditions of service; they could compete with some groups in civil society and still not behave in such a way as to lose a generally responsible attitude that we could call civic (in the broader sense). The soldier reached a level of "imperial awareness" maintained by such pillars of official military religion as Eternal Rome, the Augustan Victory, the Capitoline Jupiter (Optimus Maximus). As late as the third century A.D. the military calendar of Dura-Europos (*P.Dura,* 54 = Fink, *RMR,* 117) maintained the traditional religion of the Seven Hills on which Augustus had founded his regenerated army (Horace *Odes* 3.5.5–12). It was J. F. Gilliam, once more, who observed that even if these traditional holidays must have had little meaning for the soldier of the Severan era (and even less, I might add, for the Syrians we have met at Intercisa): "Like the rest of the soldier's routine, his use of Latin however limited, and his uniform, helped serve to distinguish him from civilians and to remind him that he was a Roman soldier."

Soldiers' epitaphs, which never fail to detail advances through the hierarchy, generally do not mention geographical peregrinations, though Aurelius Gaius, a soldier of the tetrarchs, constitutes an exception (*AE* [1981]: 777). Still, it was a well-established principle that promotions involved a change of unit. May not this silence simply mean that leaving his native province to move about the empire at every change of post, campaign, or transfer was always part of a soldier's life? And that for him no move would seem expatriation? An Egyptian soldier named Theon wrote a letter to his sister, who was concerned that he might be homesick: "Above all else, as I enjoined upon you when with you, take care of yourself so that I may have you well, and do not be anxious about me because I am away from home, for I am personally acquainted with these places and am not a stranger here" (*P.Oxy.* 8.1154). Voyages in time rivaled those through space: thus one Gaul from Vienna (now Vienne) in Gallia Narbonensis, who had enrolled as an ordinary soldier in Britannia, fifty-seven years later became a *primus pilus* (second in command) in the Legion I Italica, stationed at Novae in Moesia (*AE* [1985]: 735), a post that crowned his career as an officer up from the ranks and—somewhat late, in his case—opened the doors to the equestrian order. At this point he fulfilled the vow that he had made to the Augustan Victory when he enrolled. When he joined the army, the Roman soldier never knew whether he would see battle, but he knew what risks he was exposing himself to, and in extreme cases he hoped to encounter them.

Ancient texts never lose an opportunity to praise the separation, established by Augustus, between the military and civilians, whether the question at hand was stationing the legions at the periphery of the empire (Dio Cassius 52.27) or separate places for soldiers at the spectacles of the capital (Suetonius *Lives of the Caesars, Augustus* 44.1). For Tacitus, it was for their own good that soldiers should be sent far from the softening influence of cities, and his pronouncement "Inter paganos miles corruptior" ("The soldiers were demoralized by mixing with the civilian inhabitants") sounds like an adage from ancient lore (*Historiae* 1.53.14). Might it be that the pressing need to requisition billeting (*hospitium*) for the soldiers, permanently or occasionally, may have inspired such virtuous proclamations? Taken literally, such dispositions would have held the soldier at a distance and cut him off from civil society during the long parenthesis that often represented the greater part of his adult life. Marginalized in this manner, how could he not have developed a countersystem of values, a mind-set and a caste culture reflected both in military jargon and in his assiduity in destroying cities and slaughtering their inhabitants when civil war offered an opportunity to do so? This portrait of the Roman soldier as a marginal being, now abandoned, at least under the form that Rostovtzeff gave it, has been revived in recent years by several authors seeking to impose diachronic comparisons with the armies of medieval or modern Europe. In these views the Roman army finds the picturesque qualities that it so sorely lacked, but is that the historian's aim? Should we seek what Petronius failed to tell us in Thackeray's *Barry Lyndon*?

I shall return to the arguments that have been drawn from the *sermo militaris*. The next question is whether the sources permit us to recognize family behavior patterns in military society that are distinct from those of the civilian populations. A recent article deduces from the infrequency of military burial stones erected in Britain by relatives of the deceased that recruitment from outside the province isolated soldiers from their families. This conclusion, which is contradicted by all previous studies of the Roman army in Britain, shows the oversimplification of this reasoning. What is more important to our purposes is to understand why the family is so seldom mentioned in soldiers' funerary inscriptions.

Soldiers were automatically assured a minimal decent burial by their obligatory payments into the unit's "coffers." This institutional solidarity was backed up by a spontaneous professional solidarity in which soldiers agreed to see to one another's eventual obsequies. The most natural form of this promise was between brothers (when feasible), and indeed epitaphs often mention a brother, although this does not mean that he was the only kin nearby or that the deceased was unmarried. Indeed, the commemoration of a soldier by a brother was not normally part of the familial pattern of responsibilities for funerary honors, but it does represent the ideal form of celebration by a companion in arms, a *commilito*. Its frequency shows both the collective dimension of the choice of a military career in certain families and the result of the army's policy of putting members of a family in the same unit or at least in the same camp.

Until the reign of Septimius Severus, the soldier who was unmarried when he was inducted could not contract a marriage recognized by Roman law during his service. However, the concubinage that this prohibition created for many soldiers was legalized at their discharge, when the *peregrina* companion and the children born of such unions were accorded Roman citizenship. This meant that while maintaining a theoretically rigid principle that conceded no compromise between military service and family life, the military authorities closed their eyes to the soldier's private life. He could shift for himself.

We can see many of them living with a *hospita* (host) or a *focaria*. The latter, a term typical of military language, was no longer taken in its original meaning of "kitchen girl" but designated a woman who made the soldier's "chow" in the *canabae* outside the camp. In military testaments a soldier could bequeath a portion of his obligatory contributions to the regimental funds to his *focaria,* who otherwise would have no right of inheritance (*P.Wisconsin* 14; *BGU* 2.600; *P.Princ.* 57). Until their father's discharge from military service, any children bore their mother's name (*P.Oxy.* 3.475 = *Sel.Pap.* 337).

Other soldiers had a "slave" who evidently not only saw to their house in town but, on occasion, bore them children (who were also slaves). One veteran of the fleet at Misenum even had two female slaves for whom he provided in his will, freeing them and setting them up equally as his universal heirs, along with the daughter he had had by one of them (*BGU* 1.326 = *FIRA* 3.2.50). The dedication on a praetorian's tomb by a woman who was first his slave, then his wife, hints at a similar situation (*CIL* 6.32678). Thus the soldier was not forced to frequent prostitutes—who, incidentally, were plentiful among the population of the *canabae*.

For the most part, the papyri show soldiers established in a stable relationship in good middle-class fashion, often with the daughter or sister of another soldier, and the inscriptions confirm a widespread aspiration to leading a family life comparable to that of civilians. Such men took back, in practice, all their citizens' rights, gravely hampered by a prohibition to marry that was justified only by their exceptional status under the *ius militare*. This victory of ethical values over law led first to a neutralization and eventually to abrogation of the law. For Romans, social success was impossible without the foundation of a respectable family nucleus. Like the notables or the craftsmen in the cities, soldiers increasingly had themselves represented as family men on their funerary monuments, thus laying claim to a respectable moral and social conformity.

Backed by their cohesion and their professional solidarity—which explains certain endogamic tendencies—soldiers as a group also showed proof of a desire to be integrated into a larger society. They cultivated their primary ties with kin but also, as local recruitment became more frequent, their ties with their geographical roots. Thus it is hardly surprising to find ideological notions in the more loquacious epitaphs: "he lived honestly"; "he served without stinting"; "I have lived the time allotted to me always in the respect of good; poorly, honestly, without harming anyone, at which my bones rejoice." This last formula can be found in nearly identical form on a tomb in Rome and one in Dalmatia (*ILS* 2028, 2257).

In contrast, commentaries are notably absent from the epitaphs of soldiers who died in combat (2305–12 and elsewhere). This does not mean that the army had lost its sense of warlike virtues by multiplying its contacts with civil society. Only circumstances—unpredictable when a man entered military service—decided the existence of the Roman soldier, and he expected equal recognition of his merits, whether they found expression in works of war or of peace.

What is more striking is the absence, in the cities, of "war monuments" to the dead like the ones that existed (for instance) in the Greek cities. The epitaph of Julius Quadratus Bassus, killed in the Dacian campaign, is an exception. His body was brought back to Perga, where he had been born, and carried through the city in procession (*AE* [1933]: 268; see also *PIR*, 2d ed., 1.508). In this case the ceremony, which honored a soldier of the highest rank, took place on the initiative and at the expense of the emperor Hadrian. Should we see in the public's silence in other cases the limits of civilian patriotism and solidarity with the soldiers? More simply, perhaps the princeps encouraged civilians to celebrate the victories of his armies more than their defeats.

The fact that the soldier "belonged" to the emperor, a notion firmly established after Augustus ("*milites mei*"), defined both the soldier's obligations and his privileges. The soldier justified those privileges by the personal sacrifices for which they were the reward. The heavy price he paid provided some balm to the jealousy of civilians, and it tempered the fear that the soldier inspired in them by a feeling of condescending superiority. The heavy burdens of the soldier's lot found familiar expression in a number of metonymic terms for life in the *militia*. One of these was *sarcina,* from the name of the pack that, from the time of Marius, the soldier carried when the army was on the move. Carried over the shoulder on a forked frame, it could weigh from 45 to 110 pounds.

Another term that often recurs is *sudor*—sweat—which was the product and the proof of military *labor* and the mark of the soldier's willing gift of his person and his renunciation of civilian comforts. "Sweat, dust, and all such things let them leave to us," Marius exclaims, exhorting his troops, "to whom they are sweeter than feasts" (Sallust *Jugurthine War* 85.41). Should the soldier neglect to boast of sweat as his special privilege, civilians were quick to demand it of him: Vegetius illustrated the redemptive value of perspiration by advising generals to whip their sluggish troops back into shape making them exercise "until sweat ensues" (Vegetius *Epitoma rei militaris* 3.4). The concept passed into administrative language, where it turns an astonishing metonym into common parlance: a law of 369 was aimed at detecting soldiers who had not "sweated [*ipse sudarit*] in the armed service" but had simply served in the offices of the Palatine (*CTh* 7.20.10; see also 7.1.8, of A.D. 365).

Perspiration was by this time so inherent in the military condition that the emperor, *commilito* of his troops, felt the need to sweat to manifest his sense of duty, give an example of ancestral discipline, and inspire the unlimited loyalty of his men. Pliny celebrates Trajan's military virtues in these terms: "What shall I say now of the admiration which you won from your own men? They saw how you shared their hunger and thirst on field manoeuvres and how their commander's sweat and dust was mingled with their own." He predicts that "the day will come when posterity will clamor to see and show their youngers the earth that was soaked in your sweat" (Pliny the Younger *Panegyricus* 13.1, 15.4). The emperor's divine nature must not fear to become incarnate as a humble soldier and mingle his precious humors with those of his companions in arms, thus, by this physiological libation, sealing an unbreakable pact with them. In an inverse semantic operation, the metonym (*sudor*, the effect, for the cause, *militia*) finds concrete and hyperbolic form in the fantastic biography of the first Maximinus presented in the *Scriptores Historiae Augustae*. The emperor-soldier par excellence "would often collect enough sweat, putting it in cups or a small jar, to exhibit two or three pints of it" (*SHA, The Two Maximini* 4.3). The supposed author of this life, Julius Capitolinus, exploits his public's taste for *mirabilia*, the extraordinary phenomena so often cataloged in the late Empire, but he also amuses himself by lending an appearance of historical authenticity to a play on words probably inspired by a then-classical repertory of popular pleasantries on the subject of soldiers.

Although the transcendence of the imperial person ennobled and rehabilitated military *sudor* (as least for the duration of an official discourse), sweat did not raise civilian opinion of the profession of arms. The exaggeration underlying the praise in the text quoted from the *Scriptores Historiae Augustae*, which bears a direct relation to Maximinus' monstrous physical size and supposed barbarian origin, makes the physiological excess unbearable and emphasizes the profound ambivalence—admiration and aversion—that the image of the soldier evoked in civilian opinion. The true soldier could be measured by the sweat he emitted. But at the same time, all that sweat was repulsive: it was further confirmation of the inhumanity of the military condition, as compared to civil values, and a justification for redoubled rigor in defense against this disquieting personage.

By making sweat an immediate and legible sign of Romanness, Hollywood filmmakers have proven that they have read (or heard of) Latin texts. The mistake they make is in extending that specifically military attribute to all Romans. This should not surprise us, however, for Rome's only function in Hollywood is to support American myths, as the semiological analysis by Roland Barthes has so brilliantly demonstrated.

In an utterly anachronistic passage, Livy justified Augustus' policies by situating the introduction of military pay four centuries earlier. All labor merits a wage, he says, invoking the principle that there was a connection between *labor* and *voluptas* (toil and pleasure) (Livy 5.4.4). The less said about this pseudophilosophical disguise, the better. Following a much more down-to-earth reasoning, the emperor considered that the bargain he had struck with his soldiers for a quarter-century of their lives merited the granting of some "consolation" in exchange. In the main, public opinion was far from agreeing with him.

In Livy, the use of the term *voluptas* implied that military pay had a purchasing power covering not only necessities but also some superfluities. In a society of want in which simple subsistence was a problem for most people, *voluptas* constituted an indication of social status more than a moral concept. What became a purely moral problem, on the other hand, was the opportunity, granted to or withheld from any given social group, for legitimate access to *voluptas*. That legitimacy was denied all soldiers, regardless of their milieu of origin, because their social promotion was seen as a transgression of the established moral order. *Felix militia*, Juvenal exclaims sarcastically in his sixteenth Satire, playing on the two meanings of the adjective: happiness was not for soldiers, and they were indeed lucky to have obtained so many undeserved advantages—even more so in the case of the praetorians the poet was speaking of. A highly mythic vision of ancient times, when the traditional principles had been rigorously observed, and comparison to the current situation offered an unlimited arsenal of arguments to recall to their appropriate place soldiers who had been corrupted by the excessive liberality of the princeps. It was a wonder that such reproaches did not link soldiers to the freedmen, whose enjoyment of their insolent *felicitas* was even more scandalous.

Moreover *voluptas* was held to be incompatible with the military virtues that guaranteed the security of the civilized world. The civilians' fear of seeing the soldier become soft thanks to luxury and lose his *disciplina vetus* (old-fashioned discipline) was so strong that they reassured themselves by imagining army life to be even more spartan than it really was. In the *Scriptores Historiae Augustae,* Avidius Cassius and Severus Alexander, both of whom are presented (at times in identical terms) as paragons of disciplinary severity, take into hand particularly dissolute legions, which means Eastern legions, since for Romans the East was "the sewer of every vice." Among other abominations, the soldiers were taking hot baths! (*SHA, Avidius Cassius* 5.5; *Alexander* 53.2). As if every camp in the empire did not have its own baths, of a size and elaborateness that varied according to the unit and the available resources, situated either in an annex to the camp or within it (as was the case in Chester, Vindonissa, and Lambaesis), and that rivaled civilian baths! On occasion, their operation required heavy work duties to provide water and heating fuel, which proves the importance of an element of urban civilization that not only represented comfort but was an essential place for social exchange. Thus at Bu Ngem (formerly Gholaia), in Tripolitania, small baths were built within two years of the Romans' arrival. The centurion then in command, a fine wit, composed a dedicatory poem in iambic trimeter in honor of the goddess Salus. He states: "To the best of my ability, I have sanctified her name, and to all I have given the veritable Salutary waters, among many fires burning, in these endless sandy hills in the capricious breath of the south wind, so that their bodies may restore themselves from the ardent flames of the sun by swimming peacefully" (*IRT* 918, lines 9–13 taken from the Bruno Lavagnini translation as modified by René Rebuffat). Thus the soldier did not share the strong cultural prejudices about baths of the peasants, who, toward the end of antiquity, often took their revenge on the city by destroying thermal establishments. The civilian who refused the soldier the *voluptas* of the bath, thus condemning him to the malediction of *sudor,* also showed proof of his ignorance of the "real soldier."

More than a man given over to pleasure, the soldier was viewed as a man ruled by desires, impulses, and appetites. These terms return constantly in Tacitus, who, as we have seen, considered wrath to be the soldier's dominant passion and the inspiration for his most senseless acts.

Roman antimilitarism found a naive but efficacious way to appeal to the hungry masses by stressing bulimia—the most extreme form of appetite—in its denunciations of soldierly excesses. In popular Roman imagery, the soldier (like the monk during the Middle Ages) was commonly portrayed as a glutton or a gourmand. In the *Satyricon,* Eumolpus, a second-rate poet, declaims a poem on the civil war that is a parodic accumulation of commonplaces in which he states: "The errant soldier, arms in hand, demands all the good things the earth produces to assuage his hunger. Appetite makes him clever" (Petronius *Satyricon* 119, vv. 31–33). The fabulous *Life* of Maximinus, presented as a simple soldier who rose to the imperial purple, states that he was able to drink a Capitoline amphora (twenty-six liters) of wine and swallow down at least forty pounds of meat (*SHA, The Two Maximini* 4.3). Libanius, in an oration that carried denunciation of the army as far as the imperial majesty he addressed could tolerate, describes soldiers "in the midst of their villages who for the most part loll about or doze after having their fill of wine and meat" (Libanius *Oratio de Patrociniis* 5). And John Chrysostom, portraying a model centurion who soon after became Christian, states that Cornelius "did not waste his life in banquets and drinking and gluttony," thus implying that his habits stood out from those of his fellow soldiers (*Baptismal Instructions* 7.29, trans. Harkins, 117). It is perhaps not coincidental that such accusations increased in the fourth century, when the demands of the army were held responsible for a sharp rise in taxes.

Nonetheless, authors who were quick to denounce such a lack of measure could also present a totally different picture of camp life. The "good emperor" (Hadrian, for example) is shown sharing the soldier's mess—that is, salt pork, cheese, and vinegar and water (*SHA, Hadrian* 10.2); Caracalla (though he is decried elsewhere) is praised for grinding his own grain for the "barley cake" he cooked on the coals of the campfire and "only used what was the cheapest thing available to the poorest of his men" (Herodian 4.7.5–6); Julian "was often seen partaking of common and scanty food, sometimes standing up like a common soldier" (Ammianus Marcellinus 25.4.4). These texts clearly describe campaign rations, even though "biscuit" had long replaced unleavened bread, an archaism that once again refers to the penurious regime of the olden days that the civilians wanted to see reestablished in its full rigor. In contrast, denunciation (perhaps excessive) of luxurious eating habits echoes the most basic polemical themes: the supposed disappearance of discipline and of the spirit of self-sacrifice, and the excessive and unjustified size of the military budget. Denunciation also offered an opportunity to present the soldier as a nearly animal creature given over to his primary instincts and a stranger to the reason that ruled both the *kosmos* and the laws of the city. Thus he merited being treated with extreme severity and being put back in his true place in society.

If we leave the language of ancient political diatribe for that of a modern sociology of consumption and literary sources for documentary sources, we note that the soldier in his garrison had access to some luxury foodstuffs and was minimally aware of the gastronomic pleasures that indicated a first stage in social advancement. Assured of enough to eat by the imperial quartermasters' corps, he lost no opportunity to better his basic rations. He was particularly fond of condiments, salt meats, and pork products. His correspondence with his family or with colleagues shows the place that "delicacies" had in his life and thoughts: he speaks of oysters in Vindolanda, *garum* (a fish-based condiment), asparagus, and fowl in Egypt. The resources of the network of familial and professional solidarity were often put to the service of his table, which showed an alimentary level clearly superior to that of the masses and signified (not without some ostentation) the dignity of his rank. Archaeological excavation of camp refuse heaps shows that meat was consumed in quantity, contrary to the common notion that modern historians have inherited from Roman civilians. *Voluptates* lead us to the question of the economic level of the Roman soldier.

Was the soldier of the empire a poor wretch, successor of the proletarian soldier of the late Republic, led by dire necessity to choose a marginal existence even though he was born free and to risk his life for a barely sufficient wage? Or did the emperor guarantee him an ease that was not only enviable but envied by civilians of a comparable social level? Like ancient writers, some of whom were of the first opinion and some of the second, modern historians have disagreed on this point just as they have concerning the social origins of soldiers. Furthermore, the two questions are connected, because a badly paid army would have attracted only proletarians whereas a more middle-class recruitment would seem to have implied decent economic treatment.

The conversion of the republican army from an army of predators into a regulated, administered, and paid army undeniably counts among Augustus' principal achievements. It was a complex operation that constituted an excellent test for the solidity of the new institutions. In appearance, the soldier lost considerably: direct profits from conquest stopped when conquest stopped (or at least slowed) and booty became the right of the emperor alone; the demagogic bidding between rival "warlords" came to an end when military clientage was unified and monopolized by the emperor; the opportunity to annex lands on which to settle veterans disappeared. Henceforth the soldier could no longer hope to make his fortune in just a few years of campaigns and had to await the end of an interminable service (if he was still alive) to enjoy the full fruits of his sacrifice. After a transition period to put the new system of military finances into place, when insufficient resources had to struggle with old ways of thinking (expressed in the legion rebellion of A.D. 14), troop rotation and new sources of financing enabled the army to guarantee the soldier institutionalized, regimented advantages to replace the uncertain and risky profits of the late Republic. By appealing to a different sort of calculation and psychological motivation, the new system inevitably had an influence on the social origin of recruits.

If we consider only the soldier's official pay (*stipendium*), as certain historians have done, the inescapable conclusion is that the soldier was very badly treated. The near absence of readjustments in the pay scale to maintain the soldier's purchasing power in periods of monetary devaluation (his stipend remained unchanged from the end of the Second Punic War to Caesar, then again from Caesar to Domitian, and once more from Domitian to Septimius Severus), together with the inadequacy of what few readjustments there were, reduced the soldier's pay to the poverty scale when compared to the annual income of artisans and waged workers. Civilians nonetheless judged the increase decreed by Septimius Severus scandalously generous.

Two other considerations enter the picture. First, the soldier received only a small part of this pay, since deductions were taken for his rations and for obligatory payments into the unit's savings funds that he would get back only on discharge. Second, the range of the military pay scale from one end of the hierarchy to the other was so great that a civilian could get an extremely false notion of an ordinary soldier's pay if he judged by the life-style of the officers. A prefect of a legion received four times as much as a centurion, and a centurion earned eight times the pay of a noncommissioned officer and sixteen times the pay of a simple legionary (under the Republic, a centurion was paid only twice as much as a legionary). Even in the ranks, the pay scale varied among legionaries, auxiliary troops, and sailors, while the Praetorian Guard enjoyed a particularly high rate of pay.

Should we, then, pity the fate of the imperial soldier? Not really, and for several reasons. First, it is misleading to think of the soldiers' pay in terms of modern salaries, or even in terms of ancient salaries, given that the notion of *salarium* was ideologically quite different from the concept of *stipendium*. Furthermore, the advantages that a soldier gained from military service can only be measured on the scale of his complete military career (*militia*), from his enrollment bonus to his discharge benefits and including all intermediary gains, financial and juridical (fiscal exemptions, for example). On a previous occasion I have defined the Roman *militia* as "a sort of savings plan that paid periodic benefits during the course of the contract and built up a financial capital available at term, with accrued interest in the form of social prestige." Finally, although we should not overestimate the largess (*donativa*) periodically accorded by the emperors, which ancient "sensational literature" saw (with evident polemic intent) as fabulous, nor should we limit to his pay the money that found its way into the soldier's belt (*zonula*) (*SHA, Alexander* 52.3). Originally linked to military successes, under the Empire such liberalities came to be used to celebrate events of the reign such as the emperor's accession and the anniversary of that event (after Antoninus, jubilees and dynastic events centering on the emperor's designated successor as well). Gratuities are better known in the late Empire, when their number compensated for—or brought on—the near disappearance of the *stipendium*, a move that amounted to a simple modification of the terminology pertaining to regular pay. For the early Empire, we even have to take into account a whole series of minor gratuities about which literary sources tell us little, but that, added together, rounded out the soldier's pay considerably. These were subsidies for such things as salt (*salgamum*), shoe nails (*clavarium*), and ritual feasts (*epulum*), the list of which grew longer and longer. To these special payments, set by the calendar or by custom, and to the regular *donativa* (imperial "gifts"), we might add special gratuities to troops who had been involved in combat or even simple maneuvers supervised by the emperor, as, for example, at Lambaesis under Hadrian.

Only the cumulative effect of these advantages, realized above all at the end of a soldier's military service, can explain the patience with which soldiers bore the long-term stability of their pay—a pay reduced to insignificance in the fourth century in terms of purchasing power. It also explains the absence of military revolts to protest low pay and irregular payment—unlike the army of the republican era or, even more, the Byzantine army. In this manner, the figures for the *stipendium* are more compatible with general information transmitted to us of the relative ease of a number of soldiers and veterans. Finally we can understand better how the imperial army could attract men who were not driven to enroll by an immediate preoccupation with subsistence. Naturally, one must take into account individual differences and, even more, the unequal pay scale for the various sorts of troops. Native Roman citizens, particularly if they came from a milieu that was better off and better educated than the average, might be motivated by the hope of becoming a noncommissioned officer or even a centurion, whose pay was enviable. Their counterparts among the *peregrini,* who were not eligible for a good number of material advantages, in particular the sizable bonus on discharge, were assured—even if they had never had a chance to show off their valor in combat—that with seniority they would receive Roman citizenship, a promotion in personal juridical status that seems to have remained attractive until the time of Caracalla's edict. Finally, the profession of arms was a traditional vocation among certain peoples of the ancient world, and when service under the Roman emperor was their only opportunity, they accepted its conditions without dispute. There was a highly varied mix of social and ethnic groups, each with its own motivations, that could not be deterred from enrolling. It was understandable, however, that it was a navy infantryman, the worst-paid and least prestigious branch of service, who declared in his epitaph: "I was born in deepest poverty; later, as a soldier in the navy I served seventeen years at the side of Augustus, with no hatred and no offense, until my regular discharge" (*CIL* 5.938).

The available information on the imperial soldier's standard of living lends itself to contradictory interpretations. For example, the correspondence of soldiers with their families that has been conserved in Egyptian papyri shows them largely dependent on their kin for their equipment and clothing, to round out their rations, and to provide them with an occasional treat, particularly when they were *tirones* ("rookies") who had just entered the service or were in the early years of their *militia.* If they were also seeking advancement, gifts in kind or coin had more influence than letters of recommendation, as one Claudius Terentianus, a navy infantryman, notes with resignation to back an appeal for funds addressed to his father Claudius Tiberianus, also a soldier. He states, "And if god should be willing, I hope to live frugally and to be transferred to a cohort; but here nothing will be accomplished without money, and letters of recommendation will have no value unless a man help himself" (*P.Mich.* 8.468 lat. = Pighi, *Lettere latine,* 4). The promise of frugality may well have been only a pious wish, and this young man was perhaps living beyond his means, overestimating what a military life-style should be. He may have been a young man who, dissatisfied with familial subsidies, used the weapon of vanity when he reported his comrades' mockery: how could he be so short of cash if he was a soldier's son? (See also *BGU* 3.814.) Even taking into account that a spendthrift son may have been using an easy argument, this anecdote is significant: A soldier was expected to show by his life-style the dignity of his social position and the relative wealth that accompanied it.

I might also remark that the Egyptian legionaries stationed at the gates of Alexandria sent as many (if not more) packages to their families—foodstuffs and craft products unavailable in the villages—as they received from them. More important, the money they asked from their kin was often connected with the payment of purchases relatives had commissioned. There is an immediately observable and astonishing consumption mentality within the military milieu that supposes both a financial and a psychological penchant for spending for things well beyond strict necessity. It has long been remarked that the army camps and the military centers attracted productive and commercial activity in the Roman empire, but this notion has remained somewhat theoretical, even when it was founded on incontestable archaeological information. The soldiers' correspondence—which often contains nothing but long lists of purchases, packages sent and received, and a variety of products, comparing their price, quality, and availability from one place to another—provides us with the sociopsychological basis of the phenomenon. The close relations between soldiers and the civilian population that resulted from local recruitment allowed the army to play a role of encouraging consumption by the example of its own standard of living, but also by its intermediary role as it relied on networks of sociability to transport the rarest and most exotic products of the region to the provincials of the local hinterland. If the term "romanization" can mean the integration of local and sectorial cultures into vaster circuits of exchange, we can say that the Roman soldier was an economic agent of romanization.

From the point of view of his economic position the soldier's specificity was defined less by his wealth than by the availability of hard cash in a society where that commodity was usually lacking and in which personal loans were particularly remunerative, given the nearly usurious rates that were practiced legally. Soldiers very frequently appear as lenders in the contracts that have come down to us, and at their death soldiers and veterans seem to have much of their wealth placed in a number of personal loans. This explains the relatively small size of the legionaries' estates (*bona domestica*) registered by the Egyptian probate office. Another reason was the real estate investments made during a soldier's term of service. As for the modesty of the obligatory sums paid into the regimental coffers (*bona castrensia*) and later turned over to the soldiers' heirs, it proves that, besides his pay, the other gratuities paid to the legionary— the *donativa* in particular—were immediately available to him (the text of Vegetius cited to support the contrary position uses *donativum* in the sense of *stipendium:* Vegetius *Epitoma rei militaris* 2.20). Thanks to the soldier's opportunities for profitable investment of part of his wages, those wages were worth more in practice than their nominal value. Thus we find the Roman army in a somewhat unexpected but important role that illustrates how the soldier occupied a contact zone between the money circuit set in motion by the imperial administration and a largely self-sufficient peasant economy that often found it difficult to find the cash needed for taxes. As both a consumer and a lender of small sums, the soldier contributed to and extended the monetary economy.

Another characteristic of wealth among the military was that it was accumulated more by families than by individuals in a milieu in which a number of family members chose a military career. Thus the luckiest profited from the service of the deceased, whose inheritance was accumulated from one generation to another. If we consider that only one out of two soldiers who signed up at the age of twenty (according to the calculations of A. R. Burns) ever reached retirement age and could profit from the cumulative economic benefits that came with the completion of a military career, we can see that success for the Roman soldier meant, above all, survival—that is, living longer than the other soldiers who might be in the family and reaching the end of his period of service alive. We can also see why the average veteran in our sources was better off and more respected than the average soldier. In this lottery of life, the soldier does not seem to be more at a disadvantage than the civilian, and even seems to hold a slight advantage until the age of forty. However, he had more to lose than the civilian—economically, at least—if he drew a losing number. The imperial promise of a retirement bonus at the end of a completed *militia* had to be kept to only one-half of the men to whom it had been made, and it was an incitement to remain in the service beyond the legal tour of duty.

Given that the Roman soldier of the early Empire was more likely to meet an early death thanks to the general conditions of ancient demography than from the risks of his profession, funeral monuments provide a somewhat less imprecise gauge of soldiers' wealth.

Perhaps because of the public nature of their profession—and in Rome what was public left traces in epigraphy and monuments—but also because of their pride in their chosen profession, soldiers gave their tomb, stele, or funerary altar a relatively greater importance than did other social groups of an equivalent level. A small number mention their cost, which has enabled Richard Duncan-Jones to select twenty or more prices for comment. Funerary display in general seems to have been more competitive in Italy, where soldiers were better paid, than in Africa. Italian soldiers' tombs, during the period under consideration here, ranged from a cost of 500 to 1,250 denarii, as compared to an average price of 200 denarii in Africa (a legionary's annual pay was 300 denarii). It is true, however, that the monuments erected for soldiers and noncommissioned officers by their heirs usually kept to the minimum amount set aside for that purpose in the unit's fund or stipulated in the funerary college's death benefits. Veterans, on the other hand, usually built a tomb during their lifetime, often spending at least three times as much as heirs, the sum being limited only by the client's desires. There does not seem to be any relationship between rank and funerary expenditure: one African centurion spent as much as 15,600 denarii; one of his African colleagues only 2,500 denarii. Two African veterans, simple soldiers, spent as much (6,500 denarii) as another African centurion. Although such figures, which depend on arbitrary private decisions, prevent us from making any statistical exploitation of the data, at least they provide a measure both of the heterogeneity of personal wealth within the military and of a diversity of cultural aspirations and systems of values that reigned in the army despite strong unifying pressures.

The imperial soldier found it difficult to free himself from the label of "country bumpkin" (*rusticus, agrestis*) in the last century of the Republic; such terms bore all the pejorative connotations that city dwellers, under the influence of Greek culture, attributed to country people: naïveté, vulgarity, and stupidity. Soldiers were portrayed as unable to grasp city jokes, as the innocent butt of pleasantries, but as capable of reacting with utter brutality when pushed too far (Tacitus *Historiae* 2.88.4, 3.32.4). As late as the third century, the conventional portrait of the soldier was applied to the Pannonian, the typical soldier of the age: "The inhabitants of the district of Pannonia are tall men of fine physique, natural and fierce fighters, but intellectually dull and slow-witted when it comes to crafty words or subtle actions" (Herodian 2.9.11). These commonplaces were reinforced by the anachronistic theme of the theatrical stock character of the soldier, whose silly boasting was expressed in special speech patterns and in bombastic tirades full of whirling words and clattering consonants that evoked the clash of arms. Was the Roman soldier truly the ignorant rustic that men of letters usually present?

Ancient writers have transmitted to us some quotations—isolated terms for the most part—that actually belonged to the *sermo militaris,* the language spoken in the camps. It is a sampling distorted both by its isolation from context and by its written transcription of utterances typical of oral language. Modern scholars have been tempted to see such expressions as a mere argot, signs of mutual recognition, and a contribution to a group identity of a category marginalized by respectable society. Linguists today, however, tend to see the available corpus, highly limited though it is, as a heterogeneous set of data that sometimes reveals a "group language," at other times a "specialized language," and at still other times a "level of language." Our ignorance of Roman familiar speech, the *sermo vulgaris* commonly spoken in the empire, has led some modern scholars to exaggerate the deviance of military language from normal usage.

The most visible characteristics of the *sermo militaris*—a fondness for expressive force and concision; a taste for ironic or humorous expressions (Petronius' *iocositas: Satyricon* 82); images and metaphors pushed to the limits of grotesque distortion; an inventiveness and fantasy in neologisms—all bear the mark of a popular level of language, the point of departure of a military language that might easily seem obscure to the noninitiate when applied to technical referents specific to the military profession.

Moreover, the Roman army covered two quite distinct linguistic areas, the Latin-speaking West and the Greek-speaking East, where Latin had been imposed as the official military language for record keeping in both the auxiliary units and the legions, which meant that the soldiers responsible for written reports (the *signiferi* in particular) needed to be able to write Latin. This does not mean that some soldiers of Eastern extraction were not perfectly capable of writing a text in a respectable Latin that, at the most, bears some trace of syntactical and phonetic interference from the Greek that they spoke fluently, along with the local language. This situation gave the army an important role in exchanges and borrowings between Greek and Latin, and it made military language to some extent a language of international communication.

The early date of several of these borrowings even suggests that the Roman military chancery of the late Republic had adopted elements from the Hellenistic armies, which also provided a model of a permanent army. Among these were shorthand symbols (*notae militares*): military headquarters designated the soldiers killed in combat and the survivors with Greek letters (theta and tau, respectively). The use of the theta even gave rise to a Latinized derivation, *thetatus* (killed in combat), a good illustration of the mechanics of the *sermo militaris*. Exchanges between Greek and Latin that developed out of the circulation of soldiers in the Mediterranean area could take less refined forms, as evidenced by one soldier who, in a graffito in Pompeii, latinizes the Greek verb *binein* (in the sense of the Latin *futuere*) to glorify his erotic exploits. This example shows the slang aspect of the *sermo militaris*, but Greek freedmen who moved to the West must have used a similar language.

It would be interesting to know how many soldiers were educated and how many had only the rudiments of learning, but there are few documents that permit any statistical evaluation. One exception is a papyrus conserved in Hamburg that gives a notion of the various levels of literacy in an Egyptian cavalry unit in A.D. 179 (*P.Hamb.*, 39 = Fink, *RMR*, 76). On this scroll eighty of the some five hundred men in the unit acknowledge, one after the other, receipt of their annual allocation of hay, an exercise in written Greek that occupies on the average six lines. Thirty-six of these men wrote their own statements, eleven of them also writing for an illiterate comrade; fifty-six men had someone else write for them, although three of them could sign their names. In this auxiliary unit recruited for the most part in Egypt (thus, in principle, Greek-speaking), the writing-illiterate were in the great majority, a proportion that scarcely changes if we add the twelve hands who only wrote for others than themselves in the fragment conserved, a group composed in part of *signiferi* (noncommissioned officers and professional writers). The literate group shows a broad range of departures from the linguistic norm, certain extremely weak spellings reflecting phonetic approximations. It should be noted, however, that the soldiers illiterate in Greek may easily have been literate in Egyptian and that, in any event, the ability to write Greek was more widespread in this military unit than in the civilian population. As a point of comparison the file of requests for inclusion in the wheat dole in Oxyrhynchus (third century) presented by civilians who belonged to the middle and upper classes of the city reveals that more than two-thirds of them did not write Greek. An even smaller group could write Latin in the army in the East but this minority had access to a "vehicular" culture that was relatively uniform from one end of the empire to the other, as shown by the remarkable similarity in the way Latin was written in Egypt and in Britannia (Britain).

The scholars who have edited the wooden tablets (some wax-surfaced) found in recent years in the camp of Vindolanda remark that although some of the writing is awkward, most hands are easy and well formed, and there are even a few examples of calligraphy. It seems to me that this confirms the notion that some soldiers came from an urban, relatively wealthy, and well-educated milieu. One veteran from Ancyra (now Ankara) and his wife, for example, gave a good education to their son, who was born in the camp (and named Castrensis). On a stele they lament his death at the age of thirteen and declare him "adorned with all the forms of grace, knowledge, and culture [*paideia*]" (first half of the third century; *AE* [1981]: 784). Similarly legionaries and noncommissioned officers in the West, among other milieus, had verse epigraphs engraved on their tombs in imitation of the middle classes in the municipalities (though the aristocratic elites of the early Empire did not follow their example).

Soldiers who did not themselves come from the city came into contact with comrades who had been raised in the spirit of *urbanitas,* and since the military hierarchy for a long time mirrored the sociocultural hierarchy, each level of officers had the opportunity to associate with people of higher rank. As René Rebuffat has noted, military life was for officers "a veritable language school." If officers did not know Latin well, they (and some ordinary soldiers) learned a fluent verision of it shaped by its times and by an unlearned milieu. It was a Latin with a syntax more simplified than its vocabulary, but it gave access to a vast literary culture. In a word it was "robust."

Rebuffat's reflections were inspired by a study of the verse inscriptions of the commanders of the Severan fort of Gholaia (now Bu Ngem) in Libya. They show us a centurion of African origin, one M. Porcius Iasuchtan, who was inspired to imitate the verses—respectable classical iambic trimeters—of his predecessor Q. Avidius Quintianus, who was himself born into a Latin-speaking milieu and the brilliant product of a *grammaticus'* school. Both men had served under superior officers whose privileged sociocultural situation has recently found new confirmation in the publication of the correspondence, in Latin, between the wives of unit commanders stationed in Britain at Hadrian's Wall (this correspondence is the oldest known example of a Latin autograph text written in a woman's hand).

Thus the Roman army was not an intellectual and cultural desert. The contrary would have been astonishing in an army that drew its force from a "military culture"—a culture in the strict sense of a set of intellectual acquisitions and techniques inculcated in people in proportion to their responsibilities—and from a moral and psychological conditioning, only one aspect of which was "discipline" in the technical sense. As the geographical and sociological areas of its recruitment changed, the army contributed to the cultural unification of its new components and served as an agent of acculturation. The growing tendency toward a hereditary military profession reinforced the culturally active forces within the army, a trend that increased during the trials of the third century. When the military came to power at the end of that century, the new regime ushered in changes of a cultural sort, in that it brought to the great problems of politics and administration a more "scientific" mentality and attitudes and a rationalism more "technical" than philosophical that inevitably clashed with the idealistic, liberal, and individualistic humanism of the previous dominant culture.

To turn from discourse to images, there is a tendency today to abandon the idea of a "soldiers' art," because the soldiers' funerary monuments that include iconographic motifs (a minority) merely include references to the military among the formulas and decorative schemes commonly in use in civil society. It is probable (but not demonstrable) that in some instances the sculptor was a soldier, but if so the ideological message of the monument did not reflect his status. Soldiers also followed the fashions in funeral customs (incineration or inhumation) and commemorations (altar, stele, sarcophagus) as they varied from one period or region to another.

Soldiers' funerary representations aimed at showing military values as heroic but without cutting the soldier off from the universal essence of common humanity. The Roman soldier demanded of the artist (who complied with uneven results) that he glorify "the servitude and the grandeur" (as Alfred de Vigny said) of the military. This meant depicting the soldier's arms and uniform in their three levels of value, as regulation, function, and metonym; it meant showing professional competence and military valor (demonstrated by decorations proudly displayed). For officers it meant depicting a sense of authority, a responsible, determined attitude, and a physical bearing enhanced by the prestige of the uniform. This soldierly "authority" finds its clearest expression (but not its most grandiloquent) in high reliefs of cuirassed soldiers wearing the *lorica seg-*

mentata (ornamental breastplate) in which the figures show the direct influence of monumental statues of the emperor as a military commander and make clear the reciprocal ties between the soldier and the master of the empire. Soldier and emperor both incarnated a force that preferred tranquillity, that was sure of itself and showed the same equanimity as the "guardians" of Plato's city; a force capable of channeling potential violence—*thymos*—into appropriate aims and of keeping desires in check. The harshness and the risks of military life and its cruelty, legitimized by the soldier's function, were played down, omitted, and neutralized. The soldier clearly manifested his adherence to the organizing structure that stood opposed to barbarian disorder and a self-possession gained by conquering the violence of human nature and sustained by a *disciplina* that included both wisdom and knowledge. When the Roman chose an image to perpetuate his memory, he did not show himself in the thick of the fight amid violent combat, as was sometimes true of the Greek predecessors whose bloody themes were imitated by the auxiliary cavalry of the early Empire.

Thus the Roman soldier did not exploit the murderous efficacy of the Roman army, pitilessly deployed in the triumphal representations of official art, to intimidate civilians or affirm his own social personality. Nor does the contrast between these two sorts of iconography stop there. Whereas triumphal columns and arches have accustomed us to multiple images of an anonymous "standard" soldier without emotion or individuality (the image most likely to reassure civil society about its defense), in steles and funerary altars the Roman army became a collection of individual identities showing proof of an individualistic ideal that had informed classical civilization for some time. The "idealizing realism" of triumphal art that abandoned faces to concentrate on actions had a different function in military funerary representations. The soldiers' attachment to the "portrait"—a style particularly well developed in Italy in the late Republic that spread to provincial garrisons with the recruits from the peninsula who first served there—also existed in the East, to judge by the Egyptian recruit whose first communication to his family contained a "portrait" of himself, probably executed on papyrus (*BGU* 2.423). The prevalence of this type of representation among the soldiers of the empire, which Bianchi Bandinelli has presented as characteristic of a "democratized" art, does indeed conform with a certain "democratic" structure of the Roman army—an army that never created a closed caste and never gave rise to military "lineages," even during the period in which army careers were in practice hereditary; an army that transmitted the values of the lower or middle classes but that also adopted popularized forms of elitist culture and the classical *paideia*.

As we advance into the imperial epoch, funerary representations of soldiers in combat dress disappear, replaced by depictions of soldiers in the simple regimental dress (tunic and cloak thrown on the shoulders) that more resembled civilian dress, when they were not portrayed in the toga, the symbol of the civilian par excellence (as in Cicero's wish for peace, *cedant arma togae!* "may arms be replaced by togas"). In certain cases this dress may express the acquisition of citizenship at the end of military service. On other monuments the soldier is accompanied by his father or his son wearing the toga. Some scholars have presented this change as a reflection of a supposed mingling of the civilian and the military spheres in a later age and of an even more contestable weakening of the bellicose nature of the military profession. It is obvious that the soldier of the fourth century had not become "a craftsman or a functionary who could, when the occasion arose, take up arms again and affront a war" if we reread Ammianus Marcellinus. The military function retained its specificity, but this evolution in the image that the soldier wanted to project of himself shows his desire to share with civilians the celebration of, demand for, and practice of common cultural values—the values that the aristocracy had established as dominant. The soldier, or at least the noncommissioned officer or the centurion (who, as we have seen, at times flirted with the Muses), posed for eternity as a man of learning (*musikos anēr, vir litteratus*) and made no more reference to his earthly profession than civilians did. Like them, we can even see him holding a *volumen,* a papyrus or parchment scroll that some have interpreted as his enrollment papers but that was simply the cultural object par excellence and the form in which literary texts were transmitted until the *codex* made its appearance. Without denying their military condition these soldiers wanted to show that it had neither cut them off from the civilized world nor prevented them from knowing the "true good." At the same time, the face becomes less individualized and the clothing less realistic. When he does not wear the toga the soldier in fourth-century funerary art wears the pleated tunic of the early Empire, which by that time had been abandoned as a regulation uniform and replaced by the *camisia* (originally a term in military jargon), a sewn tunic with tube sleeves, the ancestor of modern dress. Although this new uniform is well attested in official iconography (in the Luxor fresco and in the mosaic of the "Great Hunt" at Piazza Armerina, for instance), where it immediately reduces the soldier to his military condition alone, it appears on no funerary monument.

The abandonment of realism for an idealized expressionism and the renunciation of the individual portrait in order to show membership in a broader human category (both social and spiritual) are not incompatible with a continuing military specificity and esprit de corps. What they express, and incontestably, is the soldier's need for affirmation and recognition in the cultural practice of the elites, from which civilians seemed rather hastily disposed to exclude him by continuing to regard him, in the traditional way, as a rustic. We too need to revise our judgment (the soldier-rustic is still found among modern historians) without falling into the opposite excess. Was there not some discrepancy between the representation that these military men wanted to give of themselves and their real personality? One might reply to this that a similar overvaluation must have existed among civilians. And were not the soldiers who displayed such refined tastes a wealthier minority who could afford the expense of a decorated tomb? What is more important, however, is that such representations are found at all levels of the hierarchy and in all types of military units, which shows the diffusion of the phenomenon and its potential value as an example and an incitement in a structure as integrative as the Roman army.

Moreover, the imperial soldier continued to face the problem of identity that had always plagued the Roman solider in his dual function of a protector of civilized order and a technician of primitive, impulsive violence. The problem had originally been represented, overcome, and assimilated into the individual and collective consciousness through figurations of *furor*. It is a possible hypothesis that in later ages the success in military circles of Mithraism, with its antithetical and hierarchized vision of man, aiming at the sublimation of primordial forces, was another attempt to reconcile these two elements.

One cannot help being struck by the difference between the soldier's image and discourse about himself and the civilian's view of him. As in the fable of the elephant and the blind men, "civilians" often represented the soldier on the basis of the partial and particular forms they saw of the vast organism of the Roman army, and, even more often, on the basis of the absence of the soldier as an element in their own landscape. In order to understand the sometimes disappointing superficiality of civilians' image of the soldier of the first two centuries of the Empire, we must first see under what conditions civilians might have had contact with the military.

Of all the large cities of the empire—those whose opinion counted, was expressed, and has come down to us—Rome and Alexandria were the only ones whose populations had constant contact with a massive and permanent military presence. Rome had the Praetorian Guard, the troops best treated economically and most closely connected with the vicissitudes of the Empire; Rome also had the urban cohorts, the troops most specialized in the maintenance of order; finally, it had the emperor's personal guard, which offered the most extreme image of barbarian presence in the army. This odd combination of the least characteristic forms of the Roman army did little to enlighten the population of the capital about the nature of the Roman army as a whole.

The Italian peninsula, which Augustus had to some extent kept under military pressure by establishing a number of veterans' colonies ready to lend him a hand if need be, became increasingly demilitarized from that point on. Not that it stopped contributing recruits: most of the 4,500 praetorians—10,000 with Septimius Severus—were enrolled from Italy until the Severi. Rather, the ordinary presence of soldiers became less customary on the peninsula, and civilians only saw soldiers when the latter came home on leave or returned as veterans—that is, returned to civilian life. They saw the reality of the army only in episodic but dramatic (at times traumatic) circumstances that left lasting traces in memory—when Italy became a battlefield for claimants to the imperial throne. Herodian tells us of the terror of the Italian cities in A.D. 193, when "the inhabitants of Italy had long ago abandoned armed warfare" and "were naturally panic-stricken at such as unusual event" (2.11.3–6). The memory of analogous tragic events in 69 when the armies of Vitellius and Vespasian clashed were still fresh in their minds. These, too, were not the most propitious conditions for an objective evaluation of the soldier. He became a disquieting personage, both when his passage was remembered and when the civilian imagination conjured up a being who had subsequently returned to frontiers so distant that they seemed mythical where continual frequentation with barbarians, rather than "civilizing" him, would accentuate everything that predestined him for perturbing civil life.

For the provinces, even those closer to the military frontier, the situation was not fundamentally different. After the first century, when the great concentrations of legionaries that had been established in the heart of those territories were abandoned, the soldier was still a peripheral figure whose only contact with the provincial was as an agent of repression or a scout intent on requisitioning supplies from civilian stores. There were few regions like Egypt, where the absence of frontier outposts increased opportunities for social, economic, familial, and human contacts between civilians and soldiers throughout the province. Proximity did not necessarily bring better understanding, even less osmosis, but at least the two milieus got to know one another. This is what happened in the fourth century after a thorough reorganization of military bases that instituted deep defenses, when civilians and the military were once more side by side but also in competition, given the unavoidable rigidity of this strategic but also economic and financial reorganization of the empire's resources.

In any event, civil society never admitted either the utility or the necessity for a permanent army in the form in which Augustus had created it. Nor could it ever manage to situate accurately the "social distance" of the soldier, a figure at once astonishingly close to one of the two centers of social life in the Roman world, the emperor, and astonishingly distant from the other, the city.

We can understand better, under these conditions, how the soldier lent himself so well to *topoi*. Often contradictory as circumstances and users changed, usually anachronistic because they could not keep up with a changing reality, often borrowed unchanged from an older repertory, these *topoi* nonetheless filled the void of the soldier's place in collective representations. The malaise generated by a misconception of the "real soldier" was reinforced by the realization that the army was a political entity actively monopolized by the princeps. The fact that civil society was dispossessed of its army completed the transformation of the soldier into a role—thus an abstraction—rather than a person. He was, more than ever, a *miles,* a singular with a collective sense.

Bibliography

Armées et fiscalité dans le monde antique. Actes du Colloque du Centre national de la recherche scientifique (14–16 octobre 1976). Paris: Editions du C.N.R.S., 1977.

Barthes, Roland. *Mythologies.* Paris: Editions du Seuil, 1957. Available in English as *Mythologies.* Trans. and ed. Annette Lavers. New York: Hill & Wang, 1972.

Bastien, Pierre. *Monnaie et donativa au Bas-Empire.* Wetteren: Numismatique Romaine, 1988.

Birley, Eric. *Roman Britain and the Roman Army: Collected Papers.* Kendal: T. Wilson, 1953.

Bowman, A. K., and J. D. Thomas. *Vindolanda: the Latin Writing-Tablets.* Britannia Monograph 4. London: Society for the Promotion of Roman Studies; Gloucester: Alan Sutton, 1984.

———. "New Texts from Vindolanda." *Britannia* 18 (1987): 125–42.

Breeze, David J. "The Organisation of the Career Structure of the *immunes* and *principales* of the Roman Army." *Bonner Jahrbücher* 174 (1974): 245–92.

Carrié, Jean-Michel. "L'esercito: trasformazioni funzionali ed economie locali." In *Società romana e impero tardoantico,* ed. Andrea Giardina. 4 vols. Rome and Bari: Laterza, 1986. Vol. 1, *Istituzioni, ceti, economie.* Chap. 12, 449–88, 760–79.

Christol, M. "Armées et société politique dans l'Empire romain au IIIe siècle après J.C. (de l'époque sévérienne au début de l'époque constantinienne)." *Civiltà Classica e Cristiana* 9, 2 (August 1988): 169–204.

Davies, Roy W. "The Daily Life of the Roman Soldier under the Principate." In *Aufstieg und Niedergang.* Vol. 2, pt. 1, 299–330. In the same volume, see also the articles by Jacques Harmond, Giovanni Forni, and David J. Breeze.

———. *Service in the Roman Army.* Ed. David Breeze and Valerie A. Maxfield. Edinburgh: Edinburgh University Press, 1989.

Durry, Marcel. *Les cohortes prétoriennes.* Reprint of 1938 ed. Paris: E. de Boccard, 1968.

Eck, Werner, and Martmut Wolff, eds. *Heer und Integrationspolitik: Die römischen Militärdiplome als historische Quelle.* Passauer Historische Forschungen 2. Cologne: Böhlau, 1986.

Fentress, Elizabeth W. B. *Numidia and the Roman Army: Social, Military and Economic Aspects of the Frontier Zone.* Biblioteca dell'Archivum Romanicum Int. Ser. 53. Oxford: BAR, 1979.

Fink, Robert O. *Roman Military Records on Papyrus.* Cleveland: For the American Philological Association by the Press of Case Western University, 1971.

Fitz, Jenö. *Les Syriens à Intercisa.* Collection Latomus 122. Brussels: Latomus, 1972.

Forni, Giovanni. *Il reclutamento delle legioni da Augusto a Diocleziano.* Milan and Rome: Fratelli Bocca, 1953.

Franzoni, Claudio. *Habitus atque habitudo militaris: Monumenti funerari di militari nella Cisalpina Romana.* Studia Archaeologica 45. Rome: "L'Erma" di Bretschneider, 1987.

Gabba, Emilio. *Esercito e società nella tarda Repubblica romana.* Florence: La Nuova Italia, 1973.

———. *Per la storia dell'esercito romano in età imperiale.* Bologna: Pàtron, 1974.

Gilliam, J. F. *Roman Army Papers.* Mavors Roman Army Researches, 2. Amsterdam: J. C. Gieben, 1986.

Giuffrè, Vincenzo. *Iura e Arma: Intorno al VII libro del Codice Teodosiano.* 3d ed. corr. and amp. Naples: Jovene, 1983.

Harmand, Jacques. *L'armée et le soldat à Rome de 107 à 50 avant notre ère.* Paris: A. & J. Picard, 1967.

Keppie, Lawrence. *The Making of the Roman Army: From Republic to Empire.* Totowa, N.J.: Barnes & Noble, 1984.

Le Roux, Patrick. *L'armée romaine et l'organisation des provinces ibériques d'Auguste à l'invasion de 409.* Paris: Boccard, 1982.

Mann, J. C. *Legionary Recruitment and Veteran Settlement during the Principate.* Ed. M. M. Roxan. Occasional Publication 7. London: Institute of Archaeology, 1983.

Mosci Sassi, Maria Grazia. *Il sermo castrensis.* Bologna: Pàtron, 1983.

Nicolet, Claude. *Le métier de citoyen dans la Rome républicaine.* Paris: Gallimard, 1976; 2d ed. 1979. Available in English as *The World of the Citizen in Republican Rome.* Trans. P. S. Falla. Berkeley: University of California Press, 1980.

Pighi, Giovanni Battista. *Lettere latine d'un soldato di Traiano (P.Mich. 467–472).* New crit. ed. Bologna: Zanichelli, 1964.

Pikhaus, Dorothy. "Les origines sociales de la poésie épigraphique latine: L'exemple des provinces nord-africaines." *L'antiquité classique* 50 (1981): 637–54.

Rebuffat, René. "Le poème de Q. Avidius Quintianus à la déesse Salus." *Karthage* 21 (1987): 93–105.

Roxan, Margaret M. "The Distribution of Roman Military Diplomas." *Epigraphische Studien* 12 (1981): 265–85.

Speidel, Michael. *Roman Army Studies.* Mavors Roman Army Researches 1. Amsterdam: J. C. Gieben, 1984.

Vendrand-Voyer, Jacqueline. *Normes civiques et métier militaire à Rome sous le Principat.* Clermont-Ferrand: Adosa, 1983.

Watson, G. R. *The Roman Soldier.* Ithaca, N.Y.: Cornell University Press, 1969.

5

The Slave

Yvon Thébert

GRECO-ROMAN ANTIQUITY HAS a special appeal for our sensibility. There is a general notion that our civilization has inherited from the Greeks and the Romans some of its most characteristic traits and constantly borrows their philosophical and literary themes and aesthetic forms. This familiarity is violently contradicted, however, by practices that introduce a profoundly jarring note of barbarity in what is considered as civilization par excellence. At a distance, that juxtaposition is viewed as an insurmountable contradiction. How could they invent philosophy and politics; how could they erect monuments that so perfectly embodied those new values, and at the same time make human beings fight in the amphitheater or reduce a portion of humanity to slavery?

This contradiction is not superficial. If political freedom—the fact that the notion of citizen took precedence over that of subject—seems intimately linked with the city, the same is true of slavery. Only in the world of the *polis* did slavery become the dominant form of dependence. It even reached its height in certain cities in which sweeping reforms had done away with the mass of the local subjected population. The Spartans had their Helots, but the Athenians, after reforms in the archaic age had expanded the citizen body, no longer had available in Attica a similar mass of dependents. Slaves, for the most part brought from outside, rapidly filled that gap, long before Aristotle theorized on the connection between the slave and the barbarian.

In Rome, plebeian struggles created a comparable situation. The constitution of a community of soldier–property owners—a group of citizens that included most of the population—made it necessary to exploit foreigners reduced to slavery. The slave's total loss of liberty derived from being both uprooted and excluded from the group to which he was arbitrarily attached. Inversely, it is extremely significant that before the Empire, Roman law narrowly restricted the enslavement of citizens and, in extreme cases of the sort, stipulated that the condemned person must be sold outside the city of Rome. Given the intimate connection between slavery and the *polis,* it seems logical that slavery underwent an unprecedented expansion in the most powerful city and that it declined when Rome's institutions changed radically.

The slave was defined, essentially, by antithesis. Irrespective of the profound variations brought throughout the centuries by the vicissitudes of history, he remained a negative image of the citizen. For Aristotle, man was above all a political animal, but the slave lacked the faculty of deliberation (*Politics* 1.13.7). The citizen's mode of life implied the leisure (*scholē* or *otium*) that permitted him to pursue creative activities, the first of which was politics; the slave by definition had no leisure. Like a domestic animal, he worked, and he ate and slept to renew his strength for work. He was equated with his function and was for his master what the ox was for the poor man (ibid., 1.2.5): an animated object that he owned. The same idea is a constant in Roman law, where the slave is frequently associated with other parts of a patrimony, sold by the same rules that governed transfer of a parcel of land or included with tools or animals in a bequest. Above all he was an object, a *res mobilis.* Unlike the waged worker, no distinction was made between his person and his labor.

The slave's servile status thus occupied a specific place among the various forms of dependence. It imposed precautions on a master who wanted to avoid insubordination, but it permitted a particularly intense exploitation of the subjected person. This explains why slaves existed well before the development of the city and persisted well after—in the West to the early eleventh century. It also explains the renascence of slavery in more recent epochs as a dominant mode for the exploitation of manpower in societies that often were colonial and capable of setting up extremely coercive systems.

In antiquity, the permanence of the essential components of slavery must not blind us to important changes that took place. In particular, it seems that as the system of the city ceased to be the essential framework for organizing people's lives, the fundamental opposition between free men and slaves became the major division in humanity. Aristotle's thought is still organized around the notion of the citizen. Although book 1 of the *Politics* contrasts the free man and the slave, it is clear that, for

Aristotle, man is by his nature destined to live in the city (1.2.9). More-over, Aristotle's first move in book 3 is to distinguish between the citizen and the noncitizen, using criteria that are essentially political and that amount to participation in power, albeit in a broad range of forms. This still very classical procedure sets up a major break between citizen and noncitizen, was the result that the slave, rather than being isolated, is grouped with other categories contrasted to the citizen such as metics, foreigners, dependents of various sorts, and even the young, the old, and women, who had citizenship without full enjoyment of its rights. In this sense it is significant that all that Aristotle has to say about the slave in book 1 of the *Politics* is constantly intermingled with parallel remarks about the child and the woman. The major break that passed between the citizen and the other members of his family supported an argument that there was a difference of kind between power in the city and the power of the head of family over his slaves, his wife, and his children. In the domestic sphere the man's three original relationships of master, husband, and father were all, by their nature, relations of superior to inferior.

The city remained an essential framework in the centuries that fol-lowed, but when, with the development of monarchies, cities became subjected to larger political entities, their independence was considerably reduced. The ideal of the subject entered into competition with that of the citizen. The Roman Empire accelerated this evolution, and citizenship came to mean less and less that of a specific city and more and more Roman citizenship—a state citizenship, no longer anchored to a narrow geographical base, which spread within the mass of the population until the edict of Caracalla (A.D. 212) granted citizen status to all free men.

The major dividing line among humankind shifted: rather than set-ting off the citizen from the rest of humanity, henceforth it was the slave who was isolated. Lack of freedom had become the distinguishing feature. This evolution is clearly perceptible among the jurists as early as the mid-second century A.D. Gaius begins by dividing humanity into free men and slaves; the *summa divisio personarum* (*Institutiones* 1.9). Very soon—by the third century—this essential division shifted again, to lie between *honestiores* and *humiliores*. We shall have occasion to return to them.

This radical submission of one part of humanity to benefit another part throws a harsh light on the realities of Greco-Roman society. It is not enough to renounce the idealistic approach—that is, to recognize that the remarkable achievements of antiquity rested on a ferociously exhibited exploitation—to resolve what seems to be a fundamental contradiction: how can anyone praise the liberty of the citizen and defend the principle of slavery? Before attempting to answer that question, we need to take a closer look at slavery in the ancient world.

The first thing to note is the great heterogeneity that existed among slaves. Slaves were defined by a juridical status that in a general manner deprived them of personality, transformed them into owned objects that could be bought and sold, and subjected them to the authority of a master—in short, that assimilated them to domestic animals. In the Greek cities the same law was often applied to slaves and animals, and the association can frequently be found in Roman law as well, for example in Ulpian, a jurist of the third century, who on several occasions compares the fugitive slaves to lost livestock. Between these dates, Cato follows chapters on slaves' rations with a consideration of fodder for oxen (*De agri cultura* 56–58, 59). This is not a coincidental juxtaposition. What unified the servile world was thus a juridical definition that applied to all its members. This unity was contradicted, however, by the practical uses of slaves, which could vary enormously.

Scholars have often noted an essential difference between rural slaves and those employed in the city, particularly when the latter worked in their master's household. This notion seems to hold true: the countryside rose up in the great servile revolt led by Spartacus, but there seems to have been little or no reaction from urban slaves. This is quite understandable. Most of the slaves used in the country were put to hard labor. They had little contact with their master and were often subjected to a severe discipline designed to get as much work out of them as possible. In spite of some diversity in their situations, the term *ascholoi*—without free time—applies best to the rural slaves. Cato's treatise *De agri cultura* 31.1 tells what can be done in inclement weather (*ubi tempestates malae erunt, quid fieri possit*). The spirit behind this passage is clear: what had to be avoided above all else was to leave your manpower idle, for expenses never cease. A slave who was not working was a slave who cost money instead of bringing it in.

Even the more privileged slaves were kept busy doing the tasks entrusted to them. Cato gives us an example of this in his discussion of the functions of the *vilica*, the wife of the *vilicus*, the man (usually himself a slave) who managed the property for a proprietor who was only occasionally present. The *vilica* was responsible for keeping the *villa* clean and supervising the meals of all the personnel; she took care of the chickens;

she supervised the preserving of fruits and the milling of grain (*De agri cultura* 143). To make expectations perfectly clear, Cato specifies that the *vilica* must always be present, must frequent her neighbors as little as possible, and must refuse invitations and not offer any herself. All her time was taken up by her duties, and the same was true of her companion, the *vilicus*, who must be the first to rise and the last to go to bed. He was even morally obligated to accept the wife his master gave him. The entire operation was aimed at self-sufficiency in order to avoid loss of time, which was, for the proprietor, loss of earnings.

The closed system of the *villa*, where the energies of the *familia rustica* were completely given over to productive labor, contrasted with that of the *familia urbana*, where work was organized in a radically different manner. For one thing, a number of urban slaves escaped all direct, permanent control when their master charged them with the management of a range of businesses—shops or crafts operations—for his benefit. The autonomy such slaves enjoyed was without parallel in country areas, except perhaps in the case of shepherds. Next, the many slaves who populated the master's house assumed a variety of quite specific functions. They were true domestic servants, whose main purpose was to facilitate daily life for the master and his family; thus it was the masters' pleasure that dictated work rhythms rather than anything resembling the rational management of an enterprise.

This does not mean that the slaves of the *domus* were inactive, although they clearly often enjoyed less harsh working conditions than their rural counterparts. This was particularly true because the domestic staff was there not only to assure the daily operation of the household but also to display the master's power by their number and by the specialization of the tasks to which they were assigned. Gaius specifies that a guardian should give his ward a number of slaves that corresponds to the latter's *dignitas*.

We can get an idea of the complex relationships characteristic of the *familia urbana* from the *Metamorphoses* of Apuleius, a second-century African author. In this tale we can see that a great number of slaves were a part of the normal routine of a great house: one man who is wealthy but miserly dresses like a beggar and keeps only one slave (1.21); a noble lady goes about the city attended by a large troupe of domestics, and when she gives a dinner party in her house the guests are served by slaves with specialized functions—some, magnificently dressed, who cut the meat and pass the dishes; others, curly-haired young men, who offer wine (2.2.19). Like the sumptuous furnishings, the crystal, gold, and silver chalices, or the glasses cut from precious stones, they are a part of the decor of the dwelling, which they enhance by their skills, their beauty, and their number. Later in the work, we learn that a mad dog who has gotten into a rich household bites a number of the domestic servants, among them a mule driver, a cook, a chamber man, and a private doctor (9.2). Among another master's slaves are a pastry cook and sweets maker and a cook who specializes in meats, and they are clearly not the only slaves at work in the kitchens (10.13).

The city house implied relationships between master and slaves quite different from the ones that pertained when slaves were far removed from the master and put to productive labor. In the less harsh conditions of the city, the word *familia,* which included both kin and slaves, seems to take on a genuinely affective dimension and to designate not only all the persons placed under the authority—the *potestas*—of the *pater familias* but also an "affective cell," a human group that outsiders saw as unified by privileged and real bonds. This is illustrated in the *Metamorphoses* in the complaints of the noble and unlucky girl kidnapped by brigands (4.24). She is alone, she states, torn away from an eminent house (*tali domo*) with many servants (*tanta familia*) and from dear slaves born in the house (*tam caris vernulis*) and her venerable parents (*tam sanctis parentibus*). The symmetry she establishes between the slaves and her kin reflects a parallel in her mind between the two groups in the *domus.* There are other characteristic examples of this vision of the *familia* in the *Metamorphoses.* When this same girl is set free by her fiancé, "all the people of the city," her kin, and the family slaves come running to meet them (7.13).

We must not be misled by all this, however. Such paternalistic practices had their ulterior motives: they were indispensable to guaranteeing the cohesion of a band of slaves whose tasks depended too highly on the personal needs of the master. Moreover, even in the most sentimental passages of this work, the members of the ruling class never lose a sense of their rightful place, nor of the place of slaves. The pitiful kidnapped young lady who weeps for her dear relatives and domestics is not unaware of the true fate of slaves. In fact, when she speaks of her own fate, she describes herself, rather perspicaciously, as like a slave: she is reduced to slavery; closed inside a stone prison; in a place of torture. The affective ties that supposedly bind her to her own slaves in no way keep her from a realistic appreciation of servile status.

A second anecdote that shows us Venus outraged by the liaison between Psyche and her son Cupid and threatening to replace him with one of her slaves is equally revealing and just as truculent (ibid., 5.29). Indeed, Roman law permitted disinheriting an heir to the profit of an adopted slave (who was thus freed), and on one level the anecdote can be read as evidence of the intimacy between the goddess and her *vernulae,* the young slaves born in her household. She does not mislead us for long: Venus hastens to add that her choice of a new heir to Cupid's wings and arrows was an insult, an affront aimed at wounding her son. The position of subordinates was so well established that no slave could escape the rule, even if he were part of the domestic staff of a tolerant and lenient master. When a Roman asked a friend for news of himself, his wife, his children, and his domestic slaves, these terms were by no means equivalent (1.26). The health of slaves was, above all, good news for the master's prosperity.

Moreover, the realities of slavery are not absent, even in this ancient tearjerker. Fugitive slaves are mentioned on several occasions. One *vilicus,* guilty of infidelity to the wife whom his master had given him (an infidelity that cost something to the master's revenues), is smeared with honey and exposed to ants, who slowly nibble away his flesh and his viscera (8.22). A jealous master entrusts a slave with the guard of his mistress, and although he is certain of the man's exceptional fidelity, he threatens him at length, promising him prison, chains, and a slow death by hunger if he fails him (9.17). A governor who receives word of a woman suspected of a number of murders immediately has her domestics tortured (10.28). In a mill there is a band of miserable slaves scarred by the whip and clothed in rags. They are branded and chained, a lamentable state that they share, in a suggestive parallel, with the animals who turn the mill wheel (9.12–13). The miller is otherwise a good and gentle man, however (9.14).

Two things seem clear: first, a slave was a slave—that is, basically, he was someone who had no control over his fate and whose situation, comfortable as it might be in certain circumstances, could always be changed radically simply by his master's will. Second, even if the slave's destiny was completely out of his own hands, it clearly varied a great deal.

What did slaves who worked in the mines (and who, in practice, were as good as condemned to death) have in common with slaves who were an intimate part of the master's lives, whose life followed the rhythms of their master's, and who had a chance at manumission? The heterogeneity of the servile world included not only extremes such as these but also a complete and subtle hierarchy sanctioned by practice.

Jurists such as Paulus and Ulpian, who both lived in the age of the Severi, state that slaves must be fed and clothed according to their rank (*secundum ordinem et dignitatem*). In this sense, slaves hardly constituted a social class; their status reflects a juridical and ideological vision of society much more than it does real socioeconomic conditions. Still, the term "slave" remained charged with an extremely constraining social connotation. The slaves who in part shared the intimacy or the confidence of the master were only a minority, but even they remained under the threat of disgrace, and by the simple pleasure of their owner could be given corporal punishment or relegated to heavy labor.

A second essential element in slavery is chronological change. There is still a widespread tendency to treat classical antiquity as a whole and ignore the evolutions that in fact characterized that long period. Moses I. Finley's *The Ancient Economy,* which begins with a chronological summary that ranges from the eighth century B.C. to Justinian, a span of thirteen centuries, is one illustration of this unitary conception of antiquity. Finley's entire analysis rests on a global notion of antiquity, as if precise problems could be clarified by seeking information throughout the centuries and ignoring distinctions of time and place.

More recent research on slavery has played an important role in identifying decisive changes and even real breaking points throughout ancient times. In particular, such studies have shown that antiquity was not made of a simple succession of dominating powers or changes in political systems as monarchies increasingly supplanted cities of the classical type, but rather that changes in regime were based in radical changes in social and economic organization.

The scope of such overwhelming changes is reflected in the place accorded to the slave. For several centuries, the city provided the dominant framework of Mediterranean societies—which implied communities of limited size made up, for the most part, of property owners. Naturally there were tensions within these communities, in particular those prompted by a recurrent tendency toward the concentration of landholdings. In spite of occasional crises, however, life in common was regulated within the framework of the *polis,* which embodied the common interests of the citizens. Other groups coexisted with them within the city, but their place there was determined by their relation to the citizens. This was particularly true of slaves. Although they might be the collective property of the community, for the most part they belonged to citizens and constituted an essential base in the system. By their activities, slaves

consolidated the citizens' revenues, and when the owners were small
landowners, slave and master worked side by side. Slaves also permitted
citizens partial freedom from labor, hence access to free time. The noble
image of assemblies debating common problems could not have existed
without the support of a patriarchal slavery that gave even citizens of
modest wealth an opportunity to participate in politics and in the active
governance of the city.

One break occurred in the Hellenistic age. We can place it at the
third century B.C. in Greece and the very beginning of the second century
B.C. in Italy. At that time, a completely different organization was put
into place within which the slave played a totally new role. No longer
in the service of property-owning families, henceforth he was integrated
into units of production that, to the contrary, spelled the ruin of those
families and their expulsion from the land. The scope of this break was
accentuated by another change: not only did the function of the slave
change, but also, thanks to the great wars that characterized those periods, slaves were thrown onto the market in totally unprecedented
numbers.

In Italy, the only region (according to the current state of our knowledge) in which this change reached full development, this revolution had
a profound effect on the economy. The traditional peasant smallholder
was relegated to country areas away from the coast in the north of the
peninsula, where the land was worked by the owner himself, perhaps
with the help of a few slaves or seasonal waged workers in an economy
aiming largely at self-sufficiency. In Sicily and southern Italy the predominant system was the *latifundium*—an immense estate given over to raising
livestock or worked by rent-paying peasants, many of them slaves. Finally, on the Tyrrhenian coast of central Italy from Etruria to Latium
and Campania, lands were also to a great extent monopolized by large
landholders, but they were subdivided into *villae*, units of production
smaller than the *latifundia*. Everything was new about these units. The
labor, done for the most part by slaves, was rationally organized and
supervised. The farmhold surrounded a large building, the *villa* proper,
which included sumptuous buildings for the master's use when he was in
residence, cells for the slaves, and outbuildings for agricultural purposes.
Crops were extremely specialized, grown intensively, and destined for
sale, often in distant markets. In a word, the *villa* was a true rural manufacturing system run according to paramilitary discipline.

The *villa* system was by this time the prevailing agricultural structure. It permitted generous profits, thanks to its productivity and the

commercialization of its products. The *latifundium,* which was based on extensive exploitation and required little investment, played only a secondary role—though not a negligible one, in particular because it facilitated the functioning of the *villae* by furnishing them with slaves and cereals. These two complementary modes of exploitation, based in great part on slave labor, thus radically modified the situation in rural areas in nearly two-thirds of the peninsula, marginalizing small landowners or forcing them off the land and substituting intensive commercialization of agricultural products for an economy still largely directed toward self-sufficiency.

This revolution in the organization of production methods concerned craft labor as well. The traditional, small workshops, run for the most part by a family, continued to function, but their production was confined to objects of mediocre quality destined for a very limited distribution. Henceforth, production was dominated by large workshops and, above all, by veritable urban manufacturing concerns in many ways comparable to the agricultural *villae:* their average size was the same, and both aimed at large-scale production, intensive commercialization of the product, and a rational utilization of manpower, predominantly slave labor (at least where we have sufficient information to determine worker status).

The slave thus lay at the heart of a profound economic change. In manufacturing, the new way that labor was organized made the worker a simple cog in the mechanism of an overall productive process that completely escaped his grasp. A close examination of one category of ceramics produced by these methods—the black-glazed pottery called Campanian ware—permits a clearer idea of organizational procedures.

With the appearance of Campanian ware we see a systematic simplification of the work methods. For instance, the glaze was never applied with a brush but rather by immersion. The result was less precise, and the foot of the vase, which provided a handhold when it was plunged into the liquid, was not completely glazed. This seemed a minor defect in relation to the notable gain in time it permitted. In the same spirit, the forms that were used, which were not invented but borrowed from earlier objects, were often simplified, for example by the elimination of the incised fillets that decorated its models.

A second essential principle that governed the organization of work was standardization—a principle so imperative that it seems at times to contradict the search for simplification. Thus, when these vases are decorated, they bear, stamped into their base, either a central rosette or four leaves arranged radially and surrounded by circular striae. These themes are always strictly respected: we never find several rosettes, nor a rosette surrounded by striae. Moreover, the leaf motif would require a certain amount of time, since the vase would have to be turned several times. Still, this type of decoration, which was used throughout the first half of the second century B.C., was never modified: the circle of striae was never eliminated, the leaves were never lined up in the same direction, and so forth.

An essential law of this type of production thus seems to be the suppression of all individual initiative as a way to guarantee efficiency and high productivity. All connection between the buyer and the producer, or between the producer and the object he made, was abolished. Pottery was no longer made to order; rather, a range of objects was offered that was designed to cover the market's basic needs. Signatures no longer gave the owner's or the worker's name: these were anonymous pieces. These characteristics help us to reconstruct the ways in which production was organized in these manufacturing centers, with workers set to narrowly specialized tasks, each one carrying out only one of the many operations that resulted in the finished product. It was imperative to make all actions automatic and to suppress reflection, innovation, uncertainty, and adjustments. No longer could craftsmen derive a certain pride in an object they had conceived from start to finish; no longer were they sensitive to the client's needs and desires. They were veritable human machines whose juxtaposition in the same workplace permitted a mass-produced pottery whose modest price depended on the banishment of any contribution from the imagination.

We do not know the exact status of the persons who were subjected to this strict discipline and required to renounce all individual reflection, but the decisive role of slaves in similar systems at a later date is well documented. What is particularly clear is that these manufactories directly reflected the now dominant slave model. Workers who remained free men from a juridical point of view were henceforth subjected to working conditions directly inspired by the judicious exploitation of a slave. The slave, dispossessed of control over his own person, was a decisive factor in a division of labor that resulted—for the worker—in a total loss of control over the operation in which he was engaged.

This was a revolutionary innovation. It was standard practice for the worker not to own his tools, but up to this point that fact had not modified his working conditions. His actions were roughly the same whether he cultivated land he owned or worked as a tenant farmer, whether he worked for a wage on the land or in a workshop. He still remained an integral part of a system of production whose logic he understood, even when his submission to his master's commands tended to specialize his tasks. But the worker in such rural or urban manufactories not only had lost ownership of the means of production but had also lost all control over them: he was no more than a cog in a mechanism whose beginnings and ends were completely beyond his ken. He did not need to know why any specific action would be done at a given moment; he was no longer expected to do his job conscientiously and with intelligence. On the contrary, he was told not to think, and to submit to a discipline whose ends did not concern him. Some scholars have spoken, with some reason, of scientific management of the work force—Taylorism before the fact—and it is true that this radical separation of the worker from his work was a unique case, in some ways foreshadowing elements of the capitalistic mode of production.

One obvious and essential difference is the primordial role played by machines under capitalism and their minor role in antiquity. In this perspective, even the Middle Ages appear as a period of considerable technological advance in comparison to the stagnation of the Greco-Roman period (even though antiquity saw a great deal of theoretical speculation, a necessary basis for a brilliant development in technology). Many authors have even seen slavery as the reason for that stagnation.

The organization of manufacturing operations based on slave labor permits us to take a radically different approach to the problem. First, the use of slave labor in no way contradicts a search for technological improvement. It was in the *villae* that oil presses and wine presses were used most rationally, and that technological innovations connected with such devices spread most rapidly. These were innovations of such importance that they continued to be in use, almost unchanged, into modern times.

The extraordinary efficiency of a rational exploitation of slaves has too often been neglected. As Aristotle remarked, "If thus shuttles wove and quills played harps of themselves, master-craftsmen would have no need of assistants and masters no need of slaves" (*Politics* 1.4.3). But machines of this level of sophistication are not always available even today. Who could replace a slave, subjected to his master's orders and a good musician, when it came to playing an instrument? Even in the commercial sphere, what machine, before modern times, could produce ceramics like Campanian or Arretine ware and strike as fine a balance between quality and quantity, beauty and profit? Similarly what other institution could furnish needed agricultural commodities in such great abundance and at such competitive prices?

Within the framework of the slave mode of production, the slave was remarkably efficient. He was integrated into an organization that deprived him of all initiative: his human dimension was obliterated, and he was transformed into a machine that perhaps lacked the power of our modern machines but was endowed with a skill greater than any robots now existing. The ancient world was far more reliant on machines than has been thought, and when he operated within a coherent production system based on his labor, the slave was a living machine and doubtless the prime product of that system.

In this perspective, the technical innovations of late antiquity and the Middle Ages were a regression. They permitted an economy of man-power, to be sure, but in reality rudimentary machines replaced expert human machines; a more extensive economy in which the land produced little and there were many more workshops to respond to demand replaced an intensive economy that reached a remarkable level of production obtained thanks to heavy investment in human machines.

This radical transformation in how labor was organized followed the disappearance of the slave mode of production during the second century A.D. Thus there were two great breaking points in the history of slavery in the period that interests us here: the first, around 200 B.C., marked the start of an economic system that was founded on the rational exploitation of slavery and aimed at drawing the full economic benefit from the slave's status of total dependence. The second followed the collapse of the first system during the second century A.D. Moreover, there was a watershed within these four centuries between the last two centuries of the Republic and the early Empire, periods that corresponded to the high point of the slave economy and its long and gradual decline. These long chronological spans profoundly conditioned the life of the slave in Rome.

Before the Hellenistic age, the slave who was the property of a private citizen was included in the relationships that united the various members of the *familia* under the authority of the *pater familias*. It would certainly be excessive to state that the head of the household exerted the same sort of *potestas* over his children and over his slaves. In particular, his power over his children was not transferable, whereas the transmission of power was a part of the sale of a slave. Still, the situation of the son and the slave were not radically different. The Twelve Tables, the fundamental text of Roman law drawn up around the middle of the fifth century B.C., attest that a father could sell his children. Inversely, he could adopt a slave. His enormous power tends to obliterate the differences that existed among his dependents, all the more so since, in the patriarchal system, both slaves and sons served, above all, as a valuable labor force. Other measures in ancient Roman law point in the same direction. Thus, still in the Twelve Tables, anyone judged guilty of bodily harm to someone (breaking a bone, for instance) must pay a monetary indemnity to the victim, be he free or slave. The sum varies, of course, and it was double when the victim was a free man. Still, it is striking that the juridical approach to the problem is the same in the two cases: whatever the victim's social status, he had been subjected to an *iniuria*.

We must not exaggerate, though: no matter how heavily the father's authority (*patria potestas*) weighed on the son, he was essentially different from a slave. The son would himself become a citizen and the head of a family, whereas the slave would remain a slave. Still, in this period the fundamental line of demarcation separated the citizen from the noncitizen, and those under servitude were not completely isolated from the rest of society. As Aristotle did in the context of the Greek cities, we can examine the situation of the slave during the first centuries of the Republic by comparing him to the master's sons. The two situations are not identical, but they show similarities in their contrast to the dominant reality of the master and citizen.

When the system of patriarchal slavery was replaced by a true slave system, the situation of the *servus* changed radically. To return to the question of bodily harm, the *lex Aquilia* (probably late third century B.C.) introduced a fundamental distinction between the free and the nonfree: henceforth, harm done to a slave was considered as damage, not to the slave's person but to the master's property, thus depriving the dependent of all personhood. The guilty party had to pay the slave's master a sum equal to the slave's highest estimated market value in the period immediately preceding the event. Thus the slave was included in provisions that covered all threats to goods, objects, or animals.

It was this law that underlay the complex affair in which Cicero was induced to serve as the lawyer for Quintus Roscius, an actor. Roscius had trained in the dramatic arts the slave of a certain Fannius. The man who had furnished the *servus* and the one who had trained him shared the profits, which soon became considerable because the slave charged high prices for his services. One day he was killed, and the two men, both together and singly as the affair dragged on, sued the murderer, appealing to the *lex Aquilia*. Roscius eventually accepted a compromise, receiving a parcel of land instead of the stipulated indemnity. But he was not content, and a lengthy suit between the two former partners followed, which occasioned Cicero's address to the court.

It is the spirit of this text that is interesting for our purposes. The only questions Cicero raises involve money and the interests of the owners. The assassinated slave never appears as an individual: we know nothing of his personality, and it is clear that the *iniuria* was committed not toward him but toward his masters. It seems as if no manslaughter had occurred but only dilapidation of property. The dead man is conceived of as an object, and because he was the object of a joint venture, Cicero makes a distinction between his body, which belonged to Fannius, and his training, which belonged to Roscius: *Quid erat enim Fanni? Corpus. Quid Rosci? Disciplina* (*Pro Roscio Comoedo* 10.28). Furthermore, the parts of the slave dismembered with no thought to his humanity in this fashion are immediately evaluated in sesterces. We are in the world of the slave as merchandise.

Everything belonged to the master. The slave had nothing of his own and was defined only as someone's property. The way Cicero describes this actor, appreciated though he was, is remarkably revealing. Are we to believe that the actor's fame owed nothing to his personal qualities? Although we might find it surprising, Cicero finds this an obvious conclusion. The public's favor was due to the fact that he was Roscius' pupil. The celebrity of the teacher made the fame of the disciple, and only the former's efforts gave the latter any real worth. The only thing worthy of our admiration is the patience of the teacher (or the master) in training a subject so slow to comprehend.

Law soon registered this new form of slavery. Not only did the relations between masters and slaves receive increasingly strong juridical sanction but the change in practice brought about a change in vocabulary. The old term *erus,* traditionally used to designate the master as opposed to the slave, was supplanted by that of *dominus,* one illustration of the change from a patriarchal system to a system based on the notion of property. Henceforth the word *erus* survived only among the poets, who used it to give an archaic note to their verse. Even in that protected milieu it lost its original specificity and was also applied to the owner of goods or of animals—a perfect illustration of the development of the mercantile sphere, which dissolved the singularity that had characterized the relationship between master and slave into the dominant framework of a relationship of the ownership of property.

At this point, the slave as merchandise stood in isolation as a contrast to free men. He was shackled by an entire ideology, by specific juridical measures, and by common attitudes that isolated him, cut him off from the rest of humanity, and even excluded him from humanity. Truly become a thing or an animal, he was treated as such under law.

This transformation in the slave's real condition corresponded to a profound change in all of society, but the change concerned the slave first and foremost. He became a gauge for such transformations because he was the first to suffer their consequences. We should always keep in mind that there was a high degree of heterogeneity in the servile world; still, many of the considerable mass of slaves who poured into Italy during the two last centuries of the Roman Republic were destined to work within the new constraining economic structures that were being established. The response of these uprooted and harshly exploited men lay in the revolts, in particular the great slave uprisings of the second century and the early first century B.C. Slave armies defied Roman order for some years—in Sicily from 136 to 132 and again from 104 to 101; in southern Italy with Spartacus from 73 to 71. From the figures that ancient authors have transmitted to us (and which agree a good deal more than some have claimed) we can see that some 200,000 adult male slaves lived in rural areas in Sicily at that time, many of whom participated actively in the revolt of 136.

These mass movements, which express the slaves' resistance in the clearest possible manner, were prompted both by a considerable rise in the number of slaves in certain regions of Italy and by the new condition imposed on them. Before, when he was part of the *familia,* the slave's dependence, although basic to his status, did not seem an isolated phenomenon and was mitigated by the possibility of affective relationships facilitated by the lack of specificity in his duties. Now the slave was often remote from the master and constrained to labors whose logic completely escaped him. Hence his lack of freedom weighed heavier on him, and it was often given material form in the chains he wore—a brutal version of his former ideological "chains"—and by his being lodged in slave barracks.

We can easily understand the violence and the scope of revolts of people who had little to lose. Armed resistance never ceased but after Spartacus it took new and more diffuse forms, resembling acts of brigandage more than insurrection. Some have (rightly) pointed to the decisive role of the political context of the civil wars and the growing power of the *imperatores* as two of the many causes of the disappearance of mass insurrections.

It is worthy of note that the charismatic figure of the *imperator,* the chosen of the gods, was from the outset a model for the leaders of the great slave revolts just when it was becoming increasingly important in official political life. Spartacus (to cite only one example) spread the idea that he enjoyed a privileged relationship with the gods, in particular with the Thracian god Sabazius (long associated with Dionysus), and his female companion was endowed with the gift of prophecy. The figure of Spartacus is closely comparable to that of Marius, who also had a prophetess at his side. The defeat of the slave *imperatores* did not signal the end of this politicoreligious idea among the slaves. They simply turned toward other *imperatores* who were no longer of their own.

In reality, the civil wars and the growing role of war leaders offered the slaves an alternative to unilateral revolt. One important turning point, both political and military, occurred when Marius, placed in command of the African war, restricted recruitment for the campaign of 107 B.C. to volunteers, thus opening the legion ranks to the poorest citizens, who until then were enrolled only exceptionally and, when they were enrolled, confined to special corps. This move had vast consequences. Troop levies no longer depended on coercion, and the army became a means of advancement for the destitute, who expected war to provide them with booty and land. If their hopes were to be realized, however, the army had to be victorious. The general and his soldiers were henceforth bound together and the loyalty of the troops to the *imperator* was a necessary condition of success. Both tended to become professionals. This shift blurred the notion of the citizen-soldier but also that of the magistrate general, and their places were taken by personal ties and the development of veritable clientage relations between the military leader and his troops.

The *imperatores* of the late Republic thus played an essential role in social stabilization by helping to reintegrate marginal groups. When army recruitment spread outward, reintegration took on a broader geographical dimension. One significant episode was the policy of Pompey after his victory over the pirates in 67. Instead of systematically wiping them out, he settled the pirates both in the West and in the cities of Cilicia that had fallen before him, one of which then took the name of Pompeiopolis. The pirates—outlaws par excellence—were thus transformed into colonists reviving a city that took on the name of the *imperator.*

The victorious generals' function of integration soon concerned the slave world as well. In the struggles that rent the Republic in its declining years, heads of factions engaged slaves. As early as the Social War, 21,000 slaves were freed to combat the *socii,* and later Sulla and Pompey had little scruples about similar sorts of recruitment, particularly when the need was urgent, as it often was. On occasion the slave could even obtain his liberty without having to serve in the army. Thus after the death of Caesar the triumvirs who inherited power published a list of proscribed political enemies, promising a reward to anyone who would give information on them or kill them and promising liberty to a slave who did so. Thus slaves, like other disinherited groups, found service to political leaders a more efficient way out of their condition than widespread revolt. These major political upsets were thus also accompanied by profound economic and social changes, and they had all the more impact on slavery because in the early Empire the functions of the slave were tending to evolve.

The most important changes in the slave system were economic. Beginning with the early first century A.D. the slave mode of production that was typical of much of Italy and that gave Italy a dominant role in Mediterranean trade began to stagnate and then decline. This crisis was a long-term phenomenon that extended to the late second century, and its result was not the disappearance of slavery but the disappearance of the slave-based economy.

These changes brought on a diversification in the role of the slave and new ways of exploiting slave labor in which the rigorous separation between workers and means of production specific to slave manufacturing disappeared. Manufacturing had never concerned all slaves, but the sectors involved were leading ones. Henceforth, the economic supremacy of such enterprises gradually weakened, and competing modes of exploitation not specifically reliant on slave labor were developed.

It has often been said that this process brought with it a resurgence of the old social relations. This is not all that evident. Even if older types of dependence seem to recur, the distinction between exploitation and ownership was now much more solidly established than ever before. As a result the employer had a number of specific responsibilities in exchange for rights that had little resemblance to masters' rights in the earlier rural communities. Be that as it may, the slaves' working conditions were profoundly different.

This change is clear in the countryside, where a number of landowners tended to abandon direct exploitation of their land, split it up, and give it over to dependents to exploit. Some of these dependents were slaves, for whom the management of a parcel of land implied relative autonomy and responsibility. The life of these slave tenant farmers was radically different from that of slaves caught in a system that demanded of them only that they stay alive to work on tasks assigned to them day by day. Their juridical status aside, slave farmers were in practice very close to the free men who also worked a portion of an estate in exchange for carefully specified obligations. This type of sharecropping was highly constricting for the working farmer though it guaranteed him certain rights over the land he farmed; but with its spread, by the second and third centuries, agricultural lands were in large part worked by dependents—*coloni*—whose personal juridical status became secondary to their real social position. The specificity of the slave gradually weakened, and Ulpian, a jurist of the Severan age (citing first-century predecessors), speaks of *servi qui quasi coloni in agro sunt* (slaves who are in the field like *coloni, Digest* 33.7.12.3). Thus we arrive at a regrouping, into one category, of free men and nonfree men who were still slaves but were not part of the *instrumentum fundi* (the property's equipment) because they farmed under a sort of conventional agreement.

A parallel phenomenon was an increased number of slaves who played an important role in the management of such properties, supervising their exploitation and handling money, or even farming land that they rented from the owner. Thus, along with the traditional *vilici*, who were simply agents carrying out the owner's will, there appeared *vilici* who managed the land on their own account on payment of a fee and who might farm the land themselves or rent it out in small parcels to slaves. As a general rule, supervision of the master's holdings was entrusted to an entire hierarchy of financial agents working in both city and country, who carried out the wishes of their *dominus* and whom we know from inscriptions—*procuratores, actores, dispensatores, cellarii, arcarii,* and so forth.

The urban milieu underwent a similar change. There were some specifically urban varieties of slaves such as the *insularii*, who managed the owner's rental properties, and increasing numbers of physicians and intellectuals. More generally, however, the manufacturing mode of production was in decline in the city as well as in the country. It became customary to permit a slave craftsman an autonomous activity, and masters relied on *institutores* (usually slaves) to run a workshop, supervise the sale and purchase of merchandise, handle loans, arrange transportation, and so forth. As in country areas, these practices were probably not absolutely new, but when they became widespread they took on a new meaning.

The efficacy of the slave as an agent was directly linked to his juridical status. The master could subject him to all forms of interrogation, including torture, and could take justice in his own hands. These guarantees (which a free man would not offer them) explain why the wealthy increasingly turned to slaves to administer their affairs, and why slaves even became the absolute rule when it came to the administration of money. These guarantees also explain the instances—seemingly very rare—of *ingenui* (freeborn men) who sold themselves to a wealthy man in order to administer his holdings (*ad actum administrandum* or *gerendum*). The social situation of such financial managers was enviable, but it implied servile status, which gave security to the master. In this case, entering into slavery became a means of social promotion.

This change contributed greatly to a growing heterogeneity in the slave world. From the first century, the theme of the wealthy and insolent slave paralleled that of the freedman who surpassed the aristocrat in his life-style and his power. The phenomenon was considerably intensified by the rapid rise in the number of slaves who belonged to the emperor. Not only were such slaves endowed with specific rights that distinguished them from private slaves, but also the proximity of power offered a few of them greater opportunities for social promotion, in particular, in the management of the enormous imperial patrimony or in the service of the state. Like a private master, the emperor needed people devoted to him, which meant totally dependent on him.

In practice, all these changes tended to weaken the juridical incapacity of the slave. For example, when a slave *institutor* managed an enterprise, he needed to be given a certain freedom of action. The problem then arose of the articulation between the slave's responsibilities and those of the master for whom he acted. The law was obliged to take up these questions. It stipulated that the *dominus* could relinquish his responsibility for transactions that he refused to have his slave undertake, by posting a notice in the workplace. Often, however, the *institutor* was far removed from his master and disposed of a de facto autonomy expressed—necessarily—by the validation of the contracts he entered into. The contracting parties could demand redress from the owner, but their compensation would be limited to the sums produced by the slave's activity, which meant the slave's own *peculium* and the owner's profits.

Recognition of a slave's talent for business matters thus appears to have been indispensable both to the interests of those who dealt with him

and to the interests of the master who was counting on the slave's autonomy to manage his affairs efficiently. What permitted reconciliation of
this new trust with the slave's fundamental inferiority was the development of an ancient practice, that of the slave's earnings, or *peculium*. The
practice was ancient, but it was in no way systematic, and at the start it
was an explicit manifestation of the master's pleasure. From the early
Empire (and in particular from the second century), however, the master's will was increasingly implicit. In parallel fashion, the slave could
dispose more freely of his savings, and he could both lend and borrow
money outside his master's juridical responsibility. Behind the debates
over the interpretation to give to sometimes contradictory texts, we can
discern a gradual recognition of the slave's patrimonial capacity and even
of a certain legal capacity—both direct reflections of the new functions
that he was increasingly called on to assume.

The weakening of the coercive structures surrounding the slave thus led
to a weakening of the masters' control. This was quite obviously true of
the slave elite engaged in business, but it also held true for many poor
slaves, such as the *servi quasi coloni* who took on administrative duties of
varying importance. Consequently finding new ways to supervise and
control slaves became indispensable.

These took several forms. The first was the growing importance of
the slave's *peculium*. Slaves who labored in manufacturing enterprises had
no money of their own, but for slaves who enjoyed some degree of
autonomy the *peculium* was a stimulant to a personal interest in the outcome of their activities. The slave's ultimate goal was to purchase his
liberty, but manumission was above all an operation of social integration,
as illustrated by the increasingly common practice of leaving the freed
slave in possession of his savings and by legal measures (at first glance
surprising) that protected the slave's savings from his master, thus guaranteeing that the *peculium* would have its full effect. This was the logic
behind the measures obliging the *dominus* to pay for the objects produced
or sold in the locales managed by his slave. The slave's savings were
avidly accumulated at his master's expense—a condition indispensable to
the efficient integration of subordinates. Moreover, it became common
practice that the land cultivated by the slave or the enterprise that he
administered would be included in his *peculium*. For similar reasons,
third-century laws clearly distinguish between a slave who had purchased
his freedom (even though the operation was at times fictional, since he
kept his savings) from the slave who owed his manumission to his mas-

ter's kindness. The first owed his former master nothing but respect; the second owed him a number of payments and obligations—for example, he was obligated to leave a part of his estate to his former master.

Thus we can see that the development of mercantile values had consequences that might seem somewhat unexpected. Indeed, although at first that development facilitated an unprecedented growth in human commerce, in a second phase it brought possible emancipation to slaves above the level of those forced into a system of organized labor and earning only just enough to stay alive. The passive slave-as-merchandise, an object, who could be bought and sold, became active when he purchased his own person.

The process of social integration did not stop there. Before their manumission, a minority of wealthy (or at least well-off) slaves built up a patrimony that faithfully reproduced prevailing structures. They might themselves own slaves—*vicarii*—who acted as *procuratores* or *institutores* to manage the slave's holdings, just as those slaves managed their masters'. The law specified that such slaves of slaves belonged to the latter and not to his *dominus,* and the relations between the slave and his *vicarii* were modeled on those that pertained between a free man and his slaves. The *vicarii* might be harshly exploited: Pomponius, a second-century jurist, mentions a slave who prostituted the *ancillae* (women servants) who were a part of his *peculium*. But *vicarii* might also belong to the privileged slave minority, and their own *peculium* could include slaves—that is, *vicarii* who belonged to a *vicarius.* These cascading relationships within the servile world are the best testimony to the success of the policy of social integration of the slave elites. What could be more reassuring, for the dominant class, than a text of Julian, also from the second century, that mentions *venaliciarii,* or slave merchants who were themselves slaves?

The efficacy of this policy depended on a remarkable characteristic of the Roman city—its capacity to remain open to foreign elements—that Greek cities did not share. In classical Greece, the citizen body was a closed world extremely difficult to break into. The Roman city, which often granted the freed slave citizenship, offered a social model radically different from that of the Greek city. The Roman system implied channels that led slaves to manumission and then to access to all economic activities, landownership included—something nearly unknown in the Greek world, but that in Rome underlay the efficacy of the policy of social integration of the slave elites. A second form of social integration lay in a new way of presenting the relations between masters and slaves. The governing classes became increasingly aware of the need to create moral controls over subordinates who responded less and less to strict discipline. The shock of the civil wars probably played an important role in this evolution, in the sense that it gave a number of slaves an opportunity to denounce their masters and show the hatred they bore them. More simply, the civil wars allowed them to act in accordance with their own interests. This meant that once order was reestablished and the slave world was taken in hand, alternatives to the *ergastulum* (slave barracks) needed to be found, particularly since that system for exploiting slave labor no longer corresponded to the needs of a changed economy.

It is perhaps in Seneca that we find one of the fullest attempts to reflect on the need both for new relationships between masters and slaves and for the slaves' moral submission (given that moral submission was the best guarantee of physical submission). It would be futile to seek any profound influence of Stoicism here: Stoicism was for Seneca above all a technique that enabled him to transpose social conflicts to the moral plane so that he could resolve them without challenging the established social order.

The logic of Seneca's forty-seventh letter to Lucilius, on the problem of slavery, is characteristic. Seneca began by recalling a principle that had become a commonplace in Hellenistic thought—that the equality of all men extended to slaves (*Servi sunt. Immo homines:* "'They are slaves,' people declare. Nay, rather they are men"). This equality was pure abstraction, however: we too are slaves, for we are slaves of our vices and no one is sheltered from reversals of fortune, not even Plato, who was sold. As for the slave, his soul remains free (*Servus est. Sed fortasse liber animo:* "'He is a slave.' His soul, however, may be that of a freeman"), a theme that Seneca often repeated (for example, *De beneficiis* 3.20) and that had the advantage of eluding the question of the actual liberation of the slaves. The policy Seneca advocated was simple: it is our bad treatment that transforms the slaves into enemies. We must inspire in them not fear but the respect that creates affection; we must recreate the ties that once bound the slave to the house in the days when the *dominus* was the *pater familiae* and the *servi* bore the fine name of *familiares*.

It is evident that none of these arguments ever questioned slavery; rather, they encouraged it. Recognizing that the slave had a soul permitted Seneca to locate the slave's liberty within his soul—a spiritual liberty that no one could take away from him but that in no way hampered the usual operation of social relations. It might even favor them, because a well-treated slave will not only obey but may, on his own initiative, prove devoted. The moral liberty of the slave could and must necessarily produce loyalty. As for the concept of humanity, it implied that all humankind shared submission to necessity; more precisely, to authority: the aristocrat must submit to the imperial power and the slave to the *dominus,* for revolt simply adds force to domination, as with the wild animal whose struggles tighten his bonds (Seneca *De ira* 3.16). The world cannot be changed.

Seneca's theorizing on the relationship between masters and slaves, in which a sentimental approach should permit better results than physical constraint, had a certain success, but it does not seem to have modified behavior much—beginning with Seneca's own, given that he recognized corporal punishment as useful. Indeed, his vision referred only to the privileged relations that a master might foster with a restricted circle of slaves, and, as such, it was nothing new. The attitude of Pliny the Younger offers an instructive parallel. In his correspondence he makes a show of his *humanitas* toward his dependents (8.16.3). When a senator was murdered by his slaves, however, Pliny stressed the dangers that even an indulgent master faced. Although Pliny himself describes this master as cruel his death elicits a diatribe on the wickedness of the servile world, against which not even generosity served as protection (3.14).

One might well ask, What was the purpose of such discourses if the master's goodness was a literary *topos* rather than a profound change in attitudes and if it was even considered of dubious efficacy? The answer seems to lie in the way in which the role of the state was conceived in master-slave relations.

The theoretical model was based on ancient times, when slaves had been integrated into the *familia,* where they assumed honorific duties, and when the *domus* was considered a veritable republic in miniature (Seneca *Ad Lucilium* 47.14: *domum pusillam rem publicam esse iudicaverunt;* "They held that a household was a miniature commonwealth"). This past situation (the reality of which was doubtless largely illusory) remained as a model for the new *domini* whose only thought was to scorn and crush their slaves. Thus comparisons with the state are ceaselessly reiterated: anger leads to the flight of slaves just as it prompts hatred toward the magistrate (Seneca *De ira* 3.5.4); slaves kill cruel masters just as peoples kill tyrants (Seneca *De clementia* 1.26); the slave's *peculium* belongs to the master just as everything belongs to the king; this did not mean, however, that slaves and subjects could not exercise a right to property (Seneca *De beneficiis* 7.4); for slaves, the *domus* was almost a republic, a city (Pliny *Epistulae* 8.16: *servis res publica quaedam et quasi civitas domus est;* "For the house provides a slave with a country and a sort of citizenship").

One basic conclusion can be drawn from this constant comparison of the *domus* to the state. Formerly, the *patres familias* had managed their households as they ran the city, since they were also *patres conscripti* (members of the Roman Senate). Now times had changed. Caesar was so thoroughly identified with the Republic that they had become inseparable, like the soul and the body (Seneca *De clementia* 1.4–5); now the *pater familias* needed the support of the *pater patriae* (the father of the fatherland), for those who held private and public authority were no longer one and the same. Pliny gives this notion clear expression in his *Panegyric* on Trajan (42), where he praises the emperor, whom he calls (not surprisingly) *pater patriae* for having restored the filial piety of children and the obedience of slaves, thus guaranteeing the security of the masters and the virtue of the subjected.

Formerly, the state was visible only when it repressed major revolts; now its acts were celebrated even in the bosom of the *familia,* where harmony was reestablished in the name of the public safety (*salutis publicae signo*), to quote Pliny, whose statement is more than simple rhetoric. After all, a decree of Tiberius guaranteed asylum to *servi* next to images of the emperors, not only in public places but also in private houses (Tacitus *Annales* 3.36). Imperial mediation operated even in the heart of the *domus*. Throughout the early Empire, in fact, the emperor intervened increasingly in relations between masters and slaves, following a policy inaugurated by Augustus himself. The *dominus* had to appear more liberal because changed production relations no longer allowed him as much constraint over his slaves as formerly, and he could afford that liberality because the state in part replaced him in maintaining order.

Imperial legislation thus (characteristically) took over a domain that had formerly been absent in public law—which presupposes that the bonds between masters and slaves had slackened enough to leave room for state action. One good illustration of the extent of this revolution in both law and practice is the *senatusconsultum Silanianum* of A.D. 9, which condemned to death any slave who failed to come to the aid of his master if the latter was attacked and he himself was with within earshot. In order to guarantee the efficacy of this measure, the legislator limited the power of the *domini:* the testament of an assassinated master could not be opened before an inquiry and any resulting legal action were completed, so that the man's heir could not attempt to save guilty *servi* who now belonged to him. Similarly, other laws that attempted to prevent the formation of armed bands introduced the notion of a slave's moral responsibility by stating that he was not obliged to blind obedience to his master.

There were two inseparable aspects of such imperial legislation. The first was expressed in measures to protect the slave from the violence of the owner: limits to torture; regulations concerning slaves condemned to combat with wild animals; prohibitions against killing a slave incapable of working (Claudius), then any slave (Hadrian); liberty granted to slaves who were abandoned by their master because they were ill. In the second and third centuries, this protective legislation was reinforced, increasingly taking the slave's family ties into account and backing his manumission when he was the object of juridical controversy.

The second and contrasting aspect of imperial legislation was expressed in repressive laws whose purpose was to assure the safety of the *domini*. The essential measure here was the *senatusconsultum Silanianum* just mentioned, with which the state took over repressive tasks formerly handled within the *familiae*. This essential decree was further reinforced by Nero, who extended its application to a spouse's slaves, then by Trajan, who further extended it to the freedmen of an assassinated patron. Other laws to keep slaves in their place provided for organized searches for fugitive slaves and prescribed the death sentence for any slave who attempted to join the army.

Thus, thanks to the *pater patriae*, a supreme *pater familias*, the *domus* once again became a miniature republic in which persons coexisted in harmony. The growing importance of the state in family life was also noticeable in a mimesis characteristic of new institutions. Augustus reorganized the cult of the *Lares compitales*—custodians of the crossroads—in cities and associated them with the cult of his own *genius*. On this occasion he maintained the tradition that slaves took part as *magistri* and *ministri* in these rites. The political dimension of this religious reform was clear: it was an important part of a campaign to attach the various milieus of Roman society, including the slave milieu, to the imperial person.

The imperial model was copied, for their own purposes, by landowners. The *familia rustica*, in imitation of the imperial domains, belonged to collegial bodies that had their decurions and their *magistri* and that organized the cult of the Lares of the *familia* and of the *genius* of their patron. Such colleges, which included slaves and freedmen, had their own elective magistracies and could be found in both rural and urban milieus. The possibilities for organization these offered slaves, along with election to honorific posts for some among them, facilitated a necessary integration of the servile world into society. They also directly reinforced the power of the *dominus* when the cult of the patronal *genius,* directly imitated from the official cult of the (increasingly divine) imperial *genius,* took on a supernatural dimension.

Once we have grasped the several sets of profound changes that affected the relations between masters and slaves, we can return to the question posed at the beginning of this chapter: How is a society in which the citizen and the slave coexist conceivable? Or, how can one define the *servus* in a way that justifies this system? Quite obviously, the answer varies according to the historical situation.

In a first phase, "nature" was the main concept used to justify slavery. A slave was a slave because his nature was essentially servile. This was the approach that prevailed in the Hellenistic period, not, however, without opposition from a number of currents of thought hostile to slavery. Once more, we must turn to book 1 of Aristotle's *Politics* because it was used as an authority by later authors. In the *Politics* the idea of the slave by nature rests on the affirmation that the nature of any thing is its end, and each thing has its own end because nature makes every object for one use alone. Plato stressed the same idea when he wrote that nature created men not alike but different from one another and apt for different functions (*Republic* 2.370b).

Natural differences were thus the basis for differences in status. The essential problem then remained to know the criteria by which any individual would be a master or a slave. Aristotle offered two essential criteria. The first was political: man is by nature a political animal, a civic being (*Politics* 1.2.9–10); thus only a free man is perfectly man, for only he is capable of political life (1.5.10). The master coincides with the citizen. Conversely, the slave by nature is incapable of deliberation (1.13.7); he participates in reason without possessing it himself (1.5.9).

The second criterion was closely connected with the first. Certain tasks, which imply the utilization of force alone, are servile by their essence (1.5.8, 11.6). These are the tasks appropriate to individuals who have been defined as slaves by their inability to reason.

The difference in nature that contrasted the master and the slave was thus manifest in the body (the first has a noble mien; the second is strong) and in the soul. Aristotle himself, however, stresses that it is difficult to detect beauty of the spirit, and that many have only the body of a free man without his soul. Thus the danger of one part of the citizenry reducing another part to slavery must be clearly avoided—something that the basic criteria cannot sufficiently guarantee. The solution consisted in equating the ideas of the slave and the foreigner. Thus, the city's need for slaves could be satisfied coherently—that is, without denying the nature of the city as it was fashioned by sweeping reforms that quite rightly excluded the enslavement of a portion of the indigenous population. It was even more efficacious to equate the slave and the "barbarian," and the onset of the period of great wars made this easier than it had been. This choice was justified by a political criterion given by Aristotle: the barbarian did not belong to the world of the city; thus he was by nature a degraded being incapable of proper use of language, with which man, alone among the animals, was endowed (*Politics* 1.2.9–10). This was Aristotle's eventual solution to the problem (1.2.4), and he claimed that those who refused the name of "slave" to the Greeks and reserved it for barbarians thus agreed with his own notion of the slave by nature (1.6.6). In like fashion, in the *Republic* Plato drew a fundamental connection between the slave problem and the barbarian wars (469b ff.).

These ideas provided the ideological basis for slavery in Rome. The wars that flooded the slave markets with prisoners during the last centuries of the Republic made the idea of a correspondence between foreign origin and a servile nature perfectly functional. Some changes in the Aristotelian heritage occurred, however. A new ideological geography placed Rome, the only true city, at the heart of a system that drained slaves from the entire Mediterranean world and its periphery. Liberty was still equated with city and the barbarian world with slavery, but to the advantage of Rome. The venerable Greek cities had been corrupted by allowing themselves to become part of monarchic systems in which they became subject cities. In a certain sense, they fell into a barbarian state. Henceforth, only Roman citizenship embodied liberty.

This change cannot be reduced to a shift in a center of gravity. The criterion of citizenship was gradually declining. The increasing importance of mercantile values implied a gradual shift in which the basic social distinction fell no longer between the citizen and the noncitizen but between the free and the nonfree: those who manipulated merchandise and those who were themselves merchandise. The Aristotelian criteria for the definition of the slave were evolving. The slave's body was no longer considered deformed in comparison to a beauty incarnate in the citizen but in consideration of production norms. He could have webbed hands or more than five fingers, but if he could still use his hands this was not considered a defect (*Digest* 21.1.10.2, 21.1.14.6). On the other hand, since one of the essential merits of a female slave, for production purposes, was to bear slaves (an essential source of supply that has too often been undervalued), the laws considered unhealthy any slave woman who was sterile or afflicted with a condition that might reduce her capacity for childbearing.

Once again the slave was stripped of nearly all specific physical characteristics. In Aristotle, his robust constitution destined him for servile tasks; the new approach was more realistic, recognizing that people are not born with powerful muscles but acquire them and that people set to hard labor are not naturally strong but become so or perish. The slave thus came to be defined as a person who had been bought in order to be set to servile tasks, independent of his constitution. There was a good deal less theoretical concern for his physical qualifications for his role than practical concern that he might have hidden defects (a cause for legal action). After that, the market took over, and a robust slave brought a higher price than a puny one.

From an ideological point of view, the justification of slavery that triumphed toward the end of the Republic took refuge in Aristotle's criterion of the soul. This was a clever move in the sense that it permitted any sort of statement. As Aristotle himself remarked, the soul's beauty is hard to see. It was also efficacious because the notion of the slave's lack of reason was accompanied by insistent accusations of moral perversion.

Cicero's vocabulary is characteristic of this point of view. In *Against Verres* Cicero seeks to discredit Verres and his "set"—who were not juridically slaves—by attributing servile traits to them. The overwhelming majority of the characteristics he criticizes are moral and intellectual, and he portrays these men as perverted and stupid. Cicero makes few allusions to their physical appearance, and when he does, physical characteristics appear as a consequence of an inner corruption. Servile nature, he states, is opposed to free nature much as vices contrast with virtues. There is perhaps only one passage that recalls the Aristotelian tradition directly: when Verres is accused of stripping temples of statues to put in his own house, Cicero reproaches his *operarius,* calling him "a man whose birth, whose education, whose mental and physical qualities suggest that he is much better fitted to carry statues than to carry them off" (*Against Verres* 4.126).

Once it was admitted that the servile nature could have a moral dimension it seemed clear that it was contagious. This argument underlies Cicero's attacks on Verres, Catiline, Mark Antony, and many others. This contamination was based on an inversion in values perfectly illustrated by Mark Antony. Cicero presents him as incapable of managing his property, used as a woman by men and unduly influenced by women, and so given to orgies that he turned night into day. Inversion was most decisive, however, when it broke social order by giving a dominant role to slaves and made them the accomplices of the masters they contaminated. Servile morality infected this entire milieu in which no one was in his proper place. When master and slave were so ill matched, Cicero argues, how could one still consider Mark Antony a master? (*Philippics* 2.104: *Quamquam quo modo iste dominus?*).

As long as the slave system could maintain strong constraints over the mass of the slaves, and as long as the *domini* possessed the power to keep the obedience of their dependents, it was of little consequence that the appeal to nature to define the slave was weakening. However, in the early Empire, when there were radical changes in the exploitation of slaves, this ideological ambiguity became dangerous, and the fundamental division of society into free men and slaves began to be challenged. For some time, of course, there had been currents of thought that challenged the very principle of slavery. What was new was an uncertainty apparent in practice—and in the attitudes of masters—as if the division of basic categories into free men and slaves did not seem as evident as before.

The growing diversity in slaves' functions quite obviously played a large part in this confusion. The privileged slave minority could live in a manner indistinguishable from that of the freeborn. Furthermore, was not their logical destiny manumission? Wealthy slaves were the ones who profited the most from the juridical capacities progressively granted to slaves, not only because they had better opportunities to act and the means to do so but also because the law itself recognized their special status. Thus an *iniuria* committed toward a slave that formerly was punished only insofar as it harmed the master (as in the *lex Aquilia*) might now lead to a suit even if the act had not affected the owner, because, as Ulpian wrote, the slave had suffered from it. Ulpian immediately adds, however, that this *actio iniuriarum servi nomine* was not to be appealed to in cases concerning moral damages unless the slave in question occupied a privileged position, when his *qualitas* had to be taken into consideration (*Digest* 47.10.15.44). Both in practice and in law, then, the wealthy slave was in the best position to attenuate the effects of his status and minimize the differences that separated him from the world of free men.

This evolution can make it difficult to locate the borderline between liberty and servitude in daily life. The juridical texts show increasing interest in cases that arise out of just such uncertain instances: a husband discovers that his wife is a slave (Papinian *Digest* 24.3.42.1); a freeborn woman marries a slave whom she had thought free (Ulpian *Digest* 24.3.22.13), or, conversely, a free man is arrested as a fugitive slave. Such problems arose out of real doubts as well as errors or deliberate attempts to mislead. One of Trimalchio's guests recounts that he served as a slave for forty years and that no one could ever tell whether he had originally been born free or not (Petronius *Satyricon* 57). A number of juridical texts treat of the free man who is unaware of his condition and serves as a slave, and there are indications of suits to prove freeborn status that show that in many instances this was genuinely uncertain.

Even more, the law itself might create a situation that casts doubt on the distinction between free and slave. What are we to make of the perfectly possible case of an elder brother who is a slave and a younger brother who is freeborn because the father had freed their mother, his slave, in the interim? The elder would thus not only be the *servus* of his father but could become the property of his brother at the father's death. Or what are we to think of free men who voluntarily became slaves, on one end of the scale, in order to be eligible for an important administrative post or, on the other (a more frequent case), because they were miserable wretches reduced to selling themselves in order to survive? How do we classify repeated cases of kidnapping that forced free men into chains? Or the enslavement of debtors, a practice often condemned by law but nonetheless frequent? What meaning should we give, finally, to the fragment of Paulus, a jurist of the Severan period, who states that children born malformed were not free (*Digest* 1.5.14)? One remarkable aspect of a number of these cases is that they illustrate the weakening of an essential criterion—the identification of the bulk of the slave population with foreigners. Henceforth, the chief sources for slaves included not only prisoners of war, the slave trade, and the natural process of reproduction, but also the enslavement of free men and women from inside the empire, by either kidnapping, voluntary enslavement, or the abandonment or sale of infants.

The weakening of the barrier that had served to keep the free and the slave apart caused some anxiety. It appeared less able to prevent the enslavement of free men, but also to prevent slaves from usurping free status. Some fugitive slaves managed to camouflage their real status so well that they rose to important posts, like one *servus* who became a centurion under Domitian and another who became praetor. The problem was serious enough for Ulpian to question whether the decisions handed down by a magistrate who was in fact a fugitive slave were valid (*Digest* 1.14.3).

Thus we can understand the underlying meaning of such desperate attempts to find criteria for distinguishing slaves from free men as the proposition made to the Senate that slaves dress in a special costume. Social evolution had indeed made the distinction between slave and free uncertain, both in practice and in people's minds. A text of Statius, the consolation written for Flavius Ursus, who had just lost a young slave boy who was his favorite (*Silvae* 6), is a good illustration of this uncertainty. In this quite special case of intimate relations between master and *servus,* all the borderlines seem hazy. All notions of servile nature disappear, since Statius asserts that Fortune, who had made the departed young man a slave, was no connoisseur of hearts, mistaking his qualities of mind, which showed, better than a freeborn genealogy, that he belonged among free men. His charm so contradicted his status that Statius wanders into predictable fantasies: And if he were not truly a slave? Perhaps he had illustrious ancestors? In the context of master–slave relations as in the law, guidelines were dissolving.

Although we should not forget that, even at this time, most slaves were mired in harsh servitude and no one speculated excessively about the slave's status, in this period of confusion, the law rather than the authority of the *dominus* or the notion of the slave's special nature defined the character, content, and limits of servitude. The jurists of the second and the third centuries speak in purely legal terms. They no longer speak of natural servility but only of a juridical institution. Even more, when they do appeal to the idea of nature, now it is to attach it to the free state. For Florentinus, servitude was a totally legal question and was contrary to nature (*Digest* 1.5.4.1). For Tryphoninus, natural law was clearly distinct from the law of nations: the first was the basis for liberty, the second for servitude: *libertas naturali iure continetur et dominatio ex gentium iure introducta est;* "Freedom is the condition of natural law and subjection the invention of the law of the world" (*Digest* 12.6.64). Ulpian makes a similar distinction, emphasizing that, from the viewpoint of natural law, all men are equal: *quod ad ius naturale attinet, omnes homines aequales sunt* (*Digest* 50.17.32).

This shift in juridical thought gave a legal basis to several phenomena that we have noted in the early Empire. One such was the growing importance of the slave's *peculium.* Ulpian remarks that although the slave could possess nothing according to civil law, natural law permitted him to do so. Another was the increasing responsibility of the slave. By the mid-second century, Venuleius stresses that because nature is the same for all men, the law on parricides can be applied to slaves, although they have no legal parents (*Digest* 48.2.5). To affirm the autonomy of *ius naturale* permitted the rationalization of changes in slavery, but the fact that it was subordinate to the *ius civile* and the *ius gentium* prevented it from undermining the foundations of the slave system. This proved a way, on the level of the law, to get around the contradictions between the idea of the total dependence of slaves and the fact that an increasing number of them nevertheless enjoyed a certain degree of autonomy. The natural dimension of slavery disappeared, and it became a purely juridical construction. The growing role of the state had a good deal to do with this.

The answer that could now be given to the question, What is a slave? was a good deal more solid that the one based on the vague concept of natural slavery. Slavery had become a juridical reality that could no longer be questioned without challenging the central power. It was no longer a simple topic for philosophical debate, and it no longer belonged essentially within the framework of the *familia*. It had become the business of the state. Thus what was needed was to reinforce a threatened system. Recourse to the law gave a hint of the true situation, however: as long as the slave had before him a *dominus,* he was in the same position as a domestic animal. Inequality was reinforced because it seemed natural. But when the state was obliged to intervene, relegating arguments about nature to a secondary plane, subjection became openly social. After the third century futher changes made it increasingly clear that servitude was a form of dependence that owed everything to men and nothing to nature.

The heterogeneity of the slave world must not be allowed to conceal the essential fact that the mass of slaves belonged to the lower classes of society. If we approach the question of what was a slave uniquely from the point of view of the slaves' juridical status, as the dominant ideology of the epoch invites us to do, both when it emphasized nature and when it stressed the juridical dimension of the definition of a slave, we must admit that slaves as a group showed little cohesion. If, on the other hand, we look at Roman society from the point of view of its class structure, it becomes perfectly clear that the majority of slaves were poor and were members of the dominated classes, where their juridical status gave them a special place.

There were times when the slaves themselves felt this fundamental community of condition and interests that reached beyond the differences among them. The period of the great slave revolts is an interesting case in point because these insurrections attracted a number of free men—small landowners and urban proletarians (whose participation was all the more significant since the *familiae urbanae* hardly budged). Class criteria proved more important than ideological distinctions.

Connections between the mass of slaves and the subordinate classes never disappeared. It is true that the juridical definition of the slave operated well enough to create a true barrier. A number of free men owned only one slave and were so poor that their one slave was an essential source of revenue. Paulus cites the case of an owner who pawns his slave and does not have the means to redeem him (*Digest* 9.4.22.1–2). All Roman society was so deeply imbued with slavery that the master-slave relationship was readily established. Nonetheless the profound similarity between the social position of poor free men and the mass of the slaves created bonds that reached beyond the concrete implications of juridical divisions. In the cities, freedmen and slaves mingled in the social and religious life of the urban plebs. In the political sphere, although Cicero's theme of the subversion of the state by the slaves was largely sheer propaganda, it was just such connections between the plebs and slaves that made the idea of subversion credible and permitted a condemnation not only of the servile and urban masses but of the political leaders (*populares*) who relied (at least in part) on their support. This sentiment of solidarity could often be denied. As Tacitus wrote in the context of an uprising of slave gladiators that to some extent recalled the start of Spartacus' revolt, the people were "allured and terrified as always by revolution" (*Annales* 15.46). Nonetheless, under the Empire there were several instances of this sentiment of solidarity that surfaced in revealing incidents. Under Nero, for instance, a particularly rigorous application of the *senatusconsultus Silanianum* led to condemning four hundred slaves to death. This sentence met with outspoken popular disapproval, and the executions could only take place under the protection of the army.

Bands of both slaves and free sprang up again with the insurrectional movements of the late second century. This was true of the troops of Maternus, under Commodus, and afterward the phenomenon spread. In fact, the social evolution that began toward the end of the early Empire and accelerated in the third century soon so diminished the real differences between free men and slaves that the juridical distinction between them was clearly meaningless. This happened in two ways. First, the privileged minority of slaves became increasingly integrated into the free population, thus prefiguring their social power once they were legally freed and demonstrating that no wealthy man could really be a slave. Funerary inscriptions attest to marriages between free women and slaves—*dispensatores, actores,* and *vilici*—of evident wealth. The law ended up sanctioning such marriages, and Paulus examines the relationship between the dowry and the *peculium* (*Digest* 16.3.27). In general, legislation gave increasing protection to the slave's right to his own wealth, sanctioning his objective situation as a property owner.

Second, the situation of poor free men increasingly resembled that of the mass of the slaves. In country areas, many peasants were reduced to cultivating the land of the great proprietors. What difference was there between the *colonus* and the *servus quasi colonus* when they worked the land in the same manner, owed the same obligations to the master, and were thrown together in the same colleges of the *familia* to honor the *Lares* and the *genius* of their patron? The *colonus* was driven by economic constraints; the *servus quasi colonus* by both economic and extraeconomic constraints, but they did the same things. The law soon changed in recognition of the real situation, and both the *colonus,* whatever his status, and his tools were gradually attached to the land. Finally, in the fourth century, land could not be sold separate from those who cultivated it, be they slave or free. They were in the same state of dependence, and the arbitrary division between free and nonfree was wiped out by social realities.

Legislation sanctioned this new social setup by placing its major division between the *honestiores,* the powerful, and the *humiliores,* the lower classes. Thus, in the third century the fines for kidnapping someone's slave or hiding a fugitive slave increased. More importantly, a new article stipulated further punishments that differed according to social status: *honestiores* would be exiled or have one-half their goods confiscated; *humiliores* could be crucified or sentenced to hard labor—a difference that is all the more revealing because crucifixion was typically a punishment for slaves. Similarly, a penal slavery was instituted for lower-class citizens from which the *honestiores* were exempt. In the fourth century, a text of Hermogenian shows that for the same crime of *iniuria,* slaves were flogged, *humiliores* cudgeled, and *honestiores* exiled for a limited term. Thus there was still a distinction between *humiliores* and slaves in the severity of the corporal punishment they underwent, but the kind of punishment they received set them off from the social elite.

Thus it is not the Roman slave who is our true subject but Roman slaves. This is because the servile world, beyond the unity imposed on it by its juridical definition, was extremely heterogeneous. It is also (and above all) because we need to distinguish between different historical contexts. There was a genuine difference in kind between the slave who worked the land side by side with his owner and the slave who worked in a manufactory or who was settled on the land as a *quasi colonus*. Even the slave's juridical status, which supposedly unified the category, evolved considerably. Even his relations with authority changed: at first the sole property of his master, he became also the subject of the emperor. In the final analysis, the slave's most lasting characteristic, the one that remained constant through all these changes, was the fact that the mass of the slaves always belonged to the lower classes of society. The most fundamental definition of that mass was that it was set to servile tasks. However, all who were forced to sell their physical strength in order to live performed those same tasks. Cicero was right when he connected wages and servitude: *merces auctoramentum servitutis;* their pay is "a pledge of their slavery" (*De officiis* 1.42.150).

Bibliography

Actes du colloque 1973 sur l'esclavage. Annales littéraires de l'Université de Besançon, ser. 2, 182. Paris: Belles Lettres, 1976. Also published in Warsaw and in the review *Index*.

Ariès, Philippe, and Georges Duby, gen. eds. *Histoire de la vie privée.* 5 vols. Paris: Editions du Seuil, 1985–87. Vol. 1, *De l'Empire romain à l'an mil,* ed. Paul Veyne. Available in English as *A History of Private Life.* Cambridge: Belknap Press of Harvard University Press, 1987–. Vol. 1, *From Pagan Rome to Byzantium,* trans. Arthur Goldhammer.

Bonassie, Pierre. "Survie et extinction du régime esclavagiste dans l'Occident du haut moyen âge (IVe–XIe s.)." *Cahiers de civilisation médiévale Xe–XIIe siècles* 28 (1985): 307–43.

Boulvert, Gérard. *Domestique et fonctionnaire sous le Haut-Empire romain: La condition de l'affranchi et de l'esclave du prince.* Annales littéraires de l'Université de Besançon, ser. 2, 151. Paris: Belles Lettres, 1974.

Carandini, Andrea. *L'anatomia della scimmia: La formazione economica della società prima del capitale.* Turin: Einaudi, 1979.

———. *Schiavi in Italia: Gli strumenti pensanti dei romani fra tarda repubblica e medio impero.* Rome: Nuova Italia Scientifica, 1988.

Carandini, Andrea, and Salvatore Settis. *Schiavi e padroni nell'Etruria romana: La villa di Settefinestre dallo scavo alla mostra*. Bari: De Donato, 1979.

Dumont, Jean-Christian. *Servus: Rome et l'esclavage sous la République*. Rome: Ecole française de Rome, 1987.

Finley, Moses I. *Ancient Slavery and Modern Ideology*. New York: Viking Press, 1980. Available in Italian as *Schiavitù antica e ideologie moderne*, trans. Elio Lo Cascio. Rome and Bari: Laterza, 1981. The Italian edition occasioned a debate published in *Opus* 1, 1 (1982).

Gallini, Clara. *Protesta e integrazione nella Roma antica*. Bari: Laterza, 1970.

Garlan, Yvon. *Les esclaves en Grèce ancienne*. Paris: François Maspéro, 1982. Available in English as *Slavery in Ancient Greece*. Rev. and expanded ed., trans. Janet Lloyd. Ithaca, N.Y.: Cornell University Press, 1988.

Giardina, Andrea, and Aldo Schiavone, eds. *Società romana e produzione schiavistica*. 3 vols. Rome and Bari: Laterza, 1931. The acts of this seminar, organized by the Istituto Gramsci, represent a fundamental stage in Roman studies.

Hindess, Barry, and Paul Q. Hirst. *Pre-capitalist Modes of Production*. London and Boston: Routledge & Kegan Paul, 1975.

Kolendo, Jerzy. *L'agricoltura nell'Italia romana: Tecniche agrarie e progresso economico dalla tarda repubblica al principato*. Trans. Celeste Zawadzka. Rome: Editori Riuniti, 1980. Andrea Carandini's preface is an important contribution.

Morabito, Marcel. *Les réalités de l'esclavage d'après le Digeste*. Annales littéraires de l'Université de Besançon, ser. 2, 254. Paris: Belles Lettres, 1981.

Morel, Jean-Paul. "Aspects de l'artisanat dans la Grande Grèce romaine." In *La Magna Grecia nell'età Romana*. Atti del quindicesimo convegno di studi sulla Magna Grecia (Taranto, 1975). 2 vols. Naples: Arte tipografica, 1976. Vol. 1, 263–324.

———. *Céramique campanienne: Les formes*. Bibliothèque des Ecoles françaises d'Athènes et de Rome, 244. 2 vols. Rome: Ecole française de Rome, 1981.

Ramin, Jacques, and Paul Veyne. "Droit romain et société: Les hommes libres qui passent pour esclaves et l'esclavage volontaire." *Historia* 30 (1981): 472–97.

Schiavitù, manomissione e classi dipendenti nel mondo antico. Atti del colloquio internazionale tenuto a Bressanone-Brixen dal 25 al 27 novembre 1976. Rome: "L'Erma" di Bretschneider, 1979.

Staerman, Elena Michelailowna, and Marianna Kazimirovna Trofimova. *La schiavitù nell'Italia imperiale*. Rome: Editori Riuniti, 1975. This is the Italian translation of a work published in Moscow in 1971; it gives an idea of the prevailing interests of research conducted in the Soviet Union.

Texte, politique et idéologie: Cicéron. Centre de recherches d'histoire ancienne, Table Ronde, Besançon, 4 Mars 1975. Paris: Belles Lettres, 1976.

Veyne, Paul. "L'histoire agraire et la biographie de Virgile dans les Bucoliques I et IX." *Revue de Philologie* 54 (1980): 233–57.

6

The Freedman

Jean Andreau

AS MOSES FINLEY HAS STATED, historians of the end of the last century were hesitant about speaking of slavery in the ancient world. At a time when the humanities were beginning to be challenged, they did not want to risk sullying the memory of classical antiquity. Eduard Meyer, the famous German historian of the late nineteenth century, reacted to this silence. He stressed manumission: to his mind the existence of the freedmen and their social condition proved that the ancient Romans and Greeks offered their slaves ample opportunities for liberation and social promotion, and Greco-Roman slavery was in no way comparable to slavery in the Americas in more modern times.

Although he drew much inspiration from Meyer, Mikhail Rostovtzeff's interests lay in other directions, but he too acknowledged the importance of the freedmen. To his eyes the freedman was proof that the ancient economy had known capitalistic periods. Obviously, all freedmen were not bourgeois capitalists, and, more importantly, many *ingenui*—freeborn Romans—even some of the more distinguished, were genuinely bourgeois. For Rostovtzeff, the freed former slaves were perfectly integrated into Roman society, and their economic possibilities hardly differed from those of other notables. At the same time, however, they were symbolic of the spirit of enterprise. In Petronius' comic novel, the *Satyricon,* Trimalchio, a freedman living in Campania who has sold his lands in order to devote his energies to commerce in order to get rich and who avoids strictly political hierarchies, is for Rostovtzeff the best example of changes in ways of thinking that economic expansion produced in Roman Italy.

Trimalchio, a mythical personage, set Federico Fellini's imagination to work, but he affects historians in the same manner, and not only Rostovtzeff. Like Rostovtzeff, Paul Veyne sees Trimalchio as a myth emblematic of Roman society and economy, but Veyne's interpretation is quite different.

For Veyne, Trimalchio is hardly representative of all freedmen, since the complete independence that he enjoyed at the death of his owner and patron was not true for most freedmen. Veyne insists that if we want to understand the mind-set of the freedman—rich or poor, dependent or independent—we need to plunge into a preindustrial universe of varying degrees of social status, strictly defined juridical categories, personal ties, and aristocratic values—a universe in some ways similar to the Ancien Regime. The extremely wealthy Trimalchio, who owned enormous estates in southern Italy, inherited his wealth from his former master, probably a senator; thus he owed his prosperity to personal ties that arose out of his previous condition of slavery. Profits from commerce only increased this initial fortune, and Trimalchio's fondest aspiration was to own land.

This plunge into the aristocratic mind-set, although necessary, does not explain everything, since the monarchies of early modern Europe had no social category like that of the freedmen. The freedmen, commoners who could become wealthy but could never "arrive," were a species more exotic than middle-class men striving to join the gentry. For Veyne, they were not true bourgeois, and although they lived in a world of gentlemen, they could never become gentlemen. They were strangers to their epoch: in the full range of roles in Roman society Trimalchio found none for himself.

The historiographic figure of the freedman is certainly less striking than that of the slave, and among the freedmen, caught between the world of the masters and that of the slaves, there was neither a Eunus nor a Spartacus. They have inspired brilliant analyses, however, and produced unifying myths. Veyne's interpretation is perhaps the most stimulating, as it throws new light on all of Roman society and its values.

Must we reject Veyne's interpretation because it is based on the *Satyricon*? This is Florence Dupont's thesis. She has attempted to show that the *Satyricon* is not an accurate representation of the author's world—not a realistic work but rather a work of the imagination—and she insists that it should be seen in the context of the history of the literary and philosophical genre of the Banquet, or a dinner that turns into a banquet.

Admittedly, the *Satyricon* is not a realistic work that aims at representing daily life or the life of society. There is little doubt about that. But the banquet and the party are social practices as well as literary models, and, as such, they inevitably invite the perspectives of anthropology or, more simply, of social history. Trimalchio's feast is also a satirical text in the modern sense of the word, and if the author uses dialogue and the mediation of a narrator, Encolpius, to distance himself from his text, it has something to do with his satiric intent. It is not coincidental that the guests at this feast dedicated to the body are freedmen (whereas the astonished but fascinated narrator is freeborn), or that they aspire to put on a "Platonic banquet" and are incapable of doing so. Florence Dupont speaks of an *échec des affranchis*: "They neither know how to drink, how to love, or how to speak. They need a master." It aids our comprehension of social hierarchies to note that the master of the feast, who sets up the "burlesque banquet," is the only member of the company to own an aristocratic patrimony and to play the senator even though—like the others—he was born a slave.

Florence Dupont's critique does not demolish the value of the *Satyricon* as a document of social history but rather enriches that value and gives it its true sociocultural dimension.

The fact remains that when we look attentively at all the individual cases presented by texts and inscriptions, generalizations and social myths lose their force and their seduction. What becomes obvious is the juxtaposition of extremely diverse and even totally opposite situations. Trimalchio displays the bad taste of the newly rich, but many freedmen fulfilled functions that we would qualify as intellectual or artistic or that were the contemporary equivalents of the liberal professions: they were professors, writers, physicians, architects, painters, sculptors, actors, and so forth. The greatest senators were not ashamed to have the freedman Epictetus as their philosophy teacher. Marcus and Quintus Cicero, like their peers, were fond of surrounding themselves with learned slaves and freedmen. One such was Marcus Tullius Chrysippus, who had charge of Quintus' library. In 50 B.C. Chrysippus suddenly abandoned another post he occupied, that of attendant to the son of Cicero the orator, leaving in the company of another freedman, a laborer. Cicero mocks the smattering of culture (*litterularum nescio quid*) that Chrysippus had acquired (*Ad Atticum* 7.2.8), but it is clear that Cicero was well aware of the difference between a literate man and a laborer.

Trimalchio was extremely wealthy, and he has made such an impression on our imaginations that we find it difficult to envision a poor freedman, especially during the age of the last Julio-Claudians, the emperors Claudius and Nero. Nonetheless, impoverished freedmen can be found, and even in the *Satyricon:* Gaius Julius Proculus, whose wealth had amounted to a million sesterces, is now penniless and has had to sell his furniture; Gaius Pompeius Diogenes, inversely, has become wealthy but was penniless when he was freed (*de nihilo crevit;* "he was quite a nobody": Petronius *Satyricon* 38). Furthermore many Latin texts of the late Republic and the early Empire draw a parallel between the freedman and the poor, particularly the poor of the cities. Horace writes of a certain Priscus that at times he lived in a palace and at other times under a stairwell, from which no freedman who cared about appearances could decently emerge. What is significant about this is that Horace suggests that one would expect to see a freedman coming out of a slum building. Petronius' contemporary Pliny the Elder speaks of the commonality of freedmen—the *plebs libertina*—not to distinguish between a plebeian and an aristocratic group among freedmen but to note that the *libertini,* the freedmen as a specific group in relation to other groups in the city, made up the plebs, the common people of the city (*Naturalis historia* 14.48).

The freedmen formed an urban milieu, then. This was the widespread opinion, and it undoubtedly was true. We should remember, however, that some freedmen had always lived in the countryside, or at least had been engaged in farming. The freedmen that Caesar sent to his colonies (Corinth in particular) had been given lands there that made them middling landowners (Strabo 8.6.23). We meet two other freedmen of greater wealth, but also engaged in agriculture, in Pliny. One, Remmius Palaemon, the famous grammarian, plays the gentleman farmer out of vanity and displays little knowledge of agriculture; the other, Acilius Sthenelus, shows competence. Remmius had bought some poorly maintained plots of land near Rome in the territory of Nomentum and turned them over to Acilius Sthenelus to be replanted with grapevines. After eight years the harvest brought in four hundred thousand sesterces, or two-thirds the original purchase price (*Naturalis historia* 14.49–51).

What are we to make of this diversity and these contradictory observations? Are they only appearance, or was the only thing that freedmen had in common that they had known slavery and had come out of it? Was their status as freedmen enough to bind them together, or did it contribute to dividing them into subgroups?

To answer these questions, we need to recall that the social being of the freedman was complicated and fragile. A freedman did not have the coherence of the aristocrat, who was sure of his superiority and armed with fortifying values, even if he did not always apply them in his daily life. The freedman had neither the rustic simplicity of the indigenous countryman nor the finely tuned irreverence of the domestic slave. The freedman stood where several divergent and even opposing forces intersected. On the one hand, he had been a slave, and neither he nor others could forget it. On the other, he had the status of freedman, which was in itself partly contradictory, since manumission conferred on him the same citizenship as his patron but also subjected him to a number of regulations and customs that set him apart from the freeborn *ingenuus*. Finally, every freedman occupied a specific economic and social situation, and each had his own particular geographical and cultural origin.

Some of these diverse components (which I shall take up in turn) tended to integrate the freedman into the rest of Roman society; others tended to detach him and isolate him. Some accentuated group cohesion among freedmen; others tended to fragment and decompose the group. The freedman ceaselessly swung back and forth in pendular fashion between the past and the future, citizenship and slavery, assimilation and rejection, and he was a channel for the greater part of the heterogeneities and contradictions of the society that surrounded him.

If the distance between freedmen and the freeborn were reduced as much as possible, there would not even be any sense in speaking of freedmen as a group. In one sense, this would represent total success for the freedmen, since it would prove that their former life was completely forgotten. But it would also be the end of their privileges and their chances for rapid social promotion. The Romans viewed many freedmen as men of the people, poor and deserving of scorn. Exceptional cases aside, however, those who escaped that common destiny did so thanks to personal ties and client-patron relations. Veyne shows this well in the case of Trimalchio. I might add another example, less well known but just as significant, of a Trimalchio before the fact, the fuller Clesippus, who lived in Cicero's time.

Although Clesippus was a fuller, it was not the dyers' trade that assured his social promotion. Received as a bonus in an auction sale by the wealthy Gegania, he became his mistress's lover, her freedman, and her heir, thus acquiring an immense fortune. An inscription informs us that he held the titles of *magister Capitolinorum, magister Lupercorum,* and *viator tribunicius.* This undeniable social promotion would not have been possible if he had not been a slave and Gegania's favorite. He himself was acutely aware of this, since (according to Pliny the Elder) he treated with true veneration the candelabrum with which he had been knocked down to his future mistress at the auction. If Gegania had not opened her bed and her testament to him and had merely freed him without any other legal procedures, he would have ended his life in a fuller's shop like many of his fellows.

The very juridical status of the freedman contributed to subjecting him to such pendular swings. In principle the freedman was a free man, capable of perfect assimilation into the rest of the free population of the empire. In practice, however, he was subjected to a whole series of regulations and constraints that set him off from the *ingenuus*. He was fully free: in the second century A.D. the jurist Gaius distinguished two categories of free men, the *ingenuus* and the *libertinus*—the first born free, the second liberated from slavery (*Institutiones* 1.10, 11). Manumission was not only an act in private law decided by the master (or mistress) of the slave by which he or she renounced the right of ownership; the liberty of the freedman was guaranteed by the city or by the state.

This was also the case in Greece, both in the classical age and the Hellenistic age, and after the Roman conquest. The freed slave might also be consecrated to a divinity, whose priests guaranteed his rights as a freedman. Here religious sanction replaced that of the state, but in both instances the freedman was protected against threats to his liberty.

In Greece, particularly in Athens, however, the status of the freedmen was if not identical at least highly comparable to that of the resident foreigner, or metic. In the Greek cities, freedmen were thus excluded from political life, and land ownership, a right included in citizenship rights, was forbidden them. This was absolutely not the case in Rome. In the last centuries of the Republic and under the Empire, the freedman of a Roman citizen became a Roman citizen, whatever official procedure had been used to free him. The owner's voluntary act founded an act of public sovereignty that permitted his former slave to have access to political rights along with personal liberty. The freedman of a *peregrinus*, a free subject of the empire without Roman citizenship, entered into the community of his former master with the same status of *peregrinus*. The freedmen of Roman citizens, who were themselves Roman citizens, were integrated into the system of the *comitia centuriata*, where they occupied a place that corresponded to their wealth and where they had the right to vote. The freedman of a freedman had the same status as his freed master, who in turn reflected the status of his own master.

This integration into the categories of the freeborn *ingenui* divided the freedmen into several juridical subgroups, to which we would add the *dediticii* (freedmen without citizen rights) and the Junian Latins. Con-

versely, assimilation brought the freedmen closer to the rest of the population, to the point that there seems to have been no milieu specific to
the freedmen. Their only traits in common were that they had been
slaves, were no longer, and were not freeborn.

Even for the freedmen of Roman citizens (whom the law privileged
over the other freedmen), however, this negative definition had cruel
positive juridical effects, as the freed slave owed certain obligations toward his former master. He owed him *obsequium,* the respect that a son
also owed his father. This respect had juridical effects and practical manifestations. To show their loyalty to him, the emperor's freedmen, for
example, offered dedications and votive inscriptions to appropriate divinities for the emperor's health, his happy return, or his victory. On a
somewhat more serious plane, *obsequium* forbade the freedman from su-
ing his patron under both civil and criminal law.

Aside from *obsequium,* the patron had a right to *operae*—clearly defined concrete obligations consisting in a certain number of days per year
of work that the freedman promised to perform for his patron. There
has been much debate about the extent of these promises, a question that
is all the more difficult to evaluate because the amount of the *operae*
depended on the terms of the agreement drawn up at manumission. We
know by a passage in the jurist Alfenus Varus, for example, that a physician could prohibit his freedmen who were also physicians from operating independently in the same city, as they would be in competition
with him. They either had to work with him (their aid counting as *operae*)
or leave town, paying him an indemnity equivalent to what he would
have earned from their services if they had continued to "accompany"
(*sequi*) him (*Digest* 38.1.26).

In practice, in nearly all of life's circumstances the freedman lived
under a number of limitations and juridical constraints. Moreover, these
changed from one epoch to another.

To take marriage as an example, the freedman or freedwoman of a
Roman citizen enjoyed the right of *connubium,* of contracting a legal marriage according to the forms of Roman law. In principle, the patron had
not the least right to oppose the marriage of his freedman or freedwoman.
From the late Republic, however, the master could introduce a clause in
the act of manumission stipulating that the former slave promised not to
marry after gaining his or her freedom, thus guaranteeing that the patron
would not lose the *operae.* This means, of course, that normally the
patron no longer exerted control over a married freedwoman and could
not demand *operae* from her. As her guardian, however, he would have

to have given his consent to her marriage; if not, the *liberta* would continue to owe him *operae*. If her husband should die, the patron or his sons would once more have guardianship over her, which means that her husband could not give another guardian to his freed wife before he died. Once the husband was dead, his widow, left without a guardian, would have to ask for another before she could remarry legally, as only her legal guardian could authorize her to contract a marriage. In 186 B.C., in thanks for having given evidence to the magistrates in the affair of the Bacchanalian rites, the Senate granted the freedwoman Faecenia Hispala, among other exceptional privileges, that of being able to marry without the authorization of her guardian and of being able to choose her own guardian, exactly as if her husband had named one in his testament (Livy 39.9).

In practice, the freedwoman had often been the mistress of her owner when she was a slave. On manumission, if they continued to live together he could make her his official concubine without marrying her, and in the *Digest,* concubines are often the freedwomen of their companions. The patron might also marry his former slave. If they separated, however, she could not contract a new marriage without his consent.

The married *libertus,* for his part, could not defend his conjugal honor either against his own patron or against his wife's, even in cases of persons taken in flagrante delicto. The patron, however, had authorization to kill a freedman surprised in adultery with the patron's wife.

During the Republic, were freedmen and freedwomen allowed to take a freeborn spouse? They probably could, but in Cicero's times such marriages were rare, although they were clearly permissible from the reign of Augustus on. A freedwoman could not marry a senator, however, or the son of a senator—which did not prevent her from being his concubine. In short, the *connubium* of the freedman bore little resemblance to marriage among the freeborn.

Rights of inheritance provide further illumination of the freedman's condition. Aside from its importance in the maintenance of patrimony, where it was fundamental, inheritance played a prominent political role in republican Rome, since the political participation of every citizen, his military obligations, and the direct taxes he paid (the *tributum*) were established on the basis of his total wealth. The freedman had the same right as anyone else to own land, slaves, houses, livestock, gold, silver, and art objects. He had the right to have children and to transmit his wealth to them. There is a fine passage in the jurist Gaius, however, that explains quite precisely the evolution of an inheritance system in Rome that was unfavorable to freedmen and their descendants (*Institutiones* 3.39–76). Before the final century of the Republic, the freedman of a Roman citizen might, without hindrance, bequeath none of his wealth either to his patron or to his patron's children and grandchildren. Even his wife (married *cum manu*) or his adopted children could inherit a freedman's entire estate rather than his patron. Probably toward the late second century B.C. the annual praetorian decree fixing the norms for rendering justice specified that the patron was to receive one-half of the freedman's wealth if the latter, at his death, left no direct blood descendants. Under Augustus, a law gave patrons even further rights, at least where the more wealthy freedmen were concerned. All freedmen whose wealth amounted to one hundred thousand sesterces or more were obliged to leave a part of their estate to their patron unless they had three or more children. If the freedman left two children, the patron would receive one-third of his wealth; if he left only one, the patron got one-half. What is worse, if the patron was already dead at the time of the freedman's death, the patron's sons and their sons and grandsons had the same rights over the freedman's inheritance as the patron himself.

I am speaking of male freedmen. Female freedwomen were, as Gaius states, under the guardianship of their patron, and since they needed his authorization to draw up a testament the problem hardly ever came up.

The consequences of such measures were immeasurable. Although the freedmen who were merchants and artisans constituted the beginnings of a bourgeoisie, laws such as these prevented that embryo from developing, enlarging, and freeing itself from the grasp of the landed aristocracies. Latin authors, Gaius at their head, do not present the laws in this light, however. They see them as measures working for moral equity and as an attempt to give the patron a share in his freedman's wealth that he deserved and did not have under the older law. Be that as it may, they created a brutal gap between freedmen and the freeborn where inheritance was concerned.

The freedmen of the Roman empire were much less excluded from citizenship than their counterparts in the independent Greek cities. They constituted a group apart, however, the members of which were never completely assimilated into the rest of the free population during their own lifetimes. In these conditions, how could they be taken for businessmen like any others, and, in particular, like businessmen of the aristocratic orders? How could they be called capitalists, as Mikhail Rostovtzeff calls them? Capitalists who could transmit only a part of their eventual wealth to their children?

If we turn from the law to custom and from legal texts to everyday practice, we can see these same pendular swings moving between the same poles.

Some of these were in the maintenance of ties of dependency, the souvenir of a servile past, and the unity of the freedmen as a group. The former master, and masters and patrons as a group—that is, all the better society of the empire—reserved the privilege of reminding the freedman that he was basically little different from the slave that he had been, of calling him a slave, and, in extreme cases, even of treating him like a slave.

In the juridical texts and the inscriptions dating from the third century B.C., freedmen are at times designated by the word *servus* (slave) rather than *libertus* (freedman), the term later applied to them as persons in relation to their patron. At that epoch, official mention of a freedman might well use the word *servus,* as with the *Servius Gabinius Titi servus* (literally, the slave of Titus), who was in fact Titus' freedman (*CIL* 10.8054.8). Later, *libertus* was the prevailing term in official texts, but Cicero is nonetheless capable of calling a freedman a slave, whether the man is his own freedman or someone else's and whether or not he is seeking to discredit the man. Writing to his quaestor, Lucius Mescinius Rufus, concerning the accounts of the province of Cilicia, Cicero speaks of his scribe Marcus Tullius, one of his freedmen, and with no criticism implied he calls him *meus servus scriba;* "my slave and secretary" (*Ad familiares* 5.20.1, 2). In his oration *Pro Roscio Amerino* (48.140), Cicero quite naturally calls Chrysogonus, Sulla's freedman, a slave and even "the basest of slaves." Georges Fabre rightly remarks that we do not know the status, slave or free, of many of the servants that Cicero names in his letters, and this ambiguity is symptomatic of the way he considered his freedmen, if not also of their condition and way of life.

Some two centuries later Pliny the Younger could hardly believe his eyes when passing along the Via Tiburtina, the road to Tivoli, he read the funerary inscription of Pallas, a freedman of the emperor Claudius. Scandalized by the Senate's homage to this former slave and by Pallas' condescending response to the senators, Pliny refers to him several times as a slave. It is true that he also qualified as slaves the senators who, out of fear of the emperor, showed such flagrant cowardice. The vocabulary of slavery, on the metaphorical plane, is par excellence that of baseness and unworthiness, and it might be applied to anyone. Nonetheless, it is used with particular frequency in reference to freedmen (*Epistulae* 7.29, 8.6).

In exceptional cases the freedman was treated like a slave in spite of the letter of the law. Thus, after the defeat of Vitellius in A.D. 69, his freedman Asiaticus was killed, along with several aristocrats, but because he was a freedman he was crucified, a punishment reserved to slaves: *Asiaticus (is enim libertus) malam potentiam servili supplicio expiavit;* "Asiaticus, being a freedman, paid for his baneful power by a slave's punishment" (Tacitus *Historiae* 4.11.10).

In the early Empire and the Republic alike, it was impossible to revoke a legally performed manumission. There were exceptions: according to Suetonius and the jurisconsult Marcian, the emperor Claudius decreed that certain freedmen—those guilty of ingratitude toward their patrons, for example—could be returned to slavery (Suetonius *Lives of the Caesars, Claudius* 25.3; *Digest* 37.14.5, pref., Marcian). Aside from such exceptional cases, however, and from delinquent *dediticii,* who were sold irrevocably, without manumission rights, along with all they possessed, legal manumission was never annulled. At the most, the *lex Aelia Sentia* (A.D. 4) permitted sending a freedman a hundred miles or more away from Rome or condemning him to forced labor. In spite of such provisions, and although *revocatio in servitutem* was never legally permissible, we sense that a great many patrons dreamed of it, if only as a threat to freedmen who caused them concern or annoyance. Valerius Maximus, for example, insistently praised Athens and Marseilles because those cities had laws stipulating that a freedman convicted of betraying his patron or showing ingratitude toward him could be returned to slavery (Valerius Maximus 2.6.6, 7). In his enthusiasm for Athenian law, he writes, "I could never believe useful to the city anyone who has shown himself to be a rascal toward his family. Go on, then, be a slave, since you have not known how to be free!"

When Chrysippus, Cicero's freedman, abandoned a mission entrusted to him, the orator began to seek a juridical argument that would allow him to annul his manumission. Chrysippus' servile behavior when he disappeared like a runaway slave is reflected in Cicero's opinion of him when he calls him a slave and dreams of returning him to bondage.

Under Nero, the Senate debated freedmen's behavior. Tacitus notes that many of the senators were in favor of the innovation suggested by

Cicero, for "notorious offenders deserved to be brought back to their bondage" (*Annales* 13.26–27). The emperor himself intervened, however, to recommend that the law not be changed, as indeed it was not.

Dionysius of Halicarnassus expressed strong objections to the situation in his days. The city of Rome, he complained, was full of freedmen who had bought their manumission with the wages of their crimes and their prostitution or who owed their liberty to their masters' "levity." He did not propose that any hindrance be put to their manumission, however, nor that it be annulled once granted. He suggested that the censors or the consuls inquire into the life and the merits of the freedmen as they did for those of senators and knights: if freedmen were worthy of having the rights of citizenship, they could remain in Rome; if they proved unworthy, let them leave the city to found a colony, by no means a dishonorable course (*Antiquitates Romanae* 4.24).

These writers' vigorous complaints are equaled only by the timidity of the solutions they suggest. Notables in Rome (and perhaps all the freeborn) tended to see the freedman simply as a former slave whose cheek still tingled from his blows. Freedmen made them think of slaves, and they dreamed of returning them to bondage. Still, they never made any real attempt to take away the liberty of these new citizens.

There was good reason for their caution. The freedmen were inextricably mingled with the rest of the population in many ways, notably in their economic activities.

There were in Rome, as in medieval and modern Europe, vast numbers of professions and activities. In order to grasp the social significance of the single trades, we need first to see them in a few large groups, which I shall call "labor statuses." The term refers to a relationship to labor in the broadest sense of the word, both on the institutional plane and on the representational level. It expresses the concrete organization of a life in work: how work is rewarded and the influence of remuneration on the agent's mind-set. It expresses how work is conceived in relation to the rest of life, either as principal activity and condition for survival or as one chosen activity among others. It is the way people choose a particular form of work and the way in which they can change activity. It is also the relationship with the state through work.

In ancient societies there was a gulf between the labor status of what we would call the "notable" and the "peasant." The peasant, be he landowner, tenant farmer, or hired agricultural laborer, worked the soil himself, perhaps with the aid of slaves or other peasants. Despite the harshness of his labor, however, the peasant was not seen as having a trade or profession; only those who did not live from the land were thought to have a specific profession. The notable considered agricultural revenues the interest on an invested capital, which was his landholdings. Even when he took a direct interest in the administration of his estates, he did not work with his own hands, and he had no notion of work that was not related to an entire set of social and political activities connected with his social station. Even if he was very involved in the management of his estates, he could not even conceive of submitting to any sort of professional constraint.

Shopkeepers, craftsmen, and local wholesalers and retailers had the quite different labor status of tradesmen. They made up the urban plebs, they were known by their trades, they formed professional associations (when the state permitted them), and they defined themselves, even juridically, by a function and by specific constraints.

Many slaves cultivated the soil; many freedmen did so as well. Other slaves ran a shop or a workshop; so did many freedmen. But where their labor status was concerned, the freedman had a very different place from that of the slave.

The slave enjoyed none of the four freedoms that, in the Delphic tradition, were characteristic of free men: possession of a legally recognized place in the community, protection against illegal detention, freedom of movement, freedom to chose one's work. The slave's activities depended on his master's will, and he could not change them without his master's consent or without being sold to another master. Thus although the slaves did not constitute a social class, they had the same labor status. Not only was it different from that of free men; it was of another order, for it permitted the slave, if his master were willing and if the law and custom allowed, to substitute for a free man in any and all sort of work.

The master might employ a slave in a function in principle reserved to slaves (as in the "plantation labor" of agricultural gang-work); he might employ him as a domestic servant, a worker, or a manager in his own household; or he might set him up in a sort of work also practiced by free men. Thus the slave might till the soil like a peasant, keep a shop like a tradesman, or even, exceptionally, lead the life of a notable managing his master's wealth. As for other sorts of labor status that cannot be fitted into the three principle ones just mentioned, a slave could function as an employee of the state administration: in the early Empire many imperial slaves and freedmen had such positions. But the law decreed that he could never do military service.

Whatever his occupation, a slave never had more than a borrowed title to it. Often slaves' remuneration was not equal to that of free men, and they could not legally own as much as free men. The two groups' relationship with the state was obviously not the same, and from one day to the next slaves could be obliged to leave one line of work for another.

The situation of the freedmen was totally different. To be sure, if slaves as a group did not constitute a social class, neither did freedmen. Furthermore, also like the slaves, the freedmen had access to most sorts of labor status. Freedmen, however, had that access in the same manner as the freeborn: their place was recognized legally and socially, and they could leave a post at will, like other free men, and could acquire all the advantages or drawbacks it might offer. Even when they continued to be dependent on their former master (for example, if they had borrowed money from him), even when they chose to continue to exercise functions in their patron's house that were usually reserved for slaves, it did not prevent them from exercising their activities in the same way as the freeborn.

In practice, freedmen and the freeborn were in daily contact with one another in the workplace. Nearly everywhere that the freedmen could be found we also meet the freeborn, both Roman citizens and *peregrini*.

The famous grammarian Quintus Remmius Palaemon, born a slave in Vicenza, where he spent his youth, is an excellent example of a freedman's possibilities. At first a weaver, Remmius became a teacher because his mistress gave him the task of taking her son to school (a fine illustration of the status of servile work). After he was freed he became famous as the director of a school attended by Quintilian and Persius. He led the life of a notable; he had ample wealth, mostly in land and in workshops, and he took pride in the administration of his landholdings, a pride that derived less from his own efforts than from his vanity, a trait for which he was well known (Pliny the Elder *Naturalis historia* 14.49–51; see also Suetonius *De grammaticis et rhetoribus* 23). This is why he bought the poorly maintained parcel of land near Nomentum that he turned over to Acilius Sthenelus (later acquired by Seneca, a senator).

Another freedmen whom Pliny the Elder complimented for his successes in agriculture, Vetulenus Aegialus, bought the villa at Liternum that had formerly belonged to Scipio Africanus. As Cicero explicitly states in his *Pro Balbo* (25.56), landed property has no lineage (*praediorum nullam esse gentem*), and a parcel of land in Tusculum that had belonged to Metellus later passed into the hands of Marcius Sotericus, a freedman, and was later bought by the great Crassus.

Freedmen and the freeborn also mingled in the trades and in business. Trimalchio had been a businessman and had practiced *negotiatio,* and we know from funerary inscriptions of a good many other freedmen who were traders and wholesalers. Toward the same time, maritime commerce was also practiced by Sempronius Gracchus, the son of an exiled senator and a descendant of the illustrious lineage of the Gracchi (Tacitus *Annales* 1.53, 4.13). During the triumvirate and in the early Augustan period, Vespasian's grandfather, Titus Flavius Petro, an *ingenuus,* was a banker and tax collector in Reate, but other bankers of the time were freedmen, for example Lucius Ceius Serapion of Pompeii.

In the eastern Mediterranean under the early Empire we can find a number of freeborn men among the professional bankers and financiers (*argentarii, nummularii, coactores argentarii, coactores*)—Lucius Praecilius Fortunatus of Cirta and (probably) Gaius Marcius Rufus of Portus (*CIL* 8.7156; Hilding Thylander, *Inscriptions du Port d'Ostie,* 2 vols. [Lund: Gleerup, 1951–52], A 176). We also find some freedmen of the emperor, such as Tiberius Claudius Secundus, whose son Secundinus we know had become a knight in childhood, given that he died at the age of nine (*CIL* 6.1605, 1859, 1860); some freedmen of men of senatorial families, for example Lucius Calpurnius Daphnus, a money changer and banker active in auctions in the Macellum Magnum (*CIL* 6.9183); some freedmen of freedmen such as the Caucilii of the wine market (*CIL* 6.9181–82); and *peregrini* such as two freeborn men, one from Antioch and the other from Synnada, in Phrygia, who were bankers on the Roman forum in the second century A.D. (*Archeologia Classica* 30 [1978]: 252–54). There were also some slaves, such as the future pope Calixtus I, who was the slave of the imperial freedman Carpophorus (Hippolytus of Rome *Refutatio omnium haeresium* 9.12.1–12). In the reign of Commodus and for reasons difficult to determine, Calixtus fled when he could not reimburse those who had deposited money with him. His clients sought out his master, Carpophorus, who knew nothing of the matter. Calixtus occupied the post of a free banker—freedman or freeborn—but when he ran into trouble he fled—an act typical of slaves—and his clients treated him as such when they immediately sought out his master. This episode shows that although the freeborn and the freed were closely associated in the workplace, the same, despite appearances, was not true of slaves. Freedmen's access to most types of labor status was for them an important element in their social assimilation.

This is true only up to a point, however. The *Satyricon* shows us a group of freedmen who pursued urban trades: Proculus the undertaker, Echion the old-clothes seller, Phileros the lawyer, Habinnas, who sold marble monuments. Trimalchio is enthroned among these tradesmen. He is infinitely richer than the others, according to the figures provided by the author, and on his former master's death he has had access to activities typical of a higher social rank, first in commerce and finance, then in the management of his wealth. Everything about Trimalchio evokes aristocracy—except his birth, his vulgarity, his bad taste, his political rights, and the people he frequents!

Politically, the freedman was from time immemorial excluded from the magistracies of Rome itself and from the Senate, and after the *lex Visellia* of A.D. 24 he was even excluded from magisterial posts and the decurions' councils in the municipalities. It is true that posts in the imperial cult (the *seviri Augustales*, the college of priests dedicated to Augustus, for example) were filled by freedmen. Trimalchio had been a sevir, as was his guest, Habinnas the marble dealer. But the *Satyricon* itself points out the limits to the dignity of these pseudomagistrates. The majesty that Habinnas seeks to assure himself by arriving accompanied by a lictor and a number of followers fools no one. As Agamemnon says to the narrator, Encolpius: "Control yourself, you silly fool! It's Habinnas of the priests' college." Agamemnon was not about to mistake him for a praetor! Moreover, it is interesting to note what Trimalchio and his guests, Echion in particular, have to say about local politics. Their reflections are those of plebeians—those who make use of politics but are not instrumental in making policies—men outside the narrow circles of political leadership. They are only interested in bread and the games in the circus, and (probably like most Roman citizens of their times) they measure the competence of the magistrates by the gladiators they produce and the size of the public doles they grant. Gérard Boulvert has noted that even important freedmen under the empire—extremely wealthy men who had occupied high administrative posts—rarely became the patrons of cities. Only three such are known, whereas more than eighty municipal aristocrats have been attested as city patrons.

As for social relations and ties of friendship, Paul Veyne's assessment that the *Satyricon* shows the limits of the freedmen's social integration was correct. The pendulum swings that I have spoken of integrated them into the various labor statuses of Roman society but forbade them entry into the political domain and dissuaded them from acquaintances in keeping with their economic and professional roles. Within the trades did freedmen and the freeborn have friendly private relations? It is probable that they did, even though the *Satyricon* offers no proof. In any event, however, freedmen who were notables did not frequent freeborn notables, and for good reason. A satire of Horace explains why. In Rome the notables were primarily men of the senatorial and equestrian orders, and both refused to have freedmen at their tables. Maecenas, who was more liberal than some others, accepted the company, not of freedmen (which would be too much to expect), but of the sons of freedman. He did not inquire about their fathers' birth (*quali sit quisque parente natus*), since he was persuaded that one could be a man of valor without having great ancestors and that since the age of Servius Tullius Rome had made room for men with no background. This was how he became Horace's friend. Frequenting freedmen was out of the question, however (*dum ingenuus;* "just as long as he's freeborn") (*Satires* 1.6).

Were the municipal aristocracies as exclusive as those of Rome itself? We do not know, and probably that depended on the city. In the "colony" of the *Satyricon* they seem exclusive.

Even if the notables refused to rub elbows with freedmen in private, however, that did not prevent them from granting official honors to a rich former slave who had rendered a service to the city or, in the next generation, from admitting his son into their ranks. Examples of such homage are many. Under Antoninus Pius, for example, there was Gaius Titius Chresimus, who had his own reserved seat at the theater, had a private connection to the municipal water distribution system, and was permitted to wear the distinctive symbols of a decurion for his sponsorship of public games. His son entered the municipal Senate without payment (*CIL* 10.4760). This is a perfect illustration of the enormous gap that separated the freedman from his son. There is no indication that the city magistrates willingly invited the father to dinner.

Did the freedman's place of birth, his mother tongue, his age at manumission, and his education have any effect on his character and his social life? Probably, but how? And how are we to find out how? In all that concerns freedmen, nothing is more unknown than their past—that is, what preceded their liberation—unless it is their affective and family life. How many freeborn men and women were there among them, enslaved by conquest or by slave traders? How many of them were *vernae*, born in the master's house and later freed by him? How long were the *vernae* permitted to live with their blood parents? Was a working knowledge of Latin or Greek a practical condition of manumission? Were "Eastern" slaves more at ease in the system of the cities? Were they more "civilized" or more likely to be freed? How did age at manumission affect their chances of social integration and social advancement? How many slaves continued to live in the same city from birth to liberation and considered it their *patria*?

We have isolated answers on each one of these points that, although suggestive, are too fragmentary to permit the formulation of an overall response or the definition of a prevailing practice.

It can happen that freedmen and freedwomen refer in funerary inscriptions to relatives who were slaves in terms—*pater, mater, soror*, and so forth—normally reserved to familial relations among the freeborn. Licinia Eucharis, a young freedwoman in Rome who died at the age of fourteen and who was already quite accomplished (*docta, erudita omnes artes*), complains in a verse epitaph that by dying she is losing both the love of her mistress and that of her father (*parens, genitor*), who offered the inscription (*CIL* 1, pt. 2.1214). An inscription from Aquincum, on the banks of the Danube, concerns a certain Gaius Julius Euritus, who died at the age of thirty in that city but who came from Alexandria. His two brothers, Julius Crispinus and Julius Lynx, freedmen of the same patron, offered the funerary inscription (*CIL* 3.10551).

This should obviously be interpreted as a de facto, not a legal, kinship; still, such texts testify that in certain cases servile condition did not completely obliterate the solidarity of natural bonds and that the slave child remained in contact with his blood relatives. Are these exceptions, or was this current practice? In any event, the influence of the master or the former master was extremely strong, as attested by the high number of "endogamic" marriages contracted between freedmen of the same patron. It was all the stronger when, as it often happened, the freedman married his slave concubine after having given her her freedom, in which case the patron and the husband were one and the same.

Certain freedmen recall that they were born free, but this is infrequent. I can offer two examples, one of which is very well known: one of the guests in the *Satyricon*, a freedman of the same patron as Trimalchio, claims to be a king's son. How on earth could he have been reduced to slavery? He explains that he chose slavery, preferring to become a

Roman citizen by manumission rather than continue to pay taxes as a *peregrinus* (Petronius *Satyricon* 57.4). The second example is the freedman Gaius Annius Dionysius, whose funerary inscription was found in Rome. Captured at the age of nine, he spent twelve years as a slave, and lived to the age of seventy (*CIL* 6.11712).

Under the Empire, the funerary inscriptions of *vernae* often give the name of the city in which they were born into slavery. Thus Cornelia Dionysias, who died in Puteoli at the age of thirty, was born in the same city, since she is called a *verna Puteolana* (*CIL* 10.3446).

Certain imperial freedmen state their attachment to the city or the region in which they were born (probably as slaves), which they subsequently left and to which they returned rich and powerful when they retired. This is the case with Publius Aelius Onesimus, a freedman of Hadrian's, who gives his *patria* as Nacolea, in the province of Asia, and bequeaths his city of birth the sum of two hundred thousand sesterces, to be invested and the annual interest used for public distributions of wheat and money (*CIL* 3.6998).

As far as we can ascertain, the freedmen seemed less resistant to speaking about their origins and their low birth than is sometimes said. One suspects that their masters and patrons were much less concerned about the past of their present or former slaves than the interested parties. This is logical, since the senators and knights whom we know through their writings had no genuine conception of social promotion. At the extreme limit they noted it and deplored it, but they never analyzed its stages. It hardly ever happens that one of them recounts the life of a freedman, even one who became famous, from his birth to his present prosperity. It was enough for them to state his servile origins and to give the name of his master or patron. This classified the person in question and attached him to a Roman or a senatorial lineage. Further details were deemed unnecessary.

Amid these contradictory influences, how did the freedman represent his own condition, and what idea did he seek to give of it to others, in particular to the society of masters?

It has often, and rightly, been stressed that he granted a large role to chance and to the cult of Fortune. To the freedman, everything seemed possible: the poor man could become rich in an instant and the rich man poor; a miserable wretch could suddenly be overwhelmed by good luck and the happy man by misfortune. The *Satyricon* is full of such anecdotes, and even senators could adopt this notion of liberty concerning one of their own: Pliny the Younger speaks of *fortuna* and *felicitas* in connection with Pallas, and Plutarch speaks of the *tyche* of Demetrius, a freedman of Pompey's (Pliny the Younger *Epistulae* 7.29.3–4; Plutarch *Pompey* 40). A keen sense of the vicissitudes of the human condition was obviously connected with this cult of chance, as was a certain taste for social mobility.

Everyone from the conqueror to the slave was proud of his star. His sense of luck did not prevent the freedman from seeking personal renown—*gloria* and *favor*—or from boasting of his good luck. Pallas and Remmius Palaemon rival Trimalchio in this connection.

Furthermore, the freedman was a curious hybrid of mimesis and bad taste. When he was rich, the aristocrats had a fine time laughing at this odd mixture; when he was poor they probably confounded him with the rest of the plebs and thought no more about him. For his part, the freedman did his best to imitate the freeborn, above all the aristocrat, who was the *ingenuus* par excellence.

With exquisite courtesy, one of Augustus' freedmen, a connoisseur charged with choosing the wines for the emperor's table, told a guest one day that the emperor would never drink a wine that did not come from his native region. This perfect servant (who so perfectly fulfilled his function that we do not know his name) had so thoroughly absorbed aristocratic psychology and taste that he knew that an aristocrat would be fastidious about his favorite wine—a wine from his native region (*suum cuique placet*) (Pliny the Elder *Naturalis historia* 14.72).

Toward the very end of the Republic and at the beginning of the Empire, the freedmen of Rome and of Italy—who were neither the wealthiest nor the poorest freedmen—were represented on their tombs by busts. Paul Zanker, who has studied such busts, rightly compares them with the *imagines* of aristocrats, busts that were never fixed on tombs, however, but rather carried in the funeral procession. In this instance imitation led to an original practice. It could also lead to bad taste when the freedman laid it on too thick in an overly servile imitation that sacrificed the spirit of the original to the letter. Florence Dupont has shown that the freedmen of the *Satyricon* constructed a ridiculous counterculture on the basis of the only true culture—that of the aristocracy. Even when certain freeborn members of the Senate or the equestrian order indulged in the same excesses as he, it was the freedman who was more likely to appear ridiculous. When a freedman determined to get rich by any available means he was greedy and avaricious and practiced usury. Could not the same be said of certain *ingenui,* even of certain senators? Certainly, but the senators would be reproached and the freedman mocked.

I would like to insist, in conclusion, on one or two further ideological differences between the freedmen and their patrons.

It has often been said that Roman notables viewed the freedmen's place in society with a jaundiced eye. The available documentation, taken as a whole, does not seem to me to support this conclusion. In his forty-seventh letter to Lucilius, for example, Seneca speaks of Callistus, a freedman of Caligula's who held an important post in the imperial administration under Claudius. His former master, whose name we do not know, had sold him, and when Callistus had become a powerful imperial freedman he took his vengeance by making the man wait before he would see him. This text has been interpreted as symptomatic of "the pride of the rising class" of the freedmen and an illustration of the irritation that they prompted among the aristocracy. This is not what the anecdote is all about, however: Seneca takes the part of the freedman against his former master, who simply got what he deserved (*Ad Lucilium* 47.9).

Pliny the Elder not only speaks favorably, on several occasions, of the economic activities of certain freedmen but also sets them up as models. Thus he tells how, in the early second century B.C., Gaius Furius Cresimus was victimized by neighbors with large estates because his small parcel of land had a better harvest than theirs. Accused of witchcraft, he appeared in the forum with his tools and his slaves, and the Tribes acquitted him unanimously. The episode shows that public opinion was not totally hostile either to the success of the freedmen or to their enrichment (*Naturalis historia* 18.41–43).

It might be said that stories of the sort had a moral value and that in some sense they aimed at shaming the freeborn by showing them that even freedmen could better them. This is true. But it is also true that such tales do not signify that the freedmen were held to be the equals of the freeborn. Rather, they show that when certain freedmen became wealthy and advanced in society, within well-defined limits and respecting proper time lags, their success was not considered scandalous. At one point in the reign of Nero, there was a great debate on freedmen in the Senate in which the partisans of moderation founded their argument on the place that freedmen held within the body social. The fact that a number of senators and knights were rumored to be the descendants of freedmen, instead of arousing indignation, became in this text a reason

for not being too harsh toward the *libertini* (Tacitus *Annales* 13.26–27).*
The partisans of rigor did not question the social importance of the
freedmen but rather accused them of ingratitude toward their patrons.
Whatever Tacitus' opinion might have been, this text tells us much about
the senators' favorable opinion of freedmen's efforts toward personal
affirmation. Providing they not try to move too fast, however. The
senators could accept the notion that some of their peers descended from
freedmen, but they rejected the notion that a freedman might himself
become a senator. As we have seen, moreover, in private life the freedman seldom frequented the aristocrat except in the context of patronal
relations.

The senators' tolerance may not have been shared by the freeborn
plebeians, particularly not by clients, whose recriminations are echoed in
the works of Martial and Juvenal. The senators' and the knights' *idée fixe*
was certainly not the "rise" of the "class" of the freedmen but rather the
respect of personal obligations that the former slave owed his patron. It
was the *libertus* that worried them, not the *libertinus*. In the Senate debate,
neglect of these duties was the principal argument of the partisans of
severity, and if the freedman Pallas, at the same period, received the
uncustomary recompense from the Senate that was to scandalize Pliny
the Younger a half-century later (fifteen million sesterces and praetorian
insignia), the reasons given in the *senatusconsultus* remained faithful to the
logic of senatorial ideology: Pallas had shown his attachment and his
loyalty to his patrons (*et fidem pietatemque erga patronos*); he had been a
vigilant guardian of the princeps' wealth; and every senator acknowledged his own personal (*pro virili parte*) obligation to him. We can understand why Pliny might lash out at the baseness and the servility of the
senators of that time, but at least they did not write that Pallas had served
Rome and the Empire (*Epistulae* 7.29, 8.6). No matter how wealthy he
might become, the freedman had no access to the governing aristocracy;
the best he could do was to demonstrate his gratitude and loyalty toward
his patron. Innumerable texts make this point, and patrons speak willingly of a personal relationship, often comparing it to bonds of kinship.

The freedman, for his part, might well render due homage to his
patron, but he probably tended not to insist too much on the strength of
this personal tie. The cult of chance and of Fortune was one means for

---

* *Libertinus,* "one belonging to the class of freedmen," described a person in terms of
his current social status; *libertus,* "one who has been granted his freedom," described him
in terms of his relationship to his ex-master.—ED.

attenuating the weight of a connection that the freedman did not experience as truly familial. Trimalchio, an independent freedman whose patron had died and bequeathed him his estate, was a special case, as Veyne remarks. To be free of such ties was probably a freedman's dream come true. Patrons—all patrons, not just Trimalchio's—are the great missing figures in the *Satyricon*. Still, not one of the freedmen we meet in this work tries to forget his origins or his status. One might conclude that the freedman who was a Roman citizen did his best to merge anonymously into the throng of the *ingenui,* the true *Quirites*. Nonetheless, no text attests this attitude, which would, incidentally, probably be useless, since even in a city as big as Rome it would have been difficult to remain anonymous and fool people about one's true social rank. But to return one last time to the *Satyricon,* let me repeat that the freedmen we see in it have no compunctions about recounting their past lives or giving even the most scabrous details about their careers as slaves. Even the mural decorating the vestibule of Trimalchio's house illustrates all the stages in the life of the master of the house, leaving out no detail (*omnia diligenter;* Petronius *Satyricon* 29).

The existence of a milieu of freedmen, of *libertini,* which we might even call an *ordo libertinorum,* was an obstacle to the rapid and complete social integration of the freedmen themselves, albeit not to that of their descendants. This did not seem to displease the interested parties—quite the contrary, perhaps because to some extent it detached them from the household of their former master and plunged them into a life of society.

The freedman was neither slave nor freeborn; he had been a slave, and he was free. He was not the victim of systematic juridical segregation, but neither was he completely integrated into society. Mingling with the freeborn in many activities, economic and other, he was separated from them by his origins and did not often frequent them.

In spite of these contradictions, the freedmen formed a social group. What brought them together was their juridical status, a constant constraint in their daily life, and the ways in which they experienced that status. There was also the memory of an even more constraining status that they had all known: slavery. Finally, there was the way in which both they themselves and others represented that past.

Bibliography

Boulvert, Gérard. *Les esclaves et les affranchis impériaux sous le Haut-Empire romain: Rôle politique et administratif.* Naples: Jovene, 1970.

———. *Domestique et fonctionnaire sous le Haut-Empire romain: La condition de l'affranchi et de l'esclave du prince.* Annales littéraires de l'Université de Besançon, 151. Paris: Belles Lettres, 1974.

Chantraine, Heinrich. *Freigelassene und Sklaven im Dienst der römischen Kaiser.* Wiesbaden: Franz Steiner, 1967.

Duff, A. M. *Freedmen in the Early Roman Empire.* Oxford: Clarendon Press, 1928; reissued Cambridge: W. Heffer, 1958.

Dupont, Florence. *Le plaisir et la loi.* Paris: François Maspéro, 1977.

Fabre, Georges. *Libertus: Recherches sur les rapports patron-affranchi à la fin de la République romaine.* Rome: Ecole française de Rome, 1981.

Finley, Moses I. *Ancient Slavery and Modern Ideology.* New York: Viking Press, 1980.

Lemonnier, Henry. *Etude historique sur la condition privée des affranchis aux trois premiers siècles de l'Empire romain.* Paris: Hachette, 1887.

Meyer, Eduard. "Die Sklaverei im Altertum." Lecture given and published in Dresden in 1898, available in his *Kleine Schriften.* 2d ed. 2 vols. Halle: Niemeyer, 1924. Vol. 1, 169–212.

Rostovtzeff, Mikhail. *The Social and Economic History of the Roman Empire.* Oxford: Clarendon Press, 1926. Rev. P. M. Fraser. Oxford: Clarendon Press, 1957.

Treggiari, Susan. *Roman Freedmen during the Late Republic.* Oxford: Clarendon Press, 1969.

Veyne, Paul. "Vie de Trimalcion." *Annales E.S.C.* 16 (1961): 213–47.

Weaver, P. R. C. *Familia Caesaris: A Social Study of the Emperor's Freedmen and Slaves.* Cambridge: Cambridge University Press, 1972.

Zanker, Paul. "Grabreliefs römischer Freigelassener." *Jahrbuch des deutschen archäologischen Instituts* 90 (1975): 267–315.

7

The Peasant

Jerzy Kolendo

If by "peasant" we mean someone who works land that he owns, we will find very few peasants in many periods of ancient, medieval, and early modern history. Ownership was not a necessary condition in the definition: aside from free peasants who cultivated land they owned, we need to consider large numbers of individuals who worked land that belonged to others, either fairly permanently or in less stable ways, for example seasonally. Owners and nonowners shared characteristics that have been described for other historical periods by scholars of the so-called peasant economy. One such group of workers on the land, the slaves, is treated elsewhere in this book. Here I shall limit my remarks to "free" agricultural workers, even though some categories, for instance the *coloni* of late antiquity, were, in practice, under quasi servitude.

The terms used by the Romans also invite us to define the "peasant" broadly. The basic term was *rusticus,* a form derived from *rus* (country), as opposed to *urbs* (city). But the sense of *rusticus* was not restricted to the peasant: it also meant "simple" or "modest" or, in a pejorative sense, an "oaf," "uncouth," "uncivilized," lacking in urbanity. In this instance as in others, the terminology reflects true social relations.

The other two important terms—*agricola* and *colonus*—are linked to another aspect of rural life. Both are connected with the verb *colo,* to cultivate, St. Augustine tells us, "for this word gives us the derivatives *agricolae* (cultivators of the land), *coloni* (settlers) and *incolae* (inhabitants)" (*The City of God* 10.1).

Agricola (from *ager* [land, soil] and *colo*) expresses man's direct contact with the soil. It could denote the peasant who worked a parcel of land he owned (Pliny *Naturalis historia* 1, pref. 6) or a rich landowner (Varro

De re rustica 1.4.1). The ambivalence of the term springs from the fact that members of the Roman aristocracy had a high regard for their own agricultural occupations. Senators often spent the summer in country residences, drawing pleasure from them as a refuge far from the turmoil of the city, but also supervising the heavy labors of the harvest season.

The term *colonus* has a complicated history. It is often simply synonymous with *agricola,* referring principally to the "small farmer," but it also can refer to members of the senatorial and equestrian aristocracy (Cicero, for example, calls one knight an *optimus colonus; De oratore* 2.287). *Colonus* also has several technical meanings, however, designating the inhabitant of a Roman or Latin colony (who indeed received a parcel of land to farm), or a peasant who rents his land. The latter sense is found as early as the first century B.C., but it became frequent in the beginning of the imperial age and especially in the late Empire.

The history of Roman peasants is, above all, an "external" history, in great part linked to the vicissitudes of Italic agriculture. Our viewpoint is necessarily determined by our sources, which tell us very little about the "internal" history of the peasants, given that they appear almost exclusively in the specific context of political conflict concerning the agrarian laws, as those laws were viewed by the governing class in Rome or, better, by a part of that class. Only in very exceptional instances have peasants left direct testimony about themselves.

Another thing that distorts our view of peasants is the Romans' idealization of rural life in their presentations of Italy's remote past, when great men cultivated their small fields in person, or in bucolic poetry, which presents the peasants under a variety of disguises. Often the best we can do is simply to register the presence of peasants, without being able to penetrate their world. What do we know, for example, of the "free men of the fields" who joined with the slaves in Spartacus' revolt?

Traditionally, the peasants lived within the closed world of agrarian self-sufficiency. They operated at the edges of the mercantile economy, limiting their participation in a market economy to selling produce from their farms locally and in the many small towns of central Italy. In the obscene verses dedicated to Priapus known as the *Priapea,* the poor peasant is usually shown as the owner of a small vegetable garden with a rough wooden statue of Priapus, with an erect phallus, standing guard. Peasants were not limited to cultivating small truck gardens, however, and they enhanced their income by lending a hand as day laborers during the harvest season.

Both the poverty and the primitive life-style of the peasant were proverbial. The *Moretum* attributed to Virgil portrays the peasant who rises at dawn by a cold hearth, dresses in a goatskin, and sets to hard labor at a mill. To lighten his burden he hums country songs. He has only one helper, an African slave woman with thick lips and holes in her shoes.

Virgil's *Georgica* is a didactic poem, but certainly not one aimed at a peasant audience. When he evokes the life of the peasants he had known in Mantua in his youth he has the small farmhold in mind: "Praise thou large estates, farm a small one" (*Georgica* 2.412f.). The idealized symbol of the Virgilian peasant is the famous *senex Corycius* (one of the pirates of Cilicia whom Pompey defeated and settled in southern Italy), who had created a marvelous farm out of a few jugera of abandoned land near Taranto:

> And in truth, were I not now hard on the very close of my toils, furling my sails and hastening to turn my prow to land, perchance, too, I might be singing what careful tillage decks rich gardens, singing of the rose-beds of twice-blooming Paestum; how the endive rejoices in the streams it drinks, and the green banks in the parsley; and how the gourd, winding along the ground, swells into its paunch. Nor had I been silent on the late-blooming narcissus, or the curling acanthus-stem, the pale ivy or the shore-loving myrtle. For I call to mind how under the towers of Oebalia's citadel, where dark Galaesus waters his yellow fields, I saw an old Corycian, who had a few acres of unclaimed land, and this a soil not rich enough for bullocks' ploughing, unfitted for the flock, and unkindly to the vine. Yet, as he planted herbs here and there among the bushes, with white lilies about, and vervain, and slender poppy, he matched in contentment the wealth of kings, and, returning home in the late evening, would load his board with unbought dainties. He was first to pluck roses in spring and apples in autumn; and when sullen winter was still bursting rocks with the cold, and curbing running waters with ice, he was already culling the soft hyacinth's bloom, chiding laggard summer and the loitering zephyrs. So he, too, was first to be enriched with mother-bees and a plenteous swarm, the first to gather frothing honey from the squeezed comb. Luxuriant were his limes and wild laurels; and all the fruits his bounteous

tree donned in its early bloom, full as many it kept in the
ripeness of autumn. He, too, planted out in rows elms far-
grown, pear-trees when quite hard, thorns even now bearing
plums, and the plane already yielding to drinkers the service
of its shade. (Virgil *Georgica* 4.116–48).

Virgil's aim of showing the marvelous results of hard labor in the fields
is evident. I hardly need add that reality was somewhat different.

Historical sources relating to peasants in the early and middle republican
period appear to be fairly numerous. The historians (Livy, Dionysius of
Halicarnassus) tell us of the agrarian laws and the grave conflicts connected with their promulgation. Ancient tradition has transmitted to us
a good deal of information on the most ancient phase of Roman agriculture. We also know relatively well how the Roman and Latin colonies
were founded. There is debate about the value of these sources, however.
Between the end of the last century and the beginning of our own, the
prevailing historiographical tendency was to be extremely critical of
them. It was said, in particular, that the entire tradition regarding the
agrarian laws and the *leges de modo agrorum* (which placed restrictions on
the occupation of public lands) was not trustworthy, since it was a simple
anticipation of events under the Gracchi and Sulla. Historians today tend
to be less critical and to hold that at least some information on the agrarian history of Rome in the early Republic is reliable.

Roman society in the ages of the kings and the early Republic was a
peasant society. Nonetheless, we can begin to speak of peasants only
when occupations other than agriculture make their appearance. Both
literary documentation and archaeological evidence reveal the presence
of groups of craftsmen and merchants in Rome under the kings, but these
groups were a tiny minority in the population, coming for the most part
from outside Rome.

The entire governing group during the early Republic (the fifth and
fourth centuries B.C.) was composed of "peasants." This is confirmed by
much later tradition when it speaks of the great men of the past who
labored in the fields. Cincinnatus learned of his nomination as dictator
while he was plowing. The word *viatores* (envoys) was customarily derived from *via*, since envoys had to travel far to find in their fields the
senators who had been entrusted with high office (Pliny the Elder *Naturalis historia* 18.21). This tradition lauded the simplicity of the ancestors
and thought it necessary for the senatorial aristocracy to own land.

Two of the basic questions are, when did a more or less homogeneous class of peasants form (albeit with some notable differences in wealth)? and when did a class of landowners who did not themselves cultivate the soil become separated from it? This dual phenomenon is clearly visible in the third century B.C., but it must have begun long before. The appearance of a separate group of wealthy landowners should be seen in connection with the harsh struggle between patricians and plebeians and the Roman conquest of Italy, which led to the confiscation of the greater part of the lands of the defeated populations. The confiscated lands became part of the *ager publicus populi Romani,* and they were exploited in various ways. Clashes over how the *ager publicus* was to be exploited were extremely harsh, particularly when there were no new conquests. Some wanted them used as pasture for transhumant herding; others demanded that they be put to more strictly agricultural use.

From the juridical point of view, this sizable landed patrimony might be designated for the founding of colonies and for *partitio viritim* (individual allotments) among the Roman citizens. Another possibility was to leave its distribution to the censors, who had the authority to assign land according to a number of criteria. The latter solution led to uneven results from an economic viewpoint. The largest portion was rented out in large lots or assigned in hereditary ownership on the payment of a tax. Such provisions worked to the nearly exclusive benefit of the senators (who also had the advantage of having the censors drawn from among their ranks) and, somewhat later, of the wealthiest and most influential of the equestrian class. The formation of the great landholdings began with this appropriation (with titles that varied) of the *ager publicus.*

In reality, there were limitations to this occupation of the public lands. At the beginning, the prevailing principle seemed to be that it was illegal to obtain a lot too big for the grantee to cultivate himself. In a second phase, it was permitted to acquire the amount of land that one intended to exploit. Finally, an attempt was made to fix an upper limit to individual possession; in particular, the *lex de modo agrorum* made it illegal to occupy more than 500 jugera (125 hectares; 311 acres) of the *ager publicus* or to pasture more than one hundred head of large livestock or five hundred head of small on it. It is difficult to put an accurate date to this decree, but it was probably promulgated after the Second Punic War and certainly before 167 B.C. According to tradition, the limit of 500 jugera had already figured in one of the *leges Licinae Sextiae* promulgated in 367 B.C., during the last phase of the struggles between patricians and plebeians. We cannot exclude the possibility that those laws set a maximum to the amount of land one man could occupy, but the limit of 500 jugera is too high a figure for an age in which Roman territory included only Latium and a narrow band of southern Etruria.

In practice, all dispositions to limit the size of land parcels could be gotten around, and the question of the use of the *ager publicus* remained a fundamental topic of debate and a cause for political conflict for most of the Republic.

The modest dimensions of the farms cultivated by peasants are a theme that returns frequently in tradition connected with Rome under the kings and in the early and middle Republic. Romulus was supposed to have granted every Roman a field measuring *bina iugera* (1 *iugerum* equaled one-fourth hectare). This was to be the *heredium,* the parcel of land that a man owned in full and could transmit to his heirs. In the oldest Roman colonies as well, the lots granted are reported to have been of that size. The data are discordant, however. It is also reported that the plebs, after the kings were chased from Rome, had obtained lots of 7 jugera, and another source reports that the lots assigned after the war against Pyrrhus were of the same size. The victor, Curius Dentatus (consul in 290), is supposed to have said that any citizen who found 7 jugera of land insufficient was to be considered dangerous. When Cincinnatus was called to the dictatorship, the farmhold he cultivated was supposed to be 4 jugera. Obviously, these are the traditions of legend, born during the persistent struggles for agrarian reform in the late Republic. They connect with the old principle of Roman agrarian economy that said that it was not just to own land that one could not cultivate well.

Tradition speaks of small parcels of land in the following period as well. The land grants in the Roman colonies founded in the beginning of the second century varied in size, but they were almost always of reduced scale: 5 jugera (in two instances), 6 jugera (two instances), 8 jugera (once), 10 (once), 51½ jugera (once). Only in the colonies of Latin law were larger lots assigned, the cavalry soldiers normally receiving 30 or 40 jugera and infantrymen 15 or 20. In Bononia (Bologna), however, knights received 70 jugera and the other colonists 50; in Aquileia, taken out of the Roman dominions in 183, knights obtained 140 jugera, centurions 100, and infantrymen 50.

These differences have been explained in various ways. According to the commonest hypothesis, the reason for them was to avoid the formation of large fortunes in the Roman colonies. What remains unexplained in any event is how a peasant family could survive cultivating a farmhold of barely 2 jugera, even by intensive manual labor. We must also remember that in the system of biennial crop rotation only one-half the available land was cultivated every year. It is possible that the calculation of 1 *iugerum* = 0.25182 hectares is too low. According to Livy (5.30.8), after the conquest of Veii, land was distributed in lots of 7 jugera per capita, although Diodorus speaks of 4 jugera in one instance and, according to a different tradition (also mentioned by Diodorus), of 28 jugera. These may not be simple errors but variations in area measurement.

It is generally held that the exploitation of common lands accompanied the small farmholds of the peasants of ancient Italy. The *bina iugera* of Romulus would thus have been only the kitchen garden. The same is true of the colonies, where the grantees would have had access to vast undivided lands to supplement their allotments.

These variations in the indications of lot size are a constant throughout agrarian history under the Republic. We find the same variation in the land grants of the following age, when the reforms of the Gracchi provided for lots of 30 jugera; Marius is supposed to have said that 14 jugera should suffice for a peasant family, and in the first century B.C. the highly fertile lands of the *ager Campanus* and the *ager Stellas* were divided into lots of 10 and 12 jugera.

Given this variation, it is obviously very difficult to evaluate the real living conditions of the Roman peasants. We need also to keep in mind that any general description will run counter to the extreme variety of local situations, which were further complicated after Roman conquest by differences in the juridical systems of the subject populations.

Agrarian unrest and proposals to distribute land to plebeians were thus concentrated in a few periods. Problems arose, above all, when external conquest stagnated and there was a consequent need to divide up the lands already available. It is obvious that at such times not all appetites could be satisfied. Nor were colonies founded at an even pace. This alternation between periods in which the Romans had new lands available for cultivation and periods in which they did not is another fundamental trait of the history of Rome in the early Republic, and it may explain the intensity of the resulting social conflicts.

For the patricians, who held power, acquiring land was a minor problem. But who was there to cultivate it? This question raises the question of clientage. Clients often received a parcel of land that belonged to their patron, to whom they then owed a part of the harvest. A notable quantity of manpower must also have come from individuals reduced to slavery because of debts: Varro, who calls them *obaerari* and defines them as workers "between freedom and slavery, states that in his times they were found above all in Illyricum, Asia, and Egypt (*De re rustica* 1.17.2–3).

In the second century B.C. the great Mediterranean conquests brought fundamental changes in the conditions of the peasant class. The process in fact brought a basic "modernization" of social and economic structures in which Rome began to resemble the more evolved Hellenistic countries.

In central and southern Italy, times were hard for the small-scale landholding peasant, but midsized and large property ownership reliant on slave labor increased. In a well-known passage Plutarch tells us that Tiberius Gracchus, as he traveled through Etruria, was struck by the deserted countryside, where he only saw bands of slaves.

Ancient sources point to a number of concomitant reasons for this crisis. First of all, military service removed the peasants from their fields and kept them beyond the borders of Italy for long periods of time. If the *pater familias* spent many years far away from his farm, it necessarily declined for lack of supervision and manpower, and when he returned, he was no longer used to the hard labor of field work. Furthermore, when soldiers who were recruited principally among the peasants and who had lived in a predominantly or exclusively natural economy served in the more highly developed Hellenistic countries, they came into contact with the forms of a mercantile economy. War furnished them with means, which were spent on the spot. When they returned, their "consumer" habits could no longer be satisfied. The development of the city, Rome above all, offered a better opportunity to replicate the life-style they had experienced under arms, and the agrarian population was sucked into the great urban centers. In second- and first-century B.C. Rome, the construction industry was flourishing, and the various sectors of crafts were becoming established; they all used the labor not only of slaves and freedmen but also of newcomers to the city from the country. It was also possible to survive by selling one's vote, by relying on the distributions of low-cost (later free) grain, and by means of a patron's generosity. As Sallust wrote: "The young men who had maintained a wretched existence by manual labour in the country, tempted by public and private doles had come to prefer idleness in the city to their hateful toil" (*The War with Catiline* 37.6). But the life-style of Rome still attracted peasants: "Practically all the heads of families have sneaked within the walls, abandoning the sickle and the plough, and would rather busy their hands in

the theatre and in the circus than in the grain-fields and the vineyards"
(Varro *De re rustica* 2, pref. 4).

Another reason for the peasants' abandonment of the land was competition from the great landed properties that were concentrated in the
hands of the senators, the equestrian class, and the local aristocracies. The
second century was a period of intense development of large landholdings
worked by slave labor and in large part given over to the profitable
cultivation of olives and grapes. The dominant class managed to gain
control of enormous stretches of the *ager publicus* and to transform it into
de facto private property, which they managed to exploit thanks to an
influx of slave manpower. "It costs as little as a Sardinian" was a common
saying in 177 B.C., when 65,000 prisoners were put up for sale after
military operations in Sardinia that were little better than a gigantic slave
raid—one event that can stand as an example for the phenomenon.

The cultivation of grapevines and olive trees, which was much more
profitable than that of cereals, could be undertaken only by wealthy
proprietors because of the large setup costs involved (especially in the
case of vineyards) and the long wait for the first harvests. The small
peasant farmer not only could not make the required investment, he
could not even produce grain that cost less than the grain produced on
the great properties or imported from the provinces. The mercantile
economy attracted the peasant as a consumer but it excluded him as a
producer.

Another reason for the crisis was the large landholders' usurpation
of the communal lands that had been a fundamental part of the peasants'
economic existence, in particular for pasturage.

The massive exodus of peasants toward the city also had extremely serious military consequences in the Roman Republic because recruitment
became increasingly difficult. The agrarian reforms of the Gracchi were
aimed precisely at reconstructing the peasant class by the distribution
of small land parcels of the *ager publicus*. The agrarian law of Tiberius
Gracchus promulgated in 133 B.C. and again ten years later by Gaius
Gracchus limited the amount of public land that any one person could
occupy to 500 jugera plus 250 jugera for each of a maximum of two
children, or at most 1,000 jugera in all. The public land that thus became
available for distribution was to be distributed to the peasants in inalienable lots of 30 jugera.

A three-man commission was charged with the task of assigning the lands (*triumviri agris dandis adsignandis iudicandis*), and the border stones found in a number of regions in central and southern Italy give evidence of its activities. The senatorial aristocracy stubbornly opposed the reform, however. Not only did these measures encounter violent political opposition, which on two occasions led to bloody showdowns, but technical difficulties arose: for instance, how was the true *ager publicus* to be distinguished from lands cultivated as private property?

It is difficult to evaluate the real results of this attempted reform: we do not even know how many people benefited from the triumviri's grants. Whatever their result, the reforms began to be dismantled immediately after the assassination of Gaius Gracchus. Among other things, the fundamental clause of inalienable title to the lots assigned was abolished.

The agrarian reforms of the first century B.C. were of another nature, since they assigned lands to veterans at a time when most soldiers came from the poorest parts of the population. Grants of this sort represented a sort of discharge bonus designed to guarantee survival to ex-soldiers when they were discharged from service.

The first such distribution took place during the age of Sulla. According to Appian, lands were granted to 120,000 persons. According to the more realistic estimates of modern historians, the figure should be more like 80,000. To carry out this vast operation, the territories of a number of Italic cities who had opposed Sulla were confiscated; thus we cannot state that such provisions succeeded in reconstituting the peasants as a class, because what they gave with one hand was taken away with the other. I might add that these veterans did not always want to or prove able to transform themselves into peasants, and the land was often immediately sold or leased.

The practice of distributing lands to veterans continued in the epoch of the civil wars. Pompey, Caesar, and Octavian all had recourse to such methods, but the greatest distribution of land came during the principate of Augustus.

Besides the small-scale peasant landowners who cultivated their own farms and the waged day laborers, there was also a category of persons who cultivated a parcel of land that belonged to someone else, paying the owner rent in money, produce, or labor service. The term that best fits their condition is *coloni,* providing we keep in mind that the reality behind the term is not what the model of the *colonus* became in late antiquity.

Evidence of peasants who worked lands that belonged to others can be found as early as the early Republic, but at that time such arrangements were connected with such phenomena unique to that age as enslavement for nonpayment of debts and specific sorts of clientage relations. It is thus misleading to look for a continuation of these situations in following ages.

In the late Republic, tenant farming was above all a part of the development of large landholdings. Even so, we are not always able to discern the social status concealed under the ambiguous term *colonus*. We know that some of the great landed proprietors were in the habit of assigning small parcels of land to *coloni* as well as using slave labor. Columella tells something of the criteria that entered into their choice:

> We should take pains to keep with us tenants who are country-bred and at the same time diligent farmers, when we are not at liberty to till the land ourselves or when it is not feasible to cultivate it with our own servants; though this does not happen except in districts which are desolated by the severity of the climate and the barrenness of the soil. . . . On far distant estates, however, which it is not easy for the owner to visit, it is better for every kind of land to be under free farmers than under slave overseers, but this is particularly true of grain land. (*De re rustica* 1.7.4)

According to Columella, then, the use of *coloni* complemented the use of slaves and was explained by the distance or the infertility of the terrain.

On his property in the Sabine hills, Horace had five *coloni,* who farmed small holdings. On another part of his land, eight slaves worked under the direction of a *vilicus*. Under the Empire the use of *coloni* grew, as shown by the correspondence of Pliny the Younger, whose holdings in Tifernum Tiberinum (now Città di Castello) were farmed for the most part by *coloni*.

In order to determine the position of the *coloni* vis-à-vis the property owner, it is fundamental to establish the terms of their contract and know whether it involved money, produce, or labor (although the latter arrangement, if it existed, must have been extremely rare in Italy in the early Empire).

The obligations of the *colonus* were usually established in one of two ways: either he gave the owner a fixed quantity of the harvest (in kind or in money) or he agreed to give him a payment that varied proportionally to the value of the harvest. At the time, the most widespread form of contract was an annual rent payable in money and fixed for five years—one *lustrum*. *Remissiones,* or reductions in rent, were conceded when catastrophe struck, but the sources also often speak of arrears (*reliqua colonorum*).

Payments in kind often were of secondary economic importance: the *parvae accessiones,* for example a comb of honey or some cheeses that the *colonus* brought to the owner, were more like a gift that served to reinforce the bond between the two parties.

The consignment of a portion of the harvest varying according to the value of the harvest itself is described in detail by Pliny the Younger, who was obliged to concede *remissiones* after a series of bad years that had impoverished his *coloni*. It was at their demand that he set up that sort of payment; unlike a fixed rent, it did not ruin a peasant after a bad harvest. The system had a disadvantage for the owner, however, in that some form of control was required to verify the exact value of the crop.

It is impossible to determine the extent of this form of dependence in the early empire. Nor do we know anything about the relationship between slave labor and the labor of the *coloni* in either the midsized *villae* or the *latifundia* (large estates). In particular the second and the third centuries were a time of few literary sources, and recent excavations of *villae rusticae* fail to furnish reliable information on the question. The tendency is clear, however: the number of *coloni* tended to increase, even when it was often difficult to recruit that sort of manpower (Pliny the Younger *Epistulae* 3.19.7 even speaks of *penuria colonorum*).

Even though contracts were normally drawn up for five years, the *coloni* tended to remain on their farms for longer periods, as was to the interest of both the owner and the peasants. According to Columella, the *felicissimus fundus* was the one with *coloni* born on the farm. Arrears, the *reliqua colonorum,* tied the *coloni* to the land even more, although, as Pliny the Younger attests, they did not seem to have made any great effort to pay off their debts. Despite recurrent conflicts, both parties had an interest in continuing the relationship.

In late antiquity state intervention sought to limit the mobility of the agricultural population in order to guarantee the stability of its own fiscal levies. Juridical sources give us a great deal of information on farming by *coloni* during this period. According to traditional historiography, *coloni* working on small parcels of land gradually replaced slave labor until they ultimately occupied a central role in the economic system. Some historians even see the *coloni* who farmed the land in late antiquity as an anticipation of medieval serfdom. Recent studies have criticized this unilateral interpretation and stressed the partiality of the documentation at hand. Indeed, the available documents almost exclusively regard fiscal problems, which are not all there is to say about the agricultural system of *coloni* in late antiquity. After the fiscal reform of Diocletian, every individual who was obliged to pay a head tax (*capitatio*) was inscribed in a register kept for that purpose in his place of residence. Taxpayers were grouped together, and the group was collectively responsible for paying the tax. From a fiscal viewpoint, the *coloni* were thus tied to the land on which they lived. A law of 332 established, for example, that if a landowner accepted a *colonus* who "belonged" to someone else, he not only had to return him to his former proprietor but also had to pay the head tax for the entire period during which the *colonus* had been on his land.

It is evident that the interests of the state, which was concerned about the stability of fiscal revenues, coincided with those of the proprietors, who wanted to avoid losing manpower from their estates. In late antiquity, there was more "land without men" than "men without land."

Waged day laborers also played a fundamental role in Roman agriculture. Given the seasonal ups and downs of agricultural work, it was against the economic interests of the great proprietor to satisfy this large but temporary demand for manpower by using the slaves who were part of the permanent staff of the *villa*, as they would thus inevitably have been underused for the greater part of the year.

Cato speaks of the important role of such day laborers. Among the various elements to keep in mind when acquiring a *villa*, he recalls the availability of sufficient manpower in the area (*De agri cultura* 1.3: *operariorum copia sit*). Good relations with neighbors were also important because they facilitated the recruitment of seasonal farmhands. Waged day laborers are also recorded by Varro in connection with his typology of agricultural manpower: he states that such workers should be used in unhealthy territories because the death of a day laborer did less economic harm than the death of a slave (Varro *De re rustica* 1.17.2). Day laborers were to be used for dangerous tasks as well, such as harvesting grapes planted *ad arbustum* (using trees as a support).

At times day laborers worked in teams under the direction of entrepreneurs called *mancipes*. One of these men is reputed to have been the great-grandfather of the emperor Vespasian, whose workers moved from Umbria to the Sabine hills. This is probably an instance of the migration of mountain populations to more fertile terrains situated close to Rome. Laborers of this sort were recruited among the poorest peasants, those who could not make a living from their farms alone. Their work thus integrated them into society, particularly since it had the advantage of being paid in cash, often a rare commodity in the Roman economic system.

Landowners, renters, and waged day laborers: Roman peasants were a highly variegated group in all ways. Differences between them were further accentuated by the diversity of the local situation. Still, the complexity of the picture traced here went along with a high degree of unity in a class constituted of individuals whose simple survival depended, in all cases, on labor in the fields.

Bibliography

Brunt, P. A. *Italian Manpower, 225 B.C.–A.D. 14*. London: Oxford University Press, 1971; 2d ed., Oxford: Clarendon Press, 1987.

Capogrossi Colognesi, Luigi. *La terra in Roma antica: Forme di proprietà e rapporti produttivi*. Rome: La Sapienza, 1981–. Vol. 1, *Età arcaica*.

———. *Max Weber e la società antica*. Vol. 1. Rome: 1988.

———. *Proprietà e signoria in Roma antica*. Rome, n.d.

———, ed. *L'agricoltura romana: Guida storica e critica*. Rome and Bari: Laterza, 1982.

Carrié, Jean-Michel. "Le 'colonat du Bas-Empire': Un mythe historiographique?" *Opus* 1 (1982): 351–70.

———. "Un roman des origines: Les généalogies du 'colonat du Bas-Empire'." *Opus* 2 (1983): 205–51.

De Martino, Francesco. *Storia economica di Roma antica*. 2 vols. Florence: La Nuova Italia, 1980.

Evans, John K. "*Plebs rustica*: The Peasantry of Classical Italy." *American Journal of Ancient History* 5 (1980): no. 1, 19–47; no. 2, 134–73.

Finley, Moses I. *The Ancient Economy*. 2d ed. Berkeley and Los Angeles: University of California Press, 1982.

———, ed. *Studies in Roman Property*. Cambridge: Cambridge University Press, 1976.

Gabba, Emilio, and Marinella Pasquinucci. *Strutture agrarie e allevamento transumante nell'Italia romana (III–I sec. a.C.)*. Pisa: Giardini, 1979.

Garnsey, Peter, ed. *Non-Slave Labour in the Greco-Roman World*. Suppl. vol. 9. Cambridge: Cambridge Philological Society, 1980.

Giardina, Andrea, ed. *Società romana e impero tardoantico*. 4 vols. Rome and Bari: Laterza, 1986. Vol. 1, *Istituzioni, ceti, economie*.

Giardina, Andrea, and Aldo Schiavone, eds. *Società romana e produzione schiavistica.* 3 vols. Rome and Bari: Laterza, 1981. Vol. 1, *L'Italia: Insediamenti e forme economiche.*

Giliberti, Giuseppe. *Servus quasi colonus: Forme non tradizionali di organizzazione del lavoro nella società romana.* Naples: Jovene, 1981.

Johne, Klaus-Peter, Jens Köhn, and Volker Weber. *Die Kolonen in Italien und den westlichen Provinzen des römischen Reiches: Eine Untersuchung der literarischen, juristischen und epigraphischen Quellen vom 2. Jahrhundert v.u.Z. bis zu den Severen.* Schriften zur Geschichte und Kultur der Antike 21. Berlin: Akademie-Verlag, 1983.

Kolendo, Jerzy. *Le traité d'agronomie des Saserna.* Archiwum Filologiczne 29. Trans. Janina Kasinska. Wrocław: Zakład narodowy imienia Ossolińskich, Wydawnictwo Polskiej Akademii Nauk, 1973.

———. "Il lavoro servile e i mutamenti delle tecniche agrarie nell'Italia antica dal I secolo a.C. al I secolo d.C." In *Storia sociale ed economica dell'età classica negli studi polacchi contemporanei,* ed. Izabela Biezunska-Malowist. Milan: Cisalpino-La Goliardica, 1975. Pp. 9–53.

———. *L'agricoltura nell'Italia romana: Tecniche agrarie e progresso economico dalla tarda repubblica al principato.* Trans. Celeste Zawadzka. Rome: Editori Riuniti, 1980.

Kuziščhin, Vasilii Ivanovich. *Genesis rabovladel' českich latifundij v Italii (II v. do n.e.–I v. n.e.).* Moscow, 1976. Available in Italian as *La grande proprietà agraria nell'Italia romana: II sec. a.C.–I sec. d.C..* Trans. Salvatore Arcella. Rome: Editori Riuniti, 1984.

Neeve, P. W. de. *Colonus: Private Farm-Tenancy in Roman Italy during the Republic and the Early Principate.* Amsterdam: J. C. Gieben, 1984.

———. *Peasants in Peril: Location and Economy in Italy in the Second Century B.C.* Amsterdam: J. C. Gieben, 1984.

Rostovtzeff, Mikhail. *The Social and Economic History of the Roman Empire.* Oxford: Clarendon Press, 1926. 2d ed. rev. by M. Fraser. 2 vols. Oxford: Clarendon Press, 1957.

Ruggini, Lellia. *Economia e società nell' "Italia Annonaria": Rapporti fra agricoltura e commercio dal IV al VI secolo d.C.* Milan: Giuffrè, 1961.

Sirago, Vito Antonio. *L'Italia agraria sotto Traiano.* Recueil de travaux d'Histoire et de Philologie, 4e série, 16. Louvain: Université de Louvain, 1958.

Tibiletti, Gianfranco. "Il possesso dell'*ager publicus* e le norme *de modo agrorum* sino ai Gracchi." *Athenaeum* 26 (1948): 173–236; 27 (1949): 3–41.

———. "Ricerche di storia agraria romana, I: La politica agraria dalla guerra annibalica ai Gracchi." *Athenaeum* 28, (1950): 183–266.

8

The Craftsman

Jean-Paul Morel

COULD ONE BE A CRAFTSMAN and be truly Roman? This is a necessary question, given the disdain that the Roman "intelligentsia" showed toward all that concerned artisan work and waged labor. For Cicero, the workshop was irreconcilable with the condition of a free man: "no workshop can have anything liberal about it" (*nec quicquam ingenuum habere potest officina*) and "all mechanics are engaged in vulgar trades" (*opifices omnes in sordida arte versantur*) (*De officiis* 1.42). For Seneca, the artisan's tasks were "vile" and "vulgar" and "had nothing to do with the true qualities of man" (*ad virtutem non pertinent*).

These opinions are without appeal. They eliminated crafts or manufacturing activities for any proper, self-respecting man. They relegated the craftsman to a less than human level or to the rank of a second-class citizen, and with him the artist and the technician and, more generally, all who performed labor in exchange for wages. In this we can see reflections of an entire current of thought that, in many lands and throughout the centuries, has consistently ignored those whose labor enabled societies to operate.

At the same time, however, any observers of the Roman world, if they are lucid and in good faith, cannot fail to be struck by the immense quantity of manufactured goods that were produced, exchanged, and consumed and whose less destructible vestiges—the tip of the iceberg—archaeology ceaselessly brings to light. Our observers might note, here and there, iconographic representations and inscriptions that provide scattered but revealing glimpses of an entire world of specialists and shopkeepers. They might remark that the central state or the municipal powers categorized products and controlled their price and that the legions and certain sanctuaries had their own workshops. They might see the proliferation of goods and services offered in the innumerable cities of an empire that was nearly universal and become aware of their circulation through the arteries of this immense body.

In short, the archaeologist, the historian, or the curious amateur must acknowledge that the craftsman, his wares, and his services occupied a place in the Roman world unimaginable from a reading of ancient authors, from perusing the corpus of Latin inscriptions, or from visiting most of our museums. The mere fact of wondering how we might approach that craftsman and look behind all the screens that hide his personality and his activities gives us some notion of his status, some grasp of his situation in society, and a start on imagining the sentiments that he inspired or experienced.

Although it is relatively easy to know and study the craft products of the Roman world, it is difficult to know the Roman craftsman and his behavior, so strong was the customary camouflage of *honestas* that determined what could properly be said and what one could admit without losing face. It took a *lex Metilia de fullonibus* promulgated in 220 B.C. for Pliny to admit that it was not unseemly to speak of the fullers' guild. Roman crafts appear in our sources only when laws refer to them, when a technological innovation piques the curiosity of the naturalists and the encyclopedists, when some individual owes his notoriety to wealth considered ill-gotten because it comes from trade, or when a high-placed personage takes a (necessarily) perverse pleasure in the company of artisans. Remmius Palaemon, an ex-slave who earned a considerable income from clothing manufacturing under Tiberius and Claudius, quite naturally attracted Suetonius' scorn: He was a creature lost in vices (*infamis omnibus vitiis*). His *arrogantia* and *luxuria* were insupportable; he called Varro a pig. Furthermore, it was not Verres' harsh tax levies in Sicily that inspired Cicero's famous *O tempora, O mores* (2 *In Verrem* 4.56); rather that exclamation comes at the end of a passage in which Cicero describes the proprietor of a goldsmith's workshop supervising his workers and dressed like a vulgar artisan "in a dark tunic and a grey cloak," the activity and clothing equally unworthy of a Roman.

Three sorts of documents contain the better part of what we know about Roman craftsmen: texts that speak of them, the inscriptions they have left, and the products they made. According to which one we turn to, the craftsman will seem to us a vile and shameless being or, when he is a master of his craft, a notable in his city, in which case we will have a more objective but terribly vague image of him. Not only are these three approaches contradictory, they are also inseparable, together defining the ambiguous situation of the craftsman in Roman society.

It is singularly difficult even to define the Roman craftsman. The problem lies in the fact that the word *ars* and its derivatives apply to the highest forms of knowledge as well as to the most practical sorts of ordinary tasks and that they embrace what we now distinguish as craftsmanship, technology, and art. The essential distinction, for the Romans, was not between intellectual and manual activities but between occupations that aimed only at the pleasures of the mind and those with utilitarian purposes (*animi libera oblectatio / utilitas*); between the "liberal" arts—that is, those worthy of a free man such as mathematics, rhetoric, or philosophy—and the others—all the others, from manual trades to medicine or architecture. More than one Roman could adopt as his own the opinions of Plato and Aristotle, who held craftsmen to be vulgar and ignoble persons unworthy of being considered citizens. The most competent technicians did not escape this criticism the minute they debased the liberal arts by practical application.

This is the immense brotherhood of those whom we might consider artisans, be they miserably poor or immensely rich; this is our vast field of inquiry. If we remember that we need to take into consideration more than a thousand years of history and cover a geographical area that ends up, at the height of the empire, at millions of square kilometers, we can see that the vast variety of conditions, ways of life, and behavior patterns infinitely fragment the Roman craftsman for whom we are searching and dash any hope of finding an ideal type situated anywhere other than in the simplistic judgments of the ancient authors.

When we attempt to penetrate the complexity of concrete conditions, we note that the modern concepts and terms that have provoked such intense polemics concerning ancient crafts—artisan and worker, manufacturing and industry, bourgeoisie and proletariat—are not necessarily any less functional for our task than the Latin vocabulary, which is often ambiguous.

Thus a word like *vestiarius* can designate, according to context, someone who makes clothes, someone who sells them, or even a domestic servant charged with responsibility for clothing or the upkeep of a wardrobe in a master's house. And this is simply one example among many. The distinction between the craftsman and the domestic servant is, moreover, fairly artificial in a society in which a good many craft products were made within the *domus* or the *villa*. Similarly, the artisan was often merged with the merchant in the shopkeeper's world in which an important part of the crafts life of antiquity took place. It often happened that a cobbler or coppersmith who worked at the back of his shop also sold what he had made. At least this gave such craftsmen a degree of independence and put them into permanent contact with the life of the city and the animation of its streets.

Many workers were not so lucky and did not share that opportunity. We sense another ambiguity dawning here, before which our vocabulary is often not only imprecise but misleading. We know that Roman "craftsmen" did not always enjoy even the relative autonomy and the initiative that the words "artisan" or "craftsman" evoke today. A first line of demarcation regarded the juridical definition of his social status. He might be free by birth (and in this case he could be his own boss or a waged worker, a *mercennarius*); he might be a freedman or a slave, and there is no simple rule that accounts for the infinite variety of situations that pertained in various epochs and regions. It is only partially true that the majority of craftsmen were slaves or freedmen (those mutants of Roman society). What was perhaps true of Rome in the first century B.C. was no longer true two centuries later or four centuries later; what it is probably accurate to say about Italy in the early Empire is incorrect concerning Gaul at the same time. But above all, social stratifications incongruent with this basic distinction were superimposed on it. Not only because the slave, the freedman, and the *ingenuus* might work side by side in the same workshop, where the hierarchy of tasks and responsibilities often, but not always, corresponded to that of social status, but because another line of cleavage existed between what we would call the artisan and the worker.

There were, in fact, some workshops in which the workers' tasks were not only anonymous but oppressive and broken down into limited, repetitive tasks. In ceramics, metallurgy, textiles, and other activities there were enterprises that flourished at certain epochs and in certain regions and that employed large numbers of unspecialized workers and assembly-line techniques to make wares destined for mass sale, using division of labor and standardization to satisfy criteria based on the lowest possible skill requirements and production cost. *Mutatis mutandis,* the same phenomenon was characteristic of the building trades. It is thanks to vestiges of the objects that were manufactured and the buildings that were built that we can form some idea of the "slave mode of production" whose importance and originality modern historiography so rightly emphasizes. This sort of workshop, manufactory, or building site was particularly characteristic of central Italy on the Tyrrhenian coast during the second and first centuries B.C. and, to a lesser degree, in the early Empire. We know practically nothing of the identity of the men they employed or the life the workers led: neither the objects nor the texts tell us anything explicit about them. All that one can suppose is that such workers were, in the great majority (perhaps all?), slaves. And that their condition was closer to that of the worker than to the craftsman.

A text of Diodorus Siculus gives us a glimpse of the way one of these industries—the metal industry of Puteoli (Pozzuoli)—was organized in the late Republic. Partially refined iron imported from the island of Elba was bought by "men" in that city (we are told no more about them) who had collected "a multitude of artisans in metal" to make "iron objects of every description"—armor, equipment, tools—according to carefully specified "shapes." After this, the wholesalers who had sold the iron took charge of exporting the finished products "to every region" and to "many parts of the inhabited world." With this rigorous separation between manufacturing and commerce (and between capital and labor) we are far from our usual conception of artisan work. We are also far from true craftsmanship, because these teams of laborers worked from models dictated either by the wholesalers or by the owners of the workshops and with no evident initiative of their own. Furthermore, they worked in a factory setting rather than at home or in shops. This was the fate of the Roman laborer wherever the "slave mode of production" prevailed. These conditions are interesting for their originality within Mediterranean history, but they are isolated in both time and space, since the "slave mode of production" was hardly ever exported outside Italy. In the early Empire the Gallic potters who made terra sigillata (molded relief ware) did not work under the same conditions as their Italian counterparts.

At the other end of the spectrum, the artist—the sculptor, painter, or cameo engraver—and the technician or the architect were little different from craftsmen in the eyes of those whose opinion counted. They only exceptionally emerge from anonymity. For the Romans, the true author of a work of art was not the person who fashioned it; the creator of a monument was not the one who had built it. Rather, it was the customer—the person who ordered the work and financed its realization and who had imposed his tastes or his ideology on it. Traces of this attitude can be seen in Greece as well, and Gorgias states to Socrates that the arsenals and the walls of Athens owed more to Themistocles and Pericles than to the competence of the people who built them. Nonetheless, we speak of the *Doryphorus* of Polyclitus, the *Discobolus* of Myron, and the Parthenon of Phidias, Ictinus, and Callicrates, but we also speak of the monument of Aemilius Paulus, the column of Marcus Aurelius, or the arch of Constantine, whose creators are unknown. No matter how great his talent, the *artifex* remained someone who executed the wishes of a client.

Artist or artisan? In general, for the Romans "all the arts were trades" (Jean-Pierre Waltzing), and Seneca states that for nothing in the world would he put painting on the same plane as the "liberal arts." Conversely, there were periods in Roman history when the two notions tended to merge at the upper end; when the ordinary craftsman attained a refinement and quality of execution that made his craft an art; when the artisan showed a real penchant for his trade; when worth was based on the quality of the workmanship (*opus*) instead of or as well as on the value of the raw materials (*materia*). This occurred during the brilliant epoch of early Hellenism, around 300 B.C. At that time, in Rome and in Latium as in nearly all Greek and Etruscan Italy, ceramics, terra cottas, and bronzes of exceptional quality proliferated.

The phenomenon was even more apparent during the reign of Augustus, which marked a pause in the decline of the professional dignity of the artisan. The artisan's work rarely came as close to that of the artist as during this period. All historical conditions joined to contribute to this process: civic peace returned after a long period of bloody wars; a strong central power energetically diffused an official aesthetic, backed up by a literature that indefatigably furnished ideological models and iconographic motifs; a patronage system developed to relay the suggestions of the central power; finally, the purchasing power of the middle classes rose. Although the craftsman remained in his station, his work was valued, and he could take pride in being part of a collective movement and was, so to speak, reconciled with his city. This was the case par excellence in the century of Augustus; it was true to a lesser degree in the reign of Constantine. These were exceptional moments, however, and they did not last. In general, it had become paradoxical for the Roman craftsman to seek aesthetic quality, and, at least from the second century B.C., a gulf separated the work of the run-of-the-mill craftsman and that of the other sort of artisan, the artist, who worked in closer contact with the demands of the great.

The craftsman's condition showed even greater diversity from the view-point of his economic possibilities and opportunities for personal initiative. There were few other classes in Roman society in which the range between the small and the great was so wide.

The "small" were the craftsmen scattered through the cities and towns who made or repaired both luxury items and objects used in daily life. They were also the workers in mass-production industry. Within this innumerable throng there were great differences between the free, the freed, and the slave; between work gangs and semiautonomous specialists. These differences did not count for much, however, compared to the gap between these men and women and the entrepreneurs and magnates, or to the gap between the "industrial bourgeoisie" and the noble caste.

There is debate today about the pertinence of the concept of "bourgeoisie" as applied to a Roman social class that owed its social advance to labor. Debate is even more open as to whether the Roman world had an "industrial" bourgeoisie that drew the better part of its revenues from craft or manufacturing rather than from agriculture or speculation (which remained the norm).

What is important for our purposes is that we know wealthy men who presented themselves as craftsmen, some of whom rose in society. Near the Porta Maggiore in Rome stands the curious tomb of the baker Marcus Vergilius Eurysaces, which he himself calls a *panarium*, a bread bin, some aspects of which perhaps recall the ovens and the mechanical kneading machines of his bakery. A frieze in relief crowns the monument and pictures the making of bread: workers in tunics are busy grinding grain, kneading dough, and baking and weighing loaves while figures in togas, their employer presumably among them, look on. On the tomb of the Haterii family, also in Rome, a crane with a complicated block and tackle mechanism worked by men closed inside a large wooden wheel shows that the head of the family, Quintus Haterius Tychicus, was a building contractor, a notion confirmed by a frieze representing Roman monuments in whose construction he must have had a hand, the Coliseum among them. A similar machine figures in the votive bas-relief of a certain Lucceius Peculiaris in Capua.

This category of men—who were evidently more numerous than the scant evidence of their existence that has come down to us would indicate—shared one trait: they only partially admitted to their trades because, in spite of their evident economic success, their condition alone would not have been sufficient reason for their fellow citizens' consideration. Their monuments, their inscriptions, and other indications give them as notables and interlocutors recognized by their city or the state.

Thus the epitaph of Marcus Vergilius Eurysaces calls him a *pistor et redemptor*, a baker and awarder of contracts in public markets (for example, for supplying to the army or for grain distributions to the people). Similarly, Lucceius Peculiaris is given as *redemptor prosceni* of his city of Capua, where he thus controlled the construction or the rebuilding of the stage of the theater. Haterius is also given as *redemptor* both in an inscription probably connected with his tomb and on the public monuments of Rome pictured on his tomb. This term places these men within the social hierarchy. Similarly, in the ridiculous feast that is the setting for Petronius' *Satyricon*, Habinnas, who makes his entry preceded by a lictor and followed by a number of domestics, is a marble dealer who specializes in pompous tombs, but he is also given as a priest of the imperial cult (*sevir idemque lapidarius*), which means that he was a *sevir Augustalis* thanks to his financial success as a *lapidarius* and his consequent social success. Petronius had living models for characters of this sort. We know that a certain Gnaeus Haius Doryphorus of Pozzuoli (then Puteoli) became wealthy enough as a *purpurarius* (purple-dyer) to become *Augustalis dupliciarus*, the highest local honor to which a freedman could aspire (John H. D'Arms). One member of his family was to become a decurion; another an equestrian procurator.

Even wealthier and more famous were the entrepreneurs whom we might call captains of industry. We know of them not only by the traces that they themselves left of their activities but also (and this is both singular and characteristic in Roman literature, which so often is silent on the subject of industry) from writers who mention them. Behind these mentions we can sense a public opinion that was both scandalized and fascinated by these men's ability to break away from the beaten path, by the audacity of their innovative practice, and by their lack of economic prejudices.

One such man was Vestorius, from Pozzuoli. According to Vitruvius and Pliny, he introduced *caeruleum*, a copper-based, bright blue dye, into Italy. (One particularly admired variety was in fact called *vestorianum*.) The manufacturing technique was invented in Egypt, and the product met with great commercial success. Cicero counted Vestorius among his acquaintances and, despite his scorn of everything concerning the *officina*, he could not resist calling him, perhaps with a touch of envious admiration, *homo remotus a dialecticis, in arithmeticis satis exercitatus*, thus somewhat unwillingly recognizing merit in this class of enterprising businessmen who, while the politicians and the lawyers proudly took up the front of the stage, were innovating, producing, selling, and getting rich. Vitruvius also admits, with reservations that somewhat attenuate his statement, that the sort of activity in which Vestorius had distinguished himself *satis habet admirationis* ("is admirable enough"). Vestorius was a typical representative of a manufacturing bourgeoisie of Pozzuoli in the late Republic and the early Empire that developed the economy of that cosmopolitan port by introducing a variety of techniques, many of them borrowed from the Hellenistic East, developing them, perfecting them, and assuring them a renewed commercial success on the shores of the Tyrrhenian Sea—metallurgy, red terra sigillata ware, blown glass, and dyes.

Suetonius tells us about another of these captains of industry, Quintus Remmius Palaemon. Although Suetonius insists on his real or supposed infamy, he makes us sense, as if despite himself, the dynamism and the spirit of enterprise of this personage. A former slave and a textile worker in his youth, Remmius Palaemon amassed a considerable fortune thanks to activities in what we would call the primary, the secondary, and the tertiary sectors. As a teacher of grammar he commanded high fees; he also got exceptional results from his vines thanks to the use of innovative techniques. Finally, remembering his former trade, he drew a great part of his income from his clothing workshops (*officinae promercalium vestium*), which produced some several tens of thousands of items of clothing per year. We need to keep him in mind when we are tempted to take Roman ideology literally and see domestic handwork as the prototype for Roman textile production.

Thus, among the Romans engaged in craftwork (should I say "guilty of craftwork"?), those whose activities and personality we perceive the best belonged to a "bourgeoisie" that it is hardly surprising to find in the entourage of Trimalchio. Such men speak of themselves (or prompt others to speak of them), first, because they had emerged from the common herd and had become wealthy, often by participating as *redemptores* in the allocation of contracts awarded by governmental agencies or public benefactors and, second, because their place in society was not high enough to lead them to conceal an activity and a competence that they were proud of. Still, they occupied a relatively narrow band in a spectrum that ranged from the anonymous pieceworker in mass manufacturing or the cobbler in his shop, through the specialist and the artist, to the dignitary who gave over to a manager, a proxy, or a figurehead the direction of the workshops from which he drew an important part of his income.

Such managers (*institutores, praepositi*) were key persons in Roman trades. Slaves or freedmen, they put the sums their patron gave them (in the form of a *peculium* or a loan) into manufacturing or commerce. It was notably through such men that the great had access to sources of wealth without compromising a *dignitas* that in principle forbade commerce. As Crassus (who was in a position to know) said, "Anything else was to be done for him by his slaves, but his slaves were to be governed by their master."

Some prominent people did not scorn the profits to be made from the trades. T. P. Wiseman has shown that C. Vibienus and T. Rufrenus, who owned workshops in Arezzo that made terra sigillata, belonged to senatorial families. Our best information on prominent men involved in manufacturing comes from the brick and tile industry, thanks to a curious belief among the Romans that classed the *opus doliare* as an agricultural activity, perhaps because it involved clay, hence soil. Aristocrats were thus less loathe to admit their participation, and such products often bear their imprints. As early as around 200 B.C., two clients of the powerful Licinii family bear the revealing surnames of *Tegula* and *Imbrex* ("flat tile" and "round tile"). A member of the Cicero family and a member of the Pollio family, Asinius, produced bricks stamped with the family name. Even the imperial family openly practiced brickmaking, notably all the emperors from Trajan to Caracalla. This was also true earlier of Livia, Poppaea, Agrippa, and his son Agrippa Postumus, whose name (*Pupillus Agrippa*) was stamped on tiles found in Pompeii at a time when he was only one or two years old.

It is difficult to conceive of Roman crafts as female. In their immense majority, the women engaged in crafts were at the high or the low ends of the range of possibilities. They were pieceworkers condemned to obscurity or high-placed ladies who voluntarily kept to the shadows. The best we can do is to glimpse snatches of a real situation doubtless much more widespread than it seems from our sources.

Textiles come immediately to mind when female crafts in classical antiquity are mentioned, and not without reason. Lists found on the Acropolis in Athens transmit the names and the trades of thirty-five women who were active in artisanal or commercial work around 300 B.C. and who dedicated silver paterae to Athena. Twenty-six of these women were wool weavers, which gives us an idea of the preponderance of women workers in this trade and of the importance of this trade among women workers.

In Rome a deep-rooted tradition that persisted from the kings of Rome to the imperial age saw wool-working as a *femineus labor* (Tibullus) and the ideal matron as a *lanifica,* a spinner and weaver of wool, the guardian angel of the family hearth. The epitaph of Claudia tells us *domum servavit, lanam fecit* (she watched over her home; she made wool). This moralizing rhetoric doubtless covers a kernel of truth, even if this ideal activity was increasingly delegated, especially in high society, to the *infelices ancillarum greges,* the "troops of unhappy servant women," who, according to Seneca the Rhetorician, made the clothes of the wealthy. One might also recall the great halls of the Greek, and soon the Roman, houses in which, according to Vitruvius, "mothers of families are found with the spinning-women." The *Digest* is speaking of women when it mentions the persons who made clothing on the great estates (*lanificae qui familiam rusticam vestiunt*). One notable exception was the fullers, who in the Roman world formed a specialized, more "technical," and all-male trade.

All that remains of the immense army of women who spun, wove, and clothed the Romans for a thousand years is a few pieces of documentary evidence, but these few mentions, which turn up in a number of texts, inscriptions, and graffiti, give a glimpse of a world of harsh realty. They often touch on the *pensum,* the weight of wool to be worked in a day—a sort of "piecework" typical of a craft that was considered unskilled. Thus inscriptions found in Sabinium and in Apulia mention *conservae lanipendae,* companions in slavery who gathered together to spin or weave their *pensum* of wool. A Pompeii graffito enumerates thirteen woman slaves along with the weight of the yarn that they had spun and the length of the cloth they wove. These are examples typical of the small workshops that were neither completely domestic nor truly industrial in which women textile workers spent their monotonous days. We know that many men worked in the textile industry, but in the early Empire the state weaving works were nonetheless called *gynaecea,* such was the weight of tradition in the typically female activities of spinning, weaving, and making clothes.

It is still thanks to her ties with textile work that we know of one woman and mistress of her trade much higher on the social scale, Eumachia. This Pompeii *bourgeoise* came from a family that had become wealthy from vineyards and from the *opus doliare* (amphoras, bricks, tiles), but when they became allied with another *gens* that raised sheep, they developed an interest in textiles. Under Tiberius, Eumachia, "a city priestess," built a building that gave on the Forum of Pompeii, decorated with a remarkable portrait sculpture of herself given by the fullers' corporation. This "building of Eumachia" is generally (and rightly) considered to have been the cloth market of Pompeii. Thus we see a woman distinguished by her activity, her initiative, and the esteem of her profession connected with its most professional, most "masculine" aspect, the fullers' art. She, like her male counterparts, was a notable in her city. We are far from the traditional *lanifica* here, and it is significant that Eumachia graces her edifice with a series of statues and descriptions that evoke the great men of Rome and the ideology of the Julio-Claudians, giving it a respectability that its original purpose would not have provided and making it into something like a miniature Forum of Augustus.

Textiles were not the only professional sector in which women worked. They exercised a number of other trades and were hairdressers and flower wreath–makers, workers in purple dye, and bakers. Were these specifically female occupations, or at least relatively easier work? Not necessarily, since we also find women in the pottery works. The tiles of the great temple of Pietrabbondante were made in a brickworks in which women worked, a particular that we know because they incised facetious remarks on one of them. On a more serious level, infant burials (on occasion, stillbirths) have been found in the workshops for terra sigillata ware in Lezoux (Puy-de-Dôme). Evidently some of the women workers gave birth in the workplace under the constraining conditions to which a pitiless fate chained them. "Poor potters; poor misery," Hugues Vertet wrote about such workshops, and undoubtedly the women suffered the most.

Skilled manpower was a constant problem in classical antiquity. Naturally, the problem was most acute in the more specialized professions such as stonecutting. In 173 B.C., after a censor stripped the temple of Hera Lacinia in Crotona of its marble tiles for a temple in Rome, the Senate, scandalized by this sacrilege, ordered him to put them back where he had found them, but according to Livy he could find no one capable of doing so.

Many simpler professions suffered from the same lack of manpower, however. Normally an artisan learned his craft by a slow learning process under the guidance of a master. The problem of the formation of a qualified work force unavoidably arose, however, with the great conquests of the late Republic, when the masses of slaves who flooded into Rome were unskilled or were employed in ways in which their previous experience was of no help, and when midsized and large workshops began to proliferate, weakening contact between master and apprentice.

Solutions to this problem varied. Teams of itinerant craftsmen took their skills wherever they were needed, as did the Greek marble-carvers who sculpted the bas-reliefs of the amphitheater of Lecce under Trajan and Hadrian. Sorely needed artisans were brought from afar: in the mid-second century the inhabitants of Saldae, in what is now Algeria, begged the legate of the African army to send them a famous military engineer to set right a poorly designed aqueduct. The most elegant solution to the problem, however, was to train the needed specialist oneself. This solution was, of course, reserved to the largest households, and Crassus, who was wealthy among the wealthy, "himself directed the education" of his slaves, as Plutarch tells us, "and took part in it himself as a teacher, and, in a word, . . . thought that the chief duty of the master was to care for his slaves as the living instruments of household management" (*Crassus* 544).

A specialized worker was worth his weight in gold. Plutarch also tells us that Cato, aided by his servants, earned substantial sums from the "training" of slaves whom he later sold at a good price. Atticus too formed specialists "at home" (*domi*). According to Echion, the old-clothes dealer who was among Trimalchio's guests and who had his slaves learn a variety of trades, "workmanship never dies" (*artificium nunquam moritur*). It was the owner who profited the most from this training, however, because he could sell a trained slave, rent him out, or pocket the profits from his work. Conversely, Varro advises small or mid-sized landowners against having very skilled workers, for their death or temporary indisposition would not only put the owner in a difficult spot but expose him to serious financial loss. It would be better for them to rent the services of a specialist when needed.

Another solution to the basic problem of the scarcity of qualified workers called for a division of labor that made it possible for most operations to be done, following directions so specific that relatively unskilled manpower, reduced to the level of pieceworkers, could do them, working under the guidance of a few technicians who coordinated their efforts. For a number of reasons, this tendency is particularly clear in the building trades: a great number of vestiges of building remain; the clients were more demanding; and the often public nature of such activity meant that it left more traces in epigraphy. The principal Roman technological innovation in construction—the replacement of cut stone construction (*opus quadratum*), which required highly skilled workers, with masonry made of a base of rubble or debris encased in mortar (*opus caementicium*)—meant that the operations could be directed by architects whom contemporaries usually considered semispecialized practitioners rather than high-level creators. As Pierre Gros has observed, it was in all cases the person who sponsored the project who received credit for it: *Caesar pontem fecit*. The sponsor took the initiative and, so to speak, guided the hand of the person who actually executed the project. An inscription in Pozzuoli dated 105 B.C. describes in detail how a wall in *opus caementicium* should be built: it states how much rubble to use, how much mortar to add, and how the protective roof should look. No latitude and no initiative are left either to the mason or to the entrepreneur, the *redemptor*.

At the end of the Republic and the beginning of the Empire, all these elements led to a breakup of tasks that has few equals in the world history of labor. We know, in ancient Rome, of no fewer than 160 trades mentioned in texts and inscriptions (and 225 for the whole of the Roman West), as compared with 101 and more than 99, respectively, for thirteenth-century Paris and fifteenth-century Florence, which were centers of artisan work. The same specialization was true in Capua in the bronze and iron trades: according to whether he was a *scutarius,* a *lanternarius,* or a *vascularius,* a *gladiarius,* or a *cultrarius,* a worker made shields, lanterns, vases, swords, or knives. In the very large households (where we have to take into account a certain ostentation that led to the proliferation of specialized "offices"), different slaves took charge of the upkeep of the silver and the gold tableware, with further subdivisions according to whether the pieces were for drinking or eating, of gold alone or of gold decorated with gems. Although we cannot ignore the many instances in which this phenomenon doubtless reflected the skill of highly qualified artisans who, here and there during the empire, continued to produce true masterpieces, often this "extravagant division of labor" reflected lack of training and limited competence, but also the "ingenuity of the poor Roman in finding ways to earn a living" (Susan Treggiari).

The employers whom I have called large-scale entrepreneurs attempted to avoid massive employment of unskilled labor. They invested in equipment such as the mechanical kneading machines of Vergilius Eurysaces or the relatively advanced cranes of Haterius Tychicus and Lucceius Peculiaris. The justifiable pride that they drew from these machines may show that their approach was uncommon. Economizing on manpower thanks to machines was just not in the spirit of the times, no

more than it was as late as the early nineteenth century, when A. Brong-
niart advised a brickmaker against investing in "costly" machines (simple
as they were, since they were operated by a horse) where a few workers
could do the job at lower cost.

This touches on one aspect of the rejection of technological progress
with which classical antiquity has been charged (and which, incidentally,
it would be quite unjust to exaggerate, as a large number of innovations
appeared through the centuries). There was a tendency, particularly on
the part of the state, to favor full employment, even overemployment, at
the expense of investment and profitability. When an inventor presented
Vespasian with a machine to hoist columns up to the Capitoline at little
cost, the emperor rewarded him generously but refused his offer, saying,
"You must let me feed the common people" (*sineret se plebiculam pascere*).

The craftsman's narrow specialization or lack of skills was not necessarily
reflected in his culture, which could be less restricted than his technological baggage. We are struck by the literacy of the graffiti that a population
composed in great part of craftspeople has left on the walls of Pompeii.
The jokes are often salacious, but they also show proof of a wit and a
"plebeian literature" (Marcello Gigante) that the walls of our own cities
might envy. There is astonishing documentary evidence of similar capacities among relatively unskilled workers (employed in the brickworks) in
Italy in the second and first centuries B.C. In Samnium, two female slaves,
one of whom writes in Oscan and the other in Latin, scratched a well-
turned parody of a juridical formula into the fresh clay of a tile that they
had just carried out to be dried and sealed it with an impression of their
shoes. In Pellaro, near Reggio Calabria, another tile bears a well-written
inscription in the Greek spoken in the region with echoes of Latin to
report (without vulgarity) the witticisms of a slave to his workmates,
and, speaking for his master in an expression that recalls Plautus, he calls
one companion *malempte* (bad acquisition).

Still, we must guard against idealizing a reality that was often somber, for when we speak of the texts written by Roman crafts- and trades-
people, we only have knowledge of the ones (and what proportion of
the whole did they represent?) who knew how to write and cared to
do so.

The economic aspects of the crafts and the economic life of craftsmen are
particularly hard to define. Normally, the only way we can get any
glimpse of them is in the very few texts that speak of extraordinary and

newsworthy success stories that piqued the curiosity or prompted the astonishment or the disapproval of the encyclopedists or the moralists. Other, less indirect sources such as the graffiti of Pompeii or Diocletian's *Edictum de maximis pretiis* contain scattered but valuable and trustworthy information.

Because the crafts were disdained in ancient times, we tend to underestimate their economic importance. We moderns let ourselves be misled by ancient prejudices. There are several reasons for this. First, we are inclined to think that possession of landed property alone conferred an enviable social status to the Roman, but we generally have no idea what founded the fortune that permitted the purchase of those lands, nor whether the trades had any part in it. Second, we tend to think that revenues from landed property were more certain than those from craft activities, but this is obviously untrue if we consider the vicissitudes of agriculture. Cato, whom we think of as the paragon of the landed proprietor, in fact saw the possession of pitch foundries or fullers' workshops as a much safer source of income than farming. Above all, most modern historians of classical economics see manufacturing as an annex to agriculture or a branch of agriculture, making the craftsman gravitate around agriculture like a minor satellite of Roman economic life.

It is incontestable that in classical antiquity agriculture was the only truly fundamental activity, given that subsistence had always to be assured. It is also true that craftspeople worked in great part for agriculture, for which they furnished implements, machinery, packaging, and buildings and the produce of which they transformed. It is also true, finally, that craftsmen represented a small minority of the general population. One papyrus from a town of Roman Egypt tells us that craftsmen accounted for 9.5 percent of all workers, as opposed to 68 percent of the active population who were engaged in agriculture (the remainder were in commerce or provided services). The calculations (unfortunately highly approximate) that can be made for other regions lead to comparable figures.

It would nonetheless be erroneous to link the crafts with agriculture in any systematic way or to underestimate their intrinsic economic importance. The raw materials that the artisan transformed and the clients he served often had no connection with agriculture other than the obvious general and vague dependence on a primordial activity on which there is total agreement. All that we know about Aulus Umbricius Scaurus, a Pompeian entrepreneur and notable (he was a *duumvir,* and he or possibly his father was honored with an equestrian statue), is that he made *garum,* a fish-based condiment, and had a number of workshops, some of them run by freedmen. Still, to say of him that nothing allows us to see in him the representative of an industrial oligarchy that could be distinguished from the land-owning oligarchy is begging the question and risks, precisely, concealing the existence of a manufacturing bourgeoisie that made most or all of its money from nonagricultural activities.

Furthermore, the majority of artisans worked in cities—and not only the ones who provided the services of repair, upkeep, and beautification that major population concentrations required. The chief manufacturing sites were in cities, whether for metallurgy or textiles, pottery or glass, wood or dyeing. As with all rules, there were obviously exceptions to this one. In Gaul, where the *vici*—dispersed hamlets—continued to exist despite growing urbanization, a considerable portion of the production of the terra sigillata pottery of La Graufesenque came from the *vicus* of Condatomagus, near Millau. In Italy, in Baetica, and elsewhere, amphorae to hold wine and oil for export were made outside towns or in the countryside, near the agricultural zones of production. Finally, the great estates had their own craftsmen to make and repair tools, make clothing for the estate's personnel, and construct and keep up the buildings. The development of such estates in the later Empire, at the expense of urban centers, meant that more artisans worked in rural areas, which set the jurists to wondering to what extent they should be assimilated to the *instrumentum,* the property's equipment. These are regional, chronological, or structural exceptions, however. Fundamentally the Roman artisan was a man of the city.

It is particularly difficult to estimate earnings from the crafts. There are three problems involved: first, what manufacturing might bring in to a community and especially to a city; second, what profits were made by the entrepreneurs; third, what the craftsmen themselves earned.

The first problem scarcely concerns the craftsman. Furthermore, the economic impact of a good-sized crafts establishment on an ancient city is a much-debated question. The general tendency is to minimize its importance: R. M. Cook tells us, among many other things concerning Athens, that the pottery industry, which archaeologists make much of because they find its vestiges throughout the Mediterranean world, in reality may well have played only a modest role in the city's economy as a whole. Similarly, the theories of Max Weber on the ancient city (developed subsequently by others with varying degrees of success) played down the role of crafts and saw Rome as the prototype of the "consumers' city." We need to keep things in perspective. Agriculture was the main economic pursuit of the ancient world, not manufacturing. It is nonetheless true that certain cities of Italy or the empire in which crafts played a major role manifestly drew much—at times an essential part—of their relative prosperity from those crafts. This was true of Capua, Pozzuoli, and Pompeii; of Aquileia, Lyons, and Cologne; and perhaps of Rome itself. The same was true of smaller communities. Moses I. Finley claims that Lezoux and La Graufesenque flourished only in archaeological textbooks, an attitude countered by D. Vernhet, the excavator of La Graufesenque, who states that in this potters' community the standard of living seems fairly high.

In any event, what seems sure is that crafts activities could bring in substantial revenues for the large-scale entrepreneur. Otherwise it would be difficult to explain the fortunes, reflected in costly funeral monuments, amassed by people whose principal activity was construction and manufacturing and whose rise in society was often confirmed by access to magistracies or priestly posts. It would also be difficult to explain why high state dignitaries often owned brickworks. The number of the workers, the effects of mass production, and an economy of scale play their role in this connection. These became possible only with the influx of slaves that began in the second century B.C. Before that time and before the upward surge of the Roman economy, large concentrations of craftsmen were characteristic of foreign cities, where Romans, to their astonishment and interest, discovered an economy of a type new to them.

This was true of Capua in 211 B.C., where the Roman conquerors, despite the harsh punishment they inflicted on the city, took care to retain the great number of craftsmen (*multitudo opificum*) that they found there, since such workshops were indispensable for the continuing prosperity of the rich agriculture of Campania. It was also true of Carthage, where, in 210 B.C., Scipio found two thousand craftsmen in a population of ten thousand free men. These dates are noteworthy, as they mark the beginning of the "slave mode of production" in a Rome that henceforth took these throngs of craftsmen for its own. The circumstances are also worthy of note, because they stress the role that agriculture and a wartime economy played in the beginning of this process. Thus Scipio, in an attempt to stimulate production during the height of the Second Punic War, made the two thousand craftsmen of Carthage the property of the Roman people and promised them they would soon be freed.

The very large-scale entrepreneurs also had their effect on the masses, and the tens of thousands of pieces of clothing produced annually by Remmius Palaemon suggest the enormous number of craftsmen that these enterprises required. Crassus was involved in a real-estate speculation of an ingeniousness and cynicism that struck his contemporaries, and he had access to more than five hundred architects and masons. These were exceptions, however, which were considered as such. In Arezzo, which is often taken as an "industrial center," small-scale bosses known to have had only one or two slaves were in much greater number than the relative "giants" such as Rasinius or P. Cornelius, who we know employed, respectively, sixty and seventy-five slaves. The Roman craft world was largely made up of tens of thousands of modest enterprises of this sort, which had only a few workers and at times formed constellations of small workshops clustered around a slightly larger manufacturing center.

One of the most influential factors in the cost price of such products was land transportation. Cato tells us that an oil press made in Pompeii cost 73 percent more if it was delivered in Venafrum, about seventy miles away. This meant that most Roman craftsmen had an extremely limited commercial territory. For instance, one Cutronius, a potter established in the Roman colony of Cosa, only sold his wares in that city or within a range of a few miles.

Anyone interested in exporting his wares found that having more workers in his workplace did not resolve the serious problem of transport. It was easier to move men than to transport things, so the real solution to the problem lay in the mobility of manpower. The creation of branch workshops closer to potential clients than was the original center seems to have been much more frequent than has been imagined.

Arretine terra sigillata ware offers the best example of this. One enterprising employer, Gnaeus Ateius, opened branches of his Arezzo manufactory, first in Pisa (close to the sea, which facilitated exportation), then in Lyons (nearer to the camps on the Rhine frontier, where there was a good market for his wares). He sent not only equipment from Arezzo (in particular, molds for making vases decorated with reliefs) but manpower to "launch" the new line and train locally recruited workers. Even a modest workshop for Gallic terra sigillata pottery, such as the one at Montans, in the Tarn valley, might have at least four satellite workshops within twenty or thirty miles. Two centuries earlier, at the end of the third century B.C., the potters who specialized in "Calenian" black glazed ceramics with raised relief had a complex network of workshops scattered between Etruria and Campania. Teams of sculptors moved from city to city, and in the late empire African mosaic-workers went to work in the wealthy villas of Sicily and elsewhere. Those who scorned craftsmen saw them as *sellularii*—quintessentially sedentary people riveted to their worktables. Nonetheless, in an empire in which people traveled a good deal, the administrators and soldiers, students, and idlers who frequented the roads and the ports encountered along the way specialized craftsmen and workers, who bore with them their skills and their capacity for hard work. Instead of the social mobility that modern historiography makes so much of (but which soon finds its limits), the true mobility of the Roman craftsman was often geographical.

Any investigation of the craftsman's standard of living necessarily comes down to comparing his wages and the cost of the principal foodstuffs, and here we are poorly equipped to give answers by the lack of quantitative data in the documentation we have inherited from classical antiquity. In Pompeii, where an average family spent between four and eight asses for its daily bread, a bronze bucket sold for nine asses, and modest terra cotta objects (a lamp, a plate, or a bowl for cooking porridge) cost only one as. If we take production costs into account, the craftsman's earnings barely covered the necessities. Diocletian's *Edictum de maximis pretiis* gives us more detailed information. We can gather from it that manpower was only a small part of the cost price of a good many objects, and, as a corollary, we can surmise that craftsmen earned only modest amounts in comparison to the sale price of the objects they made.

Thus under Diocletian the price of a linen tunic of the best quality was ten thousand denarii, while the most highly skilled linen weaver was paid (along with his meals) forty denarii per actual working day. The fact that these figures represent the maximum in each case does nothing to change their relative value. A worker in a brickworks earned (again, over and above his meals) two denarii for making four bricks, which would be sold for about twenty-five denarii. The least-expensive rough wool cloaks cost thirty-three times the daily pay of the weaver of the same wool, and a silk dalmatic could cost up to twenty years' pay for the silk weaver. We can see that the employer could make a considerable profit out of his workers, but we can also see how small the workers' purchasing power was. In the lowest classes true purchasing power lay in the hands of those who earned modest but sure and regular wages— that is, the soldiers. It is hardly surprising that archaeologists can find more manufactured objects and identify more imported foodstuffs in military camps than in slaves' cells or craftsmen's shops.

We cannot expect the Romans to praise craftsmen or envy their life: there is no *O fortunatos nimium!* addressed to them. As society's poor relations, craftsmen reacted at times by affirming their own status and merits, at other times by inhibition and self-effacement.

It was of course the "low profile" that prevailed. The number of lapidary inscriptions or bas-reliefs in which a craftsman presents himself as a craftsman is ridiculously small in relation to the total. Everything contributed to this self-effacement: a vague sentiment of shame or malaise, perhaps a degree of illiteracy, in all cases economic conditions that enabled only a few of their number to pay a sculptor or a stonecutter. The exceptional state of preservation of Pompeii reveals what can be seen practically nowhere else: craftsmen expressed themselves in graffiti and in painted inscriptions or signs, media that cost little or nothing. Only one inscription in stone in Pompeii mentions craftsmen, and that one is the fullers' dedication of the statue to Eumachia in the wool market that she constructed. Exceptional circumstances, a locally powerful corporation, and the need to pay honors to a notable were required in order for artisans to leave a permanent, material trace of themselves that in any other site would have been the only one to have come down to us.

Nonetheless, the general shipwreck of the Roman craftsman in the dark seas of time left a few survivors. There were, in fact, periods in Roman history and regions in the empire in which the craftsman's tranquil pride in his condition, his successful integration into society, and the pleasure he took in his finished work were given full expression. In a world in which workers, from the humblest pieceworker to the artist, were anonymous, craftsmen's signatures are the best criterion of this happier state of affairs. Not simple factory marks, which are so hard to interpret for whom they designate and what they mean, but explicit signatures. One of the earliest Latin inscriptions on a vase announces "Duenos made me"—*Duenos med feced*. The chief period for such signatures, however, was the early Hellenistic period, a brief state of grace that was ended by the trials of the First Punic War. At that time, slavery had not yet dishonored labor, mass production had not depersonalized the worker or created a gap between the craftsman and his clientele, and ordinary artisan work competed with artistic artisan work. The most favored region for this was central Italy along the Tyrrhenian coast, where the political domination of Rome (under a variety of administrative forms) was by then undisputed and where cultural influence from Magna Grecia, Etruria, and Latium mingled. At that time and in that place, the artisan knew and proclaimed who he was, what he made, and for whom he worked.

All this—the worker's secure place in a society, his satisfaction with a job well done, his direct relations with his customers, and the happy mix of influences thanks to which an artisan could move to another location without feeling uprooted—is expressed in an exemplary manner in the signature of the Ficoroni cist, the most famous of the so-called Praenestine cists (sumptuous bronze coffers for women's grooming accessories). It reads: *Novios Plautios med Romai fecid, Dindia Macolnia fileai dedit.* I could also cite an entire series of terra cotta vases and bronze objects whose stamped or incised inscriptions show the pride of a lineage of free men (*C. Paco[nius]. C.f. Q.n., L. Canoleius L.f. T.n.*) or of a family association among *ingenui* (*T.L. Alba[. . .], C.L. Staie*); pride in full and complete citizenship (*C. Ovio Ouf[entina tribu] fecit*), in being from a city (*C. Pactumeius C.f. Sues[sanus], L. Canoleios L.f. fecit Calenos*), in work done in a particular city (*Retus Gabinius C.s. Calebus fecit*), or in a specialized task (*Vibis Pilipus cailavit*).

These men, who generally but not always were free citizens of Rome or one of its colonies, fully belonged to the very highest echelons of Roman craftsmen, and they lived in a time that was perhaps the most favorable for the craftsman, the time in which he lived his condition most fully. There were other epochs, however, other regions and other circumstances in which a pride in craftsmanship reappeared. One such was northern Italy in the early Empire, where, as Giuseppe Pucci has observed, small-scale independent artisans continued to predominate. Another, somewhat later, was the part of Gaul that stretched from Berry to around Treves. Here we can find burial steles on which the craftsman declares himself a craftsman without dissimulating his condition under more flattering appellations such as *sevir* or *redemptor*, which is what contemporary entrepreneurs did in central Italy (when they could). On these monuments, which are often awkward but full of zest, we see the craftsman at work, we see him negotiating with customers, and we see his working tools. Elegant women examine the stuffs that a weaver is presenting to them; a cobbler works away surrounded by his lasts; a butcher cuts meat while his wife keeps the accounts. On one stele in Ravenna a certain Longidienus, a naval carpenter in this navy port, has

himself pictured busily making a spar, standing perched on his toolbox
(or rather on his strongbox, the symbol of his success). The inscription
proudly announces, "Publius Longidienus, son of Publius, strives hard
at his work" (*P. Longidienus P.f. ad onus properat*).

Craftsmen, men whose financial resources were precarious and whose
business dealings were fragile, felt strongly the need for divine aid. Much
solicited in archaic times, Hercules received his dues from satisfied entrepreneurs. In third-century B.C. Rome and elsewhere where his cult
flourished, potters were fond of decorating their wares with the image
of Hercules or with his triumph in Olympus, the initial of his name, or
certain of his attributes, such as his club. Later the craftsmen gods, Vulcan
and Minerva, or the gods who favored initiative—Mercury, Venus, and
Fortuna—took over. A tavern keeper in Ostia added to the traditional
divinities on his home altar—the Lares and his personal Genius—a Mercury holding a purse (and, presumably, bringing earnings). In Pompeii
a feltmaker placed an image of his workshop working at full tilt under
an effigy of Venus triumphant, the patron deity of the city. On Domitian's frieze in the Forum Transitorium it was Minerva, who was also
the emperor's tutelary divinity, who presided over women spinners and
weavers as they worked. It took the backing of state religion before the
craftsmen's preferences could appear in official art.

   This approach to religion bears the stamp of a solid confidence and
great familiarity: craftsmen and gods got along well together. More than
one temple was surrounded by shops and workshops, at times huddled
against its walls, as is the case with some churches in Rome today. The
temple of Portunus in the Forum Boarium was flanked by two rows of
tabernae (shops). This familiarity was openly expressed in the surnames
of certain divinities. Rome had a *Hercules Olivarius* whose temple, a
charming rotunda in the Forum Boarium, was offered by a wholesale oil
merchant, and an *Apollo Sandalarius* was venerated in the quarter of the
sandal makers. In the complicated topography of the *Urbs*, craftsmen
often situated themselves in relation to a temple: they called themselves
*erborarius ab Hercule Primigenio, vestiarius ab aede Cereris, lanius ab luco
Lubentinae*. Moreover we can see in the very common parlance of the
inscription on a slave's collar normal use of a religious toponym clarified
by association with a trade: "[fugitive slave] to be brought back to the
temple of Flora, where the barbers are": *reduc me ad Flora[m] ad to[n]sores*.
In short, the small world of craftsmen and merchants (who were often
one and the same person) placed itself under the divine guardianship and

the reassuring proximity of its tutelary gods. To quote Mikhail Rostovt-zeff, it was "business under the aegis of religion."

The uncertainty of the craftsman's life and his feeling of precariousness also came from the fact that he was perceived as bothersome, a perception exacerbated by his natural tendency to settle at the heart of the commu-nity, where the crowd was thickest and the chances of encountering a customer greatest. This was not always viewed with a benign eye, and it is significant that, as Athenaeus tells us, the first city of Magna Grecia that attempted to rid itself of this nuisance and to chase noisy industry from its center so that its citizens could sleep soundly was Sybaris, a city that has come down in memory as the place where the art of living was carried to excess.

The tendency toward concentration was universal. In a modest-sized city such as Alesia, metalworks proliferated right in the center of the town. The problem was particularly acute, however, in the megalopolis that Rome had become under the Republic. Throughout the centuries we can follow the efforts of the governors of the *Urbs* as they struggled with invasive crafts and commerce. It was a never-ending battle, and the results were uneven.

The fundamental unit was the shop, the *taberna*. The craftsman worked in his *taberna* and often lived in a back room or a loft. As late as the time of Septimius Severus, the *Forma Urbis,* a marble map of Rome, showed unending strings of *tabernae* lining the streets. For the aediles and for the emperor, the problem was to keep the shops from invading the entire city, or at least to confine them to certain quarters.

Contemporaries—as Plautus and Juvenal confirm—were acutely aware of the many inconveniences that the *tabernae* brought: crowding, pollution, noise, odors, danger of fires, without counting their incompat-ibility with the increasingly popular ideal of a prestigious city center. We can trace the gradual shift from the center of Rome toward the near or far periphery in some industries—pottery, for example—that were considered most hampering. The nauseating odors of the tannery works were relegated en masse *trans Tiberim.* But the shipyards, the minium works, and the gigantic storage yards and workshops for marble cutting required for the development of the *Urbs* remained in the middle of the city, in particular near the Campus Martius.

Throughout the centuries, however, the guiding idea of the men who were responsible for the urban development of Rome was to move the craftsmen out of the heart of the city, the Forum. Originally the

tabernae had been an integral part of the topography of the Forum—
tabernae veteres, tabernae novae—and it was "behind them," Livy wrote,
that the *Basilica Fulvia* was built in 179 B.C. (Later Romans and we,
following their example, would be more likely to situate the *tabernae* in
relation to—that is, in front of—the basilicas.)

The result of this policy was both to concentrate craft and commercial activities (aided by architectural and urban change) and to push them
toward the edges of the city. The authorities were intent on making the
Forum more majestic—if not the "free agora" swept clean of merchants
and craftsmen and reserved to political debate that Aristotle had dreamed
of, at least a space reserved to political and religious functions or, at
most, to such "noble" economic activities as financial exchanges. Varro,
speaking of the third century B.C., states this explicitly: "The dignity of
the Forum grew when the butchers' shops were replaced by those of the
bankers" (*forensis dignitas crevit, atque ex tabernis lanienis argentariae factae*).
The solution was to group small shops within enclosed marketplaces,
macella, thus confining the "infection." These markets moved farther and
farther away from the Forum, gathering together craftsmen and shopkeepers such as the "fuller of the market of Livia" mentioned in an
inscription.

The *macella* turned out to be inadequate to hold back the torrential
flood of commercial and crafts activities in a city like Rome. The Forum
may have been by and large free of them, but two steps away cobblers'
shops huddled at the foot of the temple of the Dioscuri, to judge from a
picturesque anecdote reported by Pliny: in the time of Tiberius, one of
these cobblers had a crow who had learned to greet the princes and the
people in the Forum. Shopkeepers and craftsmen were also forced out of
the center of the city by great public works, in particular the creation of
the imperial forums on the site of the thickly populated and industrious
Argiletum, and they flooded to the periphery in a movement that recalls
the Paris of Baron Haussmann. Even so, Martial insists on the brazen
impertinence of shopkeepers whose wares overflowed onto the sidewalk
and the street. An edict of Domitian brought order to this state of affairs:
"The barber, the tavern-keeper, the cook, and the butcher now respect
the limit of their threshold; we have gone back to the true Rome, which
until recently was but one vast shop" (*Tonsor, copo, cocus, lanio sua limina
servant. / Nunc Roma est, nuper magna taberna fuit*).

On the one hand, then, we see omnipresent small-scale and infinitely
fragmented crafts operations and commerce always ready to outgrow the
meager living space allotted them and often doing so at the expense of

the public domain. On the other hand we see the state—or the municipalities, as this phenomenon is observable in other cities than Rome—channeling and regulating this dynamism and indiscipline and assigning carefully delimited spaces to craft-related activities. In the struggle between order and laissez-faire, between containment and encroachment, the authorities won important points but never a decisive victory. One reason for this was the craftsmen's constant tendency to invade the space of both public buildings and private houses; another was that although they may have been scorned, their enterprise and vitality were among the most dynamic elements in urban society. In the Latin colony of Fregellae in the second century B.C., when an influx of manpower arrived from the mountains of Samnium, rich homes, some of them still being furnished, were suddenly transformed into fulling works and their *atria* and vestibules occupied by basins and conduits (Filippo Coarelli). In Pompeii after the earthquake that destroyed the city for the first time in A.D. 62, not only were workplaces, a necessity for the economic life of the city, among the first buildings to be rebuilt but craftsmen of all sorts settled into houses deserted by their inhabitants. In Rome, shops occupied one side nave of a basilica, thus altering its symmetry. In the third century, the fullers of Rome rose up against the threat of the *curator aquarum* to take back a *locus publicus* that they had long occupied or to make them pay for its use: "Never," they observed, "from the reign of Augustus to today have we paid rent for that place" (*ex eo tempore ex quo Augustus rempublicam obtinere coepit usque in hodiernum [num]quam haec loca pensiones pensitasse*).

Clearly, the craftsmen's unity and their numbers were important. Isolated, they could do nothing; numerous, they took courage. Together, they could claim to play a role in society that their base condition gave them little hope for. At first they tended to group together topographically by affinities—that is, by trades. This is an eternal phenomenon that holds true for the Ceramicus of Athens all the way down to the Arabian souk and to modern cities. A number of neighborhoods or places in Roman cities owe their names to a concentration of craftsmen. Just as in Rome today we can find a Via dei Giubbonari or a Via dei Baullari, in ancient Rome there was a *vicus materiarius* and a *vicus turarius,* there were *scalae anulariae* and an *atrium sutorium* for lumber sellers, perfumers, ring makers, and shoemakers. In Pozzuoli there was a *clivus vitriarius sive vicus turarius.* A house could be described as being *inter falcarios,* a sanctuary as being *inter figulos,* and so forth, thus attesting that the makers of scythes and sickles, potters, and many others grouped their shops and the work-shops in a system that combined a broad structural distribution with topographical concentration.

The craftsman felt at his ease only among his peers. The chatter among Trimalchio's guests, who were merchants and small-scale entre-preneurs, confirms this. Trimalchio himself tells "the sayings [or prov-erbs?] of the weavers" (*textorum dicta*). There is further proof of this sociability in the collective signature of thirteen wool spinners on a wall in Pompeii or, still in Pompeii, in a graffito in which "Felix, artisan in silver, greets Campanus, artisan in gems" (*Felix argentarius Campano gemmario feliciter*), or in the inscribed tiles of Pietrabbondante and Pellaro. Here we penetrate into the familiar atmosphere of a ceramic works "on a human scale" where the workers, male and female, had not yet become anonymous cogs in a great machine and treated one another with humor and irony and where conviviality was not sacrificed to fast-paced produc-tivity. Furthermore, on entering the comfortable house of an important *sagarius* (a maker of *sagae*—short cloaks) in Capua we see an inscription that gives not only the name of the owner but that of the architect, who usually is not mentioned: *P. Confuleius P.M.l. Sabbio sagarius domum hanc . . . fecit arcitecto T. Safinio T.f. Fal. Pollione.*

It was also by grouping together that craftsmen could hope to have a voice in political controversies. Pompeii contains painted inscriptions that are like "posters" from several electoral campaigns. The bakers and the pastry makers, the goldsmiths and the barbers, all "recommend" the candidates they prefer. The powerful corporation of the fullers and re-lated trades at times separated into trades (dyers, feltmakers, specialists in work clothes) and at other times acted together as *fullones universi*. The few gem engravers of the city also banded together as *gemmarii universi*.

The *collegia* were the most striking manifestation of this esprit de corps. For a Roman of humble birth, a craftsman in particular, belonging to a trade association was the best way to feel himself someone. It might happen, in the troubled times of the last decades of the Republic, that these associations took sides in the civil unrest and became pressure groups. Incidentally this led to the dissolution of some of them. When they did become a political force, Cicero (who ordinarily had no words harsh enough for the working classes and who often reproached his ad-versaries for fishing in troubled waters by courting craftsmen and shop-keepers—*opifices atque tabernarios concitare; concitator tabernariorum*) boasted of the *collegia*'s support of the move to return him from exile. There could hardly be a better expression of the Romans' ambivalence toward craftsmen: they were treated with scorn as individuals but flattered or feared the minute they banded together.

The power of Rome manipulated the force represented by craftsmen's associations throughout Roman history. From the semilegendary origins of the *Urbs*, King Numa instituted craftsmen's colleges, persuaded, Plutarch tells us, that he could use these new groups to break down the long-standing antagonism between the Romans and the Sabines. Servius Tullius listed two workers' centuries among the people in arms, a recognition of the modest but necessary role that they played in the city. A thousand years later, when a lack of slave manpower compromised the very existence of the system of general public assistance that had gradually been set up in Rome, the emperors of the third and fourth centuries requisitioned craftsmen and forced them into trade corporations that they were forbidden to leave and into which their sons were obliged to follow them. "The empire was transformed into one vast workshop" (Jean-Pierre Waltzing) in a bureaucratic monstrosity that once again illustrates the ambiguity of the craftsman, relegated to the lowest levels of society but, at the same time, indispensable to Rome's survival.

Still, it would be a mistake to reduce to these administrative and regulatory aspects either the craftsmen's *collegia* or the humble folk's *collegia tenuiorum,* which were more specifically for funerary remembrance but often grouped craftsmen by trades. The *collegia* had an important place in the dense network of groups and classes that divided Romans according to their age, their social station, their affinities, their beliefs, or their occupations. These *collegia* had aims that went beyond the purely professional, and the craftsman got from them the certainty of a decent funeral, an enjoyment of the pleasures of conviviality and of a collective participation in the life of the city, and, at times, the satisfaction of a notability proper to his station. He also found in them a dignity refused him in the tiny shops, the smoke-filled and evil-smelling workshops, and the noisy, dangerous building sites. The trade corporations, like other associations, had a headquarters, a *schola,* where the poorest craftsman could find the sort of luxury we can see in Ostia in the seat of the *fabri navales,* the shipbuilders, with its large courtyard, pool, banquet hall, mosaics and frescoes, columns, and marble pavement. In the existing archaeological and epigraphical evidence on the *scholae* of corporations, ostentation is a constant theme.

In relation to the state, which was too remote, or his city, where he could hope for only a secondary role, the single craftsman did not account for much. There were striking exceptions to this rule, but in the last analysis they placed their protagonists at the limits of the craftsman's condition. It was in the *collegium* that the craftsman could best hope to make his mark. This explains the constant temptation to use association to reconstitute a universe to his measure, where he truly felt at home and where he gained stature in his own eyes. As Waltzing has noted, "What the wealthy citizen was in the municipality, the craftsman was in the college."

This then was the Roman craftsman. His most important trait was the diversity of his condition, which ranged from the miserably poor day laborer to the fabulously wealthy entrepreneur, from the unskilled worker in mass production to the specialist whose competence and skills were much in demand, from the anonymous worker in the slave mode of production to the free and responsible artisan or the slave or freedman who managed a workshop for his patron.

Under these many different aspects, these men and women shared a few common traits. These traits are not easily discerned, for the Romans have not helped us to discover them. This is true throughout classical antiquity, but the Roman world did not even have a Leonidas of Tarentum, a poet who celebrated the world of labor in the early third century B.C. and who "gave artisans back to the history of civilization" (Marcello Gigante). The Roman craftsman was disdained by his contemporaries, he was misunderstood in the historiography of the early modern period, and he is misunderstood today by reason of the very disdain that he inspired before. Scorned when he was sunk in mediocrity, he was even more scorned when, thanks to his initiative, hard work, and success, he managed to climb the social ladder, make money, and become a notable. He was, in short, either something less than nothing or a parvenu for an opinion that was perhaps a minority opinion but that is the only one to have come down to us. At best, antiquity stooped to take an interest, either out of curiosity or to express scandal, in a few striking success stories whose protagonists were considered insolent because their wealth came from the much-scorned *officina* and depended on *artes* unworthy of a free man.

If the craftsman was "the secret hero of Greek history," in Pierre Vidal-Naquet's felicitous formula, the Roman craftsman was even more inconspicuous. It is that armor of indifference, denigration, and, on occasion, hostility toward those whom Cicero called "the craftsmen and the shopkeepers and all those dregs of the cities" (*opifices et tabernarios atque illam omnem faecem civitatum*) that we must pierce if we are to discover that the Roman craftsman was not only productive (a quality that many still grant him only halfheartedly) but also a man, neither better nor worse than others but certainly no less worthy of attention. By a curious twist of fate, archaeologists and historians are becoming increasingly aware of what is now called "material culture"—the vestiges of which have come down to us largely thanks to the labor of Roman craftsmen— and of what it can teach us about the society, the civilization, and the economy of Rome.

Bibliography

Bilinsky, Bronislaw. "Le problème du travail dans la Rome antique: L'époque royale et les premiers temps de la République." *Archeologia* 3 (1949): 45– 111. The article is in Polish; a French summary is on pp. 415–25.

Burford, Alison. *Craftsmen in Greek and Roman Society*. Ithaca, N.Y.: Cornell University Press, 1972.

Carandini, Andrea. *L'anatomia della scimmia: La formazione economica della società prima del capitale*. Turin: Einaudi, 1979.

Garnsey, Peter. "Independent Freedmen and the Economy of Roman Italy under the Principate." *Klio* 63 (1981): 359–71.

———, ed. *Non-Slave Labour in the Greco-Roman World*. Suppl. vol. 9. Cambridge: Cambridge Philological Society, 1980.

Giardina, Andrea. "Lavoro e storia sociale: Antagonismi e alleanze dall'ellenismo al tardoantico." *Opus* 1 (1982): 115–46.

Gros, Pierre. "Statut social et rôle culturel des architectes (période hellénistique et augustéenne)." In *Architecture et société de l'archaïsme grec à la fin de la République romaine*. Actes du Colloque international (Rome, 1980). Rome: "L'Erma" di Bretschneider, 1983, 425–52.

Morel, Jean-Paul. "Aspects de l'artisanat dans la Grande Grèce romaine." In *La Magna Grecia nell'età romana*. Atti del XV convegno di studi sulla Magna Grecia (Taranto, 5–10 ottobre 1975). 2 vols. Naples: Arte tipografica, 1976. Vol 1, 263–324.

———. "Les producteurs de biens artisanaux en Italie à la fin de la République." In *Les "bourgeoisies" municipales italiennes aux IIe et Ier siècles av. J.-C.* Naples: Centre Jean Bérard, Paris: Editions CNRS, 1983. Pp. 21–39.

———. "La manufacture, moyen d'enrichissement dans l'Italie romaine?" In *L'origine des richesses dépensées dans las ville antique*. Actes du Colloque (Aix-en-Provence, 1984), ed. Philippe Leveau. Aix-en-Provence: Publications, Université de Provence, 1985. Pp. 87–111.

————. "La topographie de l'artisanat et du commerce dans la Rome antique." In *L'Urbs: Espace urbain et histoire Ier siècle av. J.-C.-IIIe siècle ap. J.-C.* Actes du Colloque international (Rome, 1985). Rome: Ecole française de Rome: 1987. Pp. 127–55.

————. "Das Handwerk in augusteischer Zeit." In *Kaiser Augustus und die verlorene Republik: Eine Ausstellung im Martin-Gropius-Bau, Berlin, 7. Juni–14. August 1988.* Berlin: Kulturstadt Europas, 1988. Pp. 81–92.

Mossé, Claude. *Le travail en Grèce et à Rome.* Paris: Presses Universitaires de France, 1966. Available in English as *The Ancient World at Work.* Trans. Janet Lloyd. London: Chatto & Windus, 1969; New York: W. W. Norton, n.d.

"La place de l'artisan dans les sociétés antiques (I)." *Ktema* 3 (1978): 35–131 (six articles).

Les potiers gaulois: À la conquête du monde Romain. Special issue, *Les dossiers de l'archéologie* 6 (1974).

Pucci, Giuseppe. "La produzione della ceramica aretina: Note sull' 'industria' nella prima età imperiale romana." *Dialoghi di Archeologia* 7 (1973): 255–93.

Rémondon, Roger. "Le monde romain." In *Histoire générale du travail,* gen. ed. Louis-Henri Parias. Paris: Nouvelle Librairie de France, 1959–. Vol. 1, *Préhistoire et Antiquité* (1959). Pp. 257–369.

Treggiari, Susan. *Roman Freedmen during the Late Republic.* Oxford: Clarendon Press, 1969.

Waltzing, Jean-Pierre. *Etude historique sur les corporations professionnelles chez les Romains depuis les origines jusqu'à la chute de l'Empire d'occident.* 4 vols. Louvain: Ch. Peeters, 1895–1900.

Zimmer, Gerhard. *Römische Berufsdarstellungen.* Deutsches Archäologisches Institut Archäologische Forschungen n. 12. Berlin: Mann, 1982.

9

The Merchant

Andrea Giardina

IN ALL ANCIENT CLASSICAL LITERATURE not one single passage can be found that analyzes price formation in commercial exchanges in economic terms and avoids all ethical judgments. Yet ancient literature is literally sown with references to the figure and the profession of the merchant, to large-scale commerce, to the more modest practices of buying and selling, to the relationship between agriculture and commerce, and to the problem of the "just price." It provides a universe of mentions, metaphors, definitions of social types, inventories of virtues and of detestable practices, hierarchies of decorum, associations constructed by analogy or by difference, persistent and time-honored habits and sudden breaks—an intricate tangle in which it is difficult if not impossible to discern the parameters of an inclusive description. As a result, the disquieting images of the relationship between men and merchandise in Roman culture are more "exploded" than organized into systems; more disarticulated into multiple tensions than composed in symmetrical, seamless polarities.

The ancients were persuaded that the merchant inevitably falsified the "just price," because he raised his prices without adding any additional labor to the labor value of the objects. Paul Veyne puts the situation well:

> People are convinced that the intermediary is responsible for the dearness from which he gains. We know that matters are less simple, for the marginalists have taught us that scarcity and the market are the only sources of the value of goods. Except where there is monopoly or a cartel, an intermediary

profits from the level at which prices stand at the final stage, and does not himself increase them on the way thither; for value does not increase between the producer and the consumer but, on the contrary, follows back along the stages of distribution and manufacture. People produce and sell only the things which will find a buyer, at the price which will find a buyer. . . . The difference in value provides the merchant's profit; he gains from dearth and shortages without being responsible for them. But the naïve mind does not see matters like that. In its view, the merchant does not just slip into the gap that separates intermediate values, but himself creates that gap. For the naïve mind thinks that value arises from below. It believes in labour-value. . . . Labour-value alone is the basis for the *justum pretium*. The merchant, however, is said to falsify the just price, for he inflates it without incorporating any additional labour in the object concerned. Of course the merchant is not inactive, but the very trouble that he takes is suspect. He travels, he is an unstable person, and his efforts do not change the object he sells, wherein is embodied solely the fatigue of the honest craftsman—who, himself, does not make a fortune. (*Bread and Circuses*, 52–53)

For the ancients, commerce could not be qualified as "labor" as we understand the term. It lacked the coefficient of physical work that was expressed when raw materials were transformed and that, although it did not do much to guarantee the social decorum of the laborer, at least justified the legitimacy of his pay. The terms contrasting agricultural work and commerce reflect this concept: agricultural labor (*ponos geōrgikos*) had no direct counterpart in a "commercial labor"; there was no *ponos* of *emporia*. Instead writers invoked the "danger of commerce"—*emporias kindynos* (Basil *Sermon on Wealth* 1 in *PG* 31.280 B). Similarly the term equivalent to agricultural *labor* was not mercantile *labor* but mercantile *damna* (losses) (Ausonius 13.1.1–6). Since writers lacked terms such as *ponos* and *labor* to apply to commercial activities, they chose terms that evoked the psychological and moral characteristics of those activities: danger, an integral part of the seafaring merchant's chosen life; losses that he might sustain; or the *cura,* the anxious solicitude that reigned in a soul torn by uncertainty and driven by a will to succeed (Augustine *De opere monachorum* 15.16 in *CSEL* 41.557).

Typically, commerce was the measure of distance and diversity in contacts between human groups. In the disquieting apparition of the foreign merchant, external differences (in language, customs, skin color) added up to a more hidden menace, that of a deceitful, insidious soul. Especially in the more closed societies, where comparison with the dynamic figures of the merchants inevitably generated psychological tensions, reaction against uncontrollable earnings fixed a mental image in which the different *ethnos* was defined on the basis of irreducible defects. These were the time-honored characteristics of the merchant: cleverness, trickery, and fraud.

As early as the Homeric age the Phoenicians, "famous navigators," were called greedy for gain, as in Odysseus' account to Eumaeus of the Phoenician merchant who had tricked him. The Phoenician was a merchant in Homer, but he was also a kidnapper, a *topos* that returns in Herodotus at the beginning of book 1, where he relates the capture of Io, the daughter of Inachus. This poor reputation appears again in Roman culture, applied to the Carthaginians. Along with their merchandise, Cicero tells us, the Phoenicians of Carthage were the first to introduce "greed, luxurious living, and insatiable desires of all sorts" (*De re publica* 3, fr. 4). Cicero himself, however, seems to attenuate the ancient stigma of the Carthaginians as "given to fraud and lying" by saying that they had gotten those traits "not so much by race as by the nature of their position" since their harbors had brought them into contaminating contact with merchants and strangers (*De lege agraria* 2.95). Still, Phoenicians and Carthaginians continued to be the ethnic prototypes of crafty and unprincipled merchants.

Equating ethnic traits with mercantile traits obviously was not restricted to Phoenicians and Carthaginians. Throughout the history of ancient cultures, we can see a similar connection between the images of "different" peoples and their commercial inclinations. Julius Caesar describes the success of the god Mercury among the Gauls, who held him to be the inventor of all the arts, *dux* of *viae* and *itinera* ("the guide for every road and journey"), but, above all, gifted with exceptional influence over business dealings and trade (*The Gallic War* 6.17.1). At the decline of the ancient world (but with much earlier precedents) St. Jerome called the Syrian traders "the greediest of men" (*Letters* 130.7, 9:175 Labourt); Salvianus called the Syrians the very synonyms of *mercatores* and a race of men uniquely dedicated to "plotting, trickery and wearing falsehood bare" (*On the Government of God* 4.14, trans. Sanford); and Sidonius

Apollinaris completed the picture by defining the Syrians as living symbols of usury (*Letters* 1.8.2). Still in late antiquity the Hebrews appear not only in general as merchants but also as prototypes of unprincipled tavern keepers who water their wine (for example, in Ambrose *De fide* 3.10.65 in *CSEL* 78.132). In later examples of ethnic and mercantile *topoi*, representations became mixed: for example, Byzantine sources (especially after the crusades) present Westerners as tricky and fond of lucre, and Anna Comnena was not the only person who called the Latins a greedy and clever race (*Alexiad* 6.6.4).

Those of a different *ethnos* were always seen as greedy, thus as clever and treacherous, because in all they did the quest for unreasonable gains was an insidious weapon. Although the search for lucre shortened the physical distances between peoples, the intense commercial contacts that derived from it added to psychological distances and introduced ethnic connotations that tended to stick.

Remote and nearly unattainable geographical regions were also seen as places in which one could practice a peaceable and fair "commerce." Herodotus provides a famous case in point. When the Carthaginians went to the parts of "Libya" beyond the Pillars of Hercules, they were in the habit of unloading their merchandise on the beach, arranging it in good order. They then returned to their ships and sent up smoke signals. On seeing the signals, the natives of the place went to the shore, left a certain amount of gold, and withdrew. If the Carthaginians held that the gold was adequate for the value of the merchandise, they took it and set sail; if not, they left everything on the sand and once more returned to their ships to wait. The scene was repeated until the Carthaginians felt satisfied. Herodotus comments: "Herein neither party (it is said) defrauds the other; the Carchedonians do not lay hands on the gold till it matches the value of their cargo, nor do the people touch the cargo till the shipmen have taken the gold" (4.196).

The Romans attributed the custom of "silent barter" to other peoples as well, such as the Seres, who lived in the Far East. Fond of tranquillity, the Seres looked over merchandise spread out on the banks of a river by foreign merchants, evaluated it, and made their trades without exchanging a word (*nullo inter partes linguae commercio:* Solinus *Polyhistor* 50.2ff.). Similar trades took place between the Ethiopians and the Egyptians in the border region between their lands, where the famous Apollonius of Tyana found, at a crossways, a certain quantity of raw gold together with linen cloth, ivory, roots, unguents, and spices, all untended. Philostratus tells us, "It was a market place to which the Ethiopians bring all the products of their country; and the Egyptians in their turn take them all away and bring to the same spot their own wares of equal value" (*Life of Apollonius* 6.2).

"Silent barter," described in accounts like these and others closer to our own age, has long intrigued historians and ethnologists. Although some have denied its historical veracity, there seems to be no doubt (proofs are innumerable and convergent) that the practice must have been fairly frequent, particularly where foreign merchants entered into contact with a weaker community that had no intention either of fighting off the foreigners or granting them free access to its territory. With the exception of the account of Cosmas Indicopleustes concerning trade among the Axumites and the natives of Sasou (where "silent barter" was necessary for the simple reason that they had no interpreters), all ancient sources suggest ethical reasons for the practice.

For the ancients, in fact, this practice was an admirable example of how it could be possible, almost at the ends of the earth, in lands and situations that today we could call "frontier," to practice commerce with justice. Herodotus observes that between the Carthaginians and the Libyans "neither party . . . defrauds the other," and Philostratus, following his description of trade between the Ethiopians and the Egyptians, attributes to Apollonius a digression on the greed of the Greeks, who "pretend they cannot live unless one penny begets another and unless they can force up the price of their goods by chaffering or holding them back." He exclaims, contemplating a world in decline, "What a splendid thing then it would be, if wealth were held in less honour and equality flourished a little more!" (*Life of Apollonius* 6.2). Thus the harmonious relations that were a reality in exchanges and relations between the Seres and the foreigners, the natives of Sasou and the Axumites, Ethiopians and Egyptians, the Phoenician colonists of Carthage and their Libyan neighbors were just a memory to Apollonius.

Was it possible to transport this ideal into the heart of the city and make it real? Could one create a silent market in the *polis*? Plato indicates his belief that it was indeed possible when he imagines a decree obliging retailers to sell by fixed prices (*Laws* 917b–c), thus avoiding the artful game of negotiations and small psychological tricks principally founded on verbal skill.

The utopia of a silent market comes up again in Roman culture in the introduction of Philostratus' *Heroicus*, where a viticulturist tells a Phoenician, "You are experts in the art of navigation. In fact, you have placed in the heavens something like a second Bear and you follow it sailing. You are praised for your skill in affronting the sea, but commerce makes you odious because you are greedy for gain and voracious." The Phoenician responds that the farmer is also fond of gain, and that the end of all his labor is the sale of his produce. The grape grower cannot deny this and is forced to admit the need to buy and sell: "Agriculture needs money as well, and without it neither the farmer nor the viticulturist could live, nor could the shepherd or the goat-herd, and you would have no cup to drink or offer a toast. Even the grape harvest, the sweetest of agricultural labors, is done for gain. If this were not true, the vines would be idle, without wine, as if they were painted" (1.3.7). Up to this point the discourse has been carried on in customary fashion, but what follows is more significant. The viticulturist continues, "What I have said refers to all agriculturists in general, but my goods are much more modest. I do not trade with merchants; I do not know what a drachma is. I buy and sell in person, an ox for grain, a goat for wine, and so forth, *having said little and heard little.*" An aspiration for self-sufficiency, a scorn of money and a preference for barter, a refusal of relations with merchants— all these are typical of a nostalgia for the mythical Age of Gold. He adds another, no less important trait: the goal of a nearly mute exchange that creates, in the city market, the silences of the far-off land of the Seres.

When it was removed from the utopias and shifted from the "frontier" to the heart of the city, the relationship between goods and words created thorny problems. Clever words were mingled with an unprincipled relationship with time.

The merchant's profession was a competitive one, and sudden advantage, seizing the favorable moment (the Greeks called it *kairos*), and skill in turning others' weakness to one's own advantage all made the merchant's profession comparable to the most competitive activity—the athlete's. Participants in an endless struggle, the outcome of which always might be unpredictable and disquieting, athletes and merchants could also appear as privileged interlocutors of the magicians, and the fleeting mechanisms of success demanded the use of the most consummate techniques of the supernatural (Philostratus *Life of Apollonius* 7.39).

The chief expression of the merchant's craftiness lay in the natural inclination of an intelligence gifted for prediction that enabled him to know before others when situations were changing, goods would be scarce or abundant, or harvests would be good or disappointing.

What Cicero states concerning those who cultivate lands *in Sallentinis aut in Bruttiis*—that they received news only two or three times a year

(*Pro Roscio Amerino* 132)—could be said of many who lived in the Greek and Roman world. Not only in places where the circulation of news was extremely slow and access to information episodic but in the better-informed world of the city as well, the dynamic figure of the merchant, secure in his gain, provided a contrast to the general rule.

Romans had the same emotional reactions toward merchants as the citizens of all the other ancient cities had. Demosthenes' *Against Dionysodorus* offers as credible, around 322 B.C., an entire organization of maritime traders based in Egypt, "underlings and confederates of Cleomenes, the former ruler of Egypt," that directed grain convoys to whichever market offered the best price. These merchants used "letters and conspiracies" to promote their own interests over the objective good of the city (5–9). Early and privileged information was typical of maritime trade, but it did not exclude the more modest categories of retail merchants. In the Athens of Lysias, just before the Peace of Antalcidas (386 B.C.), retail grain merchants (whose activities and earnings were supervised by specific magistrates) speculated on the difficulty of getting supplies by raising prices day by day "as if they were making purchases medimnus by medimnus" (Lysias 22.12). They explained these price rises by a whole series of unfavorable events (ships sunk in the Pontus or captured by the Spartans, markets blocked, truces broken) that they invented or had word of before the citizens. Speculation in time (sale prices that rose day by day well beyond the cost price) went along with a monopoly of information.

In a passage in his *Natural History*, Pliny the Elder contrasts the lore of the peasant, who knows nothing of astronomy (*indocilis caeli*) and seeks in the soil signs of changes in climate, to the knowledge of the merchant, who scrutinizes astronomical phenomena and sees in the heavens, with his treacherous scheming (*cura insidiandi*), signs of an advantage to be grasped. Thus he contrasts a way of knowing that draws its inferences from what has already happened (dead leaves on the ground announce autumn) to one that anticipates (from the movement of the Pleiades) what is about to happen (*Naturalis historia* 18.225–27). We will encounter this last image again, centuries later, in Diocletian's *Edictum de maximis pretiis*, which refers to traders as "evil men engaged in business" who "actually try to predict the wind and weather by watching the movements of the stars" (prologue, 10.2, quoted from Stephen Williams, *Diocletian and the Roman Recovery*, 129).

The merchant's relations with time were not restricted to such activities. In the marketplaces buffeted by a thousand confused movements that Democritus took as a metaphor for the movement of the atoms that produce the winds, the merchant also showed proof of having a special intelligence that consisted in halting the fleeting moment to his own advantage. The merchant's reason embroidered on time and saw further than normal; not surprisingly, his earnings were later expressed by the term *captare pretium,* which expresses the rapid and astute grasp of a favorable price. Another related expression is also significant: *captare annonam* (*annona,* grain supply), which indicates speculation on rising prices in times of scarcity, natural or artificial (Ambrose *On Obligations* 3.6.42, 44).

In the judgment of the ancient world, the connection between time and trade tended to be absorbed, as we have seen, into a more general question: the weight of trickery, mendacity, and clever reasoning in relations between men. This is the way in which a noted *exemplum* of Cicero's should be read. Cicero uses an imaginary dialogue between Diogenes of Babylon and his pupil, Antipater, as an opportunity to analyze the relationship between *dolus* and *simulatio* and to discuss the use of privileged forehand information in commercial practices in the general context of the relationship between *ius civile* and *principia naturae* (*De officiis* 3.50ff.).

The *exemplum* runs like this: A *vir bonus* had loaded a large amount of wheat on a ship headed from Alexandria to Rhodes. At Rhodes, famine raged, a circumstance that offered him an opportunity to make an excellent profit. He knew, however, that other ships would arrive at that island immediately after his own: was a *vir bonus* obliged to tell the Rhodians about the imminent arrival of the other convoys, or could he keep silent in order to command a higher price? Antipater is of the opinion that he must reveal all that he knows so that "the buyer may not be uninformed of any detail that the seller knows." Diogenes states instead that the seller, even though obliged to declare any defects in the merchandise, according to the tenets of civil law, is not held to furnish other information. He has the hypothetical merchant argue, "I have imported my stock, I have offered it for sale; I sell at a price no higher than my competitors—perhaps even lower when the market is overstocked. Who is wronged?" Antipater reacts to this, recalling the duties of everyone toward human society and the principles according to which "your interest shall be the interest of the community and conversely . . . the interest of the community should be your interest as well." On the basis of such principles, it is blameworthy to hide from one's fellow men the harm that awaits them. Diogenes, however, contrasts a more realistic vision of the individual's demands to the more abstract demands of a human *societas* regulated by natural relations (*inter homines natura coniuncta societas*). He asks, "Do you mean to say that these bonds of fellowship are such that there is no such thing as private property? If that is the case, we should not sell anything at all, but freely give everything away." Cicero himself inclined to Antipater's opinion that the merchant should have informed the buyers. "Who fails to discern what manner of concealment that is and what sort of person would be guilty of it? At all events he would be no candid or sincere or straightforward or upright or honest man, but rather one who is shifty, sly, artful, shrewd, underhand, cunning, one grown old in fraud and subtlety."

Examples such as Cicero's were not exclusive to Roman thought on trade, but they can be found throughout preindustrial European tradition. The *honestas* that the merchant should have displayed, according to Antipater and Cicero, by telling buyers the true value of the wheat he was selling returns in heightened form in a saintly figure from the ninth century, St. Gerald of Aurillac, whose life was told by his biographer, St. Odo of Cluny, in a biography that, as Georges Duby has pointed out, bears all the marks of a manual of proper behavior for the powerful. Gerald's is also an exemplary case.

On arriving in Pavia from Rome, Gerald stopped in an encampment of pilgrims. Some Venetian merchants approached him as they went from tent to tent, as was their wont, to sell stuffs and foodstuffs. "I bought what I wanted in Rome," Gerald replied to their offers, "but I should like you to tell me whether I bought wisely." Among the articles he bought was one cloak of excellent quality that attracted the merchants' attention. When they learned the price Gerald had paid, one exclaimed, "If it was at Constantinople it would be worth even more!" This opinion, which would have gladdened the heart of any ordinary man, threw Gerald into despair: he had wanted to know if he had spent his money well, and he learned that he had gotten a good bargain. This dismayed him as much as if it had been a great crime (*quasi grande facinus*). Grave misfortune required a remedy, and several days later the merchant in Rome received a sum equal to the difference in price between the sale price and the price in Constantinople (Odo of Cluny *Life of Gerald* 1.27 in *PL* 133.658, trans. Sitwell, 117–18).

Their contexts differ enormously, but these two documents express substantially the same conception of the acquisition of goods. Gerald is a model of nobility and saintliness, and his scruples are manifested in an extreme way that leads him to rescind the good bargain he has unwittingly made. But even the merchant from Alexandria, as Antipater (that is, Cicero) sees him, is an ideal (hence an exaggerated) figure and the personification of a noble conscience that reflects on human *societas* and on its natural values. Both cases affirm the basic principle that in buying and selling neither party should possess more information than the other. Previous or successive knowledge of an excessive advantage to be gained or actually gained always placed the willing or unwilling protagonist of the affair in a position of moral indebtedness, a position that neither Cicero nor Odo of Cluny held to be "honest." Traditional ethics, furthermore, saw few attenuating circumstances connected with *dissimulatio*, interested reticence, as compared with *simulatio*, downright simulation (Emanuele Narducci).

Commerce involved an innate inclination to lie. It was as if *lucrum* were indissolubly linked to *fraus*. One could react to this constraint in two ways: like Cicero, one could evoke extreme ideal figures that were, as Cicero himself acknowledged, difficult to realize, and could propose an aristocratic ethical model made to fit the demands of an abstract *societas*. Or like the saintly men of late antiquity and the Middle Ages (also often aristocrats), one could demand that buying and selling had to be tempered not only by human values (love thy neighbor) but also by an appeal to heavenly values. Neither of these reactions abolished the basic fact of a connection between gain and trickery; if anything they accentuated it.

It might be said that these were extreme cases and symbolic figures of an aristocratic ethics that pertained only among extremely limited groups of people. The fact remains, however (as is always the case), that this ethics, independent of the concrete behavior patterns it spoke for, became a measure of the actions of other classes in society and the parameter of an *honestas* valued in absolute terms. It was values, furthermore, that served to measure the relative "unworthiness" of the merchant (a full appreciation in positive terms was out of the question).

The particular relationship between the merchant and time did not only consist in playing the anticipation game (deciphering celestial signs, privileged information), in his ability to grasp the moment of *kairos*, or in holding back sales while the price rose artificially. There was also another unprincipled use of time in the *statim vendere*, or "immediate sale," of retail sellers who *mercantur a mercatoribus* (buy from the merchants). Cicero found the theoretical basis for his condemnation of retail trade, the activity of the *kapēlos* and the *tabernarius*, in the relationship between time and mendacity. The rapidity with which an intermediary resold what he had bought from another merchant was directly proportional to an unprincipled use of language: "Vulgar we must consider those also who buy from wholesale merchants to retail immediately; for they would get no profits without a great deal of downright lying; and verily, there is no action that is meaner than misrepresentation." Large-scale or wholesale commerce (*magna mercatura*) "importing large quantities from all parts of the world" was a long-term activity, and the length of time justified the gain, which meant that it could be practiced without misrepresentation (*sine vanitate*); retail commerce (*tenuis mercatura*) was founded on profits that were inevitably the result of fraud (Cicero *De officiis* 1.150ff.).

Deceit, an evil intrinsic to commerce, was diluted in wholesale merchandising and to some extent balanced by other elements such as the courage of the merchant in confronting the high seas and the civic function of supplying the cities (a subject to which I shall return). In retail merchandising, however, deceit tended to be manifest in its pure state.

Condemnations of small-scale commercial activities run uninterrupted throughout Greek and Roman antiquity. Aeschylus presented *kapēloi* as men who dreamed up tricks and stratagems (*Tragicorum graecorum Fragmenta,* Nauck, fr. 322), which accorded with a tradition in which the shopkeeper's mentality was ambiguous and corrupt. According to Plato, in the orderly *polis* the task of serving as shopkeepers must be given to "those who are weakest in body and those who are useless for any other task" (*Republic* 371c). Plato's image of the mercantile function in the ideal city was in line with his definition of *mesotes* as an elite virtue:

> Small is the class of men—rare by nature and trained, too, with a superlative training—who, when they fall into divers needs and lusts, are able to stand out firmly for moderation. . . . The disposition of the mass of mankind is exactly the opposite of this; when they desire, they desire without limit, and when they can make moderate gains, they prefer to gain insatiably; and it is because of this that all the classes concerned with retail trade, commerce, and inn-keeping are disparaged and subjected to violent abuse. (*Laws* 11.918c–d)

It was the character of most men that distorted commercial practices and made them odious and detestable not the *natura* of commerce, the aim of which was to make "even and symmetrical" the distribution of goods that "before was unsymmetrical and uneven" (ibid., 918b). The natural purpose of retail trade was gain, and the merchant, the *kapēlos,* "ordained for this purpose," was "a benefactor." Plato added that if it should happen that the best men everywhere "were compelled for a certain period to keep inns or to peddle or to carry on any such trade—or even to compel women, by some necessity of fate, to take part in such a mode of life—then we should learn that each of these callings is friendly and desirable" (ibid., 918d–e).

The function of commerce that we might call "naturally democratic" (not only of *emporia* but also of *kapēlikē*) was thus altered by an almost impossible reconciliation of ethics and gain. Ethics—seeking a measured gain—would bring the merchant closer to the *polis*. But in real life that situation was not to be found.

These are the reflections of a philosopher, to be sure, but similar opinions must have found confirmation in the widespread practices of anyone who had dealings with small-scale retailers, if it is true that "the laws . . . declare that anyone who makes business in the market" was protected from "a reproach against any male or female citizen" by "penalties for evil-speaking" (Demosthenes *Against Eubulides* 30). The small retailer was treated to scorn in Rome as well and as a type was identified with the intermediary. Martial says: "The scurrilities of home-born slaves, low railing, and the foul insults of a hawker's tongue, which the broker [*proxenēta*] of shattered Vatinian glasses would reject as the price of a sulphur match, a certain skulking poet scatters abroad, and would have them appear as mine" (10.3)

The unprincipled broken-glass peddler whom Martial uses as a comparison to a poet who was distributing miserable verse and attributing it to him is called a *proxenēta*, a term that was used at the time in a technical sense to designate an intermediary, because the intermediary and the peddler aroused the same contempt. The retail seller was irremediably discredited; so was the intermediary, whose earnings Ulpian declared (in a fragment) "sordid." Ulpian seems to attenuate this traditional judgment, however, by recognizing that the intermediary was "useful in a not unreasonable way" within the context of lawful sales contracts and trade (*Digest* 50.14.3). This attenuation, born of the practice and the special perspective of the jurist, did not succeed in canceling the old condemnation, as we have seen in the semantic connection that Martial makes between the go-between and the retail merchant. As always in such cases, small dynamic statements hardly scratch the surface of the traditional image. Thus it is natural that Philostratus (a contemporary of Ulpian's) repeated the old duality of large- and small-scale commerce and put retailing on a par with the intermediary's trade, thus somewhat formalizing the ethical association between *kapēlos* and *proxenētes* hinted at in Martial's choice of words. According to Philostratus, one of the main reasons why the merchants were "wretched and ill-starred" was that they were constrained to associate "with factors and brokers" (*Life of Apollonius* 4.32).

In the Roman system of social values, large-scale commerce was never permanently included among the "sordid" professions. The preface to Cato's treatise on agriculture, often taken as exemplary for condemnation of the merchant, to the contrary contains one of the clearest instances that antiquity has left us of praise of this social figure. Not only was the merchant "bent on making money" (*studiosus rei quaerendae*), which in Cato's scheme of things was always positive, provided that certain principles were respected, but the *mercator* was also "energetic" (*strenuus*). His activities were limited only by their dangers to his person and his investments: *mercatorum periculosum et calamitosum* (the merchants' dangerous [career] and one subject to disaster).

The risks faced by the seafaring merchant formed a common *topos* harking back to the earliest days of Greek poetry. The notion was directly linked to a view of the sea as treacherous and perilous, the most "just" of the elements when no force disturbed it but the least controllable when stirred up by the winds. The "justice" of the sea, expressed in Latin as *aequor* and which Varro derived from the notion of *aequitas,* was anything but to the advantage of the sea merchant, who preferred speed, hence wind. The "equity" of the sea contrasted with its "inequity," which merchants knew all too well but nonetheless braved (see, for example, Philostratus *Heroicus* 1.2). There were a number of variations to this *topos.* In Columella it took on a philosophical and religious tone: the merchant was a man who had dared to break the pact with nature; his sacrilegious audacity provoked the ire of the elements; he was uprooted, a man without a homeland, a migratory bird. This last image recurs throughout the centuries, and indeed a wild duck was the emblem of Italian merchants in the later Middle Ages. Precisely such recourse to a naturalistic element is the clearest sign that trade on the large scale—sea trade—could be exempt from the blacklist of "sordid" professions.

The courage of the sea merchant was thus taken for granted, and it inevitably served as a plus in locating this figure on the scale of social values. The moral force of courage remained unchanged through time. For example, when John Chrysostom recommended the virtue of constancy amid trials and tribulations to Theodore, his correspondent, he said, "The worst, Theodore, is not to fall in the struggle but to stay stretched out on the ground; and it is unfortunate, not to be wounded in war, but, once wounded, to neglect one's wound out of despair." He goes on to offer as examples a list of the sorts of persons who are accustomed to the disturbing vicissitudes of the fray—the athlete, the soldiers, the martyr, and, to head the list, the merchant: "No merchant leaves off voyaging because he has been shipwrecked and has lost his cargo; he takes to the seas again, to the billows and the vast ocean, and does his best to recuperate his lost wealth" (*PG* 47.309). Incidentally passages like this demonstrate, among other things, the inaccuracy of Christian Bec's contrast between the resignation before the blows of fate supposedly represented in "Christian and pagan tradition" and the tenacious and pugnacious attitudes of the Florentine merchants of the late Middle Ages.

Another aspect of the seafaring merchant's character that attenuated social condemnation of him was his particular experience as an eyewitness, something the ancients valued highly. The question of how best to reconcile the material demands of turning a profit (with moderation) and the moral demands of a quest for cultural knowledge lies at the base of "Solon's voyages," on which Plutarch bases broader reflections:

> And there is no reason why a good statesman should either set his heart too much on the acquisition of superfluous wealth, or despise unduly the use of what is necessary and convenient. In those earlier times, to use the words of Hesiod, "work was no disgrace," nor did a trade bring with it social inferiority, and the calling of a merchant was actually held in honour, since it gave him familiarity with foreign parts, friendships with foreign kings, and a large experience in affairs. Some merchants were actually founders of great cities, as Protis, who was beloved by the Gauls along the Rhone, was of Marseilles. Thales is said to have engaged in trade, as well as Hippocrates the mathematician; and Plato defrayed the expenses of his sojourn in Egypt by the sale of oil. (*Life of Solon* 2.5–7)

Plutarch was combating the view that Solon "travelled to get experience [*polypeiria*] and learning [*historia*] rather than to make money" (ibid., 2.1) The theme must have been fraught with tension and subject to attempts at attenuation, although these could not have been of any great importance if even Aristotle stated, quite simply, that Solon had gone to Egypt "with the combined objects of trade and travel" (*The Athenian Constitution* 11.1, trans. Kenyon).

When he discusses benefits, Seneca mentions some services of great utility to others that nonetheless lose in *gratia* because they are remunerated: the physician benefits the sick, the slave trader provides a service for anyone who wants to put himself up for sale, the merchant does a service to the city (*mercator urbibus prodest; De beneficiis* 2.13.2). But the person who receives the advantage is not in a position of moral indebtedness, because if these people help others it is in order to help themselves. Things were not that simple, however, and a glimpse of the complicated and subtle distinctions of the connection between *utile* and *beneficium* in the mercantile function takes us to the heart of one of the fundamental problems in the relationship between ethics and commerce.

The merchant could not be denied a precise civic role connected to the essential problem of provisioning the city. The connection between large-scale commerce, provisioning, and the civic role of the merchant emerges in Roman documents as early as the dedication of the *aedes Mercuri* (the sanctuary of Mercury) on the Ides of May, 495 B.C. As Livy tells us:

> The consuls had got into a dispute as to which should dedicate the temple to Mercury. The Senate referred the case to the people for decision, whichever consul should, by command of the people, be entrusted with the dedication was to have charge of the grain supply [*annona*], to establish a guild of merchants, and perform the solemn rites in the presence of the pontifex. (2.27.5–6)

The anachronisms and incongruencies in Livy's account are valuable for the history of mental attitudes, because they make clear the associations that the tradition of annals used to construct a coherent account: the dedication of the temple of Mercury, the god of the merchants; the organization of the latter into a college; and responsibility for the *annona* in the end made up a series of harmonic elements in what was normally considered to be the relationship between the mercantile function and the city.

Recognition of the merchants' civic role returns in Cicero's famous discourse on honest trades and "sordid" ones:

> Trade, if it is on a small scale, is to be considered vulgar; but if wholesale and on a large scale, importing large quantities from all parts of the world and distributing to many without misrepresentation, it is not to be greatly disparaged. Nay, it

even seems to deserve the highest respect, if those who are engaged in it, satiated, or rather, I should say, satisfied with the fortunes they have made, make their way from the port to a country estate, as they have often made it from the sea into port. (*De officiis* I.151)

It is useless to raise the old problem of the senatorial order's involvement in commercial dealings on the basis of this celebrated passage from ancient literature. No one today still doubts (or should doubt) that this involvement existed and was widespread, thanks to a number of stratagems for guaranteeing members of the elite an apparent detachment from the actual goods. The moral problem was long to trouble the upper classes: "Commerce is not unbecoming to a cavalier," one of Goldoni's characters declares, "but because of men's prejudices I have found it convenient to carry it on secretly." When they "theorized" on the question, the Romans insisted on one simple and rigid distinction: selling only what one produces oneself was not commerce.

This distinction, which recurs often in Roman sources, finds expression as early as Plato (*The Sophist* 223d), who distinguishes, in the context of the *agorastikē*, between *autopolikē* (the sale of one's own products) and *metabletikē* (the sale of others' products). In other words, what was important was not to "trade with the traders," as Cicero, Philostratus, and St. Ambrose, among others, took pains to point out. Cicero stated, logically, that the only thing that made trade truly praiseworthy was when its proceeds were converted into landed property—that is, when it ceased. Cicero also showed that large-scale commerce could be integrated into the system of social values (or at least brought closer to those values) in other ways than the conversion of commercial capital into landed property. Such a conversion was so frequent that it was taken for granted and considered inevitable. Cicero expressed it as a shift from sea to port to land that ennobled the merchant's labor. This can also be seen in the discrepancy between "is not to be greatly disparaged" (*non est admodum vituperanda*), which refers to large-scale trade in itself, and "it even seems to deserve the highest respect" (*videtur iure optimo posse laudari*), which refers to commerce converted into agriculture. Cicero's thought was nonetheless based on the notion that large-scale commerce cannot be totally condemned, precisely in consideration of its civic function ("importing large quantities from all parts of the world").

As we have seen throughout the present volume, to speak of the social figures of Rome (or any other traditional society) means in large part to speak of the way in which they were seen by the social classes that produced the sources that we use. Naturally, using some of the specific categories of social history in our analysis of these sources is a good way to avoid a passive reception of stereotypes formed in antiquity, but it also is an invitation to return to the complexity of social and mental situations. The "Roman world" was also an "epigraphic civilization," and thanks to inscriptions (funerary epigraphy in particular), we can discern some of the ways in which the Romans represented themselves, sketch the values that the merchants saw as their own or said they did, and gain some slight notion of a Roman "mercantile morality."

Self-representation comes on three levels. First, there are some aspects of the dominant culture's evaluation of the mercantile function that the merchants accepted as their own; next, there are reactions to the dominant culture's criticism of mercantile behavior; finally, there are values particular to the social orders involved in various levels of commercial activities.

The courage of the sea merchant was a theme that could be treated brilliantly by the protagonists themselves. In its simplest versions, the merchant or the ship's captain (or one person performing both roles) stressed the frequency of his voyages as a sign of continuing bravery: "I have often taken voyages over the billows and the seas" (*CIL* 9.3337). Other texts offer more elaborate and downright poetic thoughts: the splendid epitaph of a merchant from Brindisi (*CIL* 9.60) combines the two themes of courage and acquaintance with many lands that we have seen in some literary sources, Columella and Plutarch in particular. It differs from them in some details and in emphasis, but danger—danger from the elements but also the risk of possible financial failure—is part of a "model" that emphasizes knowledge of many lands and the bravery of one who, though in fear, has repeatedly accepted the challenge:

> On the ships with speedy sails I have often sailed the great sea, / I have reached many lands: this is the end / that the Fates sung for me at my birth. / Here have I left off all anxieties and all toil. / Now I do not fear the stars, nor the storm-clouds, nor the cruel sea, / nor do I fear that expenses will outstrip gains.

Bravery and experience: in comparison with these virtues, lucre could even seem to be a means more than a goal, or at least it fitted into a more complex picture.

The courage and the prestige of a seafaring merchant and ship's captain were measured by the number of his voyages. The merchant Flavius Zeuxis records in Hierapolis, in Phrygia, that seventy-two times he braved the seas "from the Malea to Italy" (*Syll.* 1229). The emperor Hadrian gives as his reason for recommending that the Ephesians give two sea traders places in their city council that they have "many times sailed the sea and been useful to the homeland" (*Syll.* 838 = *Die Inschriften von Ephesos* 5.1487, 1488). These two traders have other merits as well (not the least of which is to have transported high dignitaries and, on two occasions, the princeps himself), but it is significant that Hadrian begins his presentation by recalling their two principal merits: courage, which is directly proportional to the "many times" they have faced the high seas, and civic utility, which is closely connected with that courage. As Henri Willy Pleket has noted, the emperor's intervention probably fits into a transitional phase in the history of commerce and its social evaluations: the city council of Ephesus does not seem to have been eager to welcome the two *nauklēroi* among its ranks, whereas the emperor seems to have thought this a possible social promotion and lent it his support. It is possible that this sort of co-optation had already occurred in other cities and that in still others it occurred even later, but the central position of Ephesus in the Mediterranean trade system and the social level at which this episode took place make it extremely probable that the documents do indeed express a transitional phase in the evolution of values connected with the social position of sea traders.

Sea traders and great merchants were certainly in the forefront of this type of promotion to the ranks of city councils, but the phenomenon soon involved small-scale merchants as well. In the age of the Severi the jurist Callistratus stated that vendors of merchandise for ordinary use (*utensilia*) should not be scorned as "base persons," so they could certainly aspire to a post on the city councils (*Digest* 50.2.12). One should not conclude from this that small-scale merchants were likely to find access to governmental responsibilities difficult; rather the jurist's favorable opinion was probably based on the difficulty of guaranteeing that such local, autonomous institutions would function smoothly in a period of growing financial obligations for their members. The social promotion of such categories was thus written into the history of Roman urbanism.

The distinction between retail commerce and large-scale commerce to satisfy urban needs can, of course, be found elsewhere than in cultural elaborations of reflections on the pursuit of gain and its attendant "duties." The same duality is apparent in the attitudes of the merchants themselves. An excellent illustration of this awareness is the inscription on an arch in the Forum Boarium that the *boari* and the *argentarii* dedicated to Septimius Severus, Caracalla, and Julia Domna in A.D. 204. In its first version the epigraph (*CIL* 6.1035 = *ILS* 426) contained the words *argentarii et boari huius loci* (the bankers and beef sellers of this place), but some time later (no later than the reign of Caracalla) it was changed to read *argentarii et boari huius loci qui invehent* (the bankers and beef sellers of this place who will import). Specifying *qui invehent,* which qualified the *boari* as "importers," not simple retailers, must have seemed to them indispensable. The nuance took on even greater significance by being displayed in one of the most prestigious spots in the city, thus attributing to the *boari,* as importers, a civic role that local merchants (retail or wholesale) normally did not have and would never have had in popular opinion. Some scholars who have written about the topography of craft and commerce in Rome (Jean-Paul Morel for example) have spoken of a gradual transfer of small businesses out of the more decorous parts of the central city and of their dispersion and reconstruction in a variety of new contexts. This literal "marginalization" was paralleled, in the third century A.D. in particular, by the extension of what we might call the "spaces of civic commerce"—that is, of mercantile activities (subsidized or not) endowed with a "civic" (in the ancient sense) purpose. The world of large-scale provisioning of the city, protected by imperial liberality, undermined the gritty world of *tenuis mercatura.*

This explains the use of the future tense in *invehent.* The addition, held to be indispensable, reflects a new general situation in the Forum Boarium—a formal reorganization to provide a basis for a new urban context that was to include not just simple *boari* but *boari* who would "import." If this is the case, the future tense in *invehent* stresses innovation. At the same time, it takes on another, ideological, shade of meaning: "will continue to import"—will continue to assure provisions for the Roman plebs. The nature of these provisions, the city for which they were destined, and probably also their subsidized price gave the *boari qui invehent* a highly "civic" role in comparison to simple *boari* who sold their merchandise in the city without being involved in importation.

The commercial activities of the great importers of foodstuffs who supplied the city dwellers with the wheat, meat, oil, and wine they needed, could easily seem to have a civic dimension. A boat on the horizon, its sails bellied out in the wind and its hold full of merchandise, was always a reassuring sight, at least until the bargaining began and suspicions of unwarranted gain arose.

We can verify recourse to civic credentials of this sort in the texts of inscriptions in which the merchants "speak" of themselves. These, too, were "self-representations," since we can presuppose the participation of the merchant himself, who prepared his epitaph before he died, or that of his family circle. Thus, in an inscription from Magliano (*CIL* 9.4796), the merchant L. Nerusius Mithres declared that he had been "known in the sacred city as a seller of goat-skins" (*notus in urbe sacra vendenda pelle caprina*) and that he had "displayed goods appropriate to the people's needs" (*exhibui merces popularibus usibus aptas*). Similarly the wine merchant Herennuleius Cestus added to his *curriculum*, with evident pride, that he had traded "in overseas goods of all sorts" (*mercator omnis generis mercium transmarinis; CIL* 9.4680). Here *transmarinis* seems indispensable to the prestige of the person being commemorated.

The first level of self-representation thus consisted in the merchant's deliberate appropriation of courage and a civic role, two things that, even in the extreme formulations of the dominant culture, greatly attenuated the traditional condemnation of commerce. The second level consisted in the merchants' reversal of the most radical and widespread of the criticisms aimed at them. Almost as if making an unprompted excuse, the merchant draws a reversed portrait of himself that points to virtues where his interlocutors suspected sins.

The epigraph of L. Nerusius Mithres mentioned above records that the departed always paid his taxes, that he was honest in all his transactions (*in cunctis simplex contractibus*) and fair to all, within the limits of the possible (*omnibus aequus ut potui*), and that he was ever ready to come to the aid of the needy (*subveni saepe petenti*).

In an epitaph from the last years of the Republic one Gaius Ateilius Euhodus, who sold jewels on the Via Sacra (*margaritarius de sacra via*), is remembered, among other reasons, as a *homo bonus, misericors,* and *amans pauperis* (*ILLRP* 797). "Lover of the poor": the expression has piqued scholars' curiosity and set them to musing. Hendrik Bolkestein has seen this epigraph (and others that reflect a similar sensitivity) as a manifestation of a "popular pagan morality" similar, from a sociological viewpoint, to the Jewish moral sense and, more generally, to that of Eastern peoples. Others, Martin R. P. McGuire among them, have used onomastic evidence to trace a direct influence from eastern areas under Roman domination. Both the "sociological" and the "historical" theses make the mistake of reducing the history of ancient ethical systems to the problem of the circulation of a *topos*. The same *topos*—particularly when it involves concepts that might safely be called elementary—could arise independently in a variety of historical and geographical situations. Naturally, *topoi* can also travel and can be transplanted. But what counts—in every instance—is not the simple isolated formula as much as the value that such a formula assumes in a variety of contexts.

If we look at the epitaph of Ateilius Euhodus in this light it opens a different perspective. It was opportune and in harmony with the moral code of the upper classes to remove any shadow of suspicion from the activity of the jeweler commemorated here. It is not a coincidence that celebration of the *margaritarius amans pauperis* was written in a vocabulary recalling the virtues of *bonitas* and *misericordia*—virtues that had a prominent place in the repertory of aristocratic *humanitas*. As for his particular consideration for the *pauperes,* we need to remember that, even though here it regards relations between individuals of the same social class, it was an integral part of the morality of the truly *liberalis* man. In a text as impregnated with values reflecting noble ethics as this one, we cannot exclude the possibility that *amans pauperis* should be taken in this sense, but even if that were not the case, the expression fully belongs within a vocabulary that aims at hiding the sordidness of small-scale commercial activities by emphasizing the social sensitivities of the departed.

Similarly, the *argentarius* Praecilius of Cirta was recorded for being *misertus* toward all. His epitaph (*CIL* 8.7156 = *IlAlg* 2.820) also shows a close connection between his trade, a declaration of honesty that was particularly appropriate for one who handled money, since bankers were always suspect (*Fydes in me mira fuit semper et veritas omnis*), and evidence of generous social attitudes (*Omnis communis ego: qui non misertus ubique?*).

The merchants' appropriation of noble values reached even higher and in large part unsuspected levels. An extraordinary epigraphic text (to be published by Stefano Priuli) from the very late Republic or the beginning of the Empire, found in the periphery of Rome along the Via Portuense, records a beef merchant (*bublarius*), M. Valerius Celer. The motifs of *fides* and *amicitia* recur in his praise. More surprising in a text of this sort, we also find a rejection of what today we might call a "consumer attitude" toward acquisition and savings: *plura maluit emereri quam consumere* (he much preferred to earn than to spend). The canons of traditional reproof might lead us to expect to see a merchant energetically engaged in making money and coins that circulate rapidly, generating luxury and comforts and producing new merchandise and more money. We see

nothing of the sort: Valerius Celer chose the way of cautious and systematic accumulation, saving rather than spending. He inevitably brings to
mind Cato the Elder's advice to the *pater familias* to "have the selling
habit, not the buying habit" (*De agri cultura* 2.7).

The third level of the merchant's self-representation, the farthest removed
from the vision of the upper classes, falls under the sign of *lucrum*.

To indicate gains, the Greeks used the word *kerdos,* which occupied
a central place in the vocabulary of *mētis* (intelligence, cunning). *Kerdos*
also referred to a smart move, a sudden stratagem that gave one an
immediate advantage. *Kerdo* was the name of the fox, the cleverest of the
animals. The merchant, who pursued gain by means of cleverness, was
a man of *mētis*. The word returns often in the vocabulary of Roman satire
to describe the mundane occupations of the crafts and the small-scale
retailer—categories that were often bracketed together. Prejudice against
them long remained rooted in the Western mind: the great Michelangelo
thought it well to note that he had never kept a shop: "I have always
carefully avoided it, for the honor of my family and my brothers!" In
Latin, *cerdo* was used as a term of opprobrium. Martial applied it to a
lowly and ambitious shoemaker who had provided his city with gladiatorial combats: "You should not be angry, cobbler [*cerdo*] at my book, It
was your trade, not your character, that was wounded by my verse.
Allow harmless witticisms. Why may not I be permitted to jest, if you
have been permitted to cut throats?" (Martial 3.99; see also 3.59).

Cerdo was also a collective term for the plebs—both the common
people and the sordid individuals who lived by their wits and thus by
"clever" earnings (*kerdos*) and trickery. The connection was clearly seen
by the scholiasts: in the margins of a verse of Persius, *respue quod non es,
tollat sua munera cerdo* (return to yourself, take back your gifts, riff-raff),
the commentator remarks: "By *cerdo* is meant the mass of the plebs. The
people is called thus *apo tou kerdous,* that is, from lucre" (see also, for
example, Martial 3.59, 3.99.1; Juvenal 4.153, 8.182). It is tempting to see
representations such as these as simply erudite divagations, the choices
of cultivated authors who knew Greek and used it to special effect, but
this would be an error, or at least only a partial interpretation. A very
short but valuable piece of evidence from Pompeii opens a broader perspective: *Cerdo cerdonibus salutem* (*CIL* 4.6869), which I would interpret
as a facile play on words in which a person by the name of Cerdo (a
name common among the people) was joking ironically about himself
and about the craftsmen and retailers of the city by using the same deni-

gratory epithet we have seen in Persius, Martial, and Juvenal. The by-ways of the Roman mind, in particular in this sort of commonplace regarding labor in the system of social values, are thus much more complicated than we are normally led to believe.

The connection between *kerdos* and *lucrum* leads us to a morality based on reactions—positive or negative—and to an autonomous awareness of an end to be attained and an expression of the joy to be derived from gain, the pleasures of profit, and the satisfaction of reaching an ardently desired result. Ovid recounts that on the Ides of May, the day consecrated to their god, the *mercatores* went to the *Aqua Mercurii* near Porta Capena to perform rites of purification. He portrays one merchant who sprinkles his hair with a laurel branch dipped into the spring and prays to the god, in "a voice accustomed to deceive" (*solita fallere voce*):

> "Wash away the perjuries of past time," says he, "wash away
> my glozing words of the past day. Whether I have called thee
> to witness or have falsely invoked the great divinity of Jupiter
> in the expectation that he would not hear, or whether I have
> knowingly taken in vain the name of any other god or god-
> dess, let the swift south winds carry away the wicked words,
> and may to-morrow open the door for me to fresh perjuries,
> and may the gods above not care if I shall utter any! Only
> grant me profits, grant me the joy of profit made, and see to
> it that I enjoy cheating the buyer!" (*Fasti* 5.674–88)

This scene bears the traces of an ancient ritual, brought up to date and reinterpreted. In archaic society, commercial relations had collective implications: consciously or unconsciously, the merchant might offend the *Fides* and provoke a traumatic break between the gods and the city. As Bernard Combet-Farnoux remarks, "The observation of particular rites—which were proper to the *Mercuriales* just as the *ius fetiale* was the specialty of the *Fetiales* in relations with the outside—could prevent negative consequences if a violation of the *Fides* had occurred in this sector of activity." The chief aim of the original ritual was not to purify the merchant (the aspect on which Ovid insists) but to neutralize the goods by eliminating the obligation that passed through things and was typical of the gift/exchange of archaic times. Ovid himself reveals a significant detail: the merchant also uses the laurel branch that has been dipped in the sacred fountain to sprinkle the objects that are about to find new owners.

With the growth of a mercantile economy and with the new dimensions and characteristics of exchange, the "significance" of this rite was gradually lost, and it became transformed. Ovid's verses are the sign of a transformation that has already occurred. The poet takes up the more customary themes of the condemnation of the merchant and draws up a fairly complete list: there is the spontaneous penchant to *fallere,* the tendency to swear falsely and the use of *verba* that are inevitably *perfida* and *improba;* there is the bad bargain waiting for the buyer, awareness without repentance, and an instinctive compulsion for repetition. But if the poet has a unilateral vision, there is no doubt that the merchants who practiced that rite of purification also had sentiments closer to those Ovid imagines than to those of their ancestors of the archaic age. We can sense something of their sentiments when we read, for example, the dedication of an ex-voto to Mercury in which the god is mentioned as *lucrorum potens et conservator* (*CIL* 5.6596). To merit the gratitude of his faithful, this Mercury who could favor earnings and keep them safe must have kept his part of the bargain well.

Plautus gave an excellent interpretation of the privileged relationship between his public and Mercury. At the beginning of the *Amphitruo,* Mercury enters and prefaces his invitation to hear the play thus:

> According as ye here assembled would have me prosper you and bring you luck in your buyings and in your sellings of goods, yea, and forward you in all things; and according as ye all would have me find your business affairs and speculations happy outcome in foreign lands and here at home, and crown your present and future undertakings with fine, fat profits for evermore; and according as ye would have me bring you and all yours glad news, reporting and announcing matters which most contribute to your common good (for ye doubtless are aware ere now that 'tis to me the other gods have yielded and granted plenipotence o'er messages and profits) (*Amphitruo* Prologue, lines 1–12)

This suggests profit made with joy and with no sense of guilt, a sentiment on which several documents shed a brief but illuminating light. The house of P. Vedius Siricus in Pompeii (7.1.23.47 Eschebach) welcomes visitors with a text in white tesserae in the entry hall: *salve lucru* (welcome, earnings) (*CIL* 10.874). Still at Pompeii, a graffito bears the expression *lucrum gaudium* (*CIL* 10.875), in which we might see something like a slogan, a stereotyped invocation to good luck widespread among individuals engaged in making money. We find the same sentiment, in fact, in literary texts as well, from Ovid (*facta gaudia lucro,* mentioned above) to Zeno of Verona (*lucro gaudes;* 1.41.3).

There was something like a fatal aporia in the mentality of *lucrum gaudium,* however. The great earnings that brought much joy took the merchant far from his origins. They took him closer to the social levels that traditionally held power, and they forced on him an agonizing shame.

Bibliography

This essay is a partial return to and reelaboration of two of my own essays:

Giardina, Andrea. "Le merci, il tempo, il silenzio: Ricerche su miti e valori sociali nel mondo greco e romano." *Studi storici* (1986): 277–302.

———. "L'economia nel testo." In *Lo spazio letterario di Roma antica,* ed. Guglielmo Cavallo, Paolo Fedeli, and Andrea Giardina. 5 vols. Rome: Salerno, 1989–. Vol. 1, 401–31.

The present study is dedicated almost exclusively to representations and self-representations of the figure of the merchant. For information on the organization of commercial activities and other problems (such as the social promotion and social marginalization of *negotiatores* and *tabernarii*), see in particular:

D'Arms, John H. *Commerce and Social Standing in Ancient Rome.* Cambridge, Mass., and London: Harvard University Press, 1981.

Garnsey, Peter, Keith Hopkins, and C. R. Whittaker, eds. *Trade in the Ancient Economy.* Berkeley: University of California Press, 1983.

Nicolet, Claude. *Rendre à César: Economie et société dans la Rome antique.* Paris: Gallimard, 1988.

Rougé, Jean. *Recherches sur l'organisation du commerce maritime en Méditerranée sous l'Empire Romain.* Paris: SEVPEN, 1966.

The bibliography on merchants is endless. I indicate here only works that have been utilized in the writing of this essay.

On commerce and the "just price":

Veyne, Paul. *Le pain et le cirque: Sociologie historique d'un pluralisme politique.* Paris: Editions du Seuil, 1976. Pp. 118ff. in particular. Available in English as *Bread and Circuses: Historical Sociology and Political Pluralism.* Trans. and abr. Brian Pearce. London: A. Lane, Penguin Press, 1990.

On the topography of commerce and crafts in Rome:

Morel, Jean-Paul. "La topographie de l'artisanat et du commerce dans la Rome antique." In *L'Urbs: Espace urbain et histoire Ier siècle av. J.-C. – III siècle ap.*

J.-C. Actes du Colloque international (Rome, 1985). Rome: Ecole française de Rome, 1987, 127–55.

On the *mētis* and on *kerdos:*
Cozzo, Andrea. *Kerdos: Semantica, ideologie e società nella Grecia antica.* Rome:
Ateneo, 1988.
Detienne, Marcel, and Jean-Paul Vernant. *Les ruses de l'intelligence: La mètis des
Grecs.* Paris: Flammarion, 1974. Available in English as *Cunning Intelligence
in Greek Culture and Society.* Trans. Janet Lloyd. Atlantic Highlands, N.J.:
Humanities Press, 1978.

On Cicero's views:
Narducci, Emanuele. "Valori aristocratici e mentalità acquisitiva nel pensiero di
Cicerone." *Index* 13 (1985): 93–125.

On silent commerce and maritime law:
Gentili, B. "La giustizia del mare: Solone, fr. 11 D., 12 West. Semiotica del
concetto di dike in greco arcaico." *Quaderni Urbinati di cultura classica* 20
(1974): 159–62.
Parise, Nicola F. "'Baratto silenzioso' fra Punici e Libi 'al di là delle colonne
d'Eracle.'" *Quaderni di archeologia della Libia* 8 (1976): 75–80.

On Mercury and the merchants:
Combet-Farnoux, Bernard. *Mercure romain: Le culte public de Mercure et la fonc-
tion mercantile à Rome de la République archaïque à l'époque augustéenne.*
Rome: Ecole française de Rome, 1980.

On cultural and commercial voyages in archaic Greece:
Bravo, B. "Remarques sur les assises sociales, les formes d'organisation et la
terminologie du commerce grec à l'époque archaïque." *Dialogues d'Histoire
Ancienne* 25 (1977): 1–59.

On the relationship between commercial activities and the ranks of the urban
elites:
Pleket, Henri Willy. "Urban Elites and Business in the Greek Part of the Roman Empire." In Garnsey et al., *Trade in the Ancient Economy.* Pp. 131–44.

For the dubious comparison between the passivity of ancient merchants and the
tenacity of late medieval merchants:
Bec, Christian. *Les marchands écrivains: Affaires et humanisme à Florence, 1375–
1434.* Paris and The Hague: Mouton, 1967. P. 313.

On the figure of the intermediary:
Brutti, M. *Enciclopedia del diritto.* Milan: Giuffrè 1976. Vol. 26, s.v. "Mediazi-
one (storia)."

For epigraphy and social sensitivity:
Bolkestein, Hendrik. *Wohltätigkeit und Armenpflege im vorchristlichen Altertum:
Ein Beitrag zum Problem "Moral und Gesellschaft."* Utrecht: A. Oosthoek,
1939. Esp. pp. 473ff.

Giardina, Andrea. "Amor civicus: Formule e immagini dell'evergetismo romano nella tradizione epigrafica." In *La terza età dell'epigrafia,* ed. Angela Donati. Colloquio AIEGL-Borghesi 86. Faenza: Fratelli Lega, 1988.

McGuire, Martin R. P. "Epigraphical Evidence for Social Charity in the Roman West." *American Journal of Philology* 67 (1946): 129–50.

For praise of work in funeral epigraphy:
De Robertis, Francesco Maria. *Lavoro e lavoratori nel mondo romano.* Bari: Adriatica, 1963.

The epitaph of the *bublarius* M. Valerius Celer will be published in a forthcoming work, edited by Stefano Priuli, of essays in honor of Attilio Degrassi. (My thanks to my friend Priuli for advance word.) For an introduction to the question: Virgili, P. *Bullettino Comunale* 90 (1985): 436.

The Poor

C. R. Whittaker

IF YOU WANTED TO PRAISE a Roman emperor after the second century A.D., it was almost obligatory to compare him with the great Emperor Trajan, who lived at the beginning of the century. Marcus Cornelius Fronto, courtier and confidant of Emperor Marcus Aurelius, wrote in A.D. 165 an "Introduction to History" on the exploits of the emperor's brother in which Trajan was inevitably brought into the narrative for knowing how to achieve popularity among the people. But what Fronto says is quite revealing about the way in which the Roman aristocracy viewed the lower classes in Rome:

> Based upon the very highest principles of political wisdom, the emperor did not overlook even actors and other performers of stage or circus or amphitheater. For he knew that the Roman people are held fast by two things above all, the corn supply and public spectacles. An emperor's rule is judged no less by entertainments than by serious things. Neglect of serious matters can cause greater damage, but neglect of amusements causes greater discontent. By giving out gifts only the plebs who are on the corn list are pleased and only one by one as their names are called out. But by the spectacles everyone is pleased. (17)

This passage is full of the prejudices of the Roman rich about the Roman poor, especially about their mindless devotion to bread and circuses, which the poet Juvenal (10.79–81) caricatured forever in his bitter satires. But it also contains a hint of what is less often mentioned, that a whole section of the poor in Rome, who attended the spectacles, never received the public dole of grain or cash at all. If we go one stage further in re-membering that even the greatest of all spectacles, the games at the Circus Maximus, could be seen only by about 250,000 people (only about 50,000 could get into the Coliseum), then we begin to realize that of the million to a million and a half people who lived in the city, a substantial propor-tion of the really poor saw nothing of the blandishments that supposedly corrupted the Roman plebs. The rich, of course, also flocked to the spectacles and sometimes did not disdain to queue for their grain tickets without apparent loss of esteem. The younger Pliny, in fact, praised the gladiatorial games for preparing the spectators for death and suffering.

Throughout history the rich have stereotyped the poor for their own convenience. "One of the characteristics of inequality," says a recent survey of the poor, "is that many of the people who have the most to gain from it are not conscious of it or do not want to be reminded of it." This indifference stems from a deep-seated, instinctive belief that the poor are a part—even a subhuman part—of the natural and ordained order of the world (hence poverty is structural). At the same time, and paradoxically, it is also believed that the poor are to blame for their own condition (hence poverty is conjunctural). The existence of the poor in an age of relative affluence proved to the seventeenth-century philosopher John Locke that poverty came not from "scarcity of provision" nor from "want of employment" but because of "a relaxation of discipline and a corruption of manners."

Crime, therefore, or mental and physical deformities, congenital ig-norance, and large families became part of the structural and natural features of poverty, to which there is the inevitable, convenient appendix in the minds of the rich that in the end the poor are content with their lot. The idea that poverty is conjunctural has always discouraged charity and welfare aid, however, since they are supposed to create lazy parasites and spongers who ultimately cause social and political disturbances. In the rural communities of preindustrial Europe it was regularly argued, despite evident crop failures and famine, that urban welfare aid only incited idle countrymen to flock to the city. Towns such as Bergamo in the sixteenth century or Lyons in the seventeenth excluded vagrants, migrants, and foreigners from their charity lists. The important thing about such stereotypes is not whether they are true but that they legiti-mize the rich in the enjoyment of their wealth.

It comes as no surprise, therefore, that the Greeks and Romans pro-duced almost exactly the same range of structural and conjunctural expla-nations of poverty. It is these prejudices that predominate in our sources, which were written by or for the rich. Aristotle idealized a society in which the poor "are too subservient so that they cannot command but only obey . . . a state of slaves and masters" (*Politics* 1266b). Since labor and property were mutually exclusive, Plato described both slaves and the laboring, nonpropertied poor as those who had no mastery of themselves and their natural, animal instincts (*Republic* 590c; see also *Epistles* 7.351a). The only function of manual laborers was to produce objects needed by men of virtue (Plotinus). "Wage labor," Cicero said, "is sordid and unworthy of a fine man" (*De officiis* 1.150). There was no beauty or honor in the arts of the workman (Seneca *Epistulae* 88.21). It was only natural, therefore, that the laboring classes should be poor and subject to every vice. Cheating and lying were an inevitable trait of those who had to take part in dishonorable work (Cicero *Tusculanae disputationes* 1.1–25). "In poverty," Seneca declared, "there is room for only one kind of virtue—not to be bowed down or crushed by it" (*De vita beata* 22).

Yet, despite these strong sentiments of structural poverty and these pessimistic views of labor, Romans moralized endlessly and romantically on the virtues of hard work—usually rural labor—and the culpability of the poor, who had failed in this respect. "Persistent hard labor," says Virgil, "overcomes everything" (*Georgica* 1.145), and Seneca argued that no virtue was attainable without labor (*De vita beata* 25.5). The Latin term *iners* for the man without work implies laziness, and the language of poetry and prose is filled with similar pejorative epithets attached to poverty as being "a foul and deformed evil inclined to crime." You can hear the moral disapproval of poverty in a Pompeian graffito: "I hate poor people. If anyone wants something for nothing he is a fool. He should pay for it" (*CIL* 4.9839b). A poor man was automatically suspect as a witness in court "since poverty may suggest he is out for profit" (*Digest* 22.5.3). Aristotle even gives us a hint of the very modern stereotype of the sexually improvident poor with large families when he says, "If no restriction is imposed on the rate of reproduction . . . poverty is the inevitable result" (*Politics* 1265b).

One of the most revealing sources of all is the historian and late-republican politician Sallust, who wrote a moral tract about the conspiracy of Catiline in 63 B.C. His work betrays a pathological fear and hatred of the poor and is full of phrases such as "the insanity of the poor" who "envy the good and praise the bad," who "hate the old" and "hate their own condition." Sallust expresses a typical Roman view of conjunctural poverty (much like that of the sixteenth century) when he combines a

sublime lack of concern for low-wage labor with a terror of the shame-
lessness and criminal profligacy of the *plebs urbana*. "Young men, who
had supported shortages in the countryside by being paid for their labor,
were seduced by private and public largess and came to prefer idleness
to poorly paid hard work. Hardly surprisingly, men who were down
and out with no morals and high hopes thought as little of the state as
they did of themselves" (*War with Catiline* 37).

It is an axiom of all modern studies that poverty is a condition easier
to describe than to define. All attempts to classify it are arbitrary, relative,
and built on a sliding scale of deprivation. The nineteenth-century utilitarian Jeremy Bentham defined poverty as "the state of everyone who,
in order to obtain subsistence, is forced to have recourse to labour."
Indigence, however, "is the state of him who, being destitute of property . . . is at the same time either unable to labour, or unable, even for
labour, to procure the supply of which he happens then to be in want."
Today we could not accept Bentham's elitist social view of labor, although we would have no difficulty in agreeing with the economic description of destitution. The Romans could easily have accepted the definition, but they would have added "or unwilling" to "unable."

Built into this definition of poverty is the concept of needs and wants,
and it is here that the matter becomes so difficult. It is only in the twenti-
eth century that we have established such ideas as the poverty datum line
and minimum subsistence. They have proved to be as controversial as
they are arbitrary, however. There are not even value-free scientific facts
of what are the minimum food and nutritional needs of individuals,
which we are told lie somewhere between one thousand and three thousand calories per day but are dependent on all sorts of variables such as
work, climate, leisure and sexual activity, and so forth. "Poverty," one
distinguished modern study says, is in fact "a value judgment. It is not
something one can verify or demonstrate, except by inference or suggestion." How, then, can we ever arrive at a sensible idea of who or how
many were the Roman poor?

First, we need to remember that mass poverty in both ancient and
modern preindustrial societies was (and still is) overwhelmingly a rural
phenomenon; hence it is rarely documented. An unskilled urban laborer
could earn about three sesterces a day. But on a table of landowners
from the Ligures Baebiani near Benevento, which excluded the poorest,
subsistence farmers, the lowest recorded property was one that yielded
only about two sesterces a day. I am concerned here only with urban

poverty; it is better known, sometimes more extreme, and usually more dramatic because it combines all the squalor of city life with the social and political fears of the rich.

One method of getting some idea of Rome's population is by comparing what life looked like in better-documented ages. In Florence in the thirteenth century 70 percent of the households are calculated to have had consumption needs greater than their incomes for structural reasons of family size, children, sex, and age. Detailed studies of preindustrial European cities as varied as Norwich, Lyons, Toledo, and Rome between the fifteenth and the eighteenth centuries suggest that a fairly steady 4 to 8 percent of the population were incapable of earning a living (due to handicaps, age, etc.), another 20 percent were permanently in crisis through price fluctuations and low wages, and another 30 to 40 percent were small artisans, petty officials, or shopkeepers who might temporarily, for conjunctural reasons (family, age structure, trade revisions, personal misfortune) fall below subsistence levels.

There are, of course, no statistics for ancient Rome and there is only a vague and limited notion of what was necessary to subsistence. The lawyer Gaius, for instance, says that some believe that the word *vivere* (to live) refers only to food, but others speak also of clothing and straw since "without these none can live" (*Digest* 50.16.234.2). He makes no reference to shelter. Sallust (*War with Catiline* 48) speaks only of food and clothing, and Tacitus (*Annales* 4.30) vaguely about the "necessities of life." We can see how arbitrary the definitions of the poor are from the testimony of John Chrysostom of Antioch in the fourth century. He says that the poor in need of support were one-tenth of the population but that the church could look after only a fifth of those in need, a figure he put at three thousand (*PG* 58.630).

If, however, we think of the distribution of wealth between rich and poor, the question is complicated by slavery. Estimates of how many slaves inhabited the city vary between one-third of the population (a figure that is probably too high and based upon what we know of the Greek city of Pergamum from Galen 5.49) to about one-tenth. Some of these slaves, through living in their master's house, could have been quite well housed and fed, measured by the standards of the destitute poor. Others were in the same position as petty artisans and worked independently of their masters with their own *peculium* (private savings). There is no reason, in fact, to allot a separate category of poverty to slaves, and as we shall see, they sometimes felt a social solidarity with the free poor.

There is no doubt, as we can see from epigraphic evidence on tombs, that the main category of the Roman plebs was made up of those classed socially as freedmen, ex-slaves who had been granted freedom in their own lifetime. But it is a self-evident but often forgotten fact that a freedman's son, while suffering some disadvantages from social snobbery, was regarded as a freeborn Roman. It is all the more remarkable, therefore, that the numbers of freedmen never seem to diminish much in Rome. Our epigraphic evidence records about three inscriptions of freedmen for every one freeborn, which takes no account of the people too poor to pay for a tombstone. Even in the second century, when the emperor Trajan offered state aid to encourage freeborn parents to have children, the number of children assisted was only about five thousand—just over 1 percent of the families in Rome. Therefore, if the supply of slaves was constantly being replenished as their predecessors died or were manumitted, and if the number of freedmen remained high all the time, there must have been a high death rate in the city among both slaves and freedmen—higher than the rate of reproduction and implying poor living conditions in the city. Freedmen, however, like slaves, were not a separate class of the poor. Some, as we know from great monuments in Rome such as that of the baker Eurysaces at the Porta Maggiore, were exceedingly rich and proud of their profession. Many who left no reference to their profession or trade—about half of the imperial stones—would have been among the poor or very poor of all social categories.

There undoubtedly were also a vast number of foreigners—*peregrini*—among the poor. Seneca states that there were "more *peregrini* than citizens" in Rome (*Ad Helviam de consolatione* 6.5), but this is difficult to believe, even if slaves are counted among them. Still, we have many references to large foreign communities—Egyptians, Syrians, Phoenicians, and, above all, Jews—resident in the cities, some of which counted tens of thousands of persons. According to a *topos* of Roman political rhetoric that recurs through history, foreign immigrants were the principal cause of unrest among the poor (see, for example, Herodian 7.7.1). There is no reason to believe, however, that foreigners formed a particularly depressed category, although it is true that they did not benefit from the public distributions of grain and money that the registered plebs enjoyed in Rome. It is also true, however, that many foreigners lived in Rome only temporarily and often belonged to religious and commercial associations that had financial holdings abroad. Foreigners, in short, like the slaves and the freedmen, were variously distributed between wealth and poverty.

In the end, we can be sure that all categories of poverty existed in ancient Rome just as in the later European towns and in at least the same proportions, if not greater. "How much larger is the proportion of the poor," Seneca says (although he then goes on in a way typical of the rich), "yet you will note they are in no way sadder or more anxious than the rich" (*Ad Helviam de consolatione* 12.1). Cicero gives us some idea of the differential even among the poor: "If one defends a poor man (*inops*) who is honest, however, and upright—and there is a large proportion of them among the people—then all the lowly (*humiles*) who are not dishonest will look upon the defender as a helper" (*De officiis* 2.70). Notice the word "however" between the two categories of "poor" and "lowly." Seneca goes on to speak of *opes paene inopes*—the rich on the edge of poverty—who have to be very careful how they live.

We can get some idea of the enormous difference between the rich and the poor from their relative incomes. Leaving aside the unemployed and the unemployable, an unskilled laborer earned about three sesterces per day, which was about twice what was given a military recruit in Julius Caesar's army. Seneca tells us, however, that one of Caesar's contemporaries, Cato the Younger, who sang the praises of simple living, had property valued at 4 million sesterces, which would have yielded him an income of 550–650 sesterces a day. The ratio is about 1:200. Cato's property was by no means the greatest that we know about: Seneca's property was valued at 300 million sesterces when he died (Tacitus *Annales* 13.42), and there were many fortunes of the early Empire in the 100–200 million range. In the later Empire this concentration of wealth seems to have increased. The differential between an ordinary legionary in the army, a senior centurion, and a senatorial tribune was about 1:66:400. That gives us some idea of how much greater the wealth of the upper orders was than that of even a quite well paid centurion who could expect to get equestrian status.

None of these statistics includes the very poor, the destitute who had no visible means of support. The problem of the vocabulary of poverty is to know what is meant. Usually it refers to the majority who did not have the leisure of the rich regardless of how much they earned. Words like *inopes* (resourceless), *egentes* (needy), *pauperes* (poor), *humiles* (lowly), and *abiecti* (outcast) were used without precision, and they were often given political or social significance by being combined with terms for the "mob" like *vulgus, turba, multitudo, ochlos* (in Greek), or simply *plebs*. These terms all varied according to whether the people were behaving violently or constitutionally.

Some of these poor who acted in the Roman mobs would have been totally destitute, and the Roman rich tended to think of them as criminals, but there is no way of being sure when such people were involved. For instance, the Roman historian Appian (who wrote in Greek) tells us how, in the grain riots against the young pretender, Octavian, in 40 B.C., the people threatened to burn down the houses of those who refused to join them. Obviously, at this stage the poor were persuading the less poor. But when Octavian's troops killed some of the rioters, the soldiers removed their "fine clothes" as booty, a task in which they were joined by the "criminal classes" (*Bellorum civilium* 5.68). The latter now seem not to have been part of the rioters.

From these and many similar examples, we can draw three conclusions about the definition of the poor. First, all poverty is relative. To the soldiers and the "criminal" poor and destitute, the clothes of the less poor seemed fine. Juvenal, who constantly complained of his poverty and of the insulting arrogance of the rich, thought a person poor if he had less than twenty thousand sesterces a year (9.140–41). That happens to have been almost the qualification of property income for a member of the high equestrian order, whom we think of as rich and a far cry from our laborer, who earned about one-twentieth of that. The concept of relative deprivation, however, combined with the absolute necessity for those who aspired to a position of status to maintain a minimum standard of living, makes the notion of a poor rich man credible, if misleading.

The second inference is important because it concerns the language of poverty. *Pauperes* and its synonyms can and should include not just the destitute and beggars but the relatively better-off artisans and shopkeepers who, compared to the rich, propertied classes, were certainly poor, in the sense of being on the edge of conjunctural poverty, as was the case in thirteenth-century Florence. But, as Seneca notes in his smug way, they did not necessarily consider themselves unfortunate. Petronius imagines a "ragman" (*centonarius*) who had a little house in the country and was a close friend of a man who had inherited 30 million sesterces and owned a troop of gladiators (*Satyricon* 45). Ragmen were nonetheless distinctly *humiliores* in law (*CTh* 14.8.2). In Aristophanes' play, *Ploutos*, the character of Penia (Poverty) is careful to deny that Ptochia (Beggary) is her sister. "It is the beggar's life," she says, "to live possessed of nothing, but the poor man's life to live frugally and by applying himself to work, with nothing to spare perhaps but not really in want" (551–54).

Even *ptōcheia*, which has no precise equivalent in Latin, could be used relatively, as in the case of Gorgias in Menander's play *Dyskolos*, who calls himself *ptōchos* while owning a plot of land and a slave. "It is not poverty to have nothing," says the poet Martial (11.328). When he imagines a worse poverty, he pictures an outcast who is not even permitted the company of the beggars who live under the arches of the bridges or on the beggar's hill, the *Clivus Aricinus,* fifteen miles outside Rome. This outcast has to beg even from the beggars for the bread they throw to the dogs, and in December, when he has no shelter, those who get a pauper's burial seem to him fortunate as he listens to the birds and dogs gathering around to gnaw his bones while he dies (10.5).

Exaggerated as that horrible picture may be, it stresses the gradations of poverty and the fact that there was no single class of "the poor." This is important when we come to consider the way the rich responded to poverty. From their point of view, poverty was closely tied to social status, and it is no accident that the senatorial and equestrian social orders were separated from the masses by minimum standards of wealth—the exact opposite of twentieth-century society, which has more interest in the bottom end of the social scale and tries to separate intolerable indigence from tolerable poverty by a datum line.

The term "poor," in Roman status terms, thus usually meant anyone who was not of the ruling orders, and this became institutionalized in legal theory in the Empire by the division between *honestiores* (broadly, property owners) and *humiliores* (broadly, workers). Unless, that is, it was a matter of political importance or privilege, when it became important for the rich to separate the good poor—"the people"—from the bad poor—"the mob." We have already seen that Cicero advocated cultivating the "honest" poor for election purposes. They were clearly not slaves or freedmen or noncitizens, who had little or no voting powers. The tribune Drusus was able to split the support for Gaius Gracchus in 123 B.C. by proposing that the "poorest" should be included in Gracchus' colonial law in place of "citizens already provided with means" (Plutarch *Life of Gaius Gracchus* 9). Under the Empire, when the plebs lost their direct voting power, it became a matter of importance in political demonstrations for the ruling classes to know where they could call upon support. Evidently, therefore, there was inherent in the conditions of the poor a potential for classifying them socially and economically that was not wholly unlike the way the upper classes were classed. But before we look further at this aspect, we need to consider the actual living conditions in Rome and how the poor differentiated themselves.

It is the urban poor and the conditions of urban living that always attract the attention of writers and the fears of the rich. The size of a town's population could increase dramatically in periods of economic expansion and catastrophically during periods of rural famine. Before the eighteenth century, it is reckoned, crop failures had serious repercussions in European cities about every four or five years. A town like Bergamo could treble its poor population almost overnight. In the hundred years between the sixteenth and the seventeenth centuries, many European cities—London, Marseilles, Lyons, and Rome, for example—increased their population permanently from two- to fivefold. It was these conjunctural and structural events that broke the dependent rural relations between the peasant and his feudal lord and led to the obsessive concern of sixteenth- and seventeenth-century states with the control of poor migrants by the use of cruel poor laws and selective institutional assistance.

Similar causes and effects certainly affected ancient Rome, which for an ancient city also achieved an extraordinary size and rapid growth in the late Republic and the age of Augustus. The city is estimated to have more or less doubled its size between 130 and 30 B.C., from about four hundred thousand to about eight hundred thousand inhabitants, and to have continued to increase to something over a million people in the early Empire. The rural poor, who are said to have flocked to Rome to seek a living, were dispossessed not simply by crop failures and debt but also by the influx of slave labor—an astonishing three million or so slaves—purchased by the affluent rich to replace the services of the poor and to exploit their lands. But we must take care not to exaggerate the number of such expropriated peasants who moved to Rome permanently. The profile of the population of Rome and its high number of freedmen contradicts that notion. We know, too, that many poor farmers turned to day wage labor or tenancy, which began to become a common topic in first-century B.C. jurisprudence. Many rural migrants alternated between town and country according to where they could find work, as we know concerning the time of the land law of 133, when Tiberius Gracchus' urban supporters were away bringing in the harvest. The *lex Terentia Cassia* of 73 B.C., which established a grain list probably for freeborn citizens only, recognized only 40,000 recipients (120,000–160,000 if we add in their wives and children). That was only 15 to 20 percent of the city population, many of whom, of course, were not new migrants from the countryside. The main growth in urban population therefore came from slaves, ex-slaves, and foreigners who were drawn to Rome by its service and commercial possibilities. It was slaves and foreigners who suffered first, either by expulsion or by short rations, when there were food shortages (see, for example, Livy 4.12; Dio Cassius 55.27).

It is not hard to imagine the condition of overcrowding and squalor caused by this rapid growth, through the analogy of what happened in more recent periods in cities like London or Paris. Much has been written about the slumlike rental tenements (*cenacula*) of Rome and the jerry-built apartment blocks (*insulae*) in which they were located and about the narrow streets blocked by little shops of artisans (Martial 7.61) and filthy with mud, garbage, and human excrement; about the ever-present fear of fires caused particularly by the wooden balconies (*maeniana*) of the upper stories so close to one another that one could shake hands with a neighbor across the street (Martial 1.86); and about the smoky *tabernae*, where brawling and prostitution were commonplace events. No reader of Petronius' *Satyricon* will forget the beds in the *taberna* that crawl with cockroaches while even casual spectators join in the brawl wielding candlesticks, cooking spits, and butchers' meat hooks (95). Small wonder that crime flourished and that even soldiers were frightened to enter the maze of narrow alleys (Herodian 7.12.5) that the elder Pliny calculated as totaling nearly sixty miles in length (*Naturalis historia* 3.66). "We live in a city," Juvenal declares, "propped up with gimcrack stays and beams. . . . The building is permanently balanced like a pack of cards. . . . Fires and midnight panics are common events" (3.190). In the late Republic and the early Empire there were five fires recorded in twenty years and nine floods of the Tiber in forty years.

What is striking about Roman living conditions, however, is how many of the discomforts of the streets—the noise, the stench, and the dirt—were shared by the moderately wealthy or even some of the very wealthy. Seneca tells us that, for all his wealth, he had an apartment above some public baths, where, like the poor, he was subject to all the bedlam of the noises from below of cries from bathers and vendors, not to mention the racket of carts, musicians, and knife grinders in the street and the sound from the carpenter above him who lived in the same *insula* (Seneca *Epistulae* 56).

We know more about the layout of an *insula* from Ostia than from Rome, where only one good example remains on the slopes of the Campidoglio, now partly beneath the steps leading to Santa Maria in Aracoeli. In the *insula Capitolina* (or Casa di Via Giulio Romano) a second floor above the shops and *tabernae* contained multiroomed apartments, or *do-*

mus, that were quite spacious, housing about twelve persons. This is in marked contrast to the small *cenacula*, or cells, on the three floors above, which housed as many as forty-eight persons per floor and became progressively smaller as one ascended. The ratio of space occupied by the rich *domus* owner and the poorest in their "cells" was about 1:20. In addition, poor tenants often had to share their meager rooms of ten square meters with three or more persons in order to pay the high rents demanded in Rome for a small room—rents as much as three to four times the poor worker's wage. When we hear of sixteen people in one room (Valerius Maximus 4.4.8), therefore, we begin to appreciate something of the gradations of poverty even among the poor.

The difference between a senator and a carpenter lay more in the "vertical zoning" of their houses than in isolated suburbs or quarters, as in modern cities. According to the *Regionarii*, which were fourth-century Roman gazettes of the city, there were 1,790 *domus* in Rome and 46,000 *insulae*. Although these figures are probably not trustworthy, since they would give an absurdly low average of inhabitants for each *insula*, it is probably quite accurate to say that the *domus* occupied one-third of the residential space available in Rome.

There were, of course, many senators who lived in what were also called *domus* but were palaces that effectively were rural villas in the middle of enormous gardens. Their number and splendor increased rapidly in the empire (Pliny the Elder *Naturalis historia* 36.109). There were also certain low-lying parts of Rome that were thought insalubrious and were therefore avoided by the richer—regions like the Subura, the Argiletum, the Velabrum, and Transtiberim. It is important to remember, however, that many of the really poor could not even afford to live at the top of an *insula* or in a cheap *taberna* boarding house. They survived, as we know from Martial, for instance, by finding shelter under the bridges, in the porticos, or under the stairs and in the cellars of the *insulae*. They even lived in the mausolea outside the city, which also served as brothels and lavatories (Ulpian *Digest* 47.12.3.11). When Tacitus was describing (or imagining) the Fenni of *ultima Germania*, he says that they lived in *foeda paupertas*, the worst possible poverty. They had no weapons, no horses, and no houses; they slept on the ground, ate grasses, and dressed in skins. Yet he cannot help adding, "They think themselves luckier than to groan in the fields, toil over houses, and subject their own or other people's fortunes to hopes and fears" (*De origine et situ Germanorum* 46).

There was nothing romantic about the really destitute who lived under Tacitus' nose in these same conditions. If they were lucky they could build *tuguria,* lean-to sheds that made up a sort of shantytown, perhaps on the edge of the city, sometimes above workshops or up against public buildings. The authorities regarded them as a fire risk and might tear them down (*CTh* 16.39), but they were allowed to remain if they were not obstructive, and their inhabitants were even charged rent (Ulpian *Digest* 43.8.2.17). The beggars of the Clivus Aricinus on the Appian Way were famous for congregating where the carriages of the rich had to slow down, near Aricia, and they caused fear by their aggressive demands. In the city they were probably much as Gregory of Nyssa described them in fourth-century Constantinople: "The hand out to beg is to be seen everywhere. The open air is their dwelling, their lodgings are the porticos and street corners and the less-frequented parts of the marketplace" (*PG* 46.457). The rich man was castigated by Augustine for scorning the poor man lying in his doorway (*Sermones* 345.1). Thus we see reflected in the housing of Rome the spectrum of riches and poverty—conditions that made it possible for the powerful to divide the poor and rule them. The same extremes could be found in other living conditions, in health, diet, clothing, and family life, and in ways of death.

Hygiene and sanitation in such a vast, unplanned city were, as might be expected, crude and rudimentary, despite the myth that Rome's water supply kept the population healthy. The baths that both the rich and poor used must have transmitted horrific diseases, irrespective of the bathers' status or personal wealth. Of course, this was not the way things were perceived at the time. The rich could also at times have their own private baths and filtered water (Seneca *Epistulae* 86.11). The less poor could segregate themselves from the lowest, who were diseased, and from prostitutes by having separate bathing hours (Martial 3.93), and a small entrance fee would have kept out the destitute. The rich could tap water privately from the aqueducts, while the poor *insula* dweller had to carry his water from the open *lacus,* the public fountains, which could easily become polluted. A rich *domus* could have its own latrines, while the poor had to pay for public latrines. They also used chamber pots and the urine jars, placed on street corners by the fullers, which were available for all. The very poor no doubt excreted wherever they could, since much of the community's waste went straight into the street, and the urine jars sometimes broke (Martial 6.93). There is no evidence that any house, even a rich man's house, had links to the main *cloacae* (water drains). Thus in many ways the rich were as susceptible to infection as the poor. But when epidemics or pandemics struck, as they often did, the rich had two main advantages: first, they had more food and therefore greater resistance to sicknesses associated with malnutrition; second, they could escape disease by running to their country villas. While two thousand people died daily in Rome in A.D. 189 (of malaria? It was believed they had been injected by criminals with poisoned needles) the emperor and his court were outside the city at the Villa Quintiliana near Laurentum (Herodian 1.12.2; Dio Cassius 72.14.4).

In the final analysis, however (as the last example shows), the rich did not enjoy a huge advantage in health care over the poor, because so little was known about infectious diseases or nutrition. Famine as the sole cause of death is relatively rarely recorded by Roman writers, despite numerous food crises. This is more likely to reflect the lack of interest in the destitute than to show evidence of generally good nutrition. One exception occurred during the civil wars in 40 B.C., when Sextus Pompeius cut off the grain supply to Rome and caused "many deaths" (Dio Cassius 48.18.1). No details are given, but we can assume that this meant deaths of the very poor. Livy gives a hint of the desperation of the poor when he records that, in 440 B.C., rather than endure their hunger many of the plebs committed suicide by drowning (4.12.11). Earlier in the century we are informed that the poor, "when they were short of money, survived by eating roots and grass for food" (Dionysius of Halicarnassus 7.8.3). Although we always have suspicions about the authenticity of early Roman records, the author, from his own experience, at least considered such details plausible. Hunger may not often have been a direct killer, except of the invisible poor, but as Galen, the Pergamese doctor, knew, it had a debilitating effect on resistance to disease. Obviously, in this respect the rich were greatly advantaged by their estates, which produced food locally, and by their wealth, which allowed them to corner the market or to afford high prices. It was also by the manipulation of the grain supply that the upper classes (and later the emperors) had their most potent weapon of political control throughout the history of Rome.

Once again, however, as with sanitation, the advantages enjoyed by the rich over the poor were not necessarily as great as they themselves may have perceived. The rich, who could pay for wine, were less subject to waterborne infections than the poor, who drank more water. One of the consequences of state provision of cheap wheat in the late Republic and Empire was a great increase in the purchase of wine among the less-poor plebs. But wine, which was drunk warm or boiled into a concentrated *defrutum* (must), was heated and sweetened by the use of lead-lined pans (Pliny *Naturalis historia* 14.136) and drunk from pewter vessels, with potentially disastrous long-term effects on health. The rich could also pay for more fatty red meat and white bread than could the poor, whose staple diet was coarse bread (*panis sordidus*) and olive oil. The poor thus lacked proteins, but their cholesterol intake was lower. A recent study at the Villa dei Gordiani on the Via Prenestina outside Rome, where there is a rich man's mausoleum side by side with the graves of a Christian basilica of the fourth century A.D., demonstrates the higher level of zinc and lead in the bone minerals of the rich. We must not exaggerate, however. Bodies found at Herculaneum show the inhabitants to have been taller than modern Neapolitans and the general standards of health from diet and exercise to have been quite good. But the poor, obviously, were less healthy. High rents in Rome reduced their purchasing power for food and produced chronic malnutrition. Cheap or free wheat distributions by the state therefore improved the health of the "good" plebs but did nothing for those already below subsistence levels, who did not quality for benefits.

Poverty, as Tacitus saw, was defined not only by consumption but also by clothing. To be dressed in rags was, according to Ammianus, the norm outside Aquitania (15.12.2). Relics of clothing that have survived are regularly covered with patches—hardly surprising if the clothing allowance of one tunic and one cloak per year, as Cato advocates for a slave, was also normal for a low-wage earner. Yet despite the fact that the rich mocked the cheap clothes of the poor (Juvenal 3.147–53), to the extreme poor those clothes seemed "fine" in the rioting of 40 B.C.

In these conditions, death was an everyday spectacle, and with it came a hardening of the sensibilities. Corpses were thrown into the street, the sick were left in the open to die, children were exposed on the dung heaps. Dogs and birds scavenged for food among the dead bodies and tore off their limbs. Suetonius tells the story of how a stray dog once came into the dining room of the future emperor Vespasian carrying a human hand (*Lives of the Caesars, Vespasian* 5.4). He does not tell the story to shock but only to recount the omen.

However, we can see how even in death the poor were classified. Lanciani's vivid description of the discovery of the Esquiline republican cemetery records a whole series of burial pits filled indiscriminately with animal carcasses, excreta, refuse, and human bones, often gnawed by animals. Nearby were found the celebrated boundary stones recording the praetor's order: "Let no one throw here excreta or a dead body," but on one stone someone added: "Take your shit far away or you will catch it" (*CIL* 6.31614–5). On the same site beyond the Servian Wall was a mass burial pit estimated to contain twenty-four thousand corpses, perhaps from an epidemic. These were the graves of the *miseri,* the destitute, whose bodies Horace tells us were collected from the streets by the public slaves when they had been thrown out from the cells (*Satires* 1.8.8–16).

These were not the only burials that Lanciani found on the Esquiline, however. Set off from the disgusting stench of the paupers' crypts were the orderly columbaria and cinerary urns of the less poor. They belonged to the sort of people who joined burial clubs (*collegia*), about which we have quite a lot of information from inscriptions. They were men who came together, sometimes by professions (smiths, cloth traders, etc.), sometimes by common worship of a god. They built their own chamber tombs and took part in various activities such as funeral dinners or funeral processions for their fellow members. And then there were the household slaves and servants whose masters included them in the funeral chambers of the family. In the gardens of the Statilius family, not far from the Porta Maggiore, the family columbarium contained 427 inscriptions, of which 370 were those of the slaves and freedmen of Statilius Taurus, consul of A.D. 11, and of his children. Dozens of these sorts of columbaria have been discovered in Rome, although most are now hidden again by the city.

Several facts that strike us about the working men's clubs are relevant to the theme of social differentiation. They were not for the very poor, since they required an entrance fee, which could be as much as one hundred sesterces plus an amphora of wine, and a monthly subscription of a few asses. On the other hand, they often included slaves, showing once again that poverty was not classed by status. Finally, the *collegia* were controlled by the rich. Not only were wealthy patrons included on club lists and able to exercise their influence by benefactions (one club at Lanuvium received an endowment of fifteen thousand sesterces) but the clubs were also closely regulated by law, in theory if not always in practice. Every educated Roman would remember from his reading of Cicero how dangerously close to a proletarian revolution Rome had come in the last decade of the Republic, when Publius Clodius organized the street gangs of the city into *collegia,* including the slaves and freedmen, who had little or no voting power but could wield weapons and to whom he gave solidarity by using their organizations for distributing free grain. These were the poor whom Cicero called "hired men, rogues, and destitutes" (*De domo sua* 89), "a wretched and hungry mob," "the filthy scum of the city" (*Ad Atticum* 1.16.11).

Through the terror of the propertied classes, we catch a glimpse of the collective power of the poor, before they sink back into controlled oblivion. The emperors made very sure that they themselves took charge of grain distributions, and they attempted to regulate club membership (*Digest* 47.22.1). When refusing to recognize an association of fire fighters in Bithynia, Trajan said, "It is societies like these that have been responsible for public disturbances" (Pliny the Younger *Epistulae* 10.34). Despite the surveillance, outbreaks of violence continued to occur, as happened in the circus in Pompeii in A.D. 64, which involved the *collegia* (Tacitus *Annales* 14.17).

In death, then, as in life, there were good and bad poor. It is only to be expected that the conditions of Rome led to low life expectancy in general—about twenty-five years at birth and about thirty-five for those who survived infancy. Women must have had a lower average life expectancy than men did, since many died in childbirth. We must not exaggerate the dangers of the city and glamorize the countryside, however, since the figures do not differ significantly from those for the early medieval village of Frénouville in France. What seems clear from the earlier conclusions about slaves and freedmen is that the population of Rome did not reproduce itself and had to be constantly renewed from outside. In other words, the poor majority could not afford to maintain the five or six children necessary to arrive at a steady state. Although we have no real evidence about annual income in Rome, in medieval Paris or seventeenth-century Milan even skilled artisans worked only about 250 days in the year, often less when the weather was bad or religious festivals intervened. In Rome the calendar for the early Empire marked 159 days as holidays, and that figure rose in the following centuries.

The working man existed on "an economy of makeshift" with very little capital assets. In Lyons, eighteenth-century probate inventories show that family possessions such as tools or furniture, even for skilled artisans, equaled about six weeks' earnings and were often in pawn against the rent. Given this precarious kind of existence, we now know Malthus to have been quite wrong in believing that poverty bred children—a common stereotype in the perception of the poor by the rich.

The strategies by which the poor restricted births and family size are well known. Apart from prostitution and contraception, many children were exposed at birth on the dung heap (*stercus*), from which they might sometimes be rescued and made slaves with names like Stercorius, Stercorosus, and so forth. The knowledge that some of their lost children had become slaves was perhaps one reason why the poor and slaves lived together sympathetically. Another strategy was late marriage for men, not women, which is widely adopted in poor societies. The effect is to create a large generation gap among men and many widows with young children. The church historian Eusebius reminds us that in the mid-third century the small Christian church in Rome was already maintaining fifteen hundred widows and persons in distress (*Historia ecclesiastica* 6.43.11). Examination of skeletons of women over forty from Herculaneum suggests that they had borne very few children, but the accuracy of such information from bone evidence is much disputed.

This examination of the ways of life and death of the poor shows again that poverty was not a homogeneous condition but rather incorporated an entire range of levels of wealth. The overwhelming interest for us is the acute destitution of the lowest, and it makes us forget the relative deprivation of the majority. For the Romans it was the other way around. Seneca did not like the negative words of the Greek philosopher Antipater, who said of poverty, "It is not defined by property but by its absence. . . . It does not mean possession of a little but nonpossession of a lot" (*Epistulae ad Lucium* 87.39–40). The gap between the style of life in a vast palace on the Aventine and a steaming, hot, lean-to shack in the Subura was incalculable, and rich Romans did not want to think about it. What made the gap tolerable for them and manageable politically were the "good" plebs in between. Why and how the latter accepted their relative deprivation is what we must now consider.

Modern academic discussions of poverty are divided between the extremes of those who perceive the lower-class poor as pathologically self-generating and incurable, with a distinct subculture (a view made popular in the 1960s by Oscar Lewis's *The Children of Sánchez*), and those who favor the Marxist structuralist-functionalist view of poverty as an integral part of society necessary for, and therefore maintained by, the rich. In other words, the development of free labor, which had its historical origins in the decline of feudalism and the patronage societies of preindustrial Europe, was for Marx "latent pauperism," structurally separate but sharing the values of the whole system.

Between the two extremes there is a compromise position that maintains that while the poor subscribe to and are controlled by the norms and values of the total system, they nonetheless also develop distinct subcultural patterns—a "moral economy"—which form a sort of unwritten code, different from the laws of the land but no less sensitive to natural justice when it comes to such issues as the price of bread, petty theft, and the right to demonstrate. This intermediate view (that poverty is neither cultural nor wholly structural) is compatible with Weber's concepts of "status honor" and "style of life," which concentrate on symbols and rituals. The status restrictions on social intercourse develop a "stigma" of poverty and highlight the "disreputable" poor, who are often conceptualized ethnically (Jews, orientals, etc.). But what is important from the historical point of view is that status symbols are reinforced when social mobility increases and poverty is combined with expectations. The socially mobile then will share the values of the rich—in effect fracturing the facade of a single culture of poverty and reinforcing the social controls of the powerful.

The attractive aspect of this theory is the closeness with which it fits the structural and conjunctural evidence of Roman history. It is well known that the early emperors reinforced the qualifications of the senatorial and equestrian orders by regulation and symbols of status at the very moment that status usurpation was becoming most blatant (Tacitus *Annales* 37.27). The spiteful humor of Petronius' *Satyricon* was written at the expense of a rich freedman, Trimalchio, who was trying to behave like a high-class landowner. But Trimalchio's expectations were not totally vain. A debate in the Senate in A.D. 56 frankly recognized that "very many knights and senators derived their origin from this source" (Tacitus *Annales* 13.27). By the second century, the poor's disadvantages before the law were given formal recognition by status categories of *honestiores* for the rich and *humiliores* for the lower class, with different standards of penalties for each category.

The problem for the upper classes lay in the rapid growth of Rome in the last century of the Republic, when landowners lost their direct control of patronage over their rural workers as the latter migrated to the city. The new urban plebs could be manipulated and wooed by any politician of ambition. Imperial expansion and vast wealth aroused the expectations of ordinary Romans and brought a huge influx of foreigners to join the already increasing population of slaves and freedmen in the city. It was in these conditions that Juvenal stereotyped the urban plebs as the Orontes flowing into the Tiber, but even he recognized that it was the stigma of social status that mattered most. "Unhappy poverty has nothing about it harder to bear than that it makes men the target of ridicule" (*Satires* 3.153–54). In the early Empire, Rome became obsessed with status symbols, titles designed by the rich to demonstrate to the lower orders exactly where they stood. It could have been Juvenal, but it is a recent sociologist who said, "The social barriers and inhibitions from an unequal society distort the personalities of those with high income no less than those who are poor. Trivial differences of accent, language, dress custom etc. acquire an absurd importance and contempt is engendered for those who lack social graces." "Rare is the house," said one anonymous Roman writer, "that does not scorn a lowly friend, nor contemptuously trample on a humble client" (*Laus Pisonis* 118f.).

This reference to clients is an indication of how the wealthy adjusted to the new conditions of the Roman metropolis. During the social and political disorders of the last century of the Republic, colonization was one possible solution. Cicero in his populist mood describes one occasion: "The tribune said that the urban plebs had too much power in the state and that they should be 'drained off'—that is the word he used, as though he were talking about bilgewater and not about a class of true citizens" (*De lege agraria* 2.70). Julius Caesar and Augustus made liberal use of the device to bring order to the city. At Carthage and other North African colonies, many of the early inscriptions of colonists prove to be of freedmen, but the colonies by and large needed rugged farmers. The peasants who served in the army and were seeking land were preferable to artisans and ex-slaves.

A much more potent weapon was patronage, the very reciprocal ties of dependency that were weakened by the agricultural changes of the later Republic. The rich and powerful had other means of endorsing social dependency apart from rural ties, however. Roman patrons could still be owed services by their former slaves, and although there were as many complaints that patrons' rights were neglected (as in A.D. 56; Tacitus *Annales* 13.26), cases of flagrant disrespect were still considered socially scandalous and probably were confined to richer freedmen. We may assume, in fact, that patrons regularly demanded formal services (*operae*) as part of the agreement to manumit (Modestinus *Digest* 38.1.31) quite apart from the unwritten rule that a freedman owed loyalty to his former master.

Patronage went much deeper than this, however, and the poems of Martial and Juvenal are filled with descriptions of the informal strings by which a patron could bring his poorer client to heel. Patrons did not distribute gifts and meals for the sake of charity. It stands to reason, even if it cannot be proved, that most, if not all, of the clients who thronged the halls of the rich were the "respectable" poor. The fact that many made their morning *salutatio* before daybreak suggests they were artisans who had a day's work to do. Many rich people rented out parts of their *domus* as *tabernae* (Suetonius *Lives of the Caesars*, Nero 37), and even prostitutes and gladiators lived in "cells" that were part of the rich man's house and opened directly onto the street. Family, dependents, freedmen, clients, and slaves might occupy the *cenacula* free of charge (Ulpian *Digest* 9.3.5.1). Since the law favored the owners of *insulae* against the tenant, that would in itself ensure that the poor kept on the right side of the landlord. Patronage of the *collegia,* as we have seen, gave the wealthy opportunities for euergetism, social control, and, on occasion, political agitation.

Inevitably such connections were used by the rich and powerful and by the emperor for political purposes. In 193, when Didius Julianus made a bid to become emperor, he was supported, we are told, by "a great crowd of *clientes*" (Herodian 2.6.10). On the same occasion, Herodian speaks of poor people running through the streets to tell their rich and noble friends of the assassination of the emperor Commodus and of the dangers they had escaped (ibid., 2.2.3–5). Between A.D. 180 and 238 it is possible to identify about thirty occasions on which popular agitation was involved. Many of them—the spectacular fall of the emperor's favorite, Cleander, for one—began as food riots. In spite of Juvenal's sarcastic denigration of the Roman mobs as being interested in nothing but *panis et circenses,* it is clear that complex motives lay behind grain riots. Similarly, in the eighteenth century, food riots in Britain during a period of rapid urban growth were popular actions that were regarded as legitimate protests and could be turned into stampedes against unpopular opponents. In 353 the young Caesar, Gallus, used food riots in Antioch to get rid of the governor of Syria, who was delivered to the populace for lynching (Ammianus Marcellinus 14.7.5ff.). But the story is recounted as part of the jostling for power among the successors of Constantine.

The problem lies in deciding to what extent such popular agitations were "prepolitical" manifestations of a class struggle by "primitive rebels," as some historians believe, or simply evidence of the success with which the rich controlled the poor. Certainly in the many grain riots throughout Roman history, or in the protest against taxes in Caligula's reign (Josephus *Antiquitate iudicae* 19.24–26), we have potential evidence of direct action by the people that was considered a legitimate part of their "moral economy," analogous to the French *taxation populaire* in the eighteenth century. In the eighteenth century, however, there was also extensive use of hired mobs (in the so-called church and king riots in Britain) organized by the authorities against radical dissenters.

Such ambiguities were common in Rome. Who can believe, for instance, that the "popular talk" (*vulgi sermones*) mourning for Germanicus in A.D. 19 because he had promised "to restore the liberties of the Roman people with equal rights for all" (Tacitus *Annales* 2.82) was the authentic voice of the poor, who had never enjoyed much liberty? Herodian explicitly suggests that the famous riots of 235 against the emperor Maximinus had been "prompted by Gordian's friends and household" (7.10.5). But on the other hand, one cannot miss the resentment of the people on that occasion, who turned·in fury upon the praetorian soldiers. Although those riots ended with part of the city catching fire and many rich losing their properties, Herodian's comment on such incidents is, "Disasters that occur to those who are apparently fortunate and rich do not concern the common people [ochloi] and sometimes even cause pleasure to certain worthless, malicious individuals because they envy the powerful and prosperous" (7.3.5).

Natural divisions among the poor, plus political rivalries among factions of rich patrons, therefore make it virtually impossible to disentangle genuinely popular causes from political riots stimulated from outside. So in A.D. 69, after the death of Nero, Tacitus separates "the responsible part of the people [pars populi integra], which was connected to the great families, as well as the clients and freedmen of condemned and banished persons" from "the degraded populace [plebs sordida], frequenters of the circus and theater, the most worthless of slaves and those who wasted their property" (Historiae 1.4). But there is no reason to think this an accurate definition, since many of the occasions on which political manipulation took place began in the circus and the theater. It is true that Cicero argued that at games and gladiatorial contests the authentic vox populi was heard (Pro Sestio 106), and demonstrations at the circus—"where they spare neither emperors nor citizens" (Tertullian De spectaculis 16)— were regarded as one of the natural rights of the people. Popular "acclamations" could be, and often were, orchestrated for political purposes by aristocratic factions, who were presumably considered "responsible" if they were successful, as in 190 when shouts against Cleander were led by a woman and a hired band of children at the horse races (Dio Cassius 72.13.3), leading to riots and the fall of the man detested by the nobility.

Such ambiguity lies at the heart of perception of the poor by the rich and of the latter's response to poverty. A romantic view of the virtues of poverty, chiefly rural poverty, was embedded in the Roman mentality, and it stimulated regular, ritual praise of early heroes such as Fabricius, Cincinnatus, and Ennius by moralists (for example, Cicero Tusculanae disputationes 3.23.57). Stobaeus, a Byzantine lexicographer, collected a list of such improving literary maxims: "Nothing is more fortunate than a poor man"; "The poor always believe in the gods"; "Famine never gave birth to adultery, nor shortage of money to extravagance." It was a diversion of the bored rich, according to Seneca, to play at living like the poor in their small cells, eating simple meals and sleeping on mattresses (*Epistles* 18.7). But such occasional antics, he says, gave them no idea of how the thousands of poor and slaves endured such daily privations, and even Seneca's own experiment at living for two days like the poor in the country makes unimpressive reading when he tells us that he took very few slaves—only a carriage load!—and that his food was so simple it took only one hour to prepare (ibid., 87). The affluent in every age, like Marie Antoinette, have affected to live like peasants by escaping to their own private milking parlors.

The Roman rich were no different, but the romantic merits of this rural myth modified in an important way the feelings of disgust and fear they felt for the realities of the dirt and squalor of the indigent at their doors. Just as in the period of urban boom in Europe between the sixteenth and the eighteenth centuries, Roman nobles devised principles of selective and institutionalized assistance to separate the "deserving" from the "undeserving" poor. The rich man "will give of his wealth to good men, or to those he will be able to make into good men," Seneca says, "but to some I shall not give, although in need, because, even if I should give, they would still be in need" (*De vita beata* 23.5–24.1). The poor were carefully separated, and charity (*benignitas*) was regarded as a means of maintaining patronage ties, with the aim of inculcating traditional values of deferential submission among those capable of service. Aid should only go to the "suitable poor," Cicero says, using much the same language as he applied to those of whom he approved politically (*De officiis* 2.54). The danger lay in the corruption of the poor and the encouragement of disorderly, idle mobs, which, according to many writers throughout Roman history, had happened when free or cheap grain was distributed (Appian *Bellorum civilium* 2.120). "To give to a beggar is to do him an ill service" (Plautus *Trinummus* 339) was a convenient maxim for the rich, whose interests lay not in general poverty, which they regarded with indifference, but in marginalizing extreme poverty as a form of moral degeneration.

Euergetism—the ostentatious endowment of money and services to communities or groups of individuals—was to benefit not the poor primarily but the less rich. That much was clear to Roman patrons who "are generous in their gifts not so much by natural inclination as by reason of the lure of honor; they simply want to seem beneficent" (Cicero *De officiis* 1.44). The select poor, or even the relatively rich, were assisted, while the social status of the patron was underlined. "The boast of their good deed is considered to be the motive, not the consequence," says Pliny the Younger (*Epistulae* 1.8.15), who himself was a notable benefactor in his hometown of Comum. It was rare, although not totally unknown in some Greek cities, for slaves of foreign migrants to benefit from such schemes. It was unlikely that the very poor even bothered to turn up at the public distributions of food or money. One such scheme at Syllium, in Pisidia, distributed money to everyone from the rich town magistrates to the lowest freedman or noncitizen, but in regressive proportions (which we find bizarre today) by a ratio of 50:1 in favor of the rich (*ILLRP* 3.80.1).

Given this mentality of *bono benefacito* ("do good to the good": the words of the elder Cato), we can make some observations about the state alimentary schemes that developed in Rome in the second century A.D. to assist children, and about the state *frumentationes,* a scheme that grew up in the last century of the Republic to provide cheap or free wheat to the citizens. Both have been much studied, and the comments here relate only to the problem of the poor. Most important, there is no evidence that either scheme was available, except abnormally, for the destitute. Both were explicitly limited to citizens. As we know for certain about state *frumentationes* and as we may plausibly infer about the *alimenta* from private schemes, even the very rich were eligible, although an anecdote about the senator Lucius Piso queuing up for his quota in 123 B.C. implies that it was socially degrading for the rich to be the recipients of state patronage (Cicero *Tusculanae disputationes* 3.48). The public schemes for grain distribution at Oxyrhynchus, in Egypt, however, required recipients to prove their credentials as members of the better class of citizens by birth or wealth.

Relief of distress, therefore, was only incidental to, not the aim of, such benefits. The aim was, as Trajan's scheme to feed 5,000 freeborn children in Rome reveals, to enrich the stock of Roman citizen soldiers, a fine but vain gesture of republican propaganda designed, so it was said, eventually to reduce the size of the grain lists (Pliny the Younger *Panegyricus* 28.4–5). It was in line with Augustus' stated desire to stop all free grain distributions because they encouraged rural migration and idleness (Suetonius *Life of the Caesars, Augustus* 42)—the stereotypical point of view of rich aristocrats. He and Julius Caesar reduced the recipients from 350,000 to 150,000, although up to 250,000 people were assisted irregularly by gestures of the emperor's largess. Elites, as we know, always prefer that they themselves dispense patronage if anyone is to do so. But in no cases were all the poor given food or money. The appalling existence of the poor, who were created as a consequence of slave farming practiced by wealthy landowners and whose services were also required by the rich in the city, was never a cause of concern. The emperor's only intention was to marginalize the "immoral" extremes of poverty.

How the poor conceived of the rich is far more difficult to recover from our sources, but we have some clear indications of how they felt about the grain dole. Augustus did not abolish the list of *plebs frumentaria* because he knew popular pressure would one day restore it. No emperor ever dared to neglect the supply of grain nor to control its price when fluctuations occurred. The public rioting against Claudius in A.D. 51, when it was rumored that there were grain shortages and he had to be rescued from the mob in the forum by his guards (Tacitus *Annales* 12.43; Suetonius *Life of the Caesars, Claudius* 18.2), is one of many incidents that show the "moral rights" exercised by the poor. Emperors, who purported to be the superpatrons of the plebs, were ready to sacrifice governors or their favorites when it was alleged that prices were being manipulated. In A.D. 364 Symmachus had his house in the Trastevere burned down by the people because it was rumored that he was refusing to sell his wine at the accepted price (Ammianus Marcellinus 27.3.4). The burning of houses, like the chanting of insults and noisy demonstration in the circus or elsewhere, was regarded as ritual demonstrations of popular will, precisely as was the charivari in late medieval Europe: it had quasi-legal recognition and was exploited with remarkable efficacy for his political ends by Publius Clodius in the late Republic.

Nor was food the only subject of popular morality. Popular justice did not view the law as rigidly as the rich did. Despite precautions taken by the rich to barricade their houses with iron grills, to use doors and doormen (who were sometimes chained to the entrance), it was well known that slaves would not defend their master's property at personal cost (Apuleius *Metamorphoses* 4.9). The demonstration in the theater in favor of Androcles, the runaway slave, saved him (Aulus Gellius 5.14.29). And in A.D. 61 there was a spectacular though vain riot against the mass execution of slaves after the murder of their owner, Pedanius Secundus. The protest was not against the law so much as it was a demand for mitigation because Pedanius had been so cruel a master (Tacitus *Annales* 14.42–43). Who the free citizens were who rioted we do not know, possibly freemen of the same household, but plausibly the very poor sympathized with slaves since they sold their children and themselves into slavery at times. "The wealthy," said Anaximenes, "do not show pity to the unfortunate as the poor do. Fear for themselves breeds their pity for the misfortunes of others." It is significant that the only inscription known to commemorate a dead man for being a "lover of the poor" was that of a Greek foreigner (*ILLRP* 797). Not surprisingly, when there was a political bloodbath, as in A.D. 70, the poor and the slaves turned on their rich masters (Tacitus *Historiae* 4.1).

Solidarity among the poor was institutionalized, as seen in the *collegia,* by social and religious organizations. Titles like the "friends among the builders" (*amici subaediani*) or "the carpenter brotherhood" (*fabri fratres*) protest their close ties. Those who worked at the *horrea Galbana,* the imperial warehouses by the Tiber, formed a *sodalicium* (*ILS* 3445). Patron gods were worshiped by professional clubs—Bacchus, for example, by the innkeepers. This happened prominently among the many foreign groups settled in various quarters of Rome: the Egyptians in the Campus Martius worshiped Isis and Serapis. We know of huge ghettos of Jews in various parts of the city, the largest being in the Transtiberim region, where they numbered thirty thousand or more. The offices (*stationes*) of foreign traders kept such groups in touch with their home cities and encouraged the corporate life of ethnic groups. With it, to some extent, there did exist a separate culture of the poor.

Nevertheless it was precisely the *collegia* and *sodalicia,* comprising perhaps as much as one-third of the male population of the city, that were regulated both formally by the law and informally by their social expectations and links with rich patrons. They were deliberately given a place on festivals, funerals, and other state occasions (as in A.D. 193; Dio Cassius 75.4.5–6), and they were permitted to petition the emperor. From this same class of persons, many of whom as freedmen must have had personal obligations of service to their patrons, the emperor Augustus formed the *Augustales,* who symbolically tended the cult of the emperor's *genius.* The worship was integrated into the old cults of the crossroads (*compitales*) within the newly organized *vici* (parishes), and to be elected *vicomagister* was a highly sought-after honor. These are the men who were regarded as the *pars populi integra,* "attached" (as Tacitus says) to the houses of the rich. In short, all the evidence goes to show that despite a certain moral subculture of the poor, the rich successfully imposed their own value system upon the more socially ambitious sector of the plebs, which fragmented the solidarity of the poor.

Although Augustus also instituted the first city police force, the urban cohorts, and was in part responsible for creating the fire fighters' corps, neither service could have worked effectively without some form of social control. In fact, as we can see in the riots of A.D. 235, the soldiers (in this case the praetorians) were afraid to enter the narrow streets, where they were vulnerable. In the later Empire the city cohorts seem to have disappeared entirely, leaving fire fighting to the *collegia* and law and order to the magistrate with his *apparitores*. Despite a number of riots in the fourth century, including cases in which the urban prefect's house was burned down, the disturbances have a ritual appearance and are limited in their action, much like the charivaris of the late Republic. From the events of A.D. 365, we get a clue to how this sort of damage limitation operated when we are told that the urban prefect was hated by the *plebs infima* but that he was physically protected by his "friends and neighbors" (Ammianus Marcellinus 27.3.8). This is a good example to end on, since it demonstrates clearly how the respectable poor gave their support to the social order, from which they benefited through acts of private and state patronage. The "wretched of the earth"—the really poor—received no such comfort.

Nothing has been said about Christianity—deliberately, since during the main period of Roman history it was only a marginal force within the city of Rome, although information about the extent of the charitable activities of the church toward widows in the mid-third century A.D. provokes surprise and skepticism. The early church explicitly contrasted its charity with the normal language of Roman euergetism. It was *eleēmosynē* (pity), not *philodoxia* (reputation) that motivated almsgiving; it was "to preach the gospel to the destitute [*ptōchoi*]" (Luke 4:18), not to the poor in general, that the church declared was its aim. Widows, orphans, migrants, and the sick, whom the church tended, were those whom Roman euergetism almost ignored. They were not the "deserving poor." This form of charity exercised a powerful attraction within the cities of the later Empire, and it is one explanation of the success of Christianity as civic communities disintegrated. The pagan emperor Julian offers a vivid testimony to the effectiveness of the mutual aid given by Christian and Jewish communities when he wrote to the high priest of Galatia, "It is a disgrace that no Jew is a beggar and that the impious Galileans feed our people in addition to their own, whereas ours manifestly lack assistance from us" (*Epistles* 49).

This "morality of the socially vulnerable," as it has been called, was also a reflection of the lower-class culture of poverty. The monastic movement symbolically sanctified those who labored with their hands or who begged for their living. In sum, for a short time Christianity achieved what Gramsci would have called a "counterhegemonic" world view that integrated the institutions of church and state with popular ideology. But with how much ultimate success or effect upon the destitute is another story.

C. R. Whittaker

Bibliography

Theories and attitudes regarding poverty in recent and less recent European history are reviewed in works such as E. P. Thompson, *The Making of the English Working Class* (New York: Vintage Books, 1966); Peter Townsend, *Poverty in the United Kingdom: A Survey of Household Resources and Standards of Living* (Berkeley: University of California Press, 1979); Chaim I. Waxman, *The Stigma of Poverty: A Critique of Poverty Theories and Policies,* 2d ed. (New York: Pergamon Press, 1987); Stuart J. Woolf, *The Poor in Western Europe in the Eighteenth and Nineteenth Century* (London and New York: Methuen, 1986).

There are no studies specifically on poverty in ancient Rome, but for a general picture of social life in Rome see Paul Veyne, "L'Empire romain," in *Histoire de la vie privée,* 5 vols., ed. Philippe Ariès and Georges Duby (Paris: Editions du Seuil, 1985), vol. 1, *De l'Empire romain à l'an mil,* pp. 18–223, available in English as "The Roman Empire," in *A History of Private Life,* ed. Ariès and Duby, vol. 1, *From Pagan Rome to Byzantium,* ed. Paul Veyne (Cambridge and London: Belknap Press of Harvard University Press, 1987), pp. 5–287; Ramsay MacMullen, *Roman Social Relations, 50 B.C. to A.D. 284* (New Haven: Yale University Press, 1974); Jérôme Carcopino, *La vie quotidienne à Rome à l'apogée de l'Empire* (Paris: Hachette, 1939; Livre Club du libraire, 1959), available in English as *Daily Life in Ancient Rome: The People and the City at the Height of the Empire,* ed. Henry T. Rowell, trans. Emily Overend Lorimer (New Haven: Yale University Press, 1940); Ludwig Friedländer, *Darstellung aus der Sittengeschichte Roms in der Zeit von August bis zum ausgang der Antonine* (1862–71), 10th ed., ed. Georg Wissowa (Leipzig: 1922).

Studies on topics related to poverty are Arthur Robinson Hands, *Charities and Social Aid in Greece and Rome* (Ithaca, N.Y.: Cornell University Press, 1968); Alexander Scobie, "Slums, Sanitation and Mortality in the Roman World," *Klio* 68 (1986): 399–443; Keith Hopkins, *Death and Renewal* (Cambridge and New York: Cambridge University Press, 1983); Peter Garnsey, *Famine and Food Supply in the Graeco-Roman World: Responses to Risk and Crisis* (Cambridge and New York: Cambridge University Press, 1988); Bruce W. Frier, *Landlords and Tenants in Imperial Rome* (Princeton: Princeton University Press, 1980); Frank Kolb, "Zur Statussymbolik im antiken Rom," *Chiron* 7 (1977): 239–60.

Political aspects of poverty and of the control of the poor are studied in P. A. Brunt, "The Roman Mob," in *Studies in Ancient Society,* ed. Moses I. Finley (London and Boston: Routledge & Kegan Paul, 1974), 74–102; C. R. Whittaker, "The Revolt of Papyrius Dionysius," *Historia* 13 (1964): 348–69; Mario Mazza, "Sul proletariato urbano in epoca imperiale," *Siculorum Gymnasium* 27 (1974): 237–78; Wilfred Nippel, "Die plebs urbana und die Rolle der Gewalt in der späten römischen Republik," in *Vom Elend der Handarbeit: Probleme historischen Unterschichtenforschung,* ed. Hans Mommsen and Winfried Schulze (Stuttgart: Klett-Cotta, 1981), 70–92.

The Bandit

Brent D. Shaw

"I WAS ONCE THE HEAD of a very powerful gang that laid waste the whole of Macedonia. I am none other than the famous bandit Haemus the Thracian. At the mere mention of my name the whole province shook. I am the son of Theron, who was also a bandit. I was nourished on human blood. I was educated in the fighting units of my father's band. I am the heir and rival to my father's power."

So one bandit, having fallen on bad times, boasts in reciting his oral *curriculum vitae* to the members of the new gang he hopes to join (Apuleius *Metamorphoses* 7.5). In it he emphasizes the essential characteristics of the brigand as perceived by the Roman novelist who composed this imaginary life story: an outlaw heritage, barbaric "otherness," and the assertion of a personal autonomy. This type of brigand, the one who was embedded in Roman society, the "enclosed" bandit, is the kind of outlaw with which most bandits are identified in modern popular conceptions. The lone leader with his small band of followers is our standard mental image of the brigand: a Robin Hood, a Louis Mandrin, a Jesse James, a Salvatore Giuliano.

We can compare this picture of the lone individual seeking violent employment with the following report by the biographer Plutarch on much greater troubles afflicting the Roman Empire in the 80s to the 50s B.C.:

> The power of the pirates at first emanated from Cilicia and, at the beginning, was haphazard and erratic. But their power became deliberate and daring at the time of the war with Mithradates [88–85 B.C.] because it was useful for the king's

purposes. At that time, when the Romans were engaged in civil wars at the very gates of Rome, there were no guardians over the sea. So the pirates were enticed and led on, little by little, until they no longer attacked just ships but raided whole islands and coastal cities. Soon wealthy men of power, men from distinguished families, and even those who were considered worthy for their intelligence began to take a share in this brigandage, feeling that the occupation had a certain reputation and honor. There were fortified harbor and signal stations in many places for their ships. Ships put in at these stopovers, which were full not only of trained men and skilled pilots but also of fast, light ships all well prepared for this sort of work. . . . The way they seized persons in high posts and made demands for the ransom of whole cities was a shame to Roman hegemony. . . . This power extended its operations over the whole of the Mediterranean, making sailing impossible and cutting off trade and commerce. (Plutarch *Life of Pompey* 24.1–3, 4; 25.1)

Here brigandage had become something rather different. It had developed into a large-scale threat to the state, a more permanent, collective form of violence provoked by the unusual conjuncture of state powers in the Mediterranean that permitted and encouraged its existence.

Finally, we can contrast this seaborne brigandage with the following report on the bandits in Isauria of the later Empire by the historian Ammianus Marcellinus:

It is usually the case that the Isaurians are dormant at some times, and at others throw everything into confusion with their sudden raids. This time, however, they advanced with growing audacity to commit worse deeds, and finally to burst into open war. For a long time already their rebellious spirits had been breaking out in scattered episodes of violence. But now they declared that their honor had been harmed because certain of their brothers who had been captured had been thrown to wild beasts for public entertainment in the amphitheater at Iconium—an outrage contrary to all customary treatment in the past. So they all rushed down from their impenetrable and steep mountain slopes, like a tornado, toward places near the sea. They hid themselves in trackless and shadowy passes, as dark nights came on—for the moon was still crescent shaped and therefore not yet shining with its full brilliance. . . . Later, leaving the seacoast, they retreated to that part of Lycaonia that lies next to Isauria. Here they blocked the roads with forts and lived off the wealth of the locals and of travelers. . . . Our soldiers did their best to repel the marauders who struck first here in concentrated gangs and now there in dispersed bands. But they were overcome by the sheer number and power of the brigands, who were born and raised in the remote and snaking paths of the Isaurian highlands. The bandits bounded over the mountains as though over flat and level plains, threatening with javelins and arrows any enemy who stood in their way and terrifying them with their savage howls. (14.2.1–2, 4)

As Ammianus proceeds to report the large-scale outbreaks of banditry in Isauria in the 350s and 360s, it is clear that he is describing a very long-term historical phenomenon—a sort of regional autonomy that he labels banditry, or *latrocinium*. In this case the regional autonomy was characterized by the large-scale brigandage of the mountain zones of Isauria and Cilicia in southeastern Anatolia. It was an endemic source of violence that was to plague the Roman and Byzantine empires for the entirety of their existence. Ammianus therefore gives us a good example of a type of brigandage that is at the distal end from the isolated individual bandits of popular imagery: the existence of whole regions and peoples that were considered "brigand" from the perspective of the Roman state. The highland lords and dynasts of Isauria were indeed bandits, though on a scale that dwarfed the "enclosed" bandit such as Haemus the Thracian, who is our stereotype of the brigand. But, given the range of possibilities indicated by the three cases of brigandage from Apuleius, Plutarch, and Ammianus, a question of definition emerges. Just what, or who, is a bandit?

First of all, banditry is a form of personal power. In rare instances bandits have transformed their power into more institutionalized forms of power, such as that of a state. But so long as they remain bandits they represent an assertion of the person, a type of "individual protest" as one modern historian has put it. This individual power, based on charisma, on appearance, on brute strength, and on the ties forged by way of personhood (kinship, friendship, or clientage), is probably one of the primal forms of power known to humans. As such it is both logically and historically prior to the state. If one were to examine stateless societies, as for example those reflected in the Homeric epics, one would find that "bandit" power would be normal and accepted by all participants in that society as the only way of conducting relationships. Indeed, there was no way that this type of power could be defined as something "other" than what it was by any competing forms of power. For banditry to become labeled as "unacceptable" it had to be superseded by forms of institutionalized power, such as that of the state, which were opposed to it; which wished to subordinate, to domesticate, and finally to eliminate it. In the novel situation created by the state, competing forms of personal power were disallowed, and some were labeled as ones that threaten a return to prestate anarchy. From this perspective, therefore, banditry was perceived as being at the distal end of a spectrum of possible types of power distanced by both scale and morality. As St. Augustine phrased it: "Remove justice and what are states but gangs of bandits on a large scale? And what are bandit gangs but kingdoms in miniature?" (*The City of God* 4.4). But that "kingdom," the state, must come into existence before an aberrant type of power called banditry and a delinquent social role (that of the bandit) can be recognized. Looked at from another perspective, however, the figure of the bandit can provide the modern historian with a good measure of the relative standing of the state in a whole society. By considering bandits in the Roman world, therefore, we understand more not only about these "archaic reservoirs" of personal power in the Roman world but also about the nature of the Roman state itself.

In formal Latin terminology, bandits were generally known as *latrones* (singular, *latro*) and banditry as *latrocinium*. In that half of the Roman world where the social and political elites used Greek as a koine, the comparable Greek terms *lēstai* (singular, *lēstēs*) and *lēsteia* were used to designate bandits and brigandage. As we have just demonstrated, the most primitive point of reference for these terms was a type of prestate power, the anarchy that stood before the birth of the state in time. This is symbolized in mythical stories concerning the foundation of the great political communities of Athens and Rome. In the former case, the legendary founder of Attica, Theseus, defeated *lēstai* before overseeing the great mythical unification (*synoikismos*) of Attica that was the foundation of the Athenian state (Plutarch *Theseus* 6.4, 10.2). In the case of Rome it was Romulus and Remus who shed their roles as shepherd-bandits in the process of founding the new city (Livy 1.4.9, 1.5.3; Eutropius 1.1–3). The problem for Roman thinkers, then, was to understand by what process, or qualities, primitive societies were to be distinguished from civilized ones. When Cicero counted justice as the core moral value that permitted human societies to function, he allowed that even bandit gangs obeyed its "general laws." And yet he drew a clear quantitative distinction between banditry and statehood: "Since, therefore, the power of justice is so great that it strengthens and increases the power even of bandits, how great can you imagine it to be in a state with its laws and courts?" (Cicero *De officiis* 2.11.40). But it was not merely "greater justice" that defined the state as different from the brigand. The distance between the two was, in Cicero's eyes, qualitatively absolute, as when he rhetorically demanded of his personal and political enemy, Clodius: "For what is a state? Every collection of uncivilized savages? Every group of fugitives and bandits gathered in any one place? Not so, you will certainly say" (Cicero *De Paradoxa Stoicorum* 27). Again, although justice might compel fair treatment, there was an absolute distinction between this simple behavior and the constitution of a state. The chaos of personal power that depended on nothing else than an ethic of "fair play" to produce social cohesion is taken by Cicero to be characteristic of the absence of any state—that is to say, the norms merely agreed to by a collection of men "no more deserve to be called laws than the rules to which a gang of bandits might assent in its gatherings" (*De legibus* 2.5.13).

In fact, it might be admitted, by way of illustrating the artificiality of culture and moral standards, that some "barbaric" peoples could still be found who regarded banditry as an honorable occupation. But the dominant morality held that those who engaged in banditry did so against their own innermost moral convictions—that the bandit was one who, if he could exercise his preferences, would rather acquire goods "by honorable means" rather than by robbery. The universal claims of state morality held that even those whose lifelong profession was brigandage no longer lived in a moral space apart from that of other human beings who were the subjects of states. More precisely, the claim was issued, by moralizing senators (by Seneca for one) that the moral sense of what was "wrong" (where banditry is specified as one of these wrongs) "penetrates the minds of all men; even those who do not follow truth nevertheless see her" (Seneca *De beneficiis* 4.17.4). A distraught and indignant mother in Apuleius' novel, in reproving her son, makes the same assumptions in her exclamations: "The worst sort of men, criminals, are like that; however deeply their consciences may reproach them, they never expect to be caught" (*Metamorphoses* 7.27).

One can perceive the merging of the universal moral claim and the claims of political legitimacy in the definition of bandits and brigandage issued by the Roman state. The *Digest,* in its list of standard word definitions (*De verborum significatione,* 'latrones': *Digest* 50.16.118), declares: "Enemies [*hostes*] are those who have declared war on us or on whom we have declared war; all the rest are bandits [*latrones*] or plunderers [*praedones*]." The problem for modern historians is that our categories of "bandit" and "banditry" do not match this sweeping Roman definition. The much cruder and starker Roman version held that either you were a legitimate and recognized state that was capable of fighting a regular war (*bellum*) with the Roman state or, if not, you were a bandit. The whole world was thus divided by use of harsher terms than ours, with the fine gradations of nonstate violence we recognize missing from their spectrum. Village feuding, tribal raiding, various types of urban riots (for reasons of food or belief), and so on, do not exist as part of this definition. Although we can subtract these other forms of violence from what we consider to be genuine banditry, one must remember that the Romans themselves did not draw these fine distinctions. It is we who do so.

We might begin with banditry as the small-scale, "enclosed" type of violence exemplified in the story of the unemployed Thracian brigand Haemus in Apuleius' novel quoted above. This banditry is a form of personal violence, most often carried out in small groups (though not invariably so) and characteristically found in peasant societies (though again not exclusively). It is a parasitic type of livelihood in which the acquisition of goods and services depends directly on the use of physical violence and threats. This side of banditry as a peculiar "economy of violence" was also widely recognized in antiquity. Both Plato and Aristotle recognized banditry, or *lēsteia,* as one of the common types of economic behavior, as a distinctive mode of acquiring goods that ranked along with farming, fishing, pastoralism, and hunting as one of the fundamental economic "modes of life" (*bioi*) known to man (Aristotle *Politics* 1256a–b = 1.8.6–8). Plato was more moralizing (from the perspective of the state, as one would expect) and hence classified banditry as a subtype of the hunting mode of existence, as a morally bad type of life that he contrasted with the aristocratic hunting of four-footed animals on horseback (Plato *Laws* 7.823b;e). For a long time, however, the precise relationship between the newly emerging state, on the one hand, and the old archaic world of personal power, on the other, remained dubious.

The one could be parasitic on the other. For example, it was apparently quite legal by the "laws" attributed to Solon (c. 594 B.C.) for Athenians to form "piratical associations" as long as it was to attack other cities. The nascent state was therefore quite willing to harbor reservoirs of private power within its body as long as the violence would be directed against foreign communities. There did not yet exist that Weberian "monopoly of force" that is so critical to a modern definition of banditry. Thus the historian Thucydides (1.5), though a man of the *polis* and therefore one who heartily disapproved of brigandage, admitted that there were contemporary Greek communities for whom piracy was a perfectly honorable occupation and one that, far from incurring shame, brought considerable reputation.

Unlike these "softer" ideas of the early Greek city *polis,* the "harder" mainstream political ideologies of the high Roman Empire utterly rejected the possibility of the coexistence of bandit and state power. This in spite of the fact that Cicero, for example, admitted that bandits still shared in some of the basic norms of social behavior: they had their own standards of justice, and a distribution of honors and property that paralleled those of legitimate civil society:

> The importance of justice is so great that not even those who live by evil and wickedness can live without some part of it. For if a bandit takes anything by force or by fraud from another member of his gang, he loses his status even in the gang of bandits. And if the man who is the bandit chief does not divide the loot impartially, he will be deserted or murdered by his fellow gang members. There are even, it is said, bandit laws [*leges latronum*] that must be observed and obeyed. Indeed, because of his impartial distribution of booty, Bardulis, the Illyrian *latro,* acquired great wealth and power. (Cicero *De officiis* 2.11.40)

However much Cicero was willing to exploit Bardulis the brigand for philosophical ends, he was never willing even to contemplate "brigand justice" as merging with state law. For the Roman senator, the two were absolutely distinct.

The definition of the bandit issued by the Roman state so rejected and castigated them as a type that the term "bandit" (*latro*) could be freely deployed to label those political opponents of whom one disapproved, especially bitter political enemies who offered a type of violence that threatened to return civil society to primeval chaos. One can see, for example, a clear distinction in the works of Cicero in the deployment of the language of banditry. In his historical and philosophical works the word is used to designate "real" bandits. In his speeches and rhetorical works, however, the words *latro, latrones,* and *latrocinium* are systematically used to stigmatize his most dangerous political opponents. In fact, he used the words *latro* and *latrones* as a way of labeling the threatening power of a limited number of the most terrible of his public enemies: Verres, Catiline, Clodius, and Antony. That is to say, Cicero, like other literate and educated Romans, could use the term "bandit" as a powerful label to fix on hated persons in order to stigmatize them as dangerous "destated" enemies. It was widely so used in the late Republic in times of political tension and strife within the Roman state (e.g., in 63, 56, 44–32 B.C.). Calling political enemies "bandits" continued to be a common practice in the Roman ruling elite, and was reverted to with particular frequency during times of political crisis when the authority of the central state came into question (e.g., in A.D. 68–69 and 192–93 and during the half-century of crisis in central state authority following 238). The label *latro* was used especially to brand competitors for the imperial throne as mere "pretenders"—that is, as persons who were mere holders of personal power and therefore illegitimate from the perspective of the state. Thus Octavian branded Antony and Sextus Pompeius and their followers as brigands and pirates; Septimius Severus was able to stigmatize Pescennius Niger and Clodius Albinus as *latrones.*

Although this political exploitation of the language and imagery of banditry tells us a lot about periods of crisis in the Roman state, however, it obviously sheds little light on the persons of the bandits themselves. From the perspective of an individual who was a bandit or a pirate, banditry must be seen less as an aspect of personality than as a "space" inside (or, in some cases, outside but linked to) a given state and its society where this peculiar form of personal power could subsist. This space could be a distinctive region or zone either inhabited by people who were "free" of state control or which could be entered by persons who wished to become free. Let us consider some of the physical spaces or regions first. Even at the height of the Roman empire there remained types of lands within the putative or actual frontiers of the empire that were beyond the effective control of the state. A prime example would be the many mountain zones that traversed the lands of the Mediterranean. On a more modest scale were the dense forest and impenetrable swamplands, which, though they might sometimes be located close to an urban center, might still have a topography sufficiently forbidding to prevent the effective penetration of urban institutions. Such, for example, were the dense mountain forests and the great swamplands close to the city of Antioch in Syria, which harbored gangs of brigands throughout the entire period of the empire (Liebeschuetz, in *Antioch,* 1977, 119–26).

These islands of autonomy within the frontiers of the empire harbored persons who, though stateless, shared a relative degree of autonomy. Furthermore, given the very weak structures of policing in the empire, which were at their most feeble at the local level, even a small forest, a modest swamp, or a small highland might suffice to offer a refuge. In the rather stark vision of the empire as a mosaic of urban communities dominating the surrounding countryside, the most general "space" that was weakly dominated was precisely the vast expanse of countryside that extended outward from each city, town, and village. These great areas of peasant farming and transhumant pastoralism were regions in which the officials of the central state were rarely seen and where such law and order as did exist were provided by a combination of local self-help and the enforcers employed by local landlords.

The countryside outside each town was therefore seen as being intrinsically dangerous. Travel by land often took on the aspect of "island-hopping" as groups of frightened travelers made their way from one urban center to the next. Even with these precautions, the reception at the next town might not always be predictable. Thus, in Apuleius' novel the *Metamorphoses,* set in the empire of the mid-second century A.D., a convoy of travelers approaching a small hamlet were brutally attacked by the local villagers because, in the darkness of the approaching dusk, they had been mistaken for bandits. Even though they made loud noises with trumpets and other instruments and carried lighted torches, the travelers had savage dogs set on them, while the villagers hurled rocks at them from the rooftops of their homes. Even after the wounded and beaten wayfarers were recognized as not being bandits, the wary and fearful locals still forced them to straggle on to the next village (*Metamorphoses* 8.16–18). The perceived danger of travel outside the towns provoked the practice of traveling in convoys. The dangers of road journeys produced seriocomic scenes of travel in the provinces in which one of the few official armed groups that regularly traversed the roads between provincial centers, that of the governor and his staff, was accompanied by motley bands of people who hoped that they might escape the perils of the road by huddling close to the safety represented by government on the move (Epictetus *Discourses* 4.1.94ff.). No wonder then that St. Paul considered banditry and piracy to be among the common natural dangers, along with earthquakes and sea storms, that threatened the safety of the traveler (2 Corinthians 11:26). Nor was he alone in his fear of bandit attacks as one of the ordinary dangers to be faced by the traveler. He was just echoing common assumptions (see Seneca *De beneficiis* 4.35.2).

Town walls, therefore, did not just demarcate the sacred and institutional boundaries of the urban center from its rural hinterland. They were also a defense against persistent low-level threats of local raids by brigands (ibid., 6.15.8). When the town gates shut each night, they sealed the village off from the surrounding sea of danger that threatened particularly at night, and within those walls each household bolted and barred its doors against bandit attacks (Apuleius *Metamorphoses* 1.11, 15). To want to go outside the city at night was regarded as madness or worse. When a traveler in Apuleius' novel wished suddenly to leave a town at night, he approached the town gatekeeper (*ianitor*), who warned him: "What! Surely you must know that the roads around here are infested with bandits. Why on earth would you want to go out on the roads at this time of night? Perhaps it's because you're guilty of some crime and just have a death wish—well, I tell you, don't think that we're such blockheads as to want to go out there to die just to protect you!" (ibid., 1.15).

The dangers of travel were, as the novelist suggests, ubiquitous, even (perhaps especially) for the mighty and the powerful who could provide their own armed bodyguards and escorts. Men, even of the highest status, were known simply "to disappear" while traveling on roads between major cities. The younger Pliny notes an exemplary case (*Epistulae* 6.25) in a letter addressed to his friend Baebius Hispanus: "You say that the distinguished *eques* Robustus traveled as far as Ocriculum [just north of Rome on the Via Flaminia] with my friend Atilius Scaurus and then completely vanished. Now you want Scaurus to come to help in the search. He will come, but it will probably be of no use. I suspect that the same thing has happened to Robustus as happened to my hometown friend Metilius Crispus." Pliny then goes on to say that Crispus and his retinue of slaves left Comum one day and he was never seen again. Such dangers remained ubiquitous in the empire, even in the spokelike network of roads emanating from the imperial capital itself. In the fourth century, the senator Quintus Aurelius Symmachus wrote that, although he was prefect of the city, he did not dare venture beyond its walls because the roads outside were so infested with bandits (Symmachus *Letters* 2.22).

In many ways, therefore, Rome and the other cities of Italy at the height of the Empire were in much the same situation as, say, Rome and Naples in Italy of the seventeenth to mid-nineteenth centuries of the modern era. Lack of modern communications, poor night lighting, a sparse and corrupt local administration, inadequate policing, and other such shortfalls encouraged a latent anarchy in the countryside, especially at night.

This tendency to anarchy was also a general part of the tighter links that bound town and country in the Roman world—links so pervasive that the violence of the open countryside seemed to seep into the streets of cities in the dead of night, even into the avenues of Rome itself. To journey at night in the capital was to undertake a journey of fear and to double the dangers (Juvenal *Satires* 10.19–22): "If you're carrying only a few plain silver jars with you on your night journey, you'll still tremble in fear of the sword and stick; you will shake at the quivering of a reed's shadow in the moonlight. The empty-handed traveler, however, can whistle aloud at the bandit." As Juvenal says, having nothing to take, simply being poor, was seen as one of the few protections against being attacked. The same sentiment is echoed by Apuleius' wayfarer who tried to persuade the town gatekeeper to let him out: "Don't you know that the poorest travelers are safe—what could a bandit take?" (*Metamorphoses* 1.15). But the narrator of the novel was himself attacked by upper-class ruffians while attempting to make his way home in the middle of a town one night.

There are, of course, many other examples of common attitudes shared by urban dwellers about the ubiquitous danger posed by bandits in land and sea zones beyond the immediate control of the cities. Even if we consider *latrocinium* from the perspective of texts produced by these urban-centered populations of the empire, there are clear indications of banditry as a common phenomenon that typified the social structure of the empire. Legal texts, for example, often contain declarations like: "Where something occurs by reason of old age or disease or where something is forcibly taken by bandits or some other such thing happens, it is to be held that the borrower need not answer for matters of this kind. . . . In the case of disaster . . . or by act of God, he will not be liable"; or, "If someone has been captured by bandits and mistakenly believes that he is their slave as if they were the enemy . . . it is certain that he cannot leave a *fideicommissum*" (*Digest* 13.6.5.4; 32.1, pr). Statements such as these and a host of others in the law codes portray bandits as a force that is as common as any natural disaster—like an earthquake or a storm at sea that strikes suddenly and without warning. Just like any force of nature, bandits could interrupt any sort of normal civil dealing that persons might happen to be engaged in at the moment, from making a will and getting married to closing a sale or, perhaps more to the point, making a last will and testament (see Shaw, 1984, 8n16 for references). Such themes are consistently repeated in literary sources where the author wished to exemplify a standard list of disasters commonly faced by men, where bandits are often included along with natural disasters, plagues, and earthquakes (e.g., Seneca *Ad Marciam de consolatione* 18.8). The possibility of death or damage suffered in an attack by bandits was treated as "common damage" (*commune damnum*), the equivalent of an "accident" in our terminology. The parallel is not far off the mark. When Jesus, in one of his parables (Luke 10:25–37), tells the story of the "good" Samaritan who stopped to help the victim of a bandit attack on the highway between Jerusalem and Jericho, he notes that others on this busy main route simply bypassed the scene, much as we might avoid the common scene of a traffic accident today. And in sermonizing on the fact that doing a personal favor might also involve personal risk, Seneca offers the example of a person who tries to help a man who has been surrounded by bandits, even though he would be perfectly free to pass on by in safety and to ignore the problem (Seneca *De beneficiis* 4.12.2).

Confirming this sense of a generally ubiquitous threat in the countryside are other indices of death and insecurity. There are, for example, a reasonably large number of tombstone epitaphs recording the fact that the deceased was "killed by bandits" (*interfectus a latronibus*). Typical cases are provided by the tombstone set up near Prizren, in Moesia Superior, by one Sita Dasipi for his father Scerviaedus Sitaes, who was "killed by bandits" (*CIL* 3.8242). Or there is the more elaborate inscription set up by Antonius Valentinus (junior) to his father, Antonius Valentinus, an officer in Legio XIII Gemina, who was "killed by bandits" on a road in the Julian Alps "at an accursed place" (*loco quod appellatur scelerata: ILS* 2646, Aidusinna near Tergeste). These inscriptions are found in most regions of the empire and are a small indication of a more generalized threat. This general sense of danger is further made explicit by the many military guardposts and frontier stations manned by units of the Roman army. Like the forts and associated road system protecting the southern access of the al-Qantara pass in southern Numidia, these are explicitly stated to be "for the protection of travelers on the road" (*CIL* 8.2494–95). On the inscription incised on the face of the army lookout post at Intercisa on the middle Danube (Pannonia), part of a whole series constructed along this frontier under Commodus, we find the words that it was to provide surveillance over places along the river "exposed to nighttime forays by brigands" (*CIL* 3.3385; for other references of this type see Shaw, 1984, 12n26).

So it was not without basis in fact that distant regions of the countryside were regarded, because of the very fact of their remoteness, with some trepidation as bandit lands. But within the countryside in general there were spaces that were regarded as particularly conducive to banditry, namely topographical "rough zones" such as mountains and marshes. Hence the vast swamplands in and around the Nile Delta in Egypt were thought to harbor bandits known as "cowboys" (*boukoloi;* Dio Cassius 72.4), wild men who controlled the labyrinthine networks of water channels that crisscrossed the region. They could emerge suddenly from any of these, even in disguise, to kill wayfarers and then devour them like savage cannibals (Dio Cassius 72.4). These myths have been labeled, quite correctly, as a sort of "xenophobic fantasy," as stories that "must be read from the point of view of Roman fear in Alexandria" (Winkler, 1980, 175–77). But such beliefs persisted until the end of antiquity. The *boukoloi* were believed to inhabit a no-man's-land and live quite separate from civilized society, marked by a complete lack of the good faith that typified normal social relations. Even in the late fourth century, St. Jerome could refer to "that land called *Boukolia,* where there is no Christian, but rather a very barbaric and savage people" (*Life of Hilarion* 43 = *PL* 23.52.).

Much more threatening and pervasive than any marshlands, however, were the great swaths of mountains that cut across the Mediterranean: the Atlas, the Pyrenees, and the Alps, the Apennines, the Taurus and Anti-Taurus, the Lebanon. The domineering topography of these lands, threatening enough to modern communications, formed an almost impenetrable "other world" when the Roman state was faced with the problem of taming and policing it. As good an example as any is the long-term autonomy that a whole mountain zone, that of the Taurus and Anti-Taurus in the southeastern quadrant of Asia Minor known as Isauria (part of the Roman province of Cilicia) was able to assert during the whole period of the Empire.

No amount of power exerted by the Romans ever succeeded in taming the independent "big men" of Isauria-Cilicia. Roman forces first became involved with the region between 100 and 50 B.C. because of the large-scale piracy that emanated from the coastal sites of the region. At the end of this initial phase of repression, however, we have Cicero's eyewitness reports from his governorship of Cilicia in 51–50 B.C. When he entered the region at the base of the Taurus mountains in 51, Cicero wrote to Caelius Rufus that he was now ignorant of events in the outside world because, as he put it, "I am in a region where news comes in slowly both because of its remoteness and because of banditry in the countryside" (*Ad familiares* 2.9.1). In the autumn of 51 Cicero led the Roman army into the Amanus mountains to repress widespread brigandage by the "Free Cilicians." The highlands were also serving as a refuge for fugitives from the lowlands. But Cicero's raids, though models of brutality, achieved little, and when he returned to the region in the summer of 50 B.C. he could only report "great banditry" (ibid., 2.9.1–2, 15.1.2–3, 15.4; Cicero *Ad Atticum* 5.20.5, 6.4.1). In order to assert any degree of control whatever over the highlands of Anatolia, the Romans had to come to agreements with the highland lords like Kleon of Gordium, Antipater of Derbe, and Tarkondimotus of the Amanus, all of whom, at different points in their careers, were either labeled as bandits or recognized as legitimate rulers and allies by the Roman state.

In periods of peace all the state could do to control brigandage in Isauria and elsewhere depended rather narrowly on its ability to provide adequate policing at the local levels of imperial society where bandits were most likely to be found. What policing there was, however, consisted of a combination of civil euergetism by local municipal men and the outright deployment of private enforcers, both of which systems operated only in rather tightly circumscribed areas around each city, for the most part located along the Mediterranean coast of Isauria or a little inland, up one of the few large river valleys. The amount of control the Roman state was able to exert over the montane regions therefore depended directly on the extent to which it was able to tame the "big men" of the mountains. In periods of breakdown of the central power of the Roman state, as throughout most of the third century, these bandit figures (such as Lydius—"the Lydian"—and Palfuerius under the emperor Probus in the late A.D. 270s) emerged as figures of considerable power in their own right. Controlling them demanded nothing less than the direct intervention of the Roman emperor and his armies (Zosimus *Historia nova* 1.69–70; *SHA, Probus* 16.4–6). The stories of large-scale bandit raids stemming from the mountains of Isauria retailed by the historian Ammianus Marcellinus for the whole period of the 350s through the 370s (such as the one reported at the beginning of this chapter) are only a reflection of the normal situation in this highland zone during the entire period in which it was part of the Roman empire.

Given the fact that there existed such "spaces" in the webbing of imperial power, the question must be asked: What sort of men entered these spaces, and why? There were, of course, many different types, but we shall select two prominent ones as characteristic examples: soldiers and shepherds.

Soldiers are an excellent example of how the question of the frontier separating the space of the state from bandit space was often a notional one, not fixed in a real geography. The problem here was simply one of the legitimacy of power. Soldiers were trained for a lifetime in the profession of violence and had in their hands the power of life and death. The question then was, quite simply: When were they exercising this power legitimately? The professional soldier was thus always a *potential* bandit. It was the sanction of the state that made the critical difference.

We may begin, therefore, with good examples of those soldiers who deliberately crossed that frontier of legitimacy, principally those who were veterans "gone bad" or outright deserters. The problem of lifelong professional killers who were then supposed to retire was a big one. As long as adequate retirement bonuses and opportunities were offered to veterans, most of them, we must presume, would have preferred to retire honestly. But the law codes, for example, envisage only restricted opportunities for them: either the cultivation of land or the investment of money in "honorable and honest" business enterprises. The same laws, however, note the existence of soldiers who preferred not to retire but who felt that they could make a good income by continuing to use their military skills, though now in pursuit of a career in robbery. The laws speak, with disgust, of soldiers who preferred to become bandits "because of sheer laziness" (*neglegentia vitae*). The truth is, of course, that when they came to retire (or were forced into an early retirement because of illness) they may not have had the skills or the desire to become peasant farmers or enough money to invest "in honorable businesses" (*CJ* 12.46.3; *CTh* 7.20.7). These factors, when combined with the normal harshness of army discipline, must have driven not a few soldiers into a life of brigandage.

A much greater problem in this same area, however, was that of the "enforced desertion" of huge numbers of soldiers from the cover of legality by the shifting boundaries of state power. This problem was most in evidence during extended periods of civil conflict within the state. At the end of such conflict one of the factions would seize and maintain legitimate power at the center. While the new government would, of course, try to legitimize as many units of the army of its opponents as possible, there would still be large numbers of erstwhile soldiers in the camp of the opposition who could not be absorbed so easily or who would refuse to change old loyalties. With the formation of a new central government in Rome these army units would find themselves cut off from legitimate sources of pay and supplies and so would be compelled into a life of banditry merely in order to survive. In a sense they would enter a self-fulfilling prophesy in which they would become the "bandits" which they and their leaders had already been labeled during the period of civil war. So, for example, Octavian successfully stigmatized the forces of Sextus Pompey in the civil wars between 42 and 36 B.C., many of whom were hunted down as "brigands" and "pirates" and ended their lives on crosses or as slaves, a fact that Augustus later celebrated in his *Res gestae* (25.1). It is no accident, therefore, that every period of civil strife or war in the Roman state threw up large numbers of bandits in its aftermath.

Hence the years after 49 B.C., after 44 B.C., and after 36 B.C. in the West, until Octavian finally asserted his authority over his opponents, Sextus Pompey and others, were marked by large-scale outbreaks of banditry:

> At this time Italy and Rome itself were openly infested with brigands whose actions were more like those of barefaced plunderers than those of common thieves. Sabinus was chosen by Octavian to bring the situation under control. He executed many of the bandits he captured and, within one year, established conditions of absolute law and order. At that time, according to tradition, the practice and system of night guards originated, which is still in force. Octavian elicited great astonishment by putting an end to this social evil with such unparalleled speed. (Appian 5.132)

The conditions, however, were neither as absolutely chaotic as Appian would have us believe, nor were they settled as quickly as his hagiographic statements would seem to suggest. What in fact was happening, as Augustus' biographer Suetonius (*Lives of the Caesars, Life of Augustus* 32) makes clear, is that power during this period was fragmenting in such a way that great landowners or "lords" were asserting their own rights to power and were surrounding themselves with retinues of armed men in order both to protect their interests and to take advantage of the chaotic conditions to increase their wealth (e.g., by using the armed retainers to enslave free men). The repression of banditry following any extensive period of civil war and the consequent disintegration of central state authority therefore required the reassertion of the state's authority over independent barons and their armed retainers as much as it did any hunting down of individual brigands. This is exactly what Augustus and Tiberius did by banning any such "gatherings" of armed men, by freeing all free persons who had been enslaved by them, and by establishing networks of guardposts (*stationes*) manned by units of the army to provide for security (Suetonius *Lives of the Caesars, Tiberius* 37.1). In addition to "the stick," however, there was also "the carrot." To quiet social violence in Italy in 33 B.C. Octavian offered a formal amnesty to all local barons for their *latrocinium*. Here too, however, the results were not always quick or even desired. The historian Dio Cassius remarks that the amnesty was taken by such men merely as a license to continue their brigandage (49.43.5).

Where the instances of soldiers and civil wars illustrate the case of men crossing a line into banditry and being situated in it because of the shifting frontiers of state authority, the case of shepherds better exemplifies a different and more systematic source of banditry in the existence of entire regions and peoples whose topographical location and economic life situated them on the borderline of a life of brigandage.

Shepherds, who were often slaves of landowners involved in large-scale transhumant ranching, lived in groups far removed from the towns and cities that represented centers of government control. In addition, for significant parts of the year, they were on the move with their herds and therefore beyond the immediate control of the landowner who was their nominal master. This de facto freedom of shepherds, when combined with their need to be strong men who were well enough armed to protect the herds of their master, produced a situation in which any one of them could rather easily escape the control of his master/owner (much more easily, for example, than could a peasant farmer). The autonomous shepherd could then use his indigenous skills both to assert his freedom and to prey on others for a livelihood. In fact that line was so easily crossed that slave-shepherds were the motive force behind some of the greatest slave rebellions attested in the whole of antiquity, shaking southern Italy and Sicily during the last four decades of the second century B.C. And it was crossed with such frequency that the identification of shepherd with *latro* became a very common one in Roman literature.

We know, for example, that in the fourth and fifth centuries A.D. the government was driven to extreme measures in its attempt to control the brigandage of shepherds in the southern regions of the Italian peninsula— in Lucania, Picenum, Samnium, Apulia, and Calabria. In doing so it struck at the main natural advantage shepherds possessed: their freedom of movement. All persons "except senators and high-ranking officials, administrators of provinces, veterans, decurions, and others performing imperial service under arms" were expressly denied the use of horses (*CTh* 9.30.1, 4). In recognition of the almost congenital disposition of the inhabitants of these mountain zones of Italy to brigandage, these same laws warned all persons from disposing of unwanted children by giving them to shepherds. The sure result, it was felt, was that they would be raised as the next generation of bandits (ibid., 9.31.1).

What could be done by the Roman state to confront this bandit threat, both the low-level local raids that affected towns and villages in the plains and the larger menace of the mountains? This question is obviously related to the much broader one of the ability (and the desire) of the Roman state to enforce its self-mandated monopoly of violence. At the highest level, the governors of the various provinces of the empire were seen as mandated to establish conditions of peace and order so that the tribute due to the government could be collected and the property interests of its ruling elites protected. The title of the *Digest* relating to the core duties of the provincial governor—"De officio praesidis"—makes this clear:

> It is the duty of a good and serious governor to see that the province he governs remains peaceful and quiet. This is not a difficult task if he scrupulously rids the province of evil men and assiduously hunts them down. Indeed, he must hunt down desecrators and pillagers of sacred property [*sacrilegi*], bandits [*latrones*], kidnappers [*plagiarii*], and common thieves [*fures*] and punish each one in accordance with his misdeeds. And he must use force against their collaborators [*receptores*], without whom the bandit [*latro*] is not able to remain hidden for long. (1.18.13)

This legal text was not simply a lofty ideal; it set the expectations of the actual practice of governors. Cicero wrote a letter to his brother Quintus in 60 B.C., when the latter was governor of Asia, congratulating him on a good governorship and specifying Quintus' maintenance of order in the countryside as an important part of that achievement. In the letter he makes specific reference to Quintus' repression of bandits in the region of Mysia in northwestern Asia Minor (*Ad Quintum fratrem* 1.1.25).

This practical side of governance may then be related to some of the more detailed provisions of the central government's expectations as outlined in the passage from the *Digest* quoted above. One of the main problems here was that different provincial governors faced different situations and had different resources at their command. The governor of an armed province such as Syria, Pannonia, or one of the Germanies had at his command considerable military force, whereas the governor of Pamphylia, say, Cappadocia, or Cilicia, with huge and rugged mountain masses to control, had few such forces at his disposal. Then again, the governor of Egypt might have available only one or two legions and some police forces, but the topography of the land powerfully aided him in the control of a largely fixed and highly concentrated population. Governors who did not have large military forces at their disposal, such as the governor of Asia, were forced to seek other means. A good case is provided by one Julius Senex, who is mentioned by Fronto in connection with Fronto's impending departure from Rome to govern the province of Asia (Fronto *Ad Antonium Pium* 8). The reason Fronto wished to acquire the services of Senex, an old friend from Mauretania, was to use his peculiar expertise as a "bandit hunter."

The story illustrates the fact that at the provincial level in the empire we find a rather sharp distinction between those regions or provinces in which large army garrisons were stationed and whose forces could be used by the governor in bandit-repression operations and those lightly armed provinces in which the governors had to seek "other means." The rather ironic result of this peculiar distribution of central state power was that many of the so-called dangerous frontier provinces, where army forces were ready to repel any "barbarian" threat, were probably better policed and able to control banditry than were many of the so-called peaceful "interior" provinces and regions of the empire, including, perhaps most ironically, Italy itself (Millar, 1986).

In the light-armed, interior provinces of the empire, therefore, the ability of the governor and local communities to deal with bandit raids depended directly on the strength of local policing. This too could vary greatly. In the confined, narrow, isotropic, and exposed habitat of the Nile Valley in Egypt, for instance, with its replication of myriad small face-to-face village communities, such policing as there was could be much more effective than, for example, in many mountain and hill towns in Italy. Between these two extremes, in the many small urban communities that were typical of the "core" of the empire—say, the towns and cities of Asia Minor—it is fair to state that policing was a thin line of defense in each town and city and its rural territory, a defense that at best provided for the maintenance of civic order in the towns themselves. The *phylakēs* and *paraphylakēs* (civil guards) and the eirenarchs (peace officers) formed a local gendarmerie in each town. But each municipal guard was organized and operated locally. There is no sign in these city police forces of any coordination by the provincial governor or of any systematic linkages between the police forces or between them and the army.

Towns in the western Roman empire were in much the same situation. They had *viatores* (road patrols) and *stationes* (guardposts), mainly in order to control excesses of town violence and rowdyism (Shaw, 1984, 16n34). There were also *nocturni* (night men) who, using municipal slaves as additional "muscle," patrolled the streets and the more violent neighborhoods of each town. But even here there was a need for much self-help. An incident of theft in Petronius' novel, the *Satyricon*, only merited a response when women in the marketplace raised cries of "*latrones, latrones.*" Similarly, a search for a stolen slave brought the *nocturnus* and his strongmen, but only on the insistent demand of the aggrieved party (*Satyricon* 15–17, 21–22). The bandits going on raids in Apuleius' novel specify local self-help, especially that offered by neighbors (*vicini*), as the most dangerous threat they normally faced on raids, and in fact the hue and cry raised by neighbors' loud shots and calls for action led to the loss of one of the brigands' bravest captains (*Metamorphoses* 4.10).

To judge by Cicero's advice to his brother Quintus at the time of the latter's governorship of Asia (in 60 B.C.), however, dependence on these local civic police was not the best course for the governor to follow. If the governor needed dependable and effective forces of repression, he had to have recourse to the services of vigilantes and semiprofessional killers (*diōgmitai*) already in the employ of the great landowners of the region. These "bandit hunters"—one example is Julius Senex of Mauretania—are reasonably well attested in our records. In the account of the martyrdom of Polycarp in Asia Minor about A.D. 150 we see a posse of *diōgmitai* led against local bandits by an eirenarch (Musurillo, *Acts of the Christian Martyrs*, 6–7). Or there is the specific case of one Aurelius Eirenaios ("Man of Peace") from Ceretapa in Lycia, who bragged in his epitaph of "having killed many bandits" and who was surely just such a killer (*IGRR* 4.886).

The simple point that must be emphasized here is that, despite its appearance as a state of unprecedented size, the Roman empire lacked any centrally organized police force to serve as the civic counterpart of its military rule. To control large-scale outbreaks of brigandage the state was thus dependent either on local self-help or on the use of the army. When they could not have recourse to the army to deal with serious bandit threats, however, governors of unarmed provinces seem to have been largely at the mercy of whatever local support they could muster from municipalities or powerful individuals. Both the general law codes and the more specific charters issued on the foundation of Roman cities (colonies and municipalities) contain terms that made it the responsibility of these towns to hunt down bandits in their territories and to hand them over to the provincial governor (e.g., CJ 8.40.13, A.D. 238–40, and the terms of the Lex Coloniae Genetivae Iuliae 103). A typical example of such behavior is embedded in a letter sent by the emperor Commodus to the inhabitants of Bubon, in northwestern Lycia, in A.D. 190. In it he thanked them for having hunted down local bandits, an operation in which some of the brigands were taken prisoner and others were killed. But not only such corporate entities as legally constituted towns were accorded such rights. Another measure of both the extremity of the danger and the weakness of the Empire's instruments for dealing with it is the extent to which the state was willing to contemplate transferring powers of violence to isolated individuals in order to deal with bandits. The jurists stressed that it was the duty of the individual to pursue bandits and to betray their activities to local authorities and that, in the performance of this civic obligation, such individuals were to be exempt from the normal laws governing personal assault (iniuria) and homicide (Digest 9.2.7; CJ 3.27.1–2, 9.16.13). Thus, although the Roman state did make normative claims to a monopoly of violence, it was willing, indeed compelled, to have recourse to this extreme concession of individual force, which was justified under the rubric of "public vengeance," necessary to maintain "the common peace."

A second big problem concerning the genesis of banditry was inherent in the very nature of the structure of a large unitary state such as the Roman empire. If the state mandated to itself total legitimate power and then subdivided and allotted this power to various governors who ruled areas in which their command was valid, the state at the same time had to forbid clashes between these subordinate powers and also the possible threats they might present to the center. By definition, therefore, governors could not usually move armed forces under their authority beyond the boundaries of their province; to do so was part of the very definition of "treason." Groups of armed men could therefore hope to survive, even flourish, in the "no-man's-land" of these frontier regions where the jurisdictional force of the governors was in doubt (and which, in any event, were often also areas of rough terrain).

To overcome this structural difficulty defined by its own existence, the Roman state responded, as many other large states have done subsequently, by the creation by the central government of special "bandit commands." The very frequency of these special army officers, known as *praefecti adversus latrones* or *arcendibus latronibus* (officers against, or for fending off, bandits), is one of our better indices of the ubiquity of brigandage in the empire (Shaw, 1984, 12n3). To these were added other special commands, such as that exercised by an imperial official who, "having received the procuratorship of Lower Moesia at an increased salary, and at the same time put in the command of troops drawn from the legions, was sent by the emperor to dislodge the gang of Brisean bandits on the borders of Macedonia and Thrace." This special army command illustrates both the type of extraordinary powers needed to deal with bandits and the precise fact of the interstitial location of brigands on the borders between one imperial jurisdiction and the next—a purposeful location that made their eradication so difficult.

This rather extraordinary treatment of bandits in the law raises the question of the way the state conceived their relation to common criminals. The latter were regarded as free persons and citizens (of either the imperial state or some local community in the empire) who, having committed some felony, were subject to the force of legal punishments meted out by the state. Bandits were clearly regarded quite differently. They were interstitial characters, seen neither as persons with rights in civil law nor as enemies of the state but somewhere in between. This much is clear in the Roman laws that governed the legal status of Roman citizens who became prisoners of war. If they lost their citizenship by becoming the prisoners of some enemy of the Roman state, they needed to undergo a ritualistic "reentry" into the civic world that would reactivate their citizenship, a legal act known as *postliminium*. The laws explicitly state, however, that capture by bandits did not require *postliminium*— bandits were not enemies of the state. But neither were they simple criminals. That much is made clear in the laws governing their treatment and punishment. Brigands were not to be accorded any of the protections or procedures normally accorded to criminal defendants. Torture and extreme forms of interrogation were permitted to the arresting officers, even before captured bandits were sent to the governor for sentencing. The types of crimes that bandits were believed to commit habitually (e.g., kidnapping, cattle rustling, robbery with violence) were thought to make them automatically deserving of the worst type of death penalties (the *summa supplicia*) that the Roman state could inflict: throwing to wild beasts, burning alive, and crucifixion.

The types of punishments to which bandits were subjected were admitted to be nothing less than a form of state retribution and public terrorism. Bandits who were well known in any given locale were to be executed and their bodies impaled on stakes at the spot where they had committed most of their crimes, so that the mere sight of their rotting corpses might deter others from committing similar acts. Men like the Sicilian bandit Selouros "the son of Aetna" (Etna) were purposefully sacrificed before the public as entertainment in the gladiatorial arenas of the empire (Strabo 6.2.6). Then again, there is the case of the brigand who was made to play the role of the fictional bandit Laureolus in a drama called "The Crucified Bandit" and who was murdered on stage in a variation on public entertainment as moral lesson (Suetonius *Lives of the Caesars, Caligula* 57; see Juvenal *Satires* 8.187–88; Josephus *Antiquitate iudicae* 19.94).

As with other recalcitrant persons who so rejected the norms of Roman society as to be deserving of a total outlawry (e.g., Christians), bandits were thrown to wild beasts in the great public arenas of the empire in a form of public morality that marked them as men apart. It was, as is recorded in the selection from Ammianus with which this chapter began, the special shame to which the Isaurians objected by launching a veritable war on the Roman colony of Iconium to avenge the dishonor heaped on their brothers. The whole combination of ways in which the Roman state responded to bandits in its attempts to detect them, hunt them down, and punish them placed brigands in a category different from enemies of the state, on the one hand, and common criminals, on the other.

These same laws, however, also reveal something to us of the world of the bandits themselves, for in the assumptions about how brigands were to be caught and punished there are revealed elements of the world in which bandits were presumed to live. Roman jurists assumed that bandits could not operate without a broader network of supporters and that the governor could not hope to apprehend them without first striking at this base of helpers "without whom the bandit cannot long remain hidden" (*Digest* 48.13.4.2). Implicit in the terms of all these laws is the great assumption of the principal means by which officials of the state are ultimately to apprehend brigands: by betrayal. This betrayal could be enticed or enforced.

The local support on which the bandit depended for survival was seen as divided into two basic types: the kinship links in which the bandit was enmeshed and, outside this, the broader community in which he lived. Certain laws even held that blood relations were to be treated more leniently, since it was expected that they would be compelled "by nature" to support bandits who were their relatives (*Digest* 47.16.2). In attacking these local connections, however, Roman military commanders were cautioned against the use of excessive force, which might only succeed in alienating the very people the government had to win over in order to remove the foundation of the bandits' operations (*CJ* 9.39.2.3 = *CTh* 9.29.2.3). If the bandit could be isolated within his home region or, better, compelled to move out of it, the chances of the government combining its objectives with those of a local populace hostile to the bandit were considerably increased. The physician Galen, writing in the late second century, reports just such a case: "On another occasion we saw the skeleton of a bandit lying on a rising ground by the roadside. He had been killed by some traveler who had resisted the brigand's attack. None of the local inhabitants would bury him but in their hatred of the bandit were glad enough to see his body consumed by the birds, which in a few days ate his flesh, leaving the skeleton as if for medical demonstration" (*On Anatomical Procedures* 1.2).

Roman laws further assume that the bandit, in order to survive for any length of time at all, had to establish certain types of contact with normal society. One of these contacts to which frequent reference is made in the laws is the *receptator,* or "receiver," who was the critical link needed by the bandit to assist in the disposal of stolen goods and the provision of supplies or money and, doubtless, to serve as a source of information. The laws stress that these men must be hunted down with special zeal because "*receptatores* are the very worst sort of men, since without them no man would be able to remain hidden very long. Hence receivers are to be punished exactly as the bandits themselves. In addition, all those persons who were in a position to capture bandits but who let them escape, having received money or part of the loot, are to be treated as if they were receivers" (*Digest* 47.16.1). But there is a more sinister side to the presence of "local contacts" that helps explain not only the very deeply rooted nature of brigandage but also the ability of some bandits to survive over long periods of time despite the force brought to bear on them by the central state and local municipalities. This aspect emerges rather unconsciously in laws, such as one on the punishment of cattle rustlers, that specify punishment not just for ordinary persons but even for those of high social rank (e.g., *Digest* 47.14.3.3).

Little revelations like that open up a whole other side of banditry—the systematic ties that bandits who operated successfully over long periods of time developed with powerful men such as great landowners and local persons of wealth. If a figure as highly vulnerable as a brigand who operated well within spaces dominated by Roman towns and cities was to survive for any length of time, there is every indication that he needed to be co-opted by local men in power. Laws repeatedly refer to bandits who operated under the covert (or even overt) support of landlords and powerful municipal grandees; they express concern that the state must try to have some force of its own precisely in order "to abolish the protection of the powerful over armed criminals and bandits" (*CTh* 1.29.8). Other laws consistently assume the complicity of *honestiores* or persons of high social status in operations with bandits. Laws, especially those from the later empire, constantly threaten landlords or their agents with punishments for harboring bandits on their lands or offering protection to "violent men" (*CTh* 9.29.1–2; *CJ* 9.39.2, among many others).

In fact, there is a consistent line of evidence extending from the behavior of landlords in the great slave rebellions of the late second century B.C. (in which shepherd-bandits were widely involved) to the fourth and fifth centuries A.D. that attests the consistent patronal linkage between Roman *domini* and brigands. The landlords offered their "protection" to the bandits, and, in return, the bandits offered their services as private armed retainers. But the involvement of local elites with bandits was not just a one-way thing; it was also a reciprocal and active participation. The wealthy and violent town rowdy in Apuleius' novel, the young and "noble" Thrasyllus, who had permanent links with local brigands and who occasionally went on raids with them (*Metamorphoses* 8.2), is surely not just an atypical creation in the writer's imagination.

That peculiar linkage is explained in part by hard economic reality, for bandits, like all persons, had to produce in order to survive. They represented one of the most primitive types of accumulation—what Aristotle dubbed the "bandit mode of production." Bandits lived parasitically, no less than rulers, by taking from others. The taking ran the gamut from small raids and major assaults, seizing whatever booty happened to be available at the moment, to more long-term, institutionalized demands formalized as a "tribute" taken from locals and wayfarers, mostly in return for "protection" (Strabo 16.1.27; Ammianus Marcellinus 28.2.11–

14). Robbery included the seizure of animals and humans. Kidnapping for ransom, being rather spectacular, was a favorite of novelists and affected everyone from small landowners to a Julius Caesar.

But the human body could also be treated as just another commodity for resale on the slave markets of the Mediterranean. Either as violent enforcers or as dealers in human flesh, bandits could find employment on as large a scale as the markets would support or demand. The kidnapping operations that were the staple of profits for small gangs produced, among other types of human booty, slave girls who were cast into the sordid brothels of the large cities (Apuleius *Metamorphoses* 7.10). At the other end of the scale, the Mediterranean pirates of the first half of the first century B.C. became an integral part of the massive slaving operations that provided hundreds of thousands of bodies for Italian markets. Repression of banditry therefore involved contradictory demands that were not as easily resolved at every level of government as was Pompey's "unbounded command" (*imperium infinitum*) of 67/66 B.C. that led to the final control of Mediterranean piracy. The special combination of conditions—the political conjuncture if you will—that led the political elite at Rome to concede unusual powers to one man to meet brigand and pirate threats, however, was rare. Most often, local officials of the Roman state had to cope with whatever "local arrangements" were made to "deal with" bandits.

None of this description in our source materials, however detailed it might be concerning perceptions of bandits, categorizations of their actions, and the types of measures taken to control them, tells us very much about the men and women who were brigands. They were people who, by choice or compulsion, entered into or lived in a space that was marginalized and outcast by the state and civil society. Bandit societies, whether composed of a few individuals or a large gang (or indeed a whole people or community), tended to be characterized by an absence of all "higher" civil modes of communication in writing or graphic symbols. There does not remain a single written word (of which I am aware) left to us by a bandit. We have less evidence regarding the problem than we have concerning many other marginal social groups in the Roman world, since at least *some* women, peasants, slaves, and freedmen (to name but a few) have left us *some* record of themselves. All we are left with, then, are other persons' *perceptions* of bandits, and these range from the arid philosophical asides of a Cicero or a Seneca to the hard legal definitions of the jurists and to metaphorical usages by poets, politicians, and moralists. The most extensive external views of bandits that we have, however, are "mythical" bandit tales—either the vignettes embedded in larger narratives retailed by historians or the longer and more elaborate stories embedded in Greco-Roman novels.

The strict historical veracity of bandit life in these tales is rather difficult to interpret. It can be said that the novels and their stories function on at least two distinct levels. Their writers were highly educated literati from the cultural elite of the Greco-Roman world. Apuleius, a North African from the colony of Madauros, composed his *Metamorphoses* (probably in the A.D. 160s or 170s) partly as a result of his philosophical concerns with "conversion" and magic. Much less is known of Heliodorus and Achilles Tatius, the other major novelists whose works include major bandit episodes. The former novelist, from Emesa, in Syria, was probably writing in the 230s, and he appears to be well acquainted with a wide range of the Hellenistic literary tradition. Achilles Tatius, a Greek from Alexandria writing perhaps toward the end of the third century, also reveals a strong background in classical rhetoric and legal knowledge. In addition to providing enjoyment, these novels were also meant to instruct, though in subtle and indirect ways, by reminding the reader and listener of the clash between popular and elite values and mores.

Of course, "reality" was perceived in these novels only through a strong literate and upperclass filter—a lens that powerfully refracted a "reality" that, as a result, could only be perceived as a distortion. The low and the servile demanded a systematic humorization and caricaturization as well as a great distancing from the real present to mythical "fairyland" settings. On the other hand, these novelists seem to have had access to oral traditions (or, perhaps, oral traditions that had been recorded in writing) of popular derivation that contained certain "truths" about bandit behavior and the realities of bandit life. But even so, there is a range of "reality." Heliodorus in his *Aithiopika* and Achilles Tatius in his *Leukippe and Kleitophon* represent heavily fantasized versions of bandit life closely tied to Greco-Alexandrian literary conventions. Apuleius in his *Metamorphoses,* on the other hand, though still harking back to earlier Greek models (including Lucian's *The Ass*) was also heir to a more realistic Latin tradition stemming from native Italian farce, satire, and parody (as reflected, for example, in Petronius' *Satyricon*).

Therefore, without having to make elaborate arguments about the types of reality in Apuleius or about possible "real-life" influences on his composition, we can say that Apuleius represents the source that is linked most closely to the objective realities of bandit life and organization.

Although the novel may have functioned in terms of offering entertaining reading or listening, and therefore may have had embedded in it themes derived from popular and oral culture, we cannot forget its second level of function, which was to reflect upon upper-class ideals and to implicate the listener in its categories. The novel was therefore a form of ideology. In addition to being a studied distortion of the realities of banditry, the bandit tales in the novels of Apuleius and his like also served, by the conscious use of parody and similar literary devices, to highlight inversions of the proper social order—of true (i.e., state) justice and power—in order, by inference, to stabilize the existing order of things.

In interpreting these novels and their bandit tales, we are therefore presented with a calculated mixture of "reality" and interpretation. Take, for example, the sudden appearance of bandits on a raid. The movement of a bandit gang to attack and return back to its home base after the raid is invariably portrayed as taking place in the dark of night. The raid staged by bandits on the wealthy home of Demochares in Apuleius' novel, for example, is planned to take place on a dark and moonless night precisely because it is the time when all civilized people are sunk deep in sleep: "that time of night which is best for bandits" (*Metamorphoses* 4.18; see also 4.9). The attack in which Lucius, the narrator of the novel, by now metamorphosed into an ass, is captured by bandits takes place at night, when the brigands burst into the household complex with torches and flashing swords (3.27–28). Over the next days the brigands' trek back to their hideout with their booty is carefully planned to take place at night (4.4). When a terrifying crashing of the bolted and barred door rudely awakens the sleeping Aristomenes in the dead of night, his first thought is that the break-in is a bandit raid (1.11).

Given other contextual evidence from the Roman world and comparative modern evidence, there is no reason to doubt that many bandit attacks, especially on villages and isolated farmsteads, would indeed be carried out under the cover of night. But because of the strong overlapping identification of night with blackness and death, the interpretation of bandits as signifying much more than just a party of raiders overshadows the simple meaning of them as mere criminal types.

Bandits were strongly identified with ghosts and the dead. They therefore assumed a particularly fearsome aspect. It is no accident that the most apocalyptic event for Christians, "the Day of the Lord," was to come "like a thief in the night" (1 Thessalonians 5:2–4—with strong play on the "darkness" of night; 1 Peter 4:15; Revelations 3.3, 16.15, among other texts). Or take the opening scene of Heliodorus' novel, the

Aithiopika, where we find a beautiful girl, the sole survivor of the carnage of a bandit raid somewhere on the Mediterranean shores of the Nile Delta. She looks up and sees more armed men descending on her. She is immediately struck by their "strange color" and "banditlike appearance." But as they advance toward her she is confused—perhaps they are ghosts of the dead lying all around her come back to life? "If you are living beings," she says, "then your life must be one of banditry" (*Aithiopika* 1.3.1). But the confusion remained, and not a few bandits were firmly believed to exploit the common fear, deliberately disguising themselves as ghosts in order to add to the terror of their sudden nightly incursions.

The novels present us with hybrid views that must be interpreted as capable of imparting divergent meanings. We might begin with the simple question of who became a bandit. In the novels there appears the theme of persons being compelled to enter banditry because of rejection or persecution that they have suffered in civil society. A good example is provided by the brigand chief Thyamus in Heliodorus' *Aithiopika.* He is portrayed as being "not completely barbaric," and even "a little civilized," because he belonged to a family of good background. He had only become a bandit because he had been forced into the outlaw life. As Thyamus himself tells the story: "As you know, I was the son of a priest of Memphis. When my father decided to resign his post, I was prevented from achieving his priestly office by my younger brother, a real troublemaker. It was then that I became a fugitive in the hope of avenging myself" (*Aithiopika* 1.19.4).

The dual themes of compulsion through want and desire for personal vengeance are repeated in other sources. Another perspective is given by a member of the bandit gang in Apuleius' novel, who suggests a recruiting drive to enlist new "fellow soldiers" for the gang. The man envisages two possible sources of new manpower. First, from the more general populace there are those who could be enrolled either by use of threats or by the more attractive device of rewards; or there are the poor who are seen to provide a more natural reservoir of bandits. As the man puts it, when the poor see the profits to be made from brigandage they will be more than content to leave behind their low and servile status and to assume the new position of being able to "wield tyrannical power" as part of a gang. The man then presents for inspection a new recruit whom he himself just acquired for the band, a man of noble bearing, young, and strong. The new arrival in the bandits' camp then offers them an oral version of his career as an outlaw, after which the existing members of the band inspect the new recruit and unanimously elect him as their new chief (Apuleius *Metamorphoses* 7.4–5). Even through its parody of Roman army recruiting, the scene presents a plausible interpretation of likely candidates for brigandage: those compelled into it, those drawn by its rewards, those forced to it by poverty, and those who were already living a life of banditry.

For poverty as a great motivator, we also have the testimony of the rabbinical sources: "Every man is obliged to teach his son a trade, and whoever does not teach him a trade teaches him to become a bandit" (MacMullen, *Roman Social Relations,* 97/ *Midrash,* Tract. b. Kidd 29a). So too, one of Apuleius' brigands patiently explains to one of their kidnap victims, "You see, it was poverty that forced us to take up this profession" (*Metamorphoses* 4.23). At the other end of the spectrum we find the hereditary life-style of those persons who were part of the bandit regions and peoples in the empire. This aspect is sufficiently stressed by the model *curriculum vitae* of the bandit Haemus the Thracian, quoted at the beginning of this chapter. Work experience, background, and achievements are stressed in his job résumé, exactly as they might be for any "normal" employment. But he also stresses an inherited tradition: he was born and raised in a life of banditry; his father was a well-known brigand.

Once outside recruits were accepted by existing bandits, they entered an alter world. This social mirror was seen, as St. Augustine observed, as a smaller parody of civil society. The actual size of bandit gangs is rarely specified, but it is assumed that they were relatively small, self-contained worlds. The two gangs of bandits actually on raiding expeditions described in Heliodorus are rather small, the one containing ten members and the other about thirty (*Aithiopika* 1.3). The raiding parties sent out from the cave described by Apuleius are similarly small, no more than a dozen or so in size. These small gangs sent out on plundering expeditions, however, were sometimes only small segments of a larger society, namely the entire bandit community from which they came. The most detailed description of one of these communities, found in Heliodorus, relates to the brigand country called Boukolia by the Egyptians. This "cattle country" was located on the other side of a mountain ridge, where the waters of the Nile formed a deep lake with extensive swamps all around its periphery. Here the Egyptians "of the bandit type" had their home, indeed their own political community, replete with homes, wives, and children. Each of the *boukoloi* regarded this land as his own city (*patria*). This remote country, isolated by the "wall" of the water channels that surrounded it, was also a refuge to which other persons fled from civil society precisely in order to take up "a life of this sort" (ibid., 1.5.1, 1.6.1.). Apuleius, on the other hand, offers a description that fits the other typical bandit land, the highland retreat: a cavernous home deep in the mountains with a lookout point built on top of a mountain and a mountain spring carefully channeled so as to feed sheepfolds in the valley below (*Metamorphoses*, 4.6).

The sort of society into which the prospective bandit entered and in which many already lived is presented by the novelists as a covert critique of the grotesque inequalities of regular society. At the same time, however, it is also a genuine reflection of actual practices in a world dominated by a rather pure form of personal power. In the former sense, bandit society is played upon as an inversion of regular society—as a society in which the emphasis is placed on the egalitarian participation of its members, all of whom are perceived to be equal and deserving of equal rewards and treatment. Although not actually "democratic," bandit society was seen as strongly egalitarian. So, for example, in decisions as to which man should labor or serve the others, the democratic device of selection by lot was employed (ibid., 4.8). This egalitarian distribution of power emerges not just in the assignment of equal tasks in the transport and division of booty but also in the whole attitude of bandits toward each other as "fellow soldiers" (*commilitones*) and "brothers" (*fratres*). All these ideals are expressed rather well in a speech delivered by the brigand chief Thyamus to his men:

> You judged me to be personally worthy of being your leader.
> Indeed, until this very day, since I came here I have never
> allotted myself a larger portion of booty than to any of you.
> Whenever we had money to divide, an equal division was
> always my greatest concern. Whenever there were captives to
> be sold, I always put the receipts into our common treasury.
> In fact, in my opinion a leader ought to shoulder most of the
> work load but only take an equal share of the profits. As for
> the prisoners we have taken, I have enlisted only those whose
> physical strength would be useful to us and have sold the
> weak and the feeble. I have never insulted or outraged a
> woman. Those who are of good birth I have set free for a
> ransom or simply out of compassion for their misfortune.
> Lower-class women, for whom slavery is less a consequence
> of their captivity than a necessity of their social condition, I
> have distributed equally to each of you to be your servants.
> (Heliodorus *Aithiopika* 1. 19. 4–6)

Thyamus goes on to stress (in a manner reminiscent of Agamemnon in the *Iliad*) that he could simply have seized the girl in question as part of his booty but that he wished to have the common consent of the gang to receive her as a free gift from his friends (*philoi*).

Bandit society was therefore one that put a premium on assertion of individual power and character. People in "normal society" were therefore most impressed by precisely this element of style that characterized bandit behavior. In gesture, dress, speech, and posture bandits were marked as a different breed of men. To outsiders, as in the novelists' accounts, this aspect of banditry was at once alluring and threatening. The outlaw lifestyle was also seen to be one of calculated insolence. Plutarch's greatest indignation about the pirates was reserved not for their armed assaults (which were no worse than those of any enemy) but for their insulting behavior, for by those actions alone they publicly refuted any claims to a universal morality:

> Their greatest act of insolence was this. Whenever a prisoner would shout at them that he was a Roman citizen and give his name, they would recoil in feigned fear as if they were frightened out of their wits. They would strike their sides and fall to the ground in front of the man, begging his forgiveness. The Roman would be convinced by this fake sincerity, seeing them before him acting like suppliants. Then some of them would put shoes back on his feet, while others would throw a toga over his shoulders in order, they said, so that they would not mistake his identity again. Then, after having made fun of the man for some time and having gotten their kicks out of him, they would suddenly let a rope down over the side of the ship in the middle of the sea and bid the man "farewell" and "happy journey." (Plutarch *Life of Pompey* 24.6.7–8)

Much more than this physically insulting behavior, however, it was the fact that the pirates wore flashy clothes, flaunted their fancy weaponry, and actually enjoyed themselves that was the final straw for Plutarch: "Much more annoying than the fear they created was the disgusting extravagance of their equipment: their gilded sails, purple shades, and customized silver-chased oars. But what was most irksome was the clear impression that they reveled in their evildoing and strutted about in open enjoyment of their occupation. . . . Their flutes, guitars, and drinking bouts resounded on every shore" (ibid., 24.3–4, 7).

331

Bandit society was perceived to be egalitarian precisely because it was so institutionless, so devoid of the instruments of government and formal law. Instead, it reposed on the equal consent of all and on the counterbalanced forces of the collective willpower, physical strength, and authority of each member of the gang. One the one hand, the personal friendship and camaraderie that linked the members together was seen as an operative ideal; on the other, the more sinister side of this arrangement was precisely that bandit society had to depend on these linkages alone to hold it together, and these constantly threatened to unravel under external pressures. As Heliodorus remarks, "It is the moral among bandits to place higher honor on booty, and terms such as *philia* (friendship) and *syngeneia* (brotherhood) have meaning for them only in relation to profit" (*Aithiopika* 1.32.4). That sentiment is reinforced by Apuleius, who asserted: "My view is that intelligent bandits put profit before any other consideration whatsoever, even vengeance" (*Metamorphoses* 7.9).

Bandits are portrayed as involved in a constant struggle against these forces of disorder in their own society. Their main weapon against this ever-imminent chaos was to place extraordinary emphasis on personal loyalty to the "fellow soldiers" in their gang. They never abandoned wounded comrades: they either rescued them or killed them. Even when they were caught in a trap, they never surrendered. In his *Metamorphoses* Apuleius provides us with a model case. A boy bandit disguised in a bear suit was trapped in a raid that went terribly awry. Although repeatedly stabbed by his attackers and savagely mauled by dogs, the boy never once gave up his role as a "bear" and never once betrayed his comrades. He died the death of a hero (*Metamorphoses* 4.21). The bandits were also united in close ties of ritualized personal friendships sealed with ritualistic kisses, oaths, and exchanges of the "right hand," and they were bound together by their worship of their version of the god Mars, whom the novelist knowingly labels as "the patron deity of bandits and gladiators" (4.22, 7.5).

Overshadowing all of this, however, in a system based purely on personal power, was the ever-present threat of betrayal. It is no accident that this theme merges with the assumption of the law that betrayal was a normal means by which bandits were caught. When the bandits in Heliodorus' novel were suddenly attacked in their marshland stronghold, their leader Thyamus looked around for his lieutenant and found him missing. His immediate assumption was that the man had betrayed him and was leading the attack (*Aithiopika* 1.30.1). And when Lucius, in his changed form as an ass, is driven on by the bandits, he prays that he will not metamorphose back into a man, as he knows that in that case the bandits will suspect betrayal and will kill him immediately (Apuleius *Metamorphoses* 3.19).

Finally, in both the novels and in more "factual" sources, bandits not only were identified with the dark "other side" of existing order and with ghosts and spirits of the night but also were seen as having their own forms of religion and worship, whether it be the bandit version of Mars worshiped by the brigands in Apuleius' *Metamorphoses* or the more sinister bloodletting rituals and human sacrifice imputed to the *boukoloi* by Achilles Tatius and Heliodorus. *Latrones* were seen as purposefully inverting and defiling normal religious practices. As Plutarch says of the pirates, "They raided and violated places of refuge and holy sanctuaries. . . . They offered strange sacrifices at Olympia and celebrated secret rites" (Plutarch *Life of Pompey* 24.5). In later antiquity, in a Manichaean convergence, bandits became identified with demons and demonic forces, entering into fearsome metamorphoses that took the extraordinary powers of a man as holy as St. Konon of Isauria or the spiritual powers emanating from the sanctuary of St. Thekla, also in Isauria, to contain them. Although he used divine powers to subdue the bandit/demons, St. Konon otherwise behaved just like Pompey the Great in subduing the pirates of a much earlier age: he taught them agriculture and gave them fixed abodes.

Similarly, St. Martin of Tours is reported to have lost his way in a journey through the Alps, where he was attacked and captured by bandits. The chief bandit thought that Martin would be in terror of losing his own life, but Martin remained supremely confident in his faith and trust with his Lord, preached the Word of God, and, as the hagiographer Sulpicius Severus puts it (*Life of Martin* 5), "Why make a long story of it? The brigand became a believer, escorted Martin back, and put him on the right road, asking him to pray to Our Lord for him." The lives of such saints and their great deeds, however, also strike direct links with the popular literature of the earlier empire in playing on the themes of the supposed connections between bandits, death, and ghostly apparitions. So in his *Life of Martin* (11) Sulpicius Severus recounts the story of one of his hero's miracles. In the rural lands outside Tours there was a "holy place" supposedly connected with a local Christian martyr. It was a place of profound local "superstition" and widely reputed in "popular opinion." Martin, however, had his doubts about the legitimacy of the cult. The text continues:

> Then one day he took with him a few of his brothers in Christ
> and went to the place. Standing on the grave itself, he prayed
> to Our Lord to make it known who was buried there and
> what his character had been. Then, turning to the left, he saw
> a ghost standing close by, foul and grim. He ordered him to
> give his name and status. He gave his name and confessed to
> a guilty past. He had been a bandit and had been executed for
> his crimes. But he had become an object of devotion through
> a mistake of the common people. In reality he had nothing in
> common with the martyrs. Glory was their portion, punish-
> ment was his.

Martin ordered the altar to be removed and thus "rid the common people
of the region of a false and superstitious belief."

At the opposite end of the spectrum of "integration" with local people and their beliefs, bandits in the "pagan" novels are also portrayed
as having systematic linkages and contacts with "normal" society. In
Heliodorus there is the story of the fisherman who was able to say when
the local pirates were going to attack. When asked how he came by this
knowledge, he retorts, "Look, my job regularly puts me in contact with
these men. I supply them with fish. In fact, I get more money from them
for my products than I get by selling to normal customers." He goes on
to say that he also provides the pirate with information about the coming
and going of local shipping (*Aithiopika* 5.20.4–7). Similarly, the bandits
in Apuleius' novel, after having traversed a lot of countryside and rough
lands following one of their raids, finally arrive at a small rural village
where there are some old men who are "known" and "familiar" to them.
The two groups greet one another with ritualistic kisses and embraces
and the old men share vital information with the brigands and offer them
lodging. In return the bandits share some of their loot with the villagers
(*Metamorphoses* 4.1). These observations reinforce the assumptions of the
Roman law codes about the critical normal linkages between bandits and
their kin and other intermediaries such as "receivers."

The bandit tales in the novels, however, clearly have a significance
quite apart from the plausible details they give about brigand life. They
also offer a consistent commentary on the nature of power and on the
contrast between the opposites of justice and legitimacy in the exercise
of power. Thus a brigand chief like Heliodorus' Thyamus is referred to
as being "kinglike" in bearing and yet just, fair, and equal in his treatment

of other members of his gang. In a way, therefore, the bandit tales offer a model of a just society where the just king is a model of fairness, not much more than a *primus inter pares* in a democracy of power. It is hardly surprising, then, that miniature models of these bandit tales also appear embedded in the more formal narratives produced by historians. The historians could use historical episodes of banditry to illustrate, in a symbolic way, the confrontation between legitimate and illegitimate modes of power.

Take, for example, the case of the usurper emperor Septimius Severus, who seized the throne of Rome in a coup d'état in A.D. 193. To validate his claims to power he vaunted himself as "an enemy to bandits everywhere" (*SHA, Septimius Severus* 18.6). When he was not yet emperor but governor of Syria, however, there occurred an event that portended his later ascent to imperial power: "A certain bandit named Claudius who was overrunning Judaea and Syria and was being vigorously pursued by the governor came to Severus one day disguised as a military tribune accompanied by a cavalry escort. He saluted and kissed Severus. But the trick was not found out then, nor was Claudius ever caught later" (Dio Cassius 75.2.4). Scenes such as these could be employed by historians not only to signal the dubious nature of contacts but also to mark their normalization. Thus the same historian Dio Cassius reports that in the reign of Augustus "there was a bandit named Caracotta who flourished in Spain and with whom Augustus was at first so enraged that he offered a million sesterces to the man who would capture him alive. But later, when the bandit came over to Augustus of his own accord, the emperor not only did him no harm but actually made him richer by the amount of the reward" (Dio Cassius 56.43.3). That is, rather than a state of hostility being maintained, the relationship was simply inverted with the erstwhile bandit being granted a status like that of a Roman senator by the emperor, who gave the brigand the minimum census qualification required for the superior social rank.

More startling material in this regard is offered to us by the bandit tales embedded in the histories of Herodian and Dio Cassius who relate, respectively, the stories of the bandits Julius Maternus and Bulla Felix. Julius Maternus began as a career soldier serving in the Roman army in Gaul in the middle to late decades of the second century A.D. Some time in the early 180s he deserted. The successes of his early bandit raids attracted large numbers of men to flock to his gang (Herodian 1.10). Maternus was then able to recruit even larger numbers of men by promising them "an equal share" of the loot. His raids ranged far and wide over the Gallic provinces. In a typical action he would throw open the local prisons, releasing the convicts, "regardless of their guilt," remarks the censorious Herodian. The "madness" began to afflict all Gaul and then Spain.

The story, however, is concerned not so much with the simple account of Maternus' brigand activities as with the response of the Roman emperor, Commodus. Herodian reports that on being informed of Maternus' successes Commodus flew into an uncontrollable rage and sent threatening letters to his provincial governors demanding that they do something. The three governors concerned were none other than the same men who would later contest the imperial throne following Commodus' assassination: Pescennius Niger, Clodius Albinus, and Septimius Severus. That the essential point of the historian's insertion of the bandit tale at this point in his account is precisely this contrast between types of legitimate and illegitimate power is emphasized by the fact that it is just at this juncture in the story that the historian has Julius Maternus and his men suddenly leave their home base in Gaul and make a strike for the heart of the empire to enter the city of Rome itself. Maternus, Herodian says, planned to put himself on the throne of the empire. At the last moment, however, in a leitmotif typical of bandit tales, Maternus was betrayed by his own men because, says Herodian, "they preferred a legitimate emperor to a robber tyrant." Maternus and all his followers were arrested and executed. The true emperor was safe, for the moment; but the precarious nature of his rule had been unmasked, and the not-so-covert suggestion had been made that the emperor was not much better than a robber tyrant.

It is no accident of historiography that Dio Cassius, in his account of Commodus' successor on the throne, Septimius Severus, also uses a bandit tale to much the same effect. Septimius Severus managed to seize the throne in A.D. 193 after a prolonged and bitter internecine struggle that wracked the Roman state. His assumption to power was both dubious and in need of validation. The bandit Septimius Severus had to confront bore the name Bulla Felix ("The Lucky"). Bulla, we are told, eventually headed a gang of over six hundred men, and he plundered Italy for a period of more than two years under the very nose of the new emperor, who had then ruled for barely a decade (c. A.D. 205). Although harassed by many soldiers sent out by the emperor, Bulla "was never seen when seen, never found when found, never caught when caught" (Dio Cassio 77.10.1–7.). This elusiveness is attributed to the bandit's superior craft and better intelligence, which enabled him, like the classic figure of the trickster, to outwit greater force. The tale is characterized by little vignettes of Bulla's ability to outthink and outmaneuver the clumsy "heavy" force of the state. He used disguise cleverly, for example, to pose as a military officer who requisitioned the labor of some of the bandit's own men who had been captured and taken to prison—a neat trick whereby he was able to effect their rescue.

By the same art of deception he captured the very military officer who had been delegated by the emperor to capture him, and he then proceeded to hold a mock trial, a fascinating piece of dramaturgical inversion in which Bulla put on the official robes of a Roman magistrate and sat on a tribunal in judgment of the centurion, who appeared, his head shaven like a common criminal, to face his sentence. And what was it? "Take this message back to your masters," Bulla said, "Tell them to feed their slaves so that they are not compelled to turn to a life of banditry." Septimius Severus finally managed to capture Bulla by engaging a man who was able to use the old ploy of finding a woman who would betray the bandit. Bulla was finally arrested and taken prisoner, not in a fair fight, but was captured surreptitiously while asleep in his brigand's cave.

The demise of Bulla and the disbanding of his gang form the logical completion of the bandit tale. Its use to the latter-day historian is to provide a means of questioning the distribution of power in the empire and the role of the emperor in that hierarchy as a dispenser of justice. Bulla was thrown to the beasts in an arena, there to suffer one of the supreme punishments that the state reserved for its worst outlaws. His gang of six hundred soon dispersed and disintegrated, so much did it depend on his personal authority for its cohesion. The story contains one final act, however, that is of great importance for our understanding of the role of banditry. In it Bulla the brigand is brought forward to face the emperor's right-hand man, the praetorian prefect Papinian. We are told that the following exchange occurred in this confrontation: Papinian turned to Bulla and asked, "Why did you become a bandit?" and Bulla, looking back at the man, retorted, "Why did you become praetorian prefect?"

The obvious answer that lurked just beneath the surface of those rhetorical questions was that it was the same basic power that had made both men. In the zero-sum game of which the Roman social order was constituted, the winner's gains were the loser's losses. In this highly polarized setting, the figure of the brigand was a useful one to the opposed social classes. To the elite, the bandit could be exploited as a figure to be opposed to that of the emperor. The brigand could be used as a symbol of the ultimate form of illegitimate power. The ideological burden was then imposed on the emperor to demonstrate that he was a "good ruler" (a *bonus imperator*) and not a violent and arbitrary dictator (a *tyrranus*). The brigand was a mirror opposite of the emperor, the image of what he should not be. So, in the bandit tales used by historians, the brigand, whether he be a Claudius, a Caracotta, a Bulla Felix, or a Julius Maternus, could be placed in direct confrontation with the emperor. When the brigand was successful in eluding the emperor, he did so by using intelligence and cunning, outwitting the emperor and his agents and thereby demonstrating the weakness of "illegitimate" power. The bandit embodied a physical virtue, a sexual prowess, and a simple honesty in justice that, however "illegitimate," was the standard by which those facets of personal power could be measured (and that emperors were especially supposed to exemplify).

In the popular oral stories that we can presume to have been connected with the written tales we find in upper-class historians and novelists, the bandit could be reappropriated to tell a different story about the distribution of power in the empire. So the confrontation between Bulla Felix and Papinian could be read in quite different and opposing ways. The new mass ideology of Christianity could also appropriate and exploit bandit tales within its own framework. It began to do so with its own foundation stories, with its antiking, or messiah, nailed to the cross by Roman power and framed to his right and left by two crucified bandits— the one repentant, the other contumaciously belligerent (Luke 23:33–43 and parallels). The literary production of "lives" of saints strove to perpetuate the same dichotomy, as the stories of St. Konon, St. Thekla, and St. Martin amply demonstrate.

This inexorable imbalance of power and the rude conflict between its "personal" and "institutional" manifestations were built into the very structure of the Roman empire. In periods of strife marked by chaotic conditions in the local power of the central state (often in the generation after its initial penetration into local society), marginal men such as the Spaniard Viriathus in the 140s and 130s B.C. or the African Tacfarinas in the reign of the emperor Tiberius were able to scale the ladders of local power to become minor threats to Roman power before they were successfully labeled as brigands and brutally repressed. But the Roman state was relatively weak and prone to periods of sudden fission (e.g., "civil wars") where the labeling process and the repression no longer worked.

The point in the state's repressive apparatus where it ought to have been strongest—its armed force—often turned out, ironically, to be its weakest link. "Maecenas' Advice" to the emperor Augustus, in fact a piece composed early in the third century by the historian Dio Cassius (57.27.4), gives a vivid description of the type of men whom he thought ought to be recruited into the army. They were those of greatest physical strength and who were in need of a livelihood—in other words, the very same men who were likely to become bandits. The same historian also makes clear the thin line that separated the two types of men. When the emperor Septimius Severus decided to staff the Praetorian Guard with legionaries from the provinces instead of with men from Italy, Dio remarks that "it became all too apparent that he had by that act ruined the young men of Italy, who now turned to banditry and gladiatorial combat instead of serving in the army." The new soldiers of the guard who now appeared in the city, however, seemed not much different from brigands: "He now . . . filled the city with a motley crowd of armed men, most savage in appearance, most terrifying in their speech, and most crude in their language" (Dio Cassius 75.5–6). But much of the recruiting to the Roman army of the period, especially to its so-called auxiliary formations, seems to have been determined by just such a deliberate policy: to incorporate wild and violent men such as the Mauri of the Atlas Mountains and the Ituraeans of the Lebanon Mountains, who would otherwise form reservoirs of brigandage within the empire. On some occasions emperors (Marcus Aurelius for one) were said to have recruited bandits (in his case, those of Dardania and Dalmatia) directly into the army (*SHA, Marcus Aurelius Antoninus* 21.2.7).

In periods of substantial fragmentation of central state power and authority there was very little to prevent local men of power, whom the state once successfully defined as bandits, from ascending the fissures in the structure of the state. The pattern is exemplified at the beginning of the so-called Third-Century Crisis, in the later A.D. 230s, by the career of Maximinus the Thracian. "In his early youth he was a shepherd, a young man with an impressive and noble appearance. Later he went on raids with bandits and protected local people from armed incursions. He later entered the Roman army and served his *stipendia* [tour of duty] in the cavalry. He was conspicuous for his large body size, outshone all other soldiers in bravery, was handsome in his manliness, harsh, arrogant, contemptuous, but, nevertheless, a man of justice" (ibid., *The Two Maximini* 2.1). A man who in other times would have been repressed by the state or permanently absorbed into the fringes of its armed forces now became the emperor of Rome. This is certainly not the mode by which the regular, long-serving emperors of Rome were created. Still, however short-lived and ephemeral the career of a "risen bandit" of Maximinus' sort may have been, he was as typical of the political structure of the Roman empire as any Augustus or Constantine. Examples of political brigands who were able to legitimize their own power occur again and again, especially in the period of the collapsing empire of the late fifth century, when Isaurian brigands (Zenon comes to mind) were able to become generals, consuls, and even emperors of Rome.

As for all those bandits who never "rose," however, and who represented almost all of the brigands defined by the existence of the empire, they have left us no record of their thoughts, their hopes, their demands, or their perspectives on the power networks that constituted the empire of their day. There can be no doubt that the image they projected in the minds of the common people became as much a part of popular beliefs (everyday "mythology" if you will) as did any local deity or demon. St. Martin may well have triumphed in ridding the peasants in the rural regions near Tours of a "false belief" in worshiping a local bandit as a saint. But the vignette attests to the overpowering presence of a popular belief, of "common opinions" and "local superstitions," firmly embedded in the behavior of the peasants of the region and in their local religious leaders, both priests and clerics—a belief that took nothing less than the intervention of Our Lord and his holy agent to eradicate. As for the harsh realities of bandit life and the actual deeds and works of the bandits that lie behind that worship, they are permanently obscured by the purposeful distortions and silences of the literary production of antiquity. What those men and women were really like will remain forever shrouded in myth.

Bibliography

I have myself offered a general interpretation entitled "Bandits in the Roman Empire," *Past and Present* 105 (1984): 3–52, on which this chapter offers some elaboration.

On the general connections between banditry and piracy, see Monique Clavel-Lévêque, "Brigandage et piraterie: Représentations idéologiques et pratiques impérialistes au dernier siècle de la république," *Dialogues d'histoire ancienne* 4 (1978): 17–31; and especially Yvon Garlan, "Signification historique de la piraterie grecque," in ibid., 1–16.

On the process of labeling political enemies as bandits, see Ramsay MacMullen, "The Roman Concept Robber–Pretender," *Revue Internationale des Droits de l'Antiquité,* ser. 3, 10 (1963): 221–25.

On the connection between brigandage and slave revolts, see Maria Capozza, "Il brigantaggio nelle fonti della prima rivolta servile siciliana," *Atti dell'Istituto Veneto di Scienze, Lettere ed Arti* 133 (1974–75): 27–40.

For some regional studies on the East, see Richard A. Horsley, "Josephus and the Bandits," *Journal for the Study of Judaism* 10 (1979): 37–63; Horsley, "Ancient Jewish Banditry and the Revolt against Rome," *Catholic Biblical Quarterly* 43 (1981): 409–32; and Ben Isaac, "Bandits in Judaea and Arabia," *Harvard Studies in Classical Philology* 88 (1984): 171–203.

On the policing and administration of Italy and the empire, see Fergus Millar, "Italy and the Roman Empire: Augustus to Constantine," *Phoenix* 40 (1986): 295–318. More particularly on policing in Rome and Italy, there is now the pathbreaking work of Wilfred Nippel, *Aufruhr und 'Polizei' in der römischen Republik* (Stuttgart: Klett-Cotta, 1988).

On attempts by the state to control brigandage in southern Italy in late antiquity, see two papers by Francesco Maria De Robertis, "Prosperità e banditismo nella Puglia e nell'Italia meridionale durante il basso impero," in *Studi di storia pugliese in onore di Giuseppe Chiarelli*, ed. Michel Paone. 7 vols. (Galatine: Mario Congedo, vol. 1, 972–80), 1:197–232; and De Robertis, "Interdizione dell' 'Usus Equorum' et lotta al banditismo in alcune costituzioni del Basso Impero," *Studia et Documenta Historiae et Iuris* 40 (1974): 67–98.

On brigands and pastoralists, see Angelo Russi, "I pastori e l'esposizione degli infanti nella tarda legislazione imperiale e nei documenti epigrafici," *Mélanges de l'Ecole française de Rome: Antiquité* 98, 2 (1986): 855–72.

On the bandits as identified with demonic forces in late antiquity, see G. J. M. Bartelink, "Les démons comme brigands," *Vigiliae Christianae* 21 (1967): 12–24; and Andrea Giardina, "Banditi e santi: Un aspetto del folklore gallico tra tarda antichità e medioevo," *Athenaeum* 61 (1983): 374–89.

On literary stereotypes of the brigand, see Jack Winkler, "Lollianos and the Desperadoes," *Journal of Hellenic Studies* 100 (1980): 155–81.

For studies involving both the East and the later empire, see J. H. W. G. Liebeschuetz, "Security and Justice," chapter 4.1 in *Antioch: City and Imperial Administration in the Later Roman Empire* (Oxford: Oxford University Press, 1972), 119–26; and Brent D. Shaw, "Bandit Highlands and Lowland Peace: The Mountains of Isauria-Cilicia," *Journal of the Economic and Social History of the Orient*, forthcoming.

Humanitas: Romans and Non-Romans

Paul Veyne

THE READER CAN REST ASSURED that I am as leery as he or she of the word *humanitas*. The term is both vague and laudatory: it designates persons who are worthy of the fine name of "human" because they are neither barbarian nor inhuman nor uncultivated. *Humanitas* means literary culture, the virtue of humanity, and the state of civilization. Thus our task will be to ask, What was the Roman (or what did he claim to be)? What did Romans mean by civilization? And what traits distinguished Roman (rather, Greco-Roman) civilization from other great civilizations? But were all people "humans"? Were the slave and the barbarian "men" or not? Were humanity and the human species the same thing? If so, what did the Romans think of their own imperialism? Was ancient thought universalist? Did it salute the unity of the human race?

First we need to look at the word itself. The term *humanitas* first served as an equivalent to the Greek *paideia:* "Greece, where civilization and literature [*humanitas*], and agriculture, too, are believed to have originated," Pliny the Younger said (*Epistulae* 8.24.2). Humanity distinguished the civilized man from the savage who lived on what he could gather; it also distinguished the literate (and, more generally, those who were "well brought up" and of good family—*pepaideumenos*) from the uncouth common people and from uneducated members of the propertied class who, by their lack of instruction, brought no honor to their class. *Humanitas* also corresponded to another Greek word, *philanthrōpia,* the quality of a man who was neither hard nor haughty and did more than strict justice required or did not demand his full due. In the juridical texts, for example, the humanity of a judge or that of the emperor was expressed in the sense of personal favors, by acts of clemency, or by waiving taxes (which was what "philanthropy" was for the Hellenistic kings). All mankind belonged to the human race, but, as we can see, some were more "human" than the others: either they did not live like wild animals or were not inhuman or else they were imbued with what one day would be called "the humanities."

Humanitas was thus a merit rather than a universal trait. When it was the merit of an individual it added a certain gentleness to common justice or tempered its rigor (Cicero *Ad Atticum* 4.6.1). When an entire society shared this merit it gave an outward extension to primitive simplicity: all men ate and worked, but not all had discovered the arts, technology, or belles lettres. Individuals also progressed internally. Savages were both too rigid and not rigid enough: they were unable to make concessions to humanity, but neither could they resist their impulses. *Humanitas* made them more supple, and the law taught them self-discipline (Cicero *Pro Caelio* 11.26, where he contrasts *humanitas atque leges* to *silvestris coitio;* "civilization and laws"; "savage fraternity" or "woodland pack"). One worrisome question remained, however: might humanization also be effeminizing (Caesar *Gallic Wars* 1.1.3)? Civilization, which made souls more supple, also softened them and prepared them for slavery (Tacitus *Agricola* 12.3; *see also* Tacitus *Historiae* 4.64).

Whether *humanitas* was taken as a sign of progress or a cause for concern, it nonetheless corresponded to what we still call civilization. It was an internal modification of the individual human being but at the same time an extension of human ascendancy over the external world: cities, stone houses, public buildings, agriculture, the study of eloquence (Tacitus *Agricola* 21.1–2). Like plants, human beings existed in two forms; some lived in the wild state and others were improved by culture (Caesar *Gallic Wars* 1.1.3; Cicero *De finibus* 5.19.54; *Tusculanae disputationes* 2.5.13). Certain peoples benefited from this basic division, and they discovered civilization (Vitruvius 2, pref. 5). The Greco-Roman empire, with its three and a half million square kilometers, was an island of civilization surrounded by barbarians (Strabo, end of bk. 6). Celsus, a pagan, pointed out to the Christians that if the imperial regime were to crumble, the world would become prey to ferocious and untutored barbarians (cited by Origen *Contra Celsus* 8.68 in *PL* 11.1620). St. Optatus, a Catholic, remarked to the Donatists, who were schismatics and rebels against the orders of the Christian emperor, "The State is not in the Church, but the Church is in the State, that is to say, in the Roman Empire . . . where are the holy offices of the priesthood, and modesty and virginity, which exist not amongst foreign peoples, and which, if they did exist, could not be safe from outrage" (*Against the Donatists,* tr. Vassall-Phillips, 132–33).

Are we to believe, then, that outside of the Hellenic or Hellenized peoples nothing but ignorance and savagery existed? The Greeks and the Romans, who were neither naive nor any more ethnocentric than the average, were not always sure. When they were dissatisfied with themselves they wondered whether the barbarians were not the only ones who had preserved their primordial purity and vigor. Was the empire civilized or decadent? They alternated between the hypothesis of original savagery and original authenticity. They also wondered whether primitive humanity had lived in a state of ignorance or whether, to the contrary, it had not inherited true philosophy, later forgotten or altered: certain very ancient peoples (the Egyptians, Indians, Ethiopians, Chaldeans, and even the Jews) had preserved a very ancient wisdom and an ancient religion that well merited study (which is what Apollonius of Tyana, Iamblichus, and a good many others did). Civilization was made not of inventions but of discoveries. And where did one discover something? Among foreigners, when they knew what we do not know, or in nature itself.

The ancients thus had an idea of discoveries and of the passage to civilization very different from any contemporary idea of progress. We need to take care not to read the Epicurean Lucretius, who has wrongly been taken as a precursor of our idea of progress, with modern eyes. Lucretius' thoughts were no different from Plato's or the Stoics'. Civilization's discoveries were not of a cultural order that was superimposed on nature, allowing humanity to break away from natural fatality; they were prefigured in nature, made (if I may be permitted the figure) by "following the dotted lines." Human discovery of language came about by imitating the song of the birds. Obviously the secrets of nature were well hidden; they were to be unveiled progressively, step by step, and a little at a time: *pedetentim progrediens,* as Lucretius says. This progressiveness was proof of the weakness of human genius rather than of its power. Thus, as Seneca sadly notes, many things remain unknown that will only ·be discovered in the future.

Were such progressive discoveries seen as true "progress," deserving of congratulations, as in the nineteenth century? Yes and no: they had both good and bad results. The savages died of inanition, Lucretius says, and civilized men of indigestion. Furthermore, if the philosopher is of a severe turn of mind, he will decree that what is called civilization should really be called decadence. The modern idea of progress implies the ideas of culture (as opposed to nature), invention (as opposed to discovery), and a radiant future. I intend to return elsewhere to the question of the technological innovations and achievements of ancient engineers.

Civilized, for better or for worse, the inhabitants of the Roman empire knew that the world was vast and that they were not the only civilized people in it. Merchants traveled to the distant islands, Taprobane (Ceylon) or Jaba (Java); they praised the gentle ways of the Chinese and their Great Wall—that nation, so remote that it presented no threat, prompted kindly reveries. Seneca even imagined that one day a boat sailing to the West would discover an unknown continent (Seneca *Medea* 374).

This reveals an internal contradiction in the Romans' idea of the world and of humanity considered in its totality. The Romans were not unaware that the eastern frontier of their empire did not even reach the mid point of the gigantic island that, for the science of the time, made up the lands that emerged from the sea. At the same time, however, they boasted that they held sway over the entire world, and the Greeks had long been telling them that the whole inhabited earth had fallen under their domination (Claude Nicolet, *L'inventaire du monde: Géographie et politique aux origines de l'Empire romain* [Paris: Fayard, 1988], available in English as *Space, Geography, and Politics in the Early Roman Empire* [Ann Arbor: University of Michigan Press, 1991]). This contradiction had existed from time immemorial. What was called "world" or "humanity" was usually only the *oikoumenē*—the human horizon at the center of which each civilization thought itself placed and which it could survey, looking as far as the eye can see. Indeed, when we think of the whole of humanity, we can imagine it in two nearly opposite ways: either we think of all humanity as if we held the globe at arm's length, or else we take an ethnocentric point of view. The first vision is universalist and true, but abstract and cold; the second is partial, but it engages our emotions much more because the small part of the world of which we ourselves are the center is much more important to us than the rest of humanity. This is why the discoveries of the Americas or that of prehistoric humanity, which totally upset the universalist view, affected contemporaries much less than one might suppose.

A similar contradiction inhabits ancient thought on the human species. The ancients knew that, in theory, humanity was one, but they did not want to know it. How long had they known it? How long had men thought that all humans belonged to one and the same species—Greeks and barbarians, free men and slaves? Classical philology has constructed an entire hagiographical novel on this question. It praises Cicero or Seneca for speaking of the "common society of the human race" (Cicero *De finibus* 3.19.62); it honors the Stoics for their so-called universalism; at times it affirms that, before those philosophers, the Greeks held the slave or the barbarian to be nonhuman; it sees in Terence's famous "*homo sum, humani nihil a me alienum puto*" ("I am a man, I count nothing human foreign to me") one of the great moments in history. Such is the tenacity of the idealistic—or rather the academic—illusion that confounds the reality of history with the image of that reality in the mirror of classical texts.

Actually, the discovery of the unity of humanity predated the Stoics by approximately four million years. It dates from the first hominids, since all higher animals can recognize members of their own species: a cat knows another cat as its like and knows that a dog belongs to another species. Recognizing Adam as the father of all humankind is one thing; drawing practical consequences from that notion is quite another. Aristotle speaks of an instinctive "friendship" "not only in man but also in birds and in most animals" and, more generally, "between members of the same species" (*Nicomachean Ethics* 1155a.19; see also Seneca *Ad Lucilium* 95.53). Aristotle adds that "even when travelling abroad one can observe that a natural affinity and friendship exist between man and man universally." He probably had in mind here the curiosity that inclines anyone toward the passing stranger and the laws of hospitality: who could refuse to give directions to a traveler? As Cicero declares, no one will refuse to a fellowman the water that flows in abundance, nor fire, which one can give without depriving oneself (*De officiis* 1.16.52). The virtue of humanity was thus natural, but for the common run of humankind either its visible operation was narrowly confined or it was merely an "ideological cover." As for the philosophers, I shall attempt to show the place of the unity of the human species in their systems and what conclusions they drew from it.

The simplest procedure is to take an example, that of slavery, which our own sense of the virtue of humanity and the unity of the human species finds most revolting. If we take what they say literally, Plato and Aristotle were just as universalist as the Stoics, and neither was unaware of the fact that barbarians and slaves were two-legged creatures without feathers who belonged to the human race. However, they remarked (as we do) that individuals have unequal congenital capacities. The problem for them was to decide which was more important, mankind's common nature or these inequalities between individuals? (As we shall see, the problem is totally different for us in the modern world.)

For Plato and Aristotle, a just organization of society was based on inequality: the slaves, who were individuals endowed with only mediocre talents (as one could tell at a glance), were only good for laboring and obeying. The Stoics, for their part, were concerned less with justifying society (of which they had a low opinion) than with showing the individual the way to happiness and virtue. Thus they taught that nature is well made: although physical and intellectual capacities are not equal, nature has given all individuals equal opportunity to attain virtue happily. Indeed, everyone will reach this goal if he does well in the task that Fortune has assigned to him: if he is emperor, he must do his job as emperor virtuously; if he is a slave, his slave's tasks. (St. Paul, too, declared that all men have an immortal soul and, with right conduct, can attain salvation, and he concluded that the slave should thus be virtuous and obey his master.) For the Stoics, slavery was not natural, since their only natural distinction was between wise men and "fools," and they saw the true slave as the free man who was not virtuous because he was a slave to his passions. Stoic universalism thus arrived at nearly the same conclusions as Plato or Aristotle.

At first sight it seems to us incomprehensible that the greatest thinkers were unable to see the historical reality of slavery with any sort of objectivity. In order to understand their viewpoint, we need to be aware of our own concept of universalism, which is not only original but probably one of the greatest exploits in human thought. To return to Aristotle, he writes on several occasions that slaves are men but that slavery is natural, except when freeborn Greeks had unjustly been sold as slaves when their city was taken by an enemy. As a general rule, nature destined some to be born to servitude. Aristotle found this so self-evident that he hardly bothered to spell it out: "The intention of nature therefore is to make the bodies of freemen and of slaves different—the latter strong for necessary service, the former erect and unserviceable for such occupations, but serviceable for a life of citizenship" (*Politics* 1254b.25 and, in general, chaps. 1, 3–7; for the slaves as human, see ibid., 1254a.15–16; on manual laborers as congenitally—*physei*—despicable, see Plato *Republic* 590c). Thus slaves were born strong and lowly. This rule of nature allowed exceptions, because it might happen that a slave's son be born with a weak body and an elevated soul, just as at times the proper sorts of people might fail to engender proper offspring. The laws of nature indicated the tendency; they applied in most though not all cases (Aristotle *Politics* 1254b.27: "Things that happen most of the time").

We can see how Aristotle's thought operated: he had before him slaves who were wretched specimens, and he was unable to pierce their social appearance to guess at its cause; he saw strong, humble, and ignorant men, and it never entered his head that what had really degraded and brutalized them was servitude and contempt. The idea that no one is born a slave, a serving woman, or a wretch but becomes so by socialization was scarcely developed until the nineteenth century. Furthermore Aristotle thought in terms of species and genera and showed little sensitivity to individuals.

Two things make slavery unthinkable for us. The first is our doctrine of the rights of man, which rejects the inequalities in rights among individuals and insists that all humans possess certain rights held to be fundamental. These rights, by definition, preclude personal servitude, and their possession does not depend upon individual capacities. The second is a sociological hypothesis that denies de facto inequalities from one group to another: the two sexes, the various races and classes have virtually the same average capacities for the performance of certain operations considered fundamental. Where collective inferiority exists it is not congenital but due to socialization or to the weight of the past. The ideal would thus be to give every individual his or her "chances." The origin of this hypothesis and this idea probably lies in twentieth-century historical and sociological thought: certain social and historical indices indeed suggest that groups are virtually equal in their performance. Aristotle, to return to him, held slavery as legitimate, measured fundamental rights according to individual capacities, and believed that collective incapacities were congenital.

To modern eyes, Stoic universalism is astonishingly timid; as we shall see, that timidity reveals the limits of all of ancient thought. Why were men equal only in virtue? Why did the Stoics fail to see that a slave society is unjust? Because "virtue" alone, which they defined in an extremely particular manner, made possible the mode of existence that natural determinism had foreseen for the human species. Virtue was a faculty that "nature" (almost in a biological sense) had given to representatives of the human species, just as it had provided animals with the instincts necessary to their own survival and that of their species. When classical thought turned inward, it spontaneously turned toward "nature" and the (physical) "cosmos." Its sights were not fixed, as our are, on what seems to us closer planes—"society" and "history"—which it hardly recognized. Thus when that thought drew courage and turned its sights beyond the City (as it was defined by Plato and Aristotle, with its basis in slavery), what it saw was not society but nature and cosmic destiny.

According to Stoic doctrine, everything was determined not only in the physical and biological cosmos but also within historical time: it was fated that Cypselus should rule over Corinth, that a particular naval battle should take place, that Socrates should die and that Cato should go to the Senate on a particular day. Fortune and simple chance existed only out of our ignorance of causes. The Stoics attributed everything to providence (only Cleanthes attributed moral evil to human vices rather than to god); evil was merely the inevitable counterpart of good. At the price of a sophism or two, the Stoics reconciled that fatality and that providence with human liberty (*proairesis*). Once they had stated these principles, however, they neglected to draw the consequences for history. When they gave examples of divine providence, they borrowed them from nature or anthropology in general: nature varies the seasons so that we may sow and harvest, put the soil to cultivation, and humanize it with our hands and our discoveries. When Seneca and the other Stoics spoke of political history, they saw only individual virtue struggling with Fortune (only Lucan wondered why god should will Caesar's victory over Cato). The Stoic theodicy justified the existence of physical ills, earthquakes, or shipwrecked pilgrims, but it seemed to forget historical dramas, which escaped its vision. In practice, if not in theory, all the Stoics thought like Cleanthes.

The timidity of Stoicism is highly revealing. The Stoics, as is known, considered themselves as citizens not of any human city but of the cosmos: they were "cosmopolitan." Does that mean that they considered themselves, politically, as citizens of the entire (human) world? No: the cosmos was an order of physical phenomena, the natural theater of all peoples, Greek or barbarians (see, for example, Seneca *Ad Marciam de consolatione* 18.1). As for destiny, it ruled individuals, not cities and collective entities. If a man is exiled among the barbarians, they argued, he will find the same sun, the same seasons, the same instinct to care for his children and his new fellow citizens. Slave or free, he will do his duty. Nature has given us an instinct for aiding our neighbor by taking part in public affairs (although that implied no specific political program). But suppose a foreign city declares war on Rome (for certain people are "our enemies": Seneca *Ad Lucilium* 110.14, referring to the Parthians and the silk road). When that happens, everyone will do his duty and fight for his fellow citizens, a natural virtue shared by both camps:

> What? Do you not think that the virtue of him who bravely storms the enemy's stronghold is equal to that of him who

endures a siege with the utmost patience? Great is Scipio when
he invests Numantia, and constrains and compels the hands
of an enemy, whom he could not conquer, to resort to their
own destruction. Great also are the souls of the defenders—
men who know that, as long as the path to death lies open,
the blockade is not complete, men who breathe their last in
the arms of liberty. (ibid., 66.13)

Universalism and internationalism were not the same thing.

Aristotle considered the barbarians congenitally destined to be colo-
nized by the Greeks; Plato paid little attention to barbarians. The Stoics
put more humanity and less ethnocentric prejudice into their thought,
but the final result of their universalism was little different. They never
dreamed of unifying humanity politically; it does them too much honor
to see in their doctrine the ideology of the "universal empires" of Alexander or of Rome, whose universalism was rather of the conquering variety. The cosmic city neither admitted nor denied their conquests, and
Seneca considered Alexander a madman rabid for sack and pillage. Frontiers left no traces on the cosmos, which was an order of natural things.
Plutarch hailed Alexander as the conqueror who had realized in fact what
the Stoics had only taught: it was evident that Plutarch, a faithful subject
of the Roman Empire, was well disposed to legitimize and idealize the
established political regime (Plutarch *Life of Alexander* 1.6; *Moralia* 329a).
If the term "ideology" has any useful purpose, it is to designate this sort
of edifying thought. Inversely, it was not for ideological reasons that the
great philosophies of classical antiquity were unable to focus on sociological and historical criticism. Not even philosophers can think of all things
at all times.

We need to take leave of the philosophers. The time had not yet come
when the words "humanity" or "universal rights" would shake the foundations of society. It is rather in the collective mind-set and in ordinary
morality that we can observe some of the effects of the notion of *humanitas*, which first made an appearance in fourth-century Greece under the
name of *philanthrōpia*. Such effects are noticeable but had few practical
consequences: self-awareness and vocabulary were more affected by them
than was behavior. Roman imperialism and the horrors of the Greek and
Roman war, when boasts of having shown humanity were common,
stand as proof of this.

Like any other society, Greece had always recognized and practiced certain humanitarian customs, but it gave a name to this virtue only rather late. Greece honored pity, gentleness, and goodwill. In Homer, the suppliant, the guest, and even the beggar had to be given humane treatment; the chivalric spirit alternated between resentment (the anger of Achilles) and forgiveness of offenses, even commiseration in Priam's case, since all men shared equally in misfortune. Achilles wept for his father who was soon to die; Priam wept for his son, killed by Achilles.

Aeschylus wrote, "Greece and Persia occupy two different countries and fight one another, but they are sisters of the same blood" (*Persai* 181). "Barbarian" did not designate a living species different from the Hellenes; it was a xenophobic term of opprobrium of the sort that all peoples use to speak of foreigners. During the fourth century in particular, this contempt was formed into a political theory of the superiority of the Greek nation over the Great King—a rival at once authoritarian and powerless, with whom the Greek cities allied themselves against other cities, as Christian princes were later to do regarding the Great Turk, while they waited to see who would succeed him and preached a crusade against him.

Over and above these impassioned doctrines, however, a wisdom that approached objectivity knew very well that the point of view of each individual man can be interchanged with his neighbor's, and that everyone egocentrically defends what is his. Homer's compassionate impartiality between the Achaeans and the Trojans was of this variety, and it may have served as a model for another striking exploit of human thought, Thucydides' political impartiality between the Athenians and the Peloponnesians. Nonetheless, impartiality and humanity are not the same thing: before they massacred all the citizens of Melos, the Athenians pointed out to them that justice and pity had no place in politics, and if it were in their power, the Melians would inflict the same fate on the Athenians (Thucydides 5.105.2). This explains Scipio's somber reflection as he viewed Carthage in flames: "I have a dread foreboding that some day the same doom will be pronounced upon my own country" (Polybius 38.21). In Livy's "inhuman" interpretation, Marcellus shows analogous sentiments as he weeps in sorrow to see a city as beautiful as Syracuse wiped out, and weeps for joy over his own victory (Livy 25.24.11). Such tears had nothing to do with *humanitas* or, whatever scholars might have said, with Stoicism. They reflect the egotistical sentiment of Publilius Syrus' maxim: "Whatever can one man befall can happen just as well to all" (*Cuivis potest accidere quod cuiquam potest,* cited by Seneca *Ad Marciam de consolatione* 9.5; see also *De tranquillitate animi* 11.1). The theme of the reversals of fortune runs throughout Seneca's letter on slavery (*Ad Lucilium* 47).

The virtue of humanity was composed of pity, gentleness, affability, simplicity, and interest in the fate of others. As the fourth century progressed, however, another word, *philanthrōpia*, appeared and subsumed all these attitudes into one general attitude toward others. It was just one of the abstract words that began to proliferate as philosophy became more abstract (the word *philellēn*—"philhellene"—which was older, may have served as a model). *Philanthrōpia*, which we might also call by its Latin name, *humanitas*, consisted in having a friendly attitude toward all men, not only one's political friends. We need not suppose that this neologism corresponded to a change in political relations or social relationships; humanity, like euergetism, lay in the way Menander's bourgeois treated one another, but also like euergetism it was, and eminently, an attitude of kings. *Philanthrōpia* was less an indication of a change in moral rules than an advance in reflection on morality and self-knowledge. Fourth-century Greeks had a larger number of fine ideas, and they had learned better to comment on themselves. One might say as much of Rome in the time of Cicero, where *humanitas* had become a fashionable attitude. In Rome, as in Greece three centuries earlier, this neologism was not significant by virtue of its cause (whatever that might have been); rather, it was important for its consequences, which were to give system to the idea of an attitude, hence to the attitude itself. It outlined a role to be played and that was indeed to some extent "played." The Hellenistic epoch and the last century of the Republic were an era of fine sentiments.

This attitude, carried to its logical conclusions, might, like Christian charity, become a vast program for action. Seneca sketches it out (*Ad Lucilium* 88.30; *Stoicorum veterum fragmenta* 3, no. 292 [Chrysippus?]): do good to others, share their sorrows, avoid treating the inhabitants of the provinces of the empire tyrannically. But grasp all, lose all: since always treating everyone as a friend was impossible, this virtue was applied within the narrow confines of humane gestures in ordinary relations of courtesy and in small acts that cost little. This attitude was reduced to symptomatic behavior that signified that one's basic character was full of a humanity that would be displayed more if "things" did not stand in the way. In Cicero's time, being modern meant showing one's profound *humanitas* by not giving oneself the airs of the old Cato, by a taste for Greek letters, by not continually fulminating against decadence, by imitating Xenophon rather than the more severe style of Thucydides, and by being as polite as the interlocutors in Cicero's dialogues. At the limit, one could show one's "philanthropy" by tolerating the throng at the baths or at Olympia or if one liked crowds of one's fellowman (Epictetus *Discourses* 4.4.27–28; see also 1.6.26).

Humanity was thus an art for good society, a delicacy in mutual regard: a politician should conduct politics seriously but, "within daily conjunctures," have "philanthropic" manners rather than be discourteous and haughty (Isocrates *Antidosis* 131–33). This is the true meaning of the famous *homo sum*. To recall the context: a bourgeois of friendly disposition toward another bourgeois sees the friend tiring himself out tilling the soil and suggests to him that he buy some slaves. To justify interference in someone else's business, the friendly bourgeois declares that since he is a man, like his friend, he takes an interest in the friend's lot (Terence *Heautontimorumenos* 77). Thus he invokes humanity to excuse his meddling. In another comedy, Plautus' *Trinummus* (44), a rich man asks for the hand in marriage of the sister of a bourgeois of modest wealth, but the brother thinks his wealthy acquaintance is mocking him and that the demand is not serious. "We are simply two men, you and I. I am not here to make fun of you, God bless my soul, no," the rich man responds in a courteous renunciation of superiority. *Humanitas,* in these little dialogues, is not an object of conversation; it serves to define the respective positions of the interlocutors before the serious negotiations begin. It is a "pragmatic" utterance (in the sense of current "pragmatic linguistics"). One man was as good as another, but not everyone could claim to be a proper interlocutor for everybody: neither of our bourgeois would have dared to speak to a king in that manner, nor would they have tolerated that line of argument from a slave.

Humanity was expressed not only in fine manners or in ways of speaking. It also mitigated negative attitudes. It forbade being more harsh than was necessary with slaves, for example. This is exactly where Seneca's letter on how to behave with one's slaves fits in: they should not be shown "cruel and inhuman conduct" (*crudelia, inhumana;* Seneca *Ad Lucilium* 47.5). When possible, one was to act in the same manner with a vanquished enemy. Xenophon's *Agesilaus*, a portrait that is significant for several reasons, tells us that the Spartan king "would often warn his men not to punish their prisoners as criminals, but to guard them as human beings." This "philanthropy" earned him the more ready obeisance of the vanquished (1.21–22). Agesilaus also boasts elsewhere, more conventionally, of doing as much harm to his enemies as he had done good to his friends. This inevitably brings to mind a famous and chilling passage in Augustus' political testament: "When foreign peoples could

353

safely be pardoned I have preferred to preserve rather than to exterminate them" (Augustus *Res gestae* 3.2). We need to stop and consider this statement.

It would be difficult to imagine anything more terrible than those three lines, with their fierce and merciful smile. They show a total awareness of the game they are playing with the reader and a confidence in the connivance of the Roman elite who would read them. They were also given out to the subjects of the Empire to show them that Rome's law had been passed over their heads. Not only do they reveal that Augustus was certain of his powers of collective life and death over all peoples not his own; they were written to make that fact known. If Augustus took pride in often having renounced his rights out of humanitarianism, it was to show that he nonetheless held them and would exercise them again when he thought it opportune. These few lines were much more than a warning to inform such peoples of a threat, as would be the case in our atomic age; they were the affirmation of a clear conscience, something perhaps more horrifying than the threat itself. The Greeks as well destroyed foreign cities without hesitation and without remorse: it was the common law of war. Thucydides justifies this fury in the name of a political rationale common to the victors and the victims. The Greeks also found it "philanthropic" to prefer not to destroy the defeated, but we never see them asserting their right in quite the same tone of voice as Augustus. With Augustus, that tone makes law the privilege of a master who reigns because he is who he is. It took a king-people to dare to take that stance.

The ancient East and archaic Rome destroyed their enemies, and their annals give dizzying lists of their massacres. More accurately, Rome and the East had two policies toward a vanquished collectivity: annihilation or, in calculation of their interest in enlarging their own collectivity, absorbing the vanquished. Cicero was later to claim (wrongly) that the latter was the only policy that Rome ever put into effect, attributing the fact to the welcoming and humane character of ancestral Rome (*De officiis* 1.11.35). In reality, Rome of that time took pains to show concern: for two centuries the Greeks had taught that it was a fitting way for conquerors to talk.

War in Greece and Rome was more cruel than it would be in the Middle Ages or until the nineteenth century. One collectivity fought another without distinction between military and civilians. The enemy was a scoundrel whom one fought because he had wronged you and was wronging you again by fighting you; he was guilty and needed to be punished (see the language of Augustus and Agesilaus). At the very end of the *Aeneid* the pious Aeneas, about to show mercy to the defeated enemy chief, slits his throat to punish him for killing the young Pallas in fair combat. According to the rules of war, if he so desired, the victor could sell into slavery all the inhabitants of a city he had taken (Polybius 2.58.9–10; see also 5.11, 18.3.3–4). At times all or some of the population of the city was put to the sword under the pretext (true or false) of reprisals.

The Romans added atrocities of their own invention: one of their laws stated that a city that had not surrendered to them before the first blow of the battering rams had struck its ramparts would be delivered over to the soldiers, whose orders were to massacre any living being in their path. The law was applied so ceremonially that Polybius, who had witnessed similar scenes, says of the taking of Carthage: "They do this, I think, to inspire terror, so that when towns are taken by the Romans one may often see not only the corpses of human beings, but dogs cut in half, and the dismembered limbs of other animals" (Polybius 10.15.5, Cicero *De officiis* 1.11.35). Rome also went Hellenistic warfare one better in the scale of destruction visited on cities. The destruction of Carthage and that of Corinth caused scandal; among the Greeks only Alexander had dared to annihilate a great historic city, Thebes.

When, in 221, King Antigonus Doson crushed the Spartans at Sellasia and took control of the city, he "treated the Lacedaemonians in all respects with generosity and humanity" (Polybius 2.70.1). Their city was not destroyed, any more than Athens had been in 404. Polybius credits the same thoughts to the Roman, Flaminius: brave men must wage war with courage and anger, but in victory they should show magnanimity, gentleness, and "philanthropy" (18.37.7). Polybius notes that Flaminius had another, more political, reason for leaving the kingdom of Macedonia on its feet: Macedonia served as a bulwark against the Thracians and the Galatians. Hence Rome was acting like an imperial power responsible for world order. Clemency was a new notion. On the basis of his vast reading, Plutarch summarized the impression that the intrusion of Rome into Greek politics made on the Hellenistic world: "The Romans were considered by foreign peoples to be skilful in carrying on war and formidable fighters; but of gentleness and humanity and, in a word, of civil virtues, they had given no proofs" (*Life of Marcellus* 20.11).

Henceforth they were to give such proofs and to take up the language of fine sentiments. Rome had long been a society infused with Hellenism in its material civilization, its religion, and its mythological universe, as were the Etruscan cities, Cyprus, and so forth. Politically, however, Italy and the eastern Mediterranean were separate worlds with no relation to one another. The sudden entry of Rome into Greek affairs on the morrow of its victory over Hannibal seemed as surprising as the sudden irruption in 1917 of the United States into the affairs of European states with which it had no pacts and no previous commitments. A great power finds it difficult to sit by idly while important events are taking place on the international scene. It was in this spirit that the Romans played an active role—even the leading role—in Hellenistic diplomacy. The Romans needed to adopt Hellenistic traditions and language and to prove that they knew the fine manners of the great international civilization that Hellenism represented. In 188 the Scipios assured an Ionian city, in a missive in Greek, that they had for it "all possible good will." Their Greek secretary redacted their letter in perfect Greek style: they expressed themselves like philanthropist kings (*Syll.* 618).

One had to show "philanthropy" toward kings as well. Roman military ritual dictated that the vanquished enemy leader be strangled in his prison during the triumph at the moment when the chariot of the triumphant general reached the Capitoline: Vercingetorix and Simon bar-Gioras, who had made their submissions with great ceremony to Caesar and to Titus, respectively, were put to death in that manner (Dio Cassius 40.41.3, 43.19.4; Flavius Josephus *History of the Jewish War* 6.9.4.434, 7.2.2.36, 7.5.6.153–54; Cicero *De suppliciis* 30.77: *victis vitae finem*); the head of Decebalus, who prevented the Romans from carrying out this rite by killing himself, was carried to Trajan with solemnity. These were barbarians, however: What were the Romans to do with the first civilized king who became their prisoner after his defeat? They pardoned him: after Pydna, Perseus was not put to death. The Senate decreed that he would be kept in prison in Alba Fucens so as to enhance Rome's reputation for equity (Livy 45.42.4; Diodorus Siculus 31.9). Given that spoils were a part of the laws of war, however, Epirus had been given over to pillage by the victorious army, which sacked seventy cities and reduced 150,000 men to slavery. The entire world was horrified by the magnitude of the destruction (Polybius 30.15; Livy 45.34.6; see also Plutarch *Life of Aemilius Paulus* 29).

Cicero gives elegant expression to the spirit of *humanitas* in warfare, adorning it with a Roman patriotism nearly impervious to doubt. One should not wage war, he writes, before having exhausted all possibilities for negotiation; the only just wars are wars of defense against an enemy's

injustice; an enemy city should not be destroyed unless it deserves reprisals. This, he continues, is how our ancestors always operated, and Carthage and Numantia were razed as just reprisals. "I wish they had not
destroyed Corinth," but the strategic security of Rome demanded it (Cicero *De officiis* 1.11.35; *De lege agraria* 2.32.87). If a city surrendered, it
should be spared, even if the battering rams had already touched its
walls (*quamvis murum aries percusserit*); only the leaders of the enemy camp
should be punished and the mass of the population spared (*De officiis*
1.11.35, 1.24.82). Cicero presents here an apologetica for Roman policies,
his version of which is palliated by omissions. As was appropriate for
a cultivated and humane author, he also offers one or two words of
humanitarian advice and expresses one regret, but without insistence and
without disloyalty to his homeland. His advice proves that a Roman can
be human; his regret proves that the Romans, who were human, had
destroyed Corinth only because they could not do otherwise.

Caesar ordered the hands cut off the last defenders of Gallic independence because he felt it was necessary to make an example of them; his
clemency was sufficiently famous not to be open to doubt (Caesar-Hirtius
The Gallic War 8.44.1). He could take pride in having preserved the lives
of the surviving Nervii of Brabant and in refraining from sacking their
villages and wiping out their frontiers, but the Veneti of Morbihan were
sold as slaves, in reprisal, to teach barbarians to respect ambassadors
(Caesar *The Gallic War* 2.28.3, 3.16.4). Caesar showed himself merciless
only toward barbarians who were rebellious or traitorous. The Gauls
defeated at Alesia were treated as booty and sold as slaves. The principle
was to let live an enemy that Rome was fighting for the first time (ibid.,
3.16.4; Polybius 18.37.1); the rebel who persisted in defending himself
was a different matter. The Romans, Montesquieu writes, seem to have
supposed that it was enough simply to have heard speak of them to be
obliged to submit to them.

One should declare only just wars: in another chapter of his political
testament, Augustus declared that he had never waged war unjustly
against any people. When the Republic had attacked the Dalmatians and
driven Carthage to despair, as Polybius informs us, it took care to seek
a pretext: "To the world at large they gave out that they had decided on
war owing to the insult to their ambassadors" (Polybius 32.13.9, 36.2.1).
Caesar gives the impression of conquering Gaul by chance: to hear him,
all he did was to enter into one separate operation after another, each one
in the aim of defending Rome or its allies in Gaul (*The Gallic War* 3.28.1).
My purpose here is not to reproach the Romans for a discrepancy be-

tween their acts and their words (a timeless phenomenon) but to show the unilateral and solipsistic character of Roman foreign policy. Peace and war between nations do not arise out of a rationality invariable through the centuries. The idea of a plurality of nations with equal rights was foreign to the Romans.

A justly declared war was one thing; actual warfare was quite another: it relied uniquely on strategic utility, profits from booty, and the systematic application of terror. When Romans combated barbarians, they commonly put villages to the torch and killed every living thing in their path. In the autumn of A.D. 14, Germanicus subjected Westphalia to a scorched-earth policy, setting fires and massacring everyone without regard for sex or age, for eighty miles or more (Tacitus *Annales* 1.51.1). When he had done, the name of the people who had inhabited the region, the Marsi, dropped out of history. Among civilized peoples too there were cities leveled by fire to inspire terror in the enemy: there was Artaxata, the capital of Armenia at the foot of Mount Ararat, which was burned to the ground twice within a century; Seleucia, on the Tigris, the wealthy commercial city of the Parthian empire, was destroyed under Lucius Verus to set an example; Ctesiphon, the other great Parthian city, was razed and its women and children sold as slaves; history does not tell us what happened to the men (Dio Cassius 76.9; Herodian 3.9.11).

The fate awaiting the vanquished is still another question. It was a fine thing to treat them with humanity, and one must always suppose that rebels had been sufficiently punished to have become more reasonable (Flavius Josephus *History of the Jewish War* 6.6.2.324). These were Titus' sentiments as he stood before Jerusalem and shed tears over the horrors of the war. If the enemy was stubborn, however, no general would be blamed for treating him as he deserved: in a dramatic scene, Titus himself declares to the besieged in Jerusalem that they will be treated with ultimate severity (ibid., 6.6.2.328). A century later, the column dedicated to Marcus Aurelius provided its age and the heavens with hallucinatory scenes of slaughter among the barbarians: long files of men in chains being decapitated, huts put to the torch, women and children taken in slavery whose pathetic faces the sculptor has preserved in stone. I do not believe that this note of pathos expresses any humanization or any new sensitivity. Rather, it adds to a triumphal affirmation of the force of Rome, which crushes its vanquished with just punishment. However, it also provides something for the popular taste akin to the morbid delight our contemporaries find in war films that offer a mix of the gentle pleasures of a pity without consequences and a sadism with neither danger nor remorse. As a political expression, the column of Marcus Aurelius illustrates the Roman point of view; as a work of art, it plays on the two age-old sources of emotion, terror and pity, and places itself at the viewpoint of both the massacrers and the massacred, as does the *Iliad*. It is a humanism of the imagination.

This popular sadism contrasts with the Greco-Roman art of the preceding age, which had always been more discreet concerning atrocities and had the good taste not to show its defeated populations as crushed. The reliefs of the Augustan temple of Aphrodisias still testify to this elegant style. The equestrian statue of Marcus Aurelius in the Piazza del Campidoglio originally showed the horse trampling a barbarian, as was often the case in triumphal art in Egypt and Assyria and even into later antiquity.

These massacres of barbarians who were threatening the territorial integrity of the empire occurred at a time when, exceptional circumstances aside, the imperial regime was no longer bent on conquest: "Rome, in her satiety of glory, had reached the stage when she desired tranquillity for foreign countries as well as herself" (Claudius, in Tacitus *Annales* 12.11). The empire considered itself the only state in the world and as coexistent with the civilized and humanized world. Tacitus takes care to call the Parthians barbarians. The word "barbarian" had changed meaning, no longer designating "strangers" of all sorts: such strangers were "savages" whose hordes were beating at the ramparts of the empire that represented worldwide Hellenic civilization. Philo of Alexandria was thinking of Augustus' conquests in the Alps and in Illyria when he declared that the princeps had "brought gentle manners and harmony to all unsociable and brutish nations" and "enlarged Hellas by many a new Hellas" (*Embassy to Gaius* 147; Aelius Aristides *Roman Oration* 63). The clear conscience of the soldiers massacring the vanquished on the column of Marcus Aurelius is that of men defending civilization against barbarians whose clothing and hairstyle differed from their own.

What is more difficult to understand is the imperialism of the republican epoch—the conquest of the world. The true explanation of that imperialism matters less for our purposes than the fine reasons the Romans gave themselves for it, for in the last analysis human beings believe in humanity and feel some sense of obligation to it. There is little evidence of that sense of obligation in texts of the republican era, however: Rome seems to have thought that the fact of conquest spoke for itself and did not require comment. Other societies claimed the superiority of a civilized people over inferior races and spoke of a duty to protect them, of a crusade in favor of a religion or a political principle, of a mission to assure the reign of order and peace among the nations, and so forth. Republican Rome did not even boast of being a people of superior extraction or the natural leader of plebeian peoples; its only superiority lay in its arms and the glory of its victories—that is, in the raw fact of having conquered. It did not justify its actions on a general plane, as in Thucydides, by suggesting that all peoples would prefer to have slaves than be slaves; it did not excuse its acts by claiming that every nation holds its own egotism as sacred. It says nothing. The Latin texts are mute. And Rome had reason to remain silent: Rome reigned because it was the king-people, and a king has no universal legitimacy; he reigns because he is what he is. He is superior because he is the king; he is not king in virtue of some superior merit or for reasons of collective utility.

More precisely, under the Republic the ideological justification (for there was one after all) did not concern Rome's right to command but rather the "honesty" with which it exercised its command. In a late work (*De officiis* 2.7.26–28, 30), Cicero reproaches Caesar for his wars—not the Gallic war, to be sure, but the civil war. On that occasion Caesar had oppressed not only his fellow citizens but also the people of Marseilles, the oldest and most loyal "allies" of Rome. For Cicero, the oppression of allies or subjects meant the end of Roman domination: Sparta had lost its empire because that empire was unjust—by which Cicero did not mean that it was unjust, as a matter of principle, for Sparta to have an empire but rather that Sparta had exercised its domination unjustly, which had led to its downfall. Cicero is so imbued with Rome's right to rule that in all good faith he fails to see that he mingles two different problems: the correct exercise of authority and the right of that authority to exist. (If we imagine a discussion between a capitalist and a Marxist, the Marxist would say that the capitalist elite cannot be justified either by any innate superiority or by the common good, and that it is unjust that a wage-earning class exists. The capitalist would think it a refutation of this accusation to insist that he gives honest pay to his workers and treats them humanely.) Before the abuses of the last fifty years, Cicero continues, Roman domination was maintained thanks to the benefits it offered. Subjects were treated with equity and good faith and the Senate made itself the protector of the independence of foreign states threatened by their neighbors. Rather than possessing an empire, Rome had a protectorate (*patrocinium*) over the entire world.

Because the Roman people was a king-people, its relations with its subjects or with foreigners were indeed under the sign of *patrocinium:* they were not relations with equal partners, which followed formal rules, but personal relations, unequal and informal. A king is not subject to a rule; one puts oneself in his hands with confidence in his good faith and his humanity. This is why Rome thought of international relations as analogous to patron-client relations, which also had no law other than the patron's good faith. If the foreigner, for his part, failed to behave like a loyal client, he became a rebel, a criminal.

Here I need to simplify things for brevity's sake: Rome was not totally lacking in good faith in international relations. The Roman leader who had attacked a foreign people without the accord of the Senate could be turned over to that people, and Cato proposed to the Senate that Julius Caesar be turned over to the Germans, whom he had attacked unjustly. This does not prove, however, that Rome had a notion of juridical relations among nations, in the general or the modern sense of that term, but only that it had found a means for washing its hands of responsibility in a given circumstance. Because Hostilius Mancinus had shown cowardice in concluding an armistice with the besieged population of Numantia, the Senate, which backed the war, broke the treaty and delivered Mancinus over to the Numantians.

The tranquillity with which Rome behaved as an imperialist power is only too comprehensible: It is hard to have a troubled conscience when one feels oneself the architect and possessor of the most monumental empire that ever existed. History proved that imperialism was normal. When Romans looked back to the past, they were struck by the ancient empires: Ninus, the king of Assyria, had invented imperialism and was also the first to wage a war of conquest (Justin 1.1.5–7; see also St. Augustine *The City of God* 4.6); then came the empires of the Medes, of Alexander, and of Rome itself. St. Augustine was the first to question the self-evidence of imperialism: for him, empires were nothing but vainglory. What did it matter, for our eternal salvation, whether we were the subjects of one prince or another (4.3–6, 15; 5.17)?

In comparison to a monument as indisputable as the Roman Empire, the enterprises of Rome's enemies were the furious agitation of underlings. The Latin historians, who were quite aware of the ill being said of Rome elsewhere, seem delighted to repeat these criticisms and even to use them as an excuse for bravura pieces of their own. Mithradates is quoted as saying, "The Romans have one inveterate motive for making wars on all nations, peoples and kings; namely, a deep-seated desire for dominion and for riches"; Calgacus, the Caledonian king of the Britanni, exclaimed, "Harriers of the world . . . to plunder, butcher, steal, these things they misname empire; they make a desolation and they call it peace" (Tacitus *Agricola* 30). Tacitus himself praises the conquest of Britain, however, and in a later passage shows how avidly the inhabitants, once defeated, adopted Roman civilization and Roman *humanitas.*

The twentieth-century reader finds these texts astonishing and might even be tempted to think that Calgacus and Mithradates were right. It seems impossible that a Latin writer could have put these criticisms into their mouths without some sensitivity to them and some sense of guilt. This would be a mistake, however, as the writer only reports these reproaches in order to show how far the enemies of his country could go in their hysterical rage: Mithradates may well have thought the Romans imperialist brigands, but he himself was nothing but a monster of perfidy and cruelty and his discourse was a tissue of lies. Mithradates did not have a frontier that bordered on Rome's; he clashed with Rome because he wanted to grab for himself the lands of independent peoples, his neighbors, whose defense the Senate, the defender of liberties, had taken up. In the eyes of the Romans, the true imperialist and aggressor was Mithradates. From that day on, his hatred for Rome became the one passion in his life, and for forty-six years he attempted to destroy the Empire.

The hysteria of Rome's enemies could go literally to the point of cannibalism. During the siege of Alesia, when the besieged Gauls began to lack provisions, one chieftain decried the Romans' rage for conquest and proposed to his fellows that they eat human flesh, adding that this would provide an admirable example for their descendants. (Similar cannibalistic notions can be found in Appian *The Wars in Spain* 96, and Flavius Josephus *History of the Jewish War* 6.3.4.201–19.) To the Romans, this was proof of the stubbornness and the hysteria of "rebels" who would rather eat their children than surrender.

Far from these inhuman passions, the Romans governed with humanity the monument they were so proud of. As we shall see, the name of that virtue was everywhere. In A.D. 60, Cicero sent a letter of advice to his brother Quintus, who was governor of Asia. The duty of a leader, he wrote, was to make those he governs as happy as possible. Quintus must show himself full of *humanitas* and be neither haughty nor cruel, particularly since the people he ruled over were Greeks, not an inhuman and barbarian people. May his own humanity return to them the *humanitas* (civilization) that they had initiated and that Rome and all men owed to them. Had not the new governor spent his youth in the study of *humanitas* (culture)? His province would live in harmony if, in each city, the upper class of the *optimates* was in power (Cicero *Ad Quintum fratrem* 1.1.24–25, 27–29; for the primacy of the *optimates* see also *De re publica* 1.27.43).

A century and a half later, Pliny the Younger wrote to a governor of Baetica, supposedly to congratulate him on the job he was doing but in reality to reproach him politely (*Epistulae* 9.5). This governor treated the population under his administration with much familiarity (*humanitas*), but he seemed to have forgotten that the better part of *humanitas* was respect, and he would do better to show more respect for differences in social class and not reduce all to one level.

Fifty years after Pliny, a Greek from Asia, Aelius Aristides, congratulated the Roman governor for having treated the subjects of the Empire with as much *philanthrōpia* as firmness. It is true that between Cicero's time and Aelius Aristides', relations between Rome and its subjects (or rather the governing class among its subjects) had changed. Aristides told Rome that it had no need to keep troops garrisoned in its empire because "in every city the most considerable and the most powerful men keep their city in your obedience" (*Roman Oration* 66, see 57, 64).

The true administrative unit of the Roman Empire was the city, which operated autonomously under the authority of its notables. Political sentiment included an impassioned interest in local affairs, joined to a resigned submission to the distant powers that governed the empire and whose representative was the dreaded governor of the province. Everywhere there was an air of great architecture. The central government put the notables in power less out of class solidarity than as the simplest way to keep the empire in hand in peaceable submission. When Rome noted the submission of the provinces it had conquered, it discovered its mission as peacekeeper: *paci imponere morem,* ("to set the stamp of civilized behavior on peace": Virgil *Aeneid* 6.852; the commentary of Eduard Norden, *Aeneis Buch VI,* p. 335, cites a number of parallel texts and defends the reading *paci* instead of *pacis*). What had once been felt as the personal privilege of the king-people seemed to Virgil a mission of general interest that permitted Rome to exterminate the refractory and spare only those who submitted.

The rest of the story, down to the extension of Roman citizenship to all free men of the empire in 212, is well known. The central power, with proprietary pride, sought to make its domain prosper and to further the welfare of its charges with such projects as draining marshes and establishing agrarian policies. The provinces gradually ceased appearing to Rome as outside possessions and became integral parts of the empire, with Italy itself slowly becoming the first of its provinces. Rome had passed from a "colonial" hegemony to being a centralized state. The provincials, for their part, gradually left off considering the emperor as a master of a foreign race and obeyed him as their legitimate sovereign. Dio of Prusa, a Greek patriot inspired by a xenophobic hatred of the Roman ethnos, invited the Greeks to return to their ancient pride, but at the same time, he preached obedience to the legitimate master, the emperor, who was above ethnic differences. This change in mind was of a psychological order (the habit of living under the same master), which meant that simple symbols sufficed to maintain and fortify it.

Not enough importance has been given, it seems to me, to the revolutionary aspect of Hadrian's long voyages through his empire. It was unheard of (the case of Nero aside) that the emperor leave Italy except to wage war on the frontiers; thus the presence of the princeps in Rome was proof that the Empire was at peace. Hadrian, however, nearly gave up Italy as his homeland and Rome as his capital and spent nearly half his reign in the provinces. We can imagine the effect this produced on people's minds. To confirm his intentions, Hadrian had a series of coins struck whose reverse showed, for the first time, allegorical figures representing the various provinces. The same allegories, sculpted in marble this time, adorned his temple, the Hadrianeum in Rome. His successor, Antoninus, also had a series of provincial coins struck.

This moral unification centered on an ideal of civilization. Under Augustus, when the civil wars came to an end, contemporaries noted that the world had attained a level of prosperity hitherto unknown, and their thought was articulated around a barbaric "yesterday" and a "today" that was civilized. Once, women had worked with their hands, as housewives or farm wives (Columella 12, pref. 4–5); people did not wash and smelled bad; what was considered a luxury would today seem rudimentary (Seneca *Ad Lucilium* 86.8, 12). There was certainly some truth in these impressions. According to some economists, if the gross national product is set at 20 for the two or three richest countries in the world today, it would have ranged only between 2 and 3 before the eighteenth century. This slight difference was enough to make the difference between the Athens of Pericles, where houses were built of dried clay, and Rome under Augustus or Versailles (around 1700, India and England had comparable standards of living). From our point of view, the Roman Empire was a society in which the common people went barefoot (Seneca *Ad Lucilium* 87.4), and a province passed for prosperous when the peasants were not in rags (Ammianus Marcellinus 15.12.2) and the houses had tile roofs (Strabo 13.1.27). The only province that no longer had wild animals was Crete (Plutarch *De utilitate ex inimicis capienda* 1, *Moralia* 86c). For one contemporary of Augustus, however, a progress that had started a thousand years earlier (Varro *De re rustica* 3.1.4) had led to the refinement of his own times, thanks to technological discoveries consigned to books (Vitruvius 7, pref. 1). Peace and prosperity became coextensive with the entire empire, since the regions of the empire that were still barbaric were also becoming civilized. Since Augustus had pacified the Asturians, the barbarians had learned the sentiment of human community and *philanthrōpia,* and the Gauls of Gallia Narbonensis appointed professors of rhetoric (Strabo 4.1.5.181, 183; 3.3.8.155). The latest production of a poet in vogue was exported to the very ends of the earth, to Britannia or Vienna (Vienne) in Gallia Narbonensis (Martial 7.88.2, 11.3.5).

This prosperity made the Greco-Roman Empire one unit of civilization with two international languages, confronting the barbarians. Republican Rome had taken the culture of another people, the Greeks, as its own and had not felt that culture as foreign but as being civilization itself. Similarly, in the empire and even beyond its frontiers, Greco-Roman civilization was simply civilization: those populations were not Romanized or Hellenized as much as they were simply civilized. When in 69–70 the Gallic chieftain Julius Sabinus, in revolt against Rome, attempted to carve himself an independent kingdom in Gaul, he took the title of Caesar in much the same spirit as leaders of colonial insurrections in the 1950s borrowed the title of "colonel" or "president" from their former parent state (Tacitus *Historiae* 4.67.1; Dio Cassius 66.3.1, 16.1). The central power did not seek to Romanize: even if it had wanted to do so, how could it have gone about it? The provincials spontaneously Romanized themselves, and the central power applauded the process and gave its juridical sanction to the formation of new towns. The city had always been considered the natural setting for civilized living. From time immemorial, the political system of the city was as customary in central Italy as it was in Greece: at its birth, Rome was an authentic *polis.* The civilization in question—which was indistinguishably Greek and Roman (Herod the Great proved his loyalty to Rome by founding a Greek city which he named Caesarea)—penetrated with varying degrees of depth according to the region and social class. With some exceptions, supposed resistance to Romanization came in purely negative terms as lesser penetration. An "international" category grew up of functionaries, jurists, physicians, philosophers, and so forth, whose true nationality was imperial, even if they spoke Greek and were born in Pergamum, Alexandria, or (like Favorinus) Arles. The sentiment of a common civilization made Greece imitate the customs of its conqueror, just as Rome had imitated Greece. The *Rosalia* were a western rite that came to be introduced in the East; the festivals of Chronos were remodeled after the Saturnalia; Rome, Carthage, and even Vienna (Vienne) adopted Greek games (in the third century the games in Rome rivaled those of Olympia), while the Greek East adopted gladiatorial combats and circus races.

One can either regret the narrowness of this civilization which, wherever it reigned, presupposed a man of leisure who had wealth and excluded the Jew, the Christian, and the Manichaean, or one can admire its freedom of access. (Liberty of access was true even of Hellenistic civilization: see the famous epigram of Meleager of Gadara, *Palatine Anthology* 7.417.) The Romans were an empirical people who never behaved like convinced ideologues; they naturalized foreigners and freed slaves much more readily than the Greeks, who remained faithful to their narrow principles (see the letter of Philip V to Larissa, *IG* 9.2.517; *Syll.* no. 543). In reality, this apparent liberalism can be explained by the force of clientage bonds: the patron imposed on the citizen body admission of his freedman and the stranger he protected. In general, Roman law sacrificed little to humanity and remained extremely severe toward the weak and debtors. Even historians who can least be suspected of bias speak of "class jurisprudence."

One exception was the rule of "favoring liberty." If a master manumitted a slave or slaves by testament and the terms of the document were ambiguous, the judge was instructed to adopt the more humane view and rule to free the slave (*humaniorem sententiam sequi oportet;* Ulpian *Digest* 34.5.11.1). This rule, which remained an isolated instance, can be explained by a common moral notion: a master was considered humane if he was indulgent toward his slaves (without being considered unjust if he was harsh). For example, a master often intervened to ask another master not to punish a slave (Petronius *Satyricon* 30.7–11; Plautus *Amphitruo* 540; *Asinaria* 431; Ovid *Ars amatoria* 2.287; *Digest* 21.1.17.4, 21.1.43.1). Trimalchio takes pride in liberating his slaves "because they are men" (*Satyricon* 71.1); the *Catonis Disticha* (4.44) echoes his thought: "When you buy slaves, remember they are men."

Despite the legends still attached to Cicero's noble principles (Cicero *De legibus* 1.10.29; *De finibus* 3.19.62–65; *De officiis* 1.7.20), Roman law also did not sacrifice to natural law, though it gave it nominal praise. "As far as concerns the natural law, all men are equal," wrote Ulpian, contradicting this principle in the very next line, however (Ulpian *Digest* 50.17.32). The jurists took little account of natural law: the first pages of the *Digest* are merely a noble facade unconnected to the body of the compilation, which is pure positive law. Incest is prohibited, not because it is contrary to nature but only because the law has prohibited it.

The fact remains that Roman civilization, which was fully as unjust and cruel as many other civilizations, gives (more than other civilizations) the "touristic" impression of a liberal, open, serene society. It was unaware of moral order, racism, and religious sectarianism. Before the legislation of Constantine (which seems more plebeian than Christian), only a few tyrants—Domitian among them—attempted to make moral order reign. The emperors rarely ceded to the Confucianist temptation to measure their power by the morality of individuals and did not take politics as the place to impose an ideal of individual morality. The Roman penchant for aristocracy dissolved into liberalism. Nor did distinctions between races count: Were the Antonines descended from Roman colonists in Spain or from naturalized natives? No one even asked. Septimius Severus, during whose reign the Roman Empire reached its largest territorial extent and its demographic, economic, and juridical height, was an African whose ancestors did not speak Latin and whose grandfather was Sufetulan. There is no reason to evoke Hannibal's revenge: "Roman," "Latin," or *peregrinus* designated a status, not an ethnic origin, and the Romans made no difference whatsoever between Roman citizens of Italian origin and those of provincial origin. Ethnic differences counted for so little that in late antiquity Romans showed no repugnance toward recruiting their generals from among the Germans.

Religion was no barrier either: unlike Christianity or Islam, the pagan empire did not draw any distinction between itself and the barbarians on the basis of belief. The gods of all men, civilized or barbarians, were true gods and were even perhaps the same gods under other names, just as an oak tree was an oak tree wherever it grew. Jupiter translated into Greek as "Zeus" and into Celtic as "Taranis." The pagan empire was a desacralized society: everyone was or could become pious, but the legislator imposed no religious obligations save the respect of feast days by not working. This was precisely St. Augustine's reproach to Rome in a passage that views the imperial system with a good deal of detachment. Rome was avid for conquest, harsh toward the poor, founded on clientage bonds; it cared only for peace, prosperity, and pleasure; its emperors were totally indifferent to their subjects' morality and eternal salvation (*The City of God* 2.20).

These were the appearances, then: a tolerant religion, an open civilization that the majority of the ethnic groups gathered together under the Empire hastened to adopt (unless, like the Greeks, they already possessed it); something broadly human, then, and universalist at least in intention. Unfortunately this is only appearance. The tolerance of paganism is explained above all by the difficulty involved in putting to the test a religion with little structure, and the eagerness to adopt Greco-Roman civilization was simply due to the fortunate administrative happenstance of the city system as a basic framework. On a deeper level, Greco-Roman civilization was just as intolerant and exclusive as any other civilization, as the Christians learned to their sorrow.

The apparent tolerance of paganism was by no means indifference. The popular masses always remained pious; among men of culture, the burden of proof lay with the unbelievers and the skeptics, not, as in our day, with the believers. The problem is that paganism offered no decisive point that could serve as proof that an individual was atheist. There was no church that demanded declarations of submission, no theological dogma to profess, no profession of faith to make (which meant that atheistic statements were merely swearwords, not crimes), no jealous god who demanded exclusive fidelity, no obligatory rites (public celebrations of the cult were popular feasts that people took part in out of pleasure and from which they could be absent without serious consequences). The authoritarianism and mawkish exclusivism of Catholicism had not yet poisoned the atmosphere.

Unfortunately, anyone who, instead of neglecting details, took it into his head to reject the whole of paganism and adopt a religion incompatible with it met with a violent reaction. Greco-Roman civilization was solidly entrenched within its difference. That is the true reason for the persecution of Christianity and Manichaeism. Rather than repeating a well-known story, let me recount an incident involving a Stoic philosopher. In A.D. 66, under Nero, Thrasea, a senator and a Stoic, was accused of secret opposition to Nero, of abstaining from all public acts, and of passive resistance. Worse, he was accused of being a separatist, of fleeing human society, and of avoiding "the forums, the theaters, the temples" (*fora, theatra, templa*). Here, in three words, is the "Roman way of life"; here is why Christians were execrated.

Here was also the civilization into which all the ethnic groups of the empire (including the Herodian dynasty and the Sadducees) were acculturated. In our own days, however, the difficulty of acceding to Western technology and values, although tempting, provokes the violent reactions of rejection and intransigence with which we are all familiar. Why this difference? "Tocqueville's theorem" gives the explanation: a human group adopts the values of a foreign civilization only on condition that, after its conversion, it not find itself on the very bottom level of that civilization. An Indian chief, Tocqueville wrote, would prefer to die in his defunct glory and his noble poverty rather than start cultivating the soil and find himself at the bottom of white society.

In the Roman Empire, however, the city—the local self-government—was the basic administrative district. A barbarian village that became Romanized or Hellenized was not by that token automatically on the bottom level of Greco-Roman society. Quite the contrary: it had full title and full rights as a Greco-Roman city. An African or Lycian tribe that became urbanized was not relegated to the bottom of imperial society; it became one of the constituent cells of the worldwide civilization of its time.

INDEX

Tyrrhenian Sea, 146, 218, 222,
234–35

Ulpian (Domitius Ulpianus), 98, 141,
145, 156, 167, 168–69, 256, 367
Universalism, 342, 343, 345, 346–47,
348, 350, 368
Unrest, social and political, 38,
42–43, 91, 138, 203, 205, 208,
240, 273, 277, 288, 289, 291, 292,
297, 307, 316, 339
Ursus, Flavius, 169

Valens, M. Longinius, 107
Valentinus, Antonius, 311
Valerius Maximus, 47, 185
Varro, Marcus Terentius, 105, 205–6,
211, 215, 226, 238
Vegetius (Flavius Vetius Renatus),
1–2, 6, 105, 116, 125
Veii, 205
Velleius Paterculus, Marcus, 47
Venuleius, 170
Venus, 143–44, 236
Vercingetorix, 356
Vernant, Jean-Paul, 81
Vernhet, D., 231
Verres, Gaius, 50, 166, 215, 307
Versailles, 364
Vertet, Hugues, 225
Verus, Lucius Aurelius, 358
Vespasian, Roman emperor, 134,
189, 211, 228, 286
Vesta, 57
Vestal Virgins, 57, 58, 60, 63, 87
Vestorius, 221, 222
Veterans, 30, 31, 43, 44, 45, 108,
109–10, 121, 122, 124, 125, 126,
134, 208, 291, 315
Vettius, Lucius, 50
Veyne, Paul, 176, 179, 190, 197, 245
Vibienus, C., 223

Victory, Augustan, 111, 112
Vidal-Naquet, Pierre, 242
Vienna (Vienne), 112, 365, 366
Vigny, Alfred de, 130
Vilicus, vilica, 141–42, 144, 156, 176,
209
Villa, villae, 141–42, 146–47, 149,
210, 211, 217
Villa dei Gordiani, 286
Vindolanda, 120, 129
Vindonissa, 118
Violence, 22, 23, 42–43, 131, 133,
163, 301, 302, 305, 310; state
monopoly of, 306, 317, 320
Virgil (Publius Vergilius Maro), 3,
201–2, 274, 355, 363
Viriathus, 338
Vitellius, Aulus, Roman emperor,
111, 134, 185
Vitruvius (Marcus Vitruvius Pollio),
221, 222, 224
Voisin, Jean-Louis, 4
Voting, voters, 23, 24, 27, 28, 31–32,
38, 42–42, 47, 50, 206
Vows, 59, 61, 65, 83, 112
Vulcan, 236

Waltzing, Jean-Pierre, 219, 242
War: the African, 154; the civil, 23,
29, 43, 47, 52, 315, 316, 338; the
First Punic, 28, 234; the Gallic,
360; with Hannibal, 18, 20, 24,
29, 43, 44, 46, 52; rules of, 1, 34,
39, 354–55, 356–57, 358–59; the
Second Punic, 18, 27, 28, 67, 121,
203, 231; the Social, 15, 19, 36,
38, 39–40, 155
Wars, 146, 165, 204, 219, 300, 361;
the civil, 20, 31, 43, 50, 52, 106,
153, 160, 208, 285, 301, 315, 360,
364; of religion, 3–4; second and
third Macedonian, 44